No Victor, No Vanquished

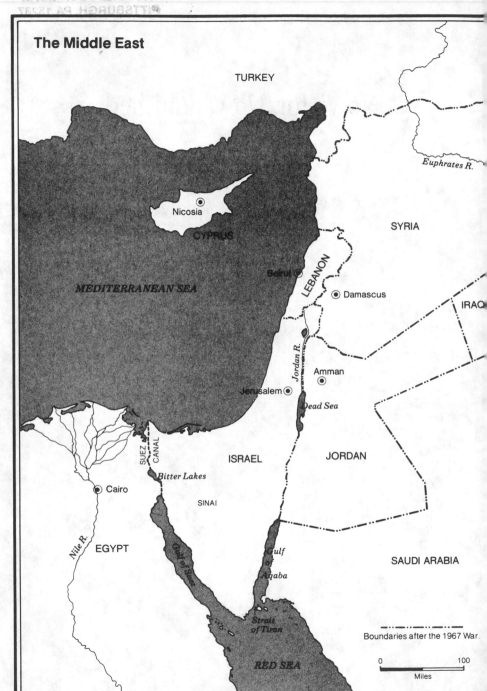

The Middle East

TURKEY

Euphrates R.

Nicosia

CYPRUS

SYRIA

MEDITERRANEAN SEA

Beirut

LEBANON

Damascus

IRAQ

Jordan R.

Amman

Jerusalem

Dead Sea

ISRAEL

JORDAN

SUEZ CANAL

Bitter Lakes

Cairo

SINAI

Nile R.

EGYPT

Gulf of Suez

Gulf of Aqaba

SAUDI ARABIA

Strait of Tiran

RED SEA

Boundaries after the 1967 War.

0   100
Miles

No Victor, No Vanquished
The Arab-Israeli War, 1973

Edgar O'Ballance

PRESIDIO

This book was originally published with the title
No Victor, No Vanquished:
The Yom Kippur War

This edition printed 1997

Copyright © 1978 by Presidio Press

Published by Presidio Press
505 B San Marin Drive, Suite 300
Novato, CA 94945-1340

Library of Congress Cataloging-in-Publication Data

O'Ballance, Edgar.
  No victor, no vanquished.
  Includes index.
  1. Israel-Arab War. 1973. I. Title.
DS128.1.02   956'.048   78-7448
ISBN 0-89141-017-1 (hardcover)
ISBN 0-89141-615-3 (paperback)

Printed in the United States of America

Contents

Illustrations

Maps

Preface

The October War brought many surprises that jolted current military thinking out of its World War II rut and provoked wide-ranging reassessments. It was a war that was not wanted by either the Israelis, the Russians, or the Americans, but once it had begun, both America and Russia felt compelled to sustain their protégés for reasons of prestige and the superpower struggle. They sent replacement arms, ammunition, and equipment in quantities that escalated widely, as neither superpower wanted to see the side it was supporting defeated completely on the field of battle. Broadly speaking, perhaps the Arabs, who wanted the war, gained the most. Despite the fact that in a purely military sense it was a dream contest, it did serve to break the almost crystalised, stultifying state of No Peace, No War, which seemed to be to everyone's advantage except their own.

This comprehensive account is compiled from the results of my interviews, researches, and visits both to the countries involved and the actual battlefields, where I "walked the course" with officers who had taken part in the fighting. With the second cease-fire, which seemed to bring more advantages to the Arabs than to the Israelis, came the myth-makers. Both Arabs and Israelis are now trying to convince themselves, and the world at large, that they won the war and, but for the intervention of the superpowers, would have won it more decisively. This is not exactly correct, and I cannot arrive at a deduction that is wholly favourable to one side or the other. Some would rather I had omitted certain information or comments, played down certain aspects and overemphasised others. This I was unable to do, as I wished to compile an accurate, contemporary, warts-and-all history, at this distance of time and in this myth-making atmosphere.

There are still grey and disputed areas, contradictory reports which are difficult to reconcile, official silences on certain details, and overeffusive explanations on others. Lips are sealed on some matters while tongues wag incessantly on others, as so many of the personalities involved, aware that they have become historical figures, are anxious that the warts first be removed before the recording pen begins to write.

Acknowledgements

Most of the information contained in this book, some exclusive at the time of writing, has been personally gained during briefings, interviews, discussions, and visits to battlefields, centers of instruction, and units. However, I would like to make grateful acknowledgement to the authors, editors, compilers, and publishers of the following works which I have read or consulted with profit and pleasure:

Deutsch, Andre. *Insight on the Middle East War*. London: Insight Team of the Sunday Times, 1974.

Glassman, Jon D. *Arms for the Arabs*. Baltimore and London: John Hopkins University Press, 1976.

Heikal, Mohammed. *The Road to Ramadan*. London: Collins, 1975.

Herzog, Chaim. *The War of Atonement*. London: Weidenfeld and Nicolson, 1975.

International Institute of Strategic Studies. *The Military Balance and Strategic Survey*. London: 1972-75.

International Symposium. *Military Aspects of the Israeli-Arab Conflict.* Tel Aviv: University Publishing Projects, 1976.

International Symposium. Various papers. Cairo: 1975.

Kalb, Marvin and Bernard. *Kissinger.* London: Hutchinson, 1974.

Meir, Golda. *My Life.* London: Weidenfeld and Nicolson, 1975.

Pajak, Roger E. *Soviet Arms Aid to the Middle East.* Washington: Center for Strategic Studies, Georgetown University, 1976.

Peres, Shimon. *David's Sling.* London: Weidenfeld and Nicolson, 1970.

1

A MIDDLE EAST
MIRAGE

*Damascus is only one hour's drive away, and
Cairo perhaps two.*

Israeli saying pre-October 1973

The war between the Arabs and the Israelis, which broke
out in the Middle East on 6 October 1973, is known to the
Arabs as the "War of Ramadan," to the Israelis as the "Yom
Kippur War," and generally to nonpartisans in the West as the
"October War of 1973." This explosion, however, was only the
most recent eruption in a history of simmering relations. Indeed,
the Arabs and the Israelis have fought five wars against each
other. The Israelis called the 1948-49 clash their "War of Independence," which brought the state of Israel into being by force
of arms as Britain relinquished the mandate for Palestine. Among
the problems it created was the question of Palestinian refugees.
The second war occurred late in 1956. President Nasser had
nationalised and then closed the Suez Canal, which led to an
Anglo-French invasion of Egypt. Taking advantage of the Egyptian preoccupation, Israeli columns moved westward across the
Sinai desert against light opposition and almost to the Suez
Canal in "One Hundred Hours." A few months later pressure
from the United Nations and especially America forced the
Israelis to grudgingly withdraw to their former boundaries.

1

The third outburst was the "Six Day War," fought in June 1967. After making a preemptive air strike on Arab airfields, the Israelis managed to destroy the air force of Jordan, almost destroy that of Egypt, and badly maul those of Syria and Iraq. Left without air cover, the Arabs were disastrously defeated. In the north, Syria lost the Golan Plateau. In the east, Jordan lost its West Bank, the more prosperous part of the Hashemite Kingdom. In the south, the Egyptians, their 90,000-strong army being routed and losing all their new Soviet weaponry and equipment, lost the Gaza Strip and the whole of the Sinai desert and peninsula. President Nasser later told Premier Mahgoub of the Sudan, "On the 9th June (1967) when I resigned, there were only 400 soldiers between Ishmailia and my house. Israeli troops could have entered Cairo if they wanted to."

The fourth clash was President Nasser's "War of Attrition" which began in 1967 virtually as soon as the Egyptian armed forces had regrouped and had received more Soviet material. The ensuing battles were fought across the Suez Canal, now the dividing line between the Egyptians and the Israelis. The ground combat included heavy artillery and mortar barrages and many commando raids. In another dimension, aircraft were used by both sides, especially the Israelis, for strategic bombing and ground support. Yet a "war of electronics" quickly developed in the air. The Soviet Union supplied Egypt with surface-to-air missiles (SAMs) for defence against Israeli aircraft. The introduction of these effective missiles redressed the situation that had developed immediately after the June defeat in which Israeli pilots had freedom of Egyptian skies. Encountering SAMs in Vietnam, the Americans had developed Electronic Counter Measures (ECM) pods, which were fixed to the wings of planes and gave the pilots warning of oncoming missiles, enabling them to take evasive action. Soon a "mad scientists' war" developed as on-the-ground, radar-directional, searching and tracking equipment improved, and in the air more advanced ECM pods enabled the pilot to jam, counter-jam and even deflect missiles aimed at him.

When the War of Attrition ended on 7 August 1970, it was very much a "drawn" contest. Israeli aircraft had been eased out from the air space over Egypt proper and their activities confined to the Suez Canal Zone. Not all observers reckon this as a "war," which accounts for the fact that some refer to the October War of 1973 as the "fourth" and others as the "fifth" Arab-Israeli war.

In any event, a major transition in the Middle East came on 28 September 1970, when President Nasser died. His last political act had been to bring about a cease-fire in Jordan between King Hussein's troops and the Palestinian Fedayeen, Freedom Fighters. Nasser's successor was Anwar Sadat. The new Egyptian leader had graduated from the (then) Royal Egyptian Military Academy in 1938. Sadat then entered the Signal Corps and at one stage was imprisoned by the British during World War II on suspicion of plotting with the Germans. He was again arrested in 1945 for complicity in an assassination attempt against the Wafdist leader, Mustafa Nahas, and, although acquitted, was dismissed from the army. His commission was restored in 1950, in time for him to take an active part in the revolution as one of the original groups of Young Officers, a secret military group that led the uprising. It was Sadat who announced over Radio Cairo that King Farouk had been deposed, and proclaimed the assumption of power by the revolutionary committee. After a period as a minister, he edited the Cairo daily newspaper *Al Goumhouriya* until 1957 when he was appointed Speaker of the (then) Egyptian National Union, later the National Assembly. One of the four joint vice presidents from 1964 to 1967, he emerged in 1969 as second only to Nasser in the hierarchy. On 16 October 1970, Sadat was elected president of Egypt for a period of six years.

At first President Sadat seemed to be trying diplomacy by giving the Roger's Peace Plan a chance. This peace initiative, proposed by United States Secretary of State William P. Rogers, in December 1969, specified Israeli withdrawal from the occupied territories in return for Arab assurance of a binding peace commitment; but it was rejected by the Israelis. At the same time Sadat continued Nasser's policy of obtaining more weapons from the Soviet Union and of improving the Egyptian armed forces. Launching a peace initiative of his own, Sadat announced on 5 February 1971 that, if the Israelis would make a partial withdrawal, the Egyptians would clear and reopen the Suez Canal. Unfortunately this proposal came to nothing, simply contributing to the undercurrent of rising discontent within the country at the continuing military inaction against Israel. This unrest rose to such a peak that Sadat promised the year would not end "without making the decision for the battle with Israel being resolved either by war or peace." Then when the year closed in the same uneasy condition of No Peace, No War, disappointment was felt by the Arabs everywhere. The Israelis merely ridiculed Sadat's famous "Year of Decision."

President Sadat also faced internal problems. He had not been in office many months when, in May 1971, he faced a power struggle as Vice President Ali Sabri and others, many with pro-Soviet views, unsuccessfully conspired against him. Six ministers and several senior members of the Arab Socialist Union (ASU), the country's only legal political party, resigned. Meanwhile Sadat formed a new government and announced a reorganisation of the ASU. For the remainder of the year he was largely preoccupied with ASU constitutional matters. On 8 September, he dissolved the National Assembly. Three days later a new constitution, being approved by a national referendum, replaced the temporary one. A new People's Assembly was elected and formally opened on 11 November.

Meanwhile, Mohammed Heikal, editor of the influential Cairo newspaper, *Al Ahram,* writing on 16 June 1971, called for an end to the situation of No Peace, No War. He warned Sadat that the inability of his regime to fulfill its promises was creating a dangerous credibility gap between the Egyptian leadership and the people. Discontent within the armed forces continued to fester during the following year (1972) as there did not seem to be any intention of attacking the Israelis to recover the "lost territories." The culmination came on 26 November, when it was reported that over 100 officers of the armoured corps had been arrested for plotting to oust President Sadat in a coup allegedly planned for the sixteenth. The Egyptian government now flatly denies there was any such attempt. On 2 November, the United States secretary of state, William Rogers, had again called for the implementation of the United Nations Resolution 242, which specified Israeli withdrawal from the occupied territories in return for Arab recognition of Israel. Yet Rogers's call received little attention.

Syria, lying just northeast of Israel, had suffered badly during the 1967 war. After the conflict, the policies of Syrian president Atassi led to isolation from other Arab governments. President Atassi had not only supported and actively encouraged the Palestinian Fedayeen, especially those of extreme, or left-wing, persuasion, but also had operated a national group of his own, the Syrian Saiqa. He had also intervened in the Jordanian civil war and had opposed the cease-fire arranged by President Nasser. In another rearrangement of power, Hafez Assad became premier of Syria in December 1970. He was then elected president by a referendum on 12 March 1971. Assad, a former regular air force officer, was more acceptable to Arab governments, and to the Soviet Union which had not liked Atassi's treatment of Syrian Communists.

Among other advantages, Assad was an Alawite, the Alawi being a heretical offshoot of Ismaili Shi'itism, which was particularly strong around the Latakia area. Representatives of the Alawite minority had effectively ruled Syria for some years, having first gained influence through the pre-1945 army. The French tended to favour this Muslim sect in a military sense, feeling that its officers and soldiers had fighting qualities considered common in mountain people. Thereafter, the Alawi produced many of Syria's politically minded officers. Dark allegations arose after the 1967 war that Alawi officers had deserted their soldiers, the majority of whom were of the Shi'ite sect. Friction developed between the Alawi and the Shi'ites as each tended to blame the other for the defeat.

While the new leaders assumed the reins, the Syrian border with Israel rocked with hostile incidents, some quite large. Aircraft clashed overhead and Syrian-based Fedayeen activity caused that country to become the object of occasional Israeli reprisals. On 10 October 1972, for example, an Israeli spokesman asserted that, since the end of the 1967 war, the Israelis had mounted ten attacks on Syria and claimed to have shot down thirty-one Syrian aircraft.

President Assad had stepped into an uneasy political heritage, one which had involved a change of government almost annually since independence in 1945. Each of these changes, often by force or coup, aggravated the internal political turmoil. Early in 1973, orthodox Muslims conducted waves of protests against alleged harsh treatment by the secular Baathist regime. On 10 June, reports circulated that Assad had been shot in the leg during an attempted coup and that some 300 officers and non-commissioned officers in "rebel units" had been arrested. During September, two more reported coups failed and deep resentment grew in some quarters against his brother, Colonel Rafat Assad, commander of the formation known as the Republican Guard. This special security, or counter-coup, force based in Damascus was designed to keep President Assad in power and had made many political arrests.

The internal problems within the individual Arab states contributed to the historic bloc disunity. After June 1967, the Arab states lapsed back into their customary and universally expected condition of disunity and disarray. Many an Arab statesman had the longtime ambition to lead a united Arab federation, but this dream had never materialised. Indeed, one of Israel's biggest advantages was a disjointed opposition. In 1958, President Nasser had managed briefly to join Egypt and Syria into the United Arab Republic (UAR), but the union was disbanded three years later. Since then nothing much was done in this respect until 1970, when a federation of Libya and Egypt was mooted.

Libya, an 810,000-square-mile country consisting mainly of desert, had a population of less than two million. In 1965 oil production began and quickly increased until by 1973 the daily output was over 2.2 million barrels. Even increasing the nation's wealth, however, did not solve the nagging internal problems. On 1 September 1969, a revolutionary committee headed by Colonel Gaddafi seized power from King Idris. Gaddafi saw the advantages of merging his country, which now had ample oil money but only a tiny population and no technical expertise, with Egypt, which had little money but ample manpower and technical knowledge. The two countries might have complemented each other admirably, if the question of political leadership could have been resolved. But Gaddafi, though personally popular with his people, demonstrated an individualistic and unpredictable character, which led Anwar Sadat to adopt a cautious attitude towards the proposition.

The subject of unity was not broached again seriously until 17 April 1971, when it was announced that a Federation of Arab Republics, of Egypt, Syria and Libya, was to come into effect on 1 January 1972. This statement proved to be premature. Although President Assad of Syria had better relations with other Arab states than his predecessor, he had only recently gained power and had problems at home to deal with first. In addition, President Sadat, uneasy as to the motives of his newly oil-rich neighbour, still hesitated. Little headway occurred during 1972, except that a statement issued on 2 August announced that a merger between Libya and Egypt was to come into force on 1 September 1973. By this time, Syria had obviously withdrawn from such a scheme, but Sadat was still being pressured by Colonel Gaddafi. However, on 1 January 1973 Gaddafi removed his detachment of Libyan troops from the Suez Canal Zone because he disagreed with Sadat's policy.

The following month, a tragic incident occurred on 21 February 1973, when a Libyan airliner strayed over the Sinai. About twelve miles east of the Suez Canal, the plane was shot down by Israelis with the loss of 106 lives. The incident caused tension as reprisals were expected from the strongly anti-Israeli Gaddafi. Finally, when the Israelis admitted their error and apologised, the situation gradually calmed down.

Gaddafi continued with his efforts to federate his country with Egypt. President Sadat visited him in June 1973, but they did not reach any agreement. A return visit by Colonel Gaddafi to Cairo in early July was no more fruitful. The impasse triggered a 1,500-mile mass march of about 4,000 Libyans on 11 July, who intended to stage a "sit-in" in the Abdine Palace, Cairo, until federation of the two countries became a fact. The crowds were halted only about 200 miles from Cairo by a train drawn across a level-crossing to block the roadway. They were then persuaded to return home.

By January 1973, President Assad of Syria had again taken up the idea of federation. On the thirty-first, he called upon all Arab countries to unify ranks to meet the "greatest threat since the Crusades." The only outward result, however, was that five months later, King Hassan of Morocco sent a small brigade of troops to Syria. While Syria and Egypt drew closer together, Egypt and Libya drifted farther apart. On 23 August, it was announced that the Egyptian-Libyan merger was "on" again, but the watching world smiled in amusement, and the Israelis regarded these diplomatic manoeuvrings with condescending contempt.

The other Arab country that had lost heavily in 1967 was Jordan, a nation also troubled by the Palestinian Fedayeen, who were living and operating from its territory. Even the cease-fire brought about by President Nasser in the civil war between the government armed forces and the Fedayeen did not last long. Fighting broke out again in January 1971 and continued until July when King Hussein finally ejected the Fedayeen from his country, an act that caused him to be banished from the Arab fold. The Jordanian border with Syria was closed and the armies of both countries clashed briefly in August. Violent outbursts continued through the fall as, in November, Palestinian Fedayeen fighters assassinated the Jordanian premier, Wasfi Tal, in Cairo.

On 15 March 1972, King Hussein made a speech to some 500 political leaders from both the East and West banks of his kingdom, announcing plans for Jordan to become the United Arab Kingdom, which would consist of two regions, the eastern one with its capital at Amman, also to be the federal capital, and the western one, with its capital at Jerusalem. This proposal was sharply rejected by both Arabs and Israelis. Egypt and Syria were especially suspicious in case King Hussein came to some independent agreement with the Israelis. Egypt reacted by severing diplomatic relations with Jordan.

The numerous undercurrents of discontent rumbling within Jordan eventually penetrated the armed forces. On 18 November 1972, over 300 Jordanian officers were arrested after an attempted coup against King Hussein, who was slightly wounded by the Jordanian pilot of a Starfighter. On 5 February 1973, King Hussein visited President Nixon in America, who agreed to provide small quantities of arms that included twenty-four U.S. F-5E, single-seater Northrop tactical fighter aircraft. While in America, Hussein admitted in a television appearance that he was prepared to enter into a separate settlement with Israel if prior agreement could be reached on several principles, "especially over Jerusalem." This made Hussein even more suspect and unpopular with his brother Arabs.

The years between 1967 and 1973 can be thought of as the Arab Fedayeen period in Middle East history. During this interval, the Palestinian "Freedom Fighters" carried out guerrilla warfare against the Israelis and staged several dramatic and spectacular incidents that also involved other nations. After unsuccessfully trying to practice Mao Tse-tung's doctrine of the guerrilla "fish" swimming in the "sea" of Arab people in the Israeli-occupied territories, and driven by hostility arising from a combination of the Palestinian refugee problem and the frustration and bitterness of the 1967 defeat, the Palestinians switched tactics, seeking to achieve enthusiastic popularity amongst Arab masses everywhere, if not always with the Arab governments themselves. Their activities became independent of governmental restraints in their host countries and led to a state of civil war in both Jordan and Lebanon. Although the Lebanese government was able to bring the Fedayeen fighters partially to heel, it was never able to completely flush them from the small portion of its territory in the south. This area adjacent to the Mount Hermon range became known as Fatahland.

Deciding to use the international stage to draw world attention to their cause, the Fedayeen hijacked three airliners on 6 September 1970 and flew them to a desert airstrip in Jordan. They kept the crew and passengers hostage for six days before the world's television cameras. Another airliner, hijacked about the same time, was blown up at Cairo International Airport. On the twelfth, the Fedayeen blew up the three airliners in Jordan after releasing some of the hostages but retaining others. Further activity followed, some dramatically spectacular, some less so, including assassinations. On 31 May 1972, for example, three members of the Japanese Red Army terrorist organisation walked through Lod (Lydda) airport in Israel, then calmly took machine guns and grenades from their cases and attacked the waiting crowd. Twenty-six bystanders were killed and another seventy-two wounded. The Fedayeen claimed that this incident proved world-wide support for their cause.

On 5 September 1972, a Palestinian Fedayeen faction known as the Black September group, so called because of their September 1970 defeat in Jordan, killed eleven Israeli athletes and a German policeman at the World Olympic Games at Munich, West Germany. Of the five Arabs involved, two were killed in the melee, but the three survivors were released by the Germans and flown to Libya where they were feted as heroes. The usual Israeli riposte to Fedayeen terrorist activities directed toward them was to launch punitive air or commando attacks into neighbouring Arab territory in the hope of hitting the guerrillas or their camps. In this instance, they retaliated with a 100-plane raid three days later on Fedayeen camps in Syria and Lebanon, causing over 100 casualties.

Elements of the Fedayeen resorted to postal warfare in which parcel-bombs and letter-bombs were dispatched to victims. On 19 September 1972, an Israeli diplomat in London was killed by such a missive. This method escalated and during the first half of November over fifty-two letter-bombs were sent to Jews living in Europe. A "James Bond" type of underground warfare also developed in which the Israelis took a full part. On 7 April 1973, three Palestinian Fedayeen leaders were assassinated in Beirut. Strong feeling over the seeming inactivity of the Lebanese army in reaction to this incident sparked a miniature nine-day civil war in Lebanon. Thinking that the Syrians might intervene, Israeli armed forces manoeuvred conspicuously on the Golan Plateau. Both Arabs and Israelis perpetrated other assassinations. Apart from the constant pin-pricking guerrilla activity along its borders, Israel also had to cope with internal Arab unrest and terrorism in the occupied territories, especially in the Gaza Strip, which it managed to contain to a certain extent, but was not able to cure.

To the watching world in September 1973, it seemed as though the Arabs, already defeated in battle three (or perhaps four) times by the Israelis, plagued with internal political unrest, having unreliable armed forces and muttering recriminations to each other, were still unable to unite to take positive action, and that their ineffective sabre-rattling was merely for home consumption. The Israelis still held the occupied territories and, if anything, were strengthening their grip by establishing settlements in them in defiance of Arab protests. It seemed that, in the centre of the shifting sands of intransigent hostility, Israel stood out like a fortress—firm, strong and solid, with well-organised armed forces, always triumphant in battle, to whom "Damascus is only one hour's drive away, and Cairo perhaps two."

It seemed as though the main danger, not only to Israel but to the world at large, came from the Palestinian Fedayeen extremist groups which hijacked aircraft, took hostages and sometimes killed them regardless of nationality, and carried out indiscriminate acts of terrorism. How to prevent hijacking of aircraft and how to deal with hijackers was an urgent world problem. The Israeli government also followed this line of thought, believing that the main danger came from the Fedayeen rather than from the armed forces of the various Arab nations. On 15 September, General Elazar, the Israeli chief of staff, maintained that the Israelis would continue to strike at "Palestinian guerrillas all over the world." This picture was largely a Middle East mirage as there was an underground current of purposeful Arab military activity not readily apparent through Israeli rose-tinted spectacles.

2

OPERATION SPARK

I told Brezhnev that we would have to fight one day.

President Sadat

In Egypt, deep thoughts were directed toward regaining military prestige and wiping out the psychological effects of the 1967 defeat. When he assumed power in September 1970, President Sadat opted against reopening the War of Attrition. He felt that it had served its purpose at the time, but that any attempt to renew the policy would simply provoke violent Israeli reaction requiring disproportionate military resources to combat. Sadat believed it would be better to arm, train and condition the armed forces so they would be capable of moving successfully against the Israelis in the Sinai. He later said, "From the day I took office on President Nasser's death, I knew I would have to fight."

President Sadat, however, always hoped that he would not have to fight. He preferred to obtain concessions in the form of an Israeli withdrawal from the occupied territories by diplomatic means. For eighteen months he anticipated that American pressure on Israel might bring this about as it had done in 1957.

Later he confirmed,

> I had some slight hopes of Secretary of State Rogers in 1970
> and 1971. But all he did was to extract more and more con-
> cessions from me and there was never a single response from
> the Israelis. Rogers thought we would never fight. The Israelis
> thought we would never fight. And they thought they could
> never be surprised. The West thought we were poor soldiers
> without good generals.

Sadat's statement probably held the key to his subsequent
course of action. The president's wounded Egyptian pride had
made him determined to one day achieve a victory that would
put Egypt on the military map of the world. Yet throughout
the sabre-rattling Year of Decision (1971), he gave instructions
that certain military reforms and reorganisation be put into
practice but apparently could not visualise a clear-cut course of
action.

He nonetheless prepared for armed intervention when in
December 1970 he concluded a military assistance agreement
with the Soviet Union and then signed a fifteen-year treaty of
friendship and cooperation with that country on 27 May 1971.
The new concords provided Egypt more arms together with
more Soviet military advisers, instructors and technicians. During 1971, the International Institute for Strategic Studies (IISS),
whose figures are not seriously disputed by either side, estimated
the armaments included at least 100 MiG-21 aircraft, 25 SU-7s,
55 MiG-17s and MiG-15s, 70 Mi-8 helicopters and unspecified
numbers of SAM-2s, SAM-3s, ZSU (quad) 23mm antiaircraft
guns and 203mm field guns. After this substantial shipment, the
arms supply tended to dry up which led Sadat to the uneasy
conclusion that America and the Soviet Union had reached some
secret agreement on arms levels in the Middle East, as both
superpowers seemed content with the No Peace, No War situation. On 5 November, President Sadat assumed supreme command of the Egyptian armed forces on the grounds that the
existing political and military situation necessitated such a step.

Egypt's seeming lack of positive action and leadership had

caused uneasiness within the armed forces, especially that section which had seen action along the Suez Canal front during the War of Attrition. The bitterness spread to the nation, producing student demonstrations on 19 January 1972, demanding war against Israel and decisive action against United States economic interests in Egypt. To soothe the students, President Sadat told them that the decision to go to war against Israel had been made. This boast was not true at the moment of speaking and Sadat later admitted that it was not until the following month that a plan began to form in his mind—an idea that eventually developed into Operation Spark (Arabic = Sharara). Operation Spark was to be in two parts, the first being a military operation seeking limited gains. The initial outbreak in turn would "spark off" an international crisis into which both the Soviet Union and the United States would be drawn. Sadat hoped that the two superpowers would then force Israel into concessions acceptable to the Arabs. Heikal, former editor of *Al Ahram,* hastened to explain that "1971 should be the year for taking a decision and not the year for implementing it." Sadat was in fact taking a leaf from the Israeli book as they had followed that strategy in the past.

With a population of thirty-six million people, Egypt had ample manpower for the imminent conflict. Indeed, the abundance of personnel facilitated selective application of the three-year period of conscription—only the best and fittest were taken. Of the 318,000 men in the armed forces, about 260,000 were in the army, which had an additional trained reserve of over a half million soldiers. After his initial service, the conscript remained in the active reserve until completing twelve years in all. Officers remained in the reserve much longer in accordance with an age-limit schedule dependent upon rank. Apart from a large regular-officer element, another class of regular officers was promoted from the ranks, but their comparatively mature age when commissioned made high rank unlikely. Still such officers formed a valuable contribution as experienced regimental commanders. An additional several thousand soldiers served for specified short and long-term regular engagements as either technicians or specialists. Many of them had served in the Air

Defence Command and as instructors at training establishments and military schools. Since the 1967 war, large numbers of officers and soldiers were retained in the armed forces after they had completed their period of conscript service.

In 1967, and years before, the rank and file of the Egyptian army had been Fellaheen, peasants from villages located mainly in the densely populated delta region. These farmers were simple, unsophisticated and unfamiliar with modern mechanisation. It took time to teach them to drive and maintain vehicles and to handle complicated weapons. By 1973, however, this was no longer the case. Although perhaps three-quarters of the soldiers were still Fellaheen, the others were largely townspeople. The population of Cairo had reached over six million people. This significant urban proportion had all their lives been familiar with modern transport, radios and mechanical gadgets. Even more important in the ranks was an element of men with a secondary education and students, who previously had been debarred from serving in the armed forces by President Nasser as he thought it politically dangerous to conscript young intellectuals. Many such men elected to remain in the ranks as a commission required a reserve liability that would have been with them for many years, whereas if they continued as enlisted soldiers their maximum military obligation remained twelve years.

Basically, the combat element of the Egyptian army was formed into three armoured, three mechanised and five infantry divisions, all on the triangular Soviet pattern, that is, three companies to a battalion, three battalions to a regiment, and three regiments to a division, plus integral supporting and logistic units. In addition there were two paratroop and sixteen artillery brigades, and twenty ranger units. The Soviet Union had replaced the weapons lost in the June 1967 war, and during the War of Attrition further quantities of munitions had been sent, including SAMs and their supporting equipment. Egypt possessed about 1,700 tanks, 1,200 light armoured vehicles, 150 self-propelled (SP) guns, and over 4,500 guns of various types and mortars, together with numbers of RPG-7s (Rocket Propelled Grenades), antitank missiles and at least twenty-four

FROG (Free Flight Over Ground) missiles, all of which were modern Soviet models.

The Air Defence Command was a completely different service within the armed forces. Early in 1972, it operated some seventy SAM-2 and fifty SAM-3 launcher sites, the latter then being entirely controlled by Soviet personnel. The majority of the SAM sites, supplemented by radar-controlled ZSU quad 23mm antiaircraft guns, were in the Suez Canal Zone, around the Aswan Dam and in other strategic locations.

The quantity of Soviet arms received by Egypt, however, was clearly not enough for Operation Spark. On 2 February 1972, President Sadat went to Moscow for two days, trying to persuade the Soviet government to provide him more "offensive" weapons. According to the current diplomatic jargon, "defensive" weapons would be antiaircraft guns and missiles, while "offensive" ones would include tanks, but not SP guns—the dividing line was incomprehensively vague. The Soviet leader, Leonid Brezhnev, reportedly said to him, "If each of your tanks had fired just one shot, the pattern of the 1967 War would have radically changed. But your guns were untouched." Sadat came away empty-handed, and the official communiqué merely referred to Soviet faith in the U.N. Resolution 242.

After publicly criticizing the Soviet Union for not providing arms, President Sadat returned to Moscow on 27 April in another attempt to obtain more arms. He later said, "I told Brezhnev that we would have to fight one day, as there was no other alternative, but he said he did not want a superpower confrontation." This time Sadat was partially successful. The official communiqué stated only that the Arabs had the right to use means, other than peaceful, to recover the "lost territories," but Sadat announced in a 1 May speech in Alexandria that "within a reasonable period of time the Soviet Union would supply the offensive power to liberate our lands."

On 14 May 1972, Marshal Grechko, the Soviet defence minister, who had previously visited Egypt from 18 to 21 February, again went to Cairo. After his three-day stay, the noncommittal official communiqué simply asserted that military cooperation was satisfactory. In the course of the year Sadat received some arms from the Soviet Union, but only defensive types. The Soviets believed that, should diplomacy and negotiation fail, a lack of sufficient offensive weapons would help restrict Egyptian options in any hostilities against Israel. The Cairo newspaper, *Al Ahram,* gave details of the Soviet arms supplies which angered both President Sadat and the Soviet government.

While relations between the Egyptian and Soviet governments worsened, the lack of sufficient modern arms was causing some dissatisfaction within the armed forces. Sadat later said, "The Russians prevaricated throughout the summer and autumn of 1972. They said they were waiting for the U.S. elections in November. Don't forget that when I was in Moscow in April 1972, they did not know whether Nixon would come back [to them in Moscow, or not], though he did go to Moscow after that, following his trip to China." On 13 July, Premier Aziz Sidki was sent to Moscow to smooth the troubled relations between the two countries. Still the Soviet Union would not agree to the Egyptian demand for more arms and the independence to use them. Moscow also wanted its personnel to remain in Egypt, feeling no doubt that they were in a good position to monitor all Egyptian military movements and perhaps control or even stop any projected military adventure.

The year 1972 was generally one of *detente* between the two superpowers. Neither wanted an embarrassing war in the Middle East in which they would have to take sides. President Sadat believed that, at the time President Nixon and First Secretary Brezhnev signed the SALT (Strategic Arms Limitation Talks) agreement on 26 May, they had also made a secret promise not to provide Egypt with offensive arms. This conclusion led to Sadat's next dramatic action of ejecting Soviet personnel from Egypt. Numbering approximately 20,000 in all, about 15,000 Soviet soldiers were manning and guarding fifty SAM-3 sites; about 4,000 others were distributed among various headquarters, formations and units; and there were over 200 pilots with their supporting ground crews. Soviet personnel had virtual control over the airfields at Alexandria, Janaklis (near Alexandria), Cairo West, Mansoura, Inchas, Mersah Matruh and Port Said, and had strong naval detachments at Port Said, Alexandria, Mersah

Matruh and Sollum. The exodus began on 17 July, and including dependents some 40,000 people left Egypt within a few days. The Egyptians simply took control and President Sadat declared that all Soviet military installations and equipment in the country were now the property of the Egyptian government.

Explaining his drastic action in a speech to the Central Committee of the Arab Socialist Union, President Sadat said that use of the arms in its possession was a matter for Egypt alone. He explained that he had ejected the Russians because they "felt they had a presence on our soil, even if they kept out of the way. I expelled them to give myself complete freedom of manoeuvre. Some did return with the task, carried out well behind Suez, of teaching us how to use the new missiles, especially the SAMs." He added that "Egypt had never sought a confrontation between Russia and America, and that nobody has ever imagined that any soldiers but our own will fight the battle for our land, our rights, our dignity." An estimated 1,000 Soviet personnel quietly returned to Egypt as instructors to complement the few who had remained all the time.

After the majority of Russians had left, the Egyptians made improvements and modifications to certain equipment. They had not been able to make these changes to the SAMs and radar amid the Soviet technical presence. The T-34 tank, for example, was modified so it could travel 4,000 kilometres on its tracks instead of only 1,000. In general, the standard Soviet expectation of tank track mileage was halved in the Middle East. The climate, sand and atmosphere reduced the T-54 and T-55 tank tracks from some 6,000 kilometres in Europe to only 2,500 kilometres in Egypt. Engine and transmission wear was twice as much in the Middle East as in Russia. Other modifications such as attaching grenade cannisters to the T-54 tank were simpler.

When, in November 1972, Richard Nixon was reelected for a second term as president of the United States, Sadat realised that American foreign policy, especially in relation to the Middle East, would not change. Therefore no extra pressure would be applied to the Israelis to make the vital concession of giving up the occupied territories. Sadat now saw no alternative but to implement the first part of Operation Spark.

On 14 November 1972, addressing a closed session of the Central Committee of the ASU, President Sadat said, "After the November election [when] Mr. Nixon was returned, I had a letter from Mr. Brezhnev, saying they wished to support the policy of *detente,* and they advised me to accept the situation. They said they could not increase their normal arms supplies. We started planning [for war] from that moment." Sadat confirmed on 3 April 1974 that "the decision to go to war was a 100 percent Egyptian decision, against the will of the two superpowers . . . but it took the Kremlin some time to realise the decision was Egyptian and not a dagger thrust in the Soviet Union's back in collaboration with the U.S.A."

Actually, Sadat had been coming to his Operation Spark decision for some time. During the previous weeks he had been quietly selecting and assembling a high-level planning team for the military part of the operation. The Egyptians had considered such plans as dropping a paratroop brigade in the Sinai and then immediately asking the United Nations for a cease-fire; another involved using fifty aircraft to bomb Sharm El-Sheikh. These proposals, however, were all vetoed by Minister of War Mohammed Sadik, who favoured a wider strategical aim over limited military action. General Sadik had become extremely popular with the Egyptian armed forces because of his resistance to Russian interference and pressure. But Sadat, suspecting that he was also too politically minded, removed Sadik and replaced him with Ahmed Ismail Ali.

Regarded as a brilliant tactician, Major General Ahmed Ismail was promoted to the rank of general on 26 October 1972 and appointed to be both minister of war and commander in chief of the Egyptian armed forces. In consultation, President Sadat and General Ismail agreed upon the form of limited military operation required to "spark off" the international crisis.

Commissioned into the Egyptian infantry in 1938, Ismail was an intelligence officer in the western desert in World War II. He later served in the 1948 war as a company commander and was the brigadier in command of the Abu Ageila area in the 1956 war. The battle which took place in his area was, according to Moshe Dayan, the only one in the campaign "in which the

Egyptians fought well, and the Israelis badly." Immediately after the June 1967 war, President Nasser appointed Ismail to hold the Suez Canal front and he was the main architect of the initial Egyptian defences there.

After General Riad was killed in action on the Suez Canal front, Ismail was appointed chief of staff in his place. The promotion was shortlived, however, as Ismail was dismissed from the army after the Israelis in their "Ten Hour War" raided the Egyptian side of the Gulf of Suez on 9 September to seize two new Soviet T-62 tanks. In May 1971, President Sadat recalled the former officer as director of intelligence, a post that allowed him to exercise his analytical talents. Ismail was one of the first Egyptian "military technocrats." Despite his extensive active service experience he succeeded as a military thinker and strategic planner, rather than as a battlefield commander. He had attended courses of instruction in both the Soviet Union and Britain, been commandant of the Nasser Military Academy and briefly, in 1961, served as military adviser to Patrice Lumumba in the Congo.

General Ismail was complemented by his chief of staff, Lieutenant General Saad el Shazli, the ideal military "hero-figure" for any nation. He was commissioned into the infantry in 1939, and, after a training course in America, he became the commander of the first and (then) only Egyptian paratroop battalion in 1956. After ranger training in America, he was appointed to command the Egyptian Special Forces. He united traditional rivals, the paratroops and the rangers, in a single elite unit and became known as "King Mena" after the ancient Egyptian king who had united Lower and Upper Egypt. But when Shazli left to command the Red Sea district, the paratroops and the rangers became separated again. Shazli also commanded the paratroop battalion when it was with the United Nations force in the Congo in 1960, was Egyptian military attaché in London in 1961, took part in the war in the Yemen, and also visited the Soviet Union for a training course. In 1967 he commanded the special "Shazli Force" in the Sinai and was one of the few Egyptian senior officers to survive that war with his reputation intact. Having a strong but pleasant personality, this natural leader was immensely popular with the junior officers and soldiers. Yet these feelings did not always extend to his seniors and contemporaries. Friction developed partly because of Shazli's rapid promotions; he was ranked thirtieth on the major generals' list when promoted to lieutenant general.

The director of operations was Lieutenant General Mohammed el-Gamasy, who had been confirmed in the post in December 1972 after serving in an acting capacity since February. A former tank officer, he had been appointed director of intelligence in September 1969, after which he was responsible for coordinating the Planning Section. Eventually he was put in charge of the Joint Military Planning Department which, in theory at least, embraced the Egyptian, Syrian and Libyan forces. Born in 1921, at El-Batanoon in the Monofia governorate, and graduating from the Royal Military Academy in 1939, Gamasy had an impressive list of commands and appointments to his credit, commencing with command of the 5th Reconnaissance Regiment in 1955 and including commander of the 2nd Armoured Brigade in 1959, commandant of the Armoured School in 1961, head of the Army Operational Branch in 1966, commander of the Operational Group on the Syrian front in 1970, and commandant of the Armed Forces Training Department in 1971.

Generals Ismail, Shazli and Gamasy worked together in a complementary relationship and maintained close liaison with other senior officers, including Air Vice Marshal Mohammed Mubarak, commander of the air force; Major General Mohammed Ali Fahmy, commander of the Air Defence Command; Rear Admiral Fuad Zukri, commander of the navy; Major General Omah Hussein Gohak, director of armaments and organisation; Major General Ali Mohammed, commander of the Engineer Corps; and Major General Fuad Nasser, director of intelligence.

Since 1967, there had been a vague plan to cross the Suez Canal to seize a bridgehead on the east bank. The various modifications to the offensive were code-named Liberation I, II or III. After the Air Defence Barrier had been established on the west bank of the canal in 1970, President Nasser ordered a plan to be made for an advance as far as the Sinai passes. This more ambitious operation became known as Granite I "after the hard rock of Aswan from which so many Egyptian monuments have been made." When General Sadik became minister of war, adding a more strategical than tactical mind, he enlarged the plan into a broad sweep towards the pre-June 1967 borders and this became Granite II. Granite III envisaged moving into the Gaza Strip.

The successive plans meant changing and differing demands on the Soviet Union for arms and equipment. Heikal wrote, "The Russians would never discuss operational plans with the Egyptian authorities; nor would they take any part in the basic studies behind those plans: they were willing to help with material, but regarded the method by which the occupied territory was liberated as being entirely up to Egypt."

Many lessons had been absorbed from the 1967 defeat and attempts made to correct some things and to improve others. In 1967 and 1968, a massive purge removed senior and incompetent officers but, even so, under President Nasser's regime, the armed forces remained tarnished by political interference. Not until Sadat became president did the political influences and the presence of a number of politically minded officers disappear, and a new, hard-working, dedicated Egyptian officer cadre began to emerge. The newcomers were quietly determined to ensure that a 1967-type debacle would never recur. An important innovation was the encouragement given the officers to study the Israelis (a policy banned by Nasser), to learn all about them, and even to speak Hebrew.

Some preliminary work had been done for the Liberation and Granite plans. About eighty Bailey-type bridges had been erected across the Sweet Water Canal, a tributary carrying fresh water from the River Nile near Cairo to the villages on the west bank of the Suez Canal. In addition, a number of fords were constructed across the canal to enable vehicles to cross quickly in numbers. Yet little else of military importance had been accomplished.

The meager preparation did not reflect the designs of General Ismail, who said, "Let the strike against the enemy be really big." Having ample manpower, he decided to assault all along the length of the Suez Canal instead of only at selected points, pressuring Israeli defences everywhere. They would not know where the main thrust was coming from and, accordingly, would not know exactly where to put the full weight of their counterattacks. The basic plan called for the Egyptians to cross the canal in strength, overcome the Bar Lev Line (a string of Israeli forts defending the east bank), advance eastward, and then dig in to wait for and repulse the Israeli counterattack before making a further advance—although it was obliquely hoped that by that time superpower or United Nations intervention would enforce a cease-fire. This plan was strongly influenced by the fact that the Egyptian air force was not yet equal to that of the Israelis. The strong Air Defence Barrier of SAMs and antiaircraft guns on the west bank of the canal would be able to cover the bridges erected after the initial crossing for up to ten miles over the east bank but could offer little protection beyond that.

One of the main Egyptian problems was an adequate supply of oil in time of war. In April 1973 President Sadat discussed the projected needs with his minister of oil. Sadat then approached Saudi Arabia and Algeria for the petrol required for the campaign. Both governments, when told of the purpose, sent large, unspecified quantities of oil. Libya was also asked for oil but Colonel Gaddafi replied that he would send it to Egypt when war broke out, not before. Libya did send oil to Egypt during the October War, charging commercial rates and cutting off the supply when the fighting ceased.

From 17 to 20 February 1973, President Sadat conferred with General Ismail and his senior planning officers. He approved Ismail's outline plan and on the twenty-seventh left for Moscow where he remained until 4 March, explaining the plan and asking for more arms, especially the mobile SAM-6. The offensive relied upon missiles to destroy or neutralise the Israeli air force, and so the Air Defence Barrier had to be thick and deadly. The expected Israeli superiority in armour dictated that the missiles also be used to neutralise or destroy tanks. Sadat asked for increased numbers of the Soviet BRDM armoured antitank missile carriers plus quantities of antitank missiles.

President Sadat prepared a diplomatic deception plan and, in

February 1973, dispatched Hafez Ismail, his national security adviser, on a tour of foreign capitals including Moscow, Bonn, London and Washington. Ismail also visited the United Nations' headquarters in New York on a "peace offensive." He met with President Nixon on 23 February but no official statement was issued. During the same period Mohammed Zayyat, the Egyptian foreign minister, visited New Delhi and Peking to lobby support for the deception plan. By mid-March, it was obvious to the world that Sadat's peace offensive had failed, but he had created the impression that a peaceful solution was being sought.

General Ismail stated that "in war there are two plans, one an operations plan and the other a decoy plan." The latter included the construction of strong and obvious defensive positions along the west bank of the canal, especially in the south, to deceive the Israelis into thinking that the Egyptians expected an attack. He also instituted a series of studies under the coordination of Chief of Staff Shazli of factors affecting the plan such as the nature of the canal itself and the construction of the Bar Lev Line. Meanwhile experiments were begun to see how to overcome some of the apparent difficulties.

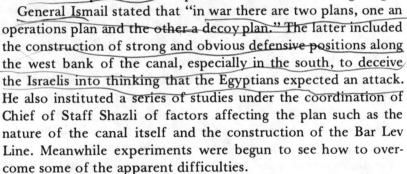

One of the most serious problems General Ismail had to overcome was what he called "trench fever," the defensive mentality caused by fighting the static War of Attrition and six years of "manning the trenches." He had to instill into both officers and soldiers an offensive spirit and confidence. The first he achieved by telling them the war was inevitable, so they must prepare for it, get used to the idea, and perform well when it came. To give them confidence, he coined the slogan, "It is the man and not the gun that matters," preaching that a bullet comes out of the barrel of a gun whether the gun is old or new. A good soldier can use an old weapon with effect, while a poor soldier can be ineffectual with a modern weapon. Ismail said, "I wanted to change the old concept that 'arms make the man' to 'the man makes the arms.' Unless our men were confident in themselves their arms would never protect them, but, on the other hand, if they were confident in themselves then any arms in their hands would protect them."

Next, General Ismail had to build the soldiers' confidence in their officers, some of whom had not demonstrated leadership ability in the 1967 war. The replacement of the old, incompetent or lazy with young, energetic and hard-working officers gave a new atmosphere to the officer corps. A new attitude toward the care of the soldiers arose. Commanders of all ranks now remained with their formations or units in the desert, in defensive positions or on training exercises, until they got used to "eating sand," and the habitual long weekends in Cairo became a thing of the past. In January 1971, more stringent conditions were introduced regarding commissioning officers, and a number of soldiers who had done well in action were promoted from the ranks. It was generally made easier for those soldiers who had gained specialist qualifications or who had shown officer-leadership potential to gain commissions.

One of the first tasks the energetic General Shazli faced was that of raising morale and infusing an offensive spirit into an army traditionally brought up on caution and defence. To do this he developed a doctrine referred to as the "calculated risk." Previously, if an unexploded bomb obstructed the roadway, everything else stopped and the whole area was evacuated until the experts were brought in to deal with it. This procedure would obviously hamper any canal-crossing operation as the Israelis frequently dropped delayed-action bombs for this purpose. The point was forcibly brought home to Shazli when an army truck, full of soldiers, ran off the road and overturned, killing five and seriously injuring others. Such road accidents were considered to be unfortunate, but simply "one of those things that happen all the time." This rationalization led him to the conclusion that if casualties of that order were accepted by civilians without due alarm in normal times, they should also be accepted by soldiers in war.

Shazli tested this theory using a quantity of old shells and explosives in a decayed and dangerous condition that had long been isolated and discarded in a desert dump. Explaining his calculated risk doctrine, General Shazli ordered his soldiers to remove them. The task was accomplished quickly and without any casualties, which surprised everyone including Shazli himself. The experiment more than proved his doctrine and he insisted that all soldiers must continue their missions whatever the apparent dangers. Thereafter, even though a bridge was being attacked from the air, a convoy moving across it, with vehicles spaced at thirty-yard intervals, must not stop as it would hold up some of the 3,000 odd vehicles crossing the bridge. Men working on an airfield on which a delayed-action bomb had been dropped would continue and not evacuate the area. Concern for individual safety would no longer delay an operation or training.

When he became chief of staff, General Shazli found that the Egyptian army lacked standardised scales as to the equipment or ammunition that each individual or unit should automatically take on active service or into battle. He knew from his training as a paratrooper that the weight and bulk of items were important and that certain gear was essential. More important, it was imperative that vital equipment be clearly specified so that none would be forgotten or overlooked. The general quickly set out to correct this situation, assembling staff officers to examine the problem and to determine which items and what quantity were to be carried by soldiers in combat. He also believed that every soldier should be thoroughly trained for his own particular task in the operation, and he held the view that it was better for an individual to know one job thoroughly than to have an imperfect knowledge of several.

After nearly three months of gruelling research and staff work, Shazli issued his famous "Directive No. 41" on 21 March 1973, defining the exact task of every soldier and establishing precise scales of weapons, ammunition, equipment, rations, water or other items to be carried by each individual. Officers had only to read the relevant part of the directive to find out just what they and the men in their command were expected to do in the operation, and to know exactly how to train and equip their soldiers. Such order and precision had never been seen in the Egyptian army and training was soon under way. Individual and unit drill was tough, repetitious and continuous. Working under the Shazli directive, everyone practiced the one particular task he was to carry out once the battle was joined so he could do it without difficulty.

Further studies were instituted by teams of staff officers, mainly under the coordination of General Gamasy, on a scientific basis to determine and analyse factors that might influence the canal crossing. Both the selection of the day to begin the offensive and the probable Israeli reaction were considered. Three special military problems had to be studied to find the best solution: the actual crossing of the waterway, breaching the Bar Lev Line defences, and quickly tearing huge gaps in the high sand rampart on the east bank. A military deception plan also had to be formulated.

Since World War II, the Russians had concentrated their training upon "assaulting across water obstacles" techniques. Although the Egyptians had learned a lot from them in this respect, they soon found that the Suez Canal presented special problems. Far from being a placid inland waterway, it had both a strong tide and a fast current that changed direction every six hours, as well as other seasonal hydrographical disturbances. These conditions were due basically to a longitudinal sea meeting a lateral one through the narrow funnel of the canal, and were increased by the breaking up of the canal proper by stretches of open water, such as Lake Timsah and the Bitter Lakes. The canal tide in the north rose (and fell) only sixty centimetres but increased to two metres in the south, 175 kilometres away. The speed of the current was eighteen metres a minute in the north, increasing to ninety metres a minute in the south. Problems in bridging, or even simply rowing a straight course across it to land at a certain point on the other side, quickly became apparent. A special study was made of the Canal Authority records going back several years to determine the most suitable dates to launch the operation.

Some 2,500 small assault boats were assembled for the crossing. Each craft was designed to carry eight combat soldiers in full battle order and was propelled by two others paddling manually. Soldiers selected as crew practiced rigorously on the western part of the El Ballah "loop," where both banks were in Egyptian possession, the El Ballah "island" being about five miles in length. When General Ali Mohammed, commander of the Engineer Corps, later stated, "There were water currents in our training ground which had the same speed as the currents in the Suez Canal," he was referring to the El Ballah loop. He also maintained that his men practiced their crossing and bridging tasks over 300 times.

The next problem was how to breach the Bar Lev Line. This string of fortifications had developed from the original chain of small observation posts, established on the east bank after the 1967 war, into a formidable obstacle. Heavy artillery barrages and aerial bombardments during the War of Attrition had caused the Israelis to harden their defences, and a number of the posts were converted into large, several-storied, bomb and blast-proof "forts" protected by thick concrete slabs overhead, supported by rails torn up from the adjacent abandoned railway lines and bolstered by sand and bales of large stones held together by wire mesh.

There had always been a sandbank on the east bank consisting of spoil brought up by perpetual dredging and deposited on that side only. The Israelis had regularised and increased this sandbank to a height of up to sixty feet or more and moved its forward apron to the edge of the canal. There was no footpath or foothold by the water's edge, and this forward slope was mined, booby-trapped and laced with concertina and barbed wire. It became a sand rampart with a gradient of forty-five degrees or more. Amphibious vehicles, generally capable of a thirty to thirty-two degree ascent, could not mount it. The Bar Lev Line forts were actually built into this huge sand rampart and included gun emplacements, revetted communication trenches, shelters for vehicles, ammunition and stores, and sleeping quarters. Reports differed on the exact number of forts, the Egyptians saying there were thirty-one in twenty-two defensive complexes while the Israelis insisted there were only sixteen forts plus other defensive positions or alternative outlying ones. It seems to be a matter of biased interpretation as to what exactly was considered a fort and what was a defensive position only, but close observation reveals twenty-six "fortress" positions worthy of that name on the canal and lake sides and also one each on the coasts of the Mediterranean and the Gulf of Suez.

The forts themselves, surrounded by minefields and barbed

wire, were linked only by patrols and radiotelephone and line communication. Behind this sand rampart was a smaller, irregular one between 300 and 500 yards away, which formed a secondary line of defence. Scattered along its length were 240 "pads" of concrete or stone, used for SP (self-propelled) guns to give indirect fire over the primary sand rampart onto the west bank. About thirty of these pads were occupied by guns at any one time. Also scattered along this secondary sand rampart were a large number of other pads for tanks to employ in an emergency to provide either indirect fire westward or to use their machine-guns to catch any invaders between the two ramparts. In the sectors covering the three main east-west routes in the area of Kantara, Ismailia and Port Suez, a third sand rampart lay farther back and contained more defensive positions and vehicle pads.

To surmount the Bar Lev Line Egyptian troops were trained on accurate models constructed on the banks of canals branching off the River Nile. They experimented with several methods trying to find the best one, using scaling ladders, rope ladders, bamboo poles and ropes. The loose, soft sand was difficult to scale quickly, especially when the soldiers were wearing equipment, carrying weapons and were additionally burdened with ammunition, rations and other extra items amounting in weight to almost sixty pounds. The assaulting infantry carried the maximum amount of ammunition and three days' water and food.

The Israelis estimated that, should the Egyptians succeed in crossing the canal, it would take them at least twelve hours to tear gaps in the primary sand rampart to enable bridges to be established and vehicles brought through them. The interval would give ample warning to mobilise and take counteraction with their armour and aircraft. They anticipated the Egyptians would have to use conventional means such as explosives, rockets or earth-moving machinery to breach the rampart. The Egyptians, however, found a quicker and better method. Many months before, in the construction of the Aswan Dam, they had successfully moved large quantities of sand for making concrete from the desert some miles away to the dam site by forcing it through a large pipe with water pressure. At the site, the water drained away and only the sand was left. Experimenting, the Egyptians found they could move quantities of loose sand quickly with ordinary high-pressure water pumps and hoses. In all, 348 experiments were made and, when adequate pumps were obtained, a gap could be water-blasted in the equivalent of the primary sand rampart within three or four hours—a third of the time anticipated by the Israelis. About eighty special detachments were formed and trained for this purpose.

From sixty-foot high watchtowers at each Bar Lev Line defensive complex, the Israelis could see twenty-five miles across the canal over the west bank in some places. The Egyptians, therefore, could not place much reliance upon being able to conceal their preparations. They relied on deceptive measures, including the construction of a large sandbank on the west bank which, though not quite as high as that of the Israelis, still enabled them to build pads under its shelter for both guns and tanks. Also, at about fifty-yard intervals along much of the canal, the Egyptians built concrete slipways to enable vehicles to enter the water. They made about sixty-five in all to confuse the Israelis and to make it almost impossible to calculate which might be used.

At intervals near the intended assault crossing points and about 100 yards back from the canal, the Egyptians built huge, horseshoe-shaped sandbanks, higher than, and overlooking, the Israeli primary sand rampart. Just below its rim, a track ran the length of the horseshoe, the sides sloping to the ground at the rear ends which enabled tanks to mount the track and from their positions near the summit give direct covering fire to the assaulting troops. The Israelis could not understand the purpose of all this work or of the "pyramids," as they called them, but as this feverish sand-moving, earth-shifting and bulldozing was in progress for months, they became accustomed to it and believed that it was simply a morale project to keep the bored Egyptian troops busy. Later, General Ismail admitted that this construction had been "expensive and difficult—but very necessary."

3

OPERATION
BADR

*They [the Russians] are drowning me in new
arms.*

President Sadat

At the beginning of 1973, President Assad expressed a
definite interest in the plan and Operation Spark was widened
to include Syria. On 21 January, General Ismail was appointed
commander in chief of the Federated Armed Forces of both
Egypt and Syria. This enabled Ismail to broaden his military
operation and to plan to attack Israel simultaneously on two
fronts. In Egypt on 26 March, President Sadat assumed the
office of premier for "a limited period and for a specific mission," and the following day he named a new cabinet, retaining
General Ismail as minister of war.

Ismail began to forge a common strategy with Lieutenant
General Mustafa Tlas who had three days previously been appointed Syrian minister of war. One of the many politically
minded officers in the Syrian army, Tlas had been appointed
president of the Damascus Military Tribunal in 1964, had served
as GOC (General Officer Commanding), 5th Division in Homs,
which was not involved in the 1967 war, and was appointed
chief of staff in 1968. He had visited Moscow, Peking, and

Hanoi and had written a book on guerrilla warfare and another on the campaigns of the prophet Mohammed.

Both Egypt and Syria wanted more sophisticated weapons, especially SAMs, from the Soviet Union, and to this end General Tlas visited Marshal Grechko, the Soviet defence minister, in Moscow on 6 December 1972. In February, he was followed by General Ismail who asked for SAMs and SCUDs, the latter being ground-to-ground missiles with a range of over 180 miles which would enable the Egyptians to strike Israeli cities. Ismail succeeded, and on 9 April Sadat said, "I have received from the Russians what I want and now I am satisfied." He told Heikal, "They are drowning me in new arms. Between December 1972 and June 1973 we received more arms from them than in the whole of the two preceding years." Most important, Sadat had received twenty-four SCUDs with Soviet crews, the counter-threat to any Israeli bombing of Egyptian cities. Sadat had really wanted MiG-23s but the Soviet Union would supply them only on the condition that they never be used without express Soviet permission; this Sadat found unacceptable.

On 2 April, the first joint Egyptian-Syrian meeting to formulate military strategy was held in Damascus, and political and military cooperation between the two countries began to blossom. A later meeting of the Arab chiefs of staff, held in Cairo on 21 and 22 April 1973, was attended by both General Tlas and General Ismail. A military appraisal given by Ismail listed the advantages of Israel as air superiority, technological skill, efficient training and reliance on quick aid from America; disadvantages cited were long lines of communication that were difficult to defend although they were interior, limited manpower which would not permit heavy losses, an economy that could not afford a long war, and the "wanton evil of conceit."

In Israel, General Ariel Sharon, GOC, Southern Command, had been quoted as saying, "Israel is now a military superpower. All the forces of the European countries are weaker than we are. We can conquer in one week the area from Khartoum to Baghdad and Algiers." This statement was indicative of the general attitude of the Israeli nation at the time. General Ismail emphasised that a common Arab strategy was essential to exploit

Israeli weaknesses. At the end of the Arab conference, General Shazli suggested that the contributions of some "unnamed" Arab countries were unsatisfactory.

During its short, troubled existence since independence, the Syrian army had been both a powerhouse and a means to achieve political power. Many officers had enlisted for that sole reason, which acted to the detriment of military efficiency. The army contained rival sects and cliques which had been involved in several coups and attempted coups, resulting in debilitating purges and dismissals. In spring of 1972, President Assad began weeding out politically oriented officers from the armed forces, and, although he made some progress, in 1973 it remained basically an army in which the officer cadre considered politics more important than strategy and tactics.

The Syrian chief of staff was Major General Yusif Shakkour, an Alawite, while the director of operations was Major General Abdul Razzaq Dardary, whose deputy was Brigadier Abdullah Habeisi, a Christian. Christians generally avoided politics in the army and thus tended to be more efficient. The commander of the Air Defence Command was Colonel Ali Saleh.

With a population of just over six million and a thirty-month period of conscription, about 110,000 men served at any one time in the Syrian armed forces. Of this number about 100,000 were in the army, which in an emergency could be expanded by about 200,000 reservists. The combat element of the army consisted of two armoured and three mechanised infantry divisions, seven artillery regiments, a paratroop and a Special Forces brigade. The Syrian armed forces had also suffered badly in the 1967 war, losing much equipment. The Soviet Union replaced the lost munitions, however, and by the end of 1972, Syria possessed, in round figures, 800 tanks and SP guns, 500 other light armoured vehicles, 800 guns and 8 batteries of SAMs. To participate in Operation Spark more sophisticated weapons were needed, and in this respect Syria was more fortunate than Egypt as President Assad had better relations with the Soviet government.

On 2 May, Assad visited Moscow and was favourably received. Syria was promised more weapons and by the end of the month had received at least forty MiG-21s. The Soviet Union organised a crash programme which supplied Syria between forty and fifty batteries of SAMs within a few weeks, enabling an entire air defence system of SAM-3s, SAM-6s and the ZSU quad-23mm antiaircraft guns to be installed. Syria also received an unspecified number of new Soviet T-62 tanks, with a 115mm smoothbore gun, deadly accurate at 1,000 yards. Firing a HEAT (High Explosive Anti-Tank) shell which was "fin-stabilised" and did not spin in flight, this gun had greater penetrative power against tanks. The concentrated fire of several T-62s, each firing three to four rounds a minute, could destroy an Israeli tank at a range of 2,500 yards.

Marshal Grechko, accompanied by the commanders of the Soviet air force and navy, visited Syria from 10 to 14 May. On the thirteenth an agreement was signed for additional military assistance, but no details were released. It was generally thought at the time that the Soviet air force commander was there to select Syrians for air force training—but there was more involved. The following month, Syria received ten missile boats. United States sources estimated that during 1972 the Soviet Union had supplied Syria with $150 million worth of armaments, and another $185 million worth in the first half of 1973. With the Soviet arms went Soviet personnel who were thought to number at least 2,000 by October. It was estimated that by October 1973 the Syrians possessed 1,100 tanks (T-62s, T-55s and T-54s), 1,000 other armoured vehicles, 2,000 guns, over 50 batteries of SAM-2s and SAM-3s, as well as 10 of the new SAM-6s, and many ZSU quad-23mm antiaircraft guns known as Shilukas.

By May 1973, President Sadat and the Egyptian armed forces, which had been in a state of almost complete mobilisation since 1967 and had retained the majority of conscripts, were ready for battle. Studies prepared in great detail by General Gamasy also indicated that this was an advantageous month in which to cross the canal. But the Syrians, more recently included in Operation Spark, needed more time to receive and absorb the new Soviet weapons. The Israelis certainly seemed to be anticipating an Arab attack in May and had mobilised to meet it.

Sadat had intended to attack in this month but postponed it because of "political reasons," that is, the projected meeting between Brezhnev and Nixon which took place in America from 17 to 25 June and led to the United States-Soviet agreements on prevention of nuclear war and limitation of strategic offensive arms. A more convincing reason was that he now had to consider Syrian capabilities and views. The delay meant the operation would have to wait until the autumn for favourable conditions to recur in the Suez Canal.

During May 1973, both President Sadat and General Ismail visited Damascus. On the twenty-second further military studies enabled Ismail to issue a Federated General Directive to both the Egyptian and Syrian armed forces for the strategical offensive against Israel, outlining certain procedures and allocating preparatory tasks, each with a time limit. Both Y Day (Yom, meaning Day in both Hebrew and Arabic) and S Hour (Sifr, meaning Zero) were discussed but it was decided that more information was required before a decision could be made. After consulting with General Tlas in Cairo in June, General Ismail issued further directives dealing with the reserves available on each front and with mobilisation plans. Major General Bahi eddin Mohammed Nofal, an Egyptian officer who was chief of staff of the Federal Operational General Staff, was appointed liaison officer with the task of ensuring smooth cooperation between the Egyptian and Syrian planning groups.

Basic disagreement existed between Egypt and Syria on the goal of Operation Spark. By accepting United Nations Resolution 242, Egypt had virtually recognised the existence of Israel, but Syria had not and refused to do so. President Sadat's aim for the operation was simply to recover the occupied territories, while Syria's goal was to dismantle the State of Israel. Disagreement on this point was resolved on 12 June, when Sadat persuaded Assad to accept the limited aim of "recovering the territories lost in 1967."

It now remained to agree on a time schedule for Y Day. At the beginning of August the planning groups of both Egypt and Syria attended a lengthy conference in Alexandria and examined the degree of readiness, efficiency and coordination of the two armed forces, and also appraised conditions inside Israel. Still, no agreement could be reached, so the decision was deferred until the working study groups reported their findings and recommendations.

From the Egyptian point of view, the main factor affecting the choice of Y Day was the need for moonlight for the first part of the night to enable them to establish bridges across the Suez Canal, with illumination fading later at night to provide a cover of darkness for the crossing of men and vehicles. The Syrians on the other hand favoured a daylight advance across the Golan Plateau. The climate should be temperate, especially from the Syrian point of view, avoiding the heavy rains in the Golan Plateau in November and the snow on the Mount Hermon range in December. For the Egyptians, hydrographical conditions at sea must be favourable for naval operations, while the tides and currents in the Suez Canal should be moderate. These many factors necessitated careful and thorough planning by the Arabs, which contradicted the generally accepted foreign view that the Arabs were incapable of such meticulous attention to detail.

The Y Day decision was a political one. Presidents Sadat and Assad chose 6 October, a day when several factors were most favourable to the Arabs. This date fell during Ramadan, the month in which, according to the dictates of the Koran, Muslims fasted during the hours of daylight, and when the Israelis would probably least expect to be attacked. The 6 October was also Yom Kippur, the holiest day in the Hebrew calendar, although the planners later insisted that this fact was of minimal importance. As 6 October was the Tenth Day of Ramadan, the traditional anniversary of the Battle of Badr won by the prophet Mohammed in the year A.D. 626, accordingly, the military part of Operation Spark now became known as Operation Badr. The Syrians had called their part of the plan Operation al-Owda, translated as "homing all the way," but agreed to adopt the code name Operation Badr.

The exact date of Y Day was a tightly held secret, known at first to perhaps only Sadat, Assad, Ismail, Tlas, Shazli, Shakkour and Gamasy, and not shared with others until just before the operation began. Then it was grudgingly given out on a "need to know" basis to certain key personnel and commanders. S Hour was still not decided.

Military deception was not forgotten and, on 4 June, General Ismail crossed the Suez Canal at its northern extremity to visit the small triangle of Egyptian-held territory around Port Fuad to inspect the causeway that was slowly creeping eastward. Normal instructions were given for the annual autumn manoeuvres to be held in September and October, as had been the practice for many years. They were to terminate as in the previous four years with an "assault crossing of a water obstacle, an attack on a strong defensive line and advance into the desert." To the watching Israelis it seemed as though the Egyptians were conforming to a set pattern, an almost traditional one which they had come to mechanically repeat, although the American Central Intelligence Agency (CIA) noted that this year for the first time the Egyptian army was exercising in divisional-sized formations.

Meanwhile, Jordan remained diplomatically isolated from some Arab countries because of King Hussein's attitude toward and action against the Palestinian Fedayeen. On 13 May 1973, Hussein, having some inkling of the coming events, sent a secret memorandum to officers of his armed forces saying the Arabs were preparing for war but that he thought the battle would be premature. Perhaps this was an indication that he had no intention of taking part in the offensive. Both Sadat and Assad, however, realised how advantageous it would be to include Jordan in Operation Badr so that pressure could be exerted against Israel from a third front.

In August 1973, President Sadat visited King Feisal in Saudi Arabia. In the course of discussions, Sadat outlined his master plan without revealing any precise detail. He was able to persuade Feisal to use the oil weapon in his support in due course and also for him to make overtures to King Hussein. Through the good offices of King Feisal and others, King Hussein attended an Arab summit meeting in Cairo on 10 September where he was told the broad outline of operations Spark and Badr. Jordan's armed forces were judged too small to successfully mount an attack on the Israelis on the West Bank of the kingdom, but Hussein agreed to cooperate by moving troops towards the River Jordan to alarm the Israelis and commit some of their formations. As gestures of good faith, Syria reopened its frontier with Jordan; on the nineteenth, King Hussein released 970 Fedayeen fighters he had imprisoned after the 1971 war, including Abu Daoud, a prominent Fedayeen leader; and President Sadat dropped charges against over 200 dissident students and journalists.

With a population of nearly two and one-half million and a two-year conscription period in force, the armed forces of Jordan numbered about 70,000, of whom over 65,000 were in the army. Apart from the conscript element, there was a high proportion of long-service regulars in the army. Many of these had roots on the East Bank* of Jordan and King Hussein relied on them to counterbalance the Palestinian, or West Bank soldiers. The Jordanian army basically consisted of three divisions—one armoured, one mechanised and one infantry—together with three artillery regiments, an independent infantry brigade and a royal guards armoured unit. Jordan possessed about 140 British Centurion tanks; 190 American M-47s, M-48s and M-60s; 550 light armoured vehicles; 200 guns and 200 M-42 SP antiaircraft guns.

By this time basic thoughts on operations Spark and Badr had crystalised. Syrian soldiers would seize the whole of the Golan Plateau including the western escarpment and gain a foothold on the west bank of the upper River Jordan. Egyptian troops would cross the canal, storm the Bar Lev Line and advance to the three passes which were up to thirty-five miles from the waterway. Meanwhile Jordan would merely pose a third front threat. In the second, and political, part of Operation Spark, Israel would be pressured into making concessions to the Arabs that would require the evacuation of the occupied territories. If the superpowers failed to intervene or were unable to force the Israelis to make the demanded concessions, the Arabs were to revert to "meat grinder" tactics against the over-

---

*Separated by the River Jordan, the East Bank was the former Emirate, later Kingdom, of TransJordan, while the West Bank was the Arab part of Palestine which had been annexed by King Abdullah in December 1948. The combined territories were known as the Hashemite Kingdom of Jordan.

stretched Israeli forces, that is, continue fighting them for weeks or months, if necessary, until they were exhausted and would have to agree to the Arab conditions.

In the interim, the "normal state of friction" between the Israelis and the adjacent Arab states continued with frequent artillery exchanges across the Golan cease-fire line and many small border infiltrations and incidents. This conflict extended to the air and the sea. According to Arab reports, on 9 August, Egyptian aircraft intercepted six Israeli planes in Egyptian air space and claimed to have hit one, although the Israelis denied this. On the thirteenth, six Israeli patrol boats trying to approach the Egyptian coast in the Gulf of Suez were attacked by Egyptian aircraft and withdrew.

On 13 September, a big air battle occurred over Tartous, in Syria. The Israelis claimed to have brought down thirteen Syrian jets. While the Syrians admitted losing eight of their own aircraft, they claimed five Israeli planes. In this battle the Syrians had wanted to fire their SAMs, but the Soviet advisers held the vital fuses and would not allow the missiles to be used, a refusal that exacerbated the touchiness between Syrians and Russians. This battle, however, quashed any hesitation or second thoughts the Syrians might have had regarding Operation Badr. In fact, on the fourteenth, they asked if the date could be advanced, but General Ismail, after conferring with senior Egyptian officers, maintained that preparations were not complete and insisted that the timetable be rigidly followed. Had the SAMs been used, perhaps the Israelis would have been prematurely alerted to the new deadly effectiveness of the Arabs.

Although diplomatic relations between Syria and the Soviet Union were satisfactory, friction existed between Soviet personnel in Syria and the Syrian people. This was partly because of a lack of Soviet understanding of the Arabs, but perhaps as much because of an inherent, and freely admitted, drawback in the Syrian character—a pride and stubborn independence, verging at times on arrogant aloofness—which made it difficult for them to seek or accept advice from foreigners. Soviet personnel in Syria were subjected to a number of irritating restrictions, which, among others, limited their movements and kept them away from cities and towns. On 28 September, the Syrian foreign minister, perhaps prompted by the refusal of Soviet officers to allow SAMs to be used against attacking Israeli aircraft, complained to the Soviet ambassador that "the attitude of the Soviet experts, which is proof of their indiscipline, is creating a state within a state." This caused further restrictions to be placed on Soviet personnel. The following day a number of Syrian officers were arrested for voicing opposition to their government's policy of depending on Soviet technicians. Soviet pressure was then brought to bear and President Assad was informed that, if he wanted a continual flow of arms, he must accept Soviet technicians as well.

On 6 September, General Ismail had issued a Federal General Directive placing both Egyptian and Syrian armed forces on a "five-day alert" beginning on 1 October, and on 30 September he sent a cautious message to General Tlas directing him to be certain everything was ready. As early as the twenty-fourth, Syrian troops had begun a slow build-up against the Golan front, but this movement was interpreted by the Israelis as part of *detente* with Jordan, and that Syrian formations were being withdrawn from the Jordanian border to foster better relations between the two countries.

On 1 October, General Ismail confirmed that Operation Badr was definitely "on." Syrian armed forces were placed in a "full state of readiness" and the following day reservists began to be recalled. Various degrees of alert were maintained in the Egyptian, Syrian and Israeli forces. The slow movement of men and vehicles of three divisions began, but they seemed to be deploying near the cease-fire line in a "defensive posture," that is, with tanks dug in and the artillery well back as if anticipating an Israeli attack; therefore no undue alarm was felt by the watching Israelis.

On the Egyptian side, the armed forces were placed in a "state of alert." The annual manoeuvres, known as "Tahir 23" (Tahir means liberation), scheduled between the first and the seventh, began. This time, however, brigade-sized formations moved eastward toward the canal in the mornings, but in the evenings only one battalion returned westward and the other two remained under cover near the waterway. Guns, heavy equipment and ammunition were moved forward at night to be buried in the sand or otherwise hidden. Egyptian soldiers were told it was a full-scale mobilisation exercise in which the Engineer Corps would strengthen the canal defences and also work on the northern road being constructed as a feint. General Ismail later said, "I believe we succeeded in planning our decoy plan at a strategical and mobilisational level, and fixed for it timings and tables which marched parallel with the operational plan."

A variety of other deception measures were taken by the Arabs. The announcement was made on 2 October, in *Al Ahram*, that lists were open for officers who wished to make the Oomrah, or Little Pilgrimage to Mecca. On the third, about 2,000 reservists were demobilised. On the sixth, several ministers were out of the country on state business, including the economic minister, who was in London, the commerce minister in Spain, the information minister in Libya, and the acting foreign minister in Vienna. In the diplomatic field, the "on-off" merger of Egypt and Libya diverted attention and drew cynical smiles. In the immediate future, on the seventh, an RAF Comet was due to fly from Cyprus to test the airstrips at Abu Simbal and Luxor in preparation for the forthcoming visit of Princess Margaret to Egypt and, on the eighth, the Rumanian defence minister was to visit General Ismail.

Another act of deception, perhaps the most successful of all and to which President Sadat had only reluctantly given his assent, involved the use of the Syrian Fedayeen, the Saiqa. Sadat was not in favour of terrorist activities. President Assad had also recently cooled towards the Palestinian Fedayeen, having in fact, on 14 September, withdrawn the radio station facilities for the "Voice of Palestine," sponsored by the Palestine Liberation Organization, objecting to its anti-Hussein tone. The deception plan was carried out on 28 September: two gunmen of the Syrian Saiqa hijacked a train in Austria, took hostages, and demanded the closure of Schonau Castle near Vienna, which was being used as a transit camp for Jews leaving the Soviet Union. The Austrian chancellor, himself a Jew, agreed—a decision that caused anger and bitterness in Israel. Following this act of terrorism it was believed that the Israeli General Staff was planning a strike against the Arabs in retaliation, so the Egyptian and Syrian "defensive measures" appeared authentic in light of this anticipated Israeli attack.

Surprisingly enough in view of the meticulous planning so far, S Hour, upon which much depended, had not yet been decided. No agreement had been reached as the Syrians wanted an early morning hour and the Egyptians the late afternoon, because both wanted the sun behind them and shining into the eyes of the Israelis at this critical moment. On 2 October, General Ismail went to Damascus, a compromise was made and agreed to by President Assad: S Hour was to be at 2:00 P.M.

On 3 October, the Soviet Union launched a reconnaissance satellite, COSMOS-596, the first of a series, from the Plesetsk Cosmodrome near Archangel into orbit over the Middle East. Each day its path was altered slightly so it covered the two Israeli fronts. The Americans had already launched an Agenda D satellite from Vandenberg Air Force Base, California, on 27 September, so both superpowers were ready for battlefield surveillance should war break out in the Middle East in the immediate future.

Realizing that President Sadat seemed determined to mount an attack on Israel despite Soviet advice to the contrary, Brezhnev asked if he could withdraw all Soviet personnel in Egypt and Sadat reluctantly agreed. The Soviet Union sent in twenty planes and, beginning on the evening of the fourth, Soviet personnel and their families were quietly taken in coaches from their residences on Gizera Island, Cairo, to the airport and flown out. The Czech advisers and technicians also left about the same time, and Soviet ships moved out of Alexandria and Port Said harbours. Only seventy Russian technicians remained in Egypt. In Syria, the exodus of Russian families began on the fifth.

During the night of the fourth, the three mechanised divisions near the cease-fire line on the Syrian front changed from a defensive to an offensive posture, that is, guns were brought to the front and tanks came out of their dug-outs, ready to roll forward. On the same evening, on the Egyptian front, trucks and trailers carrying bridging equipment moved forward to the Suez Canal, while SAMs were brought up to within four miles of it. At dawn on the sixth, the FROG tactical missiles were placed on their firing pads. Later that morning, chemically treated uniforms designed to reduce the effects of napalm, which had been used liberally by the Israelis in 1967, were issued to the Egyptian soldiers. These special uniforms were never issued on exercises and could be worn only once—a fact known by the Israelis. On the morning of the sixth, the water in the Sweet Water Canal was lowered to prevent flooding in case any Israeli bombs or shells broke its banks.

On the night of the fifth, and during the early hours of the sixth, Egyptian rangers and frogmen quietly crossed the canal and nullified Israel's "secret weapon." Each Bar Lev Line fort, except those on the Bitter Lakes and the coasts, had a large tank containing about 200 gallons of oil, with pipes (thirty-nine in all) descending to the water's edge and nozzles either just below the surface of the water or just above it at low tide. In event of a mass Egyptian attack across the canal, the oil would be released onto the water and set afire by a thermite, or similar, bomb or by electrical means to incinerate the attackers. Despite formal Israeli denials, I saw ample evidence of this secret weapon, and its existence is admitted by Chaim Herzog, who was an official Israeli military commentator during the October War.

The Egyptians had seen the Israelis experimenting with this incendiary device in the Great Bitter Lake on 28 February 1971. The amount of oil available, if released onto the water, would burn an estimated thirty to forty minutes with temperatures of some 700 degrees centigrade and flames rising to a height of over four feet. It would not form a complete fire barrier along the length of the canal, but would produce floating islands of fire that would drift with the tide. The Egyptians experimented with methods of quickly quenching such flames but had not devised a successful countermeasure. It was therefore decided that should the rangers and frogmen be unable to nullify this weapon, the initial assault waves would be delayed until the oil patches had burned out.

The mission was successful: all the oil pipes were blocked

with wet cement or cut part way up the sand rampart so the oil would be absorbed into the sand. The Egyptians claimed that many of them would not have worked anyway because they had been made "oversecure" by garrison troops nervously tightening, and overtightening, the cocks and valves until they could not be turned manually. The Israelis were unaware that their secret weapon had been disarmed. Later, General Shazli asserted that "the operation was a complete success. Not a single fire was ignited on the canal and the stores were captured intact. The Israeli engineer who had designed the whole system was taken prisoner and testified during interrogation that he had arrived in the area only the day before on an inspection trip." The failure of the secret weapon was a result of both Egyptian preemptive action and Israeli oversecurity, and not, as one authority* claimed, that "a fire barrier based on the use of petroleum to set the canal water on fire remained unused, apparently for fear the Egyptians would resort to gas."

It now became necessary to share the secret of Y Day with more people, and on the evening of the fifth the staff of the headquarters of the assaulting divisions were told. Several groups of officers made the solemn pact to succeed or die in the attempt on the morrow. Brigade commanders were not generally told until about 8:00 A.M. on the sixth and, with certain exceptions, the men in the forward infantry companies did not know they were to attack until about 12:30 P.M. Air force pilots were briefed at noon.

Egyptian and Syrian commanders, staff officers and all personnel aware of the operation, synchronised their watches at noon by the normal time signal given over radios Cairo and Damascus. At 1:30 P.M., President Sadat entered the General Command Operations Centre, known as "Centre Number Ten" (there was an alternative known as Centre Number Three), and took his seat on the rostrum, flanked by generals Ismail and Shazli, and other senior officers. At 1:40 P.M., the order was

---

*Edward Luttwak was an Israeli officer who fought in the 1967 war. When the October War began, he was in Israel writing a book, *Israeli Army*, and remained there in a journalistic capacity.

given to stop all civilian air and sea traffic, which had been moving normally as part of the deception and surprise. At 2:00 P.M., S Hour, Egyptian and Iraqi aircraft crossed over the Suez Canal flying eastward. (Iraqi MiG-21 aircraft had been serving with the Egyptian air force for almost a year.) On the northern front Syrian guns fired the opening shots of a barrage and Syrian aircraft attacked Israeli targets, while at 2:05 P.M. Egyptian bombs dropped into the Sinai and Egyptian guns opened up along the length of the canal. In their planning estimates, the Egyptians anticipated 30,000 casualties, including 10,000 killed, in this assault operation.

The Israelis, caught completely by surprise, were initially driven back on both fronts. In the General Command Operations Centre, somewhere to the east of Cairo, reports came in that various missions and tasks had been completed successfully. President Sadat checked them off on his schedule.

4

FORTRESS
ISRAEL

They [the Israelis] thought they had safely drawn the map of the Middle East for the next 100 years.

General Ahmed Ismail

Small, alone and outnumbered by the surrounding Arabs, the Israelis had built a strong military state both to ensure survival and to dominate adjacent weaker Arab states. The Israeli strategic concept was that of attack. Bolstered by previous successes, it relied upon the air force, its "long arm," the best in the Middle East at the time, to reach out and smartly rebuke any Arab state that became too arrogant, and upon the armoured corps to launch punitive campaigns into adjacent territory when necessary to subdue any Arab government. In 1973, "Fortress Israel" preened itself as it looked around the Middle East, feeling secure from conventional military attack by surrounding countries, either individually or in coalition. General Ismail told me, "They thought they had safely drawn the map of the Middle East for the next 100 years." On 19 April 1973, United States Secretary of State Rogers again urged Israel and the Arab countries to negotiate a peace settlement, but neither was interested—for opposite reasons. The Arabs were preparing to strike, while Israel was confident the Arabs did not have the capability.

49

Looking toward Egypt, Premier Golda Meir of Israel thought
that President Sadat had alternately tried sabre-rattling and
diplomacy, both ineffectually. On 6 May 1973, the anniversary
of the founding of Israel, she replied to a question on the possi-
bility of Sadat's starting a war that "he can gain nothing by war.
He knows this. But all the same we believe he may act. If so we
are ready." It is doubtful that she really thought Sadat would
launch an attack on Israel, but, speaking from a position of
strength, this statement served as a warning to the Egyptians
not to attempt any military adventures. Israeli Defence Minister
Moshe Dayan believed that "the canal is the best defence line
we could hope for." His policy, in brief, was to remain behind
the Bar Lev Line and wait for the Arabs to make peace, feeling
that Israel could indefinitely sustain a condition of No Peace,
No War. In this frame of mind, the Israelis either overlooked,
ignored or brushed aside as trivial many of the more obvious
signs of Arab military preparation.

The Israelis believed the real danger lay in guerrilla warfare
and terrorism rather than conventional attack. The intelligence
service therefore neglected its efforts in Arab countries after the
June 1967 victory, recalling many of its agents. Instead, the
Israeli intelligence organisation concentrated on penetrating the
various Palestinian Fedayeen groups. The Israeli government did
not believe that the Arabs could conduct a campaign of guerrilla
warfare and terrorism and at the same time attack Israel. Official Israeli briefings indicated that Arab leaders were not prepared for war and almost casually warned that a miscalculated
Arab attack would be as quickly defeated as that in 1967. Israel,
it was emphasised, was not interested in war.

The Israelis knew that both President Sadat and General Ismail
had requested Soviet arms, with reasonable success. But when
the Russian and Czech advisers and technicians were ejected in
July 1972, the Israelis relaxed as they felt the Egyptians could
not handle a sophisticated air defence system without Soviet
assistance. The Israeli General Staff estimated that the Egyptians
would not be able to launch an attack on Israel before the end
of 1975.

Although isolated in the Middle East, the Israelis always cultivated one major ally, which at various times had been Britain and France, and was now America. A formal treaty of alliance or friendship had not been signed by the two countries, but it was assumed that American support would be forthcoming in an emergency. Israel could not produce the supply of sophisticated weaponry needed to retain military dominance and in recent years most of this equipment had come from the United States. In December 1971, President Nixon had promised more combat aircraft and also aid for the Israeli arms industry.

The Israelis were pleased, and relieved, when President Nixon was reelected in November 1972, as it meant a continuation of present American policy toward Israel. Premier Meir confirmed in a visit to Washington on 1 March 1973 that the Israeli government could still rely on this powerful ally. Press reports indicated that the Israeli premier had asked for thirty Phantoms, thirty Skyhawks, Cobra helicopters, Smart (laser-guided) bombs and technical assistance to develop the Israeli infant air industry; and, on the fourteenth, it was made known that the United States would provide to Israel twenty-four Phantoms, twenty-four Skyhawks, assistance to develop the Israeli Barak aircraft (basically a Mirage, a French multimission aircraft), and aid in the development of the new Israeli Galil automatic rifle.

The Israelis had become overconfident and almost contemptuous of the Arabs. It seemed as though the Arabs were merely preparing to repel an attack, rather than launch one. On 9 August 1973, in a lecture to the Israeli Army Staff College entitled "Transition from War to Peace," Defence Minister Dayan said, "The overall balance of forces is in our favour. Our military superiority is the dual outcome of Arab weakness and our strength. Their weakness stems from factors that will not change soon . . . low level of their soldiers' education, technology and integrity . . . disunion among the Arabs . . . and the decisive weight of extreme nationalism."

President Sadat's vaunted Year of Decision (1971) had passed without an attack and the uneasy truce continued the following year. Therefore, obvious warnings such as Sadat's statement on 28 March 1973, when he became premier, that "the stage of total confrontation has become inevitable and we are entering it whether we like it or not," or the declaration on 28 September that "Egypt may have to fight," were not given serious consideration by the Israelis.

Arab interest in diplomacy also deceived the Israelis. On 19 August, reports indicated that Egypt intended to embark upon a new diplomatic offensive against the Israelis in the following month. On 28 September, Arab envoys met with United States Secretary of State Henry Kissinger to discuss the procedure for negotiations and it was agreed that Kissinger should meet the Israelis sometime in November for the same purpose. The return of King Hussein to the Arab fold did not worry the Israelis. In the past, Hussein and Arafat, chairman of the Palestine Liberation Organisation and leader of the El Fatah Palestinian guerrilla group, had kissed and then shortly afterward resumed their deadly enmity. The Israelis had no reason to think his new friendship with Sadat and Assad would be any more durable.

The confidence exhibited by the Israelis did not mean they were completely without anxieties. Their major concerns centered on Soviet hostility, the Arab Fedayeen campaign, Arab terrorist activities, and obtaining sufficient modern arms from America. Other worries included the perpetual border friction; an internal Arab security problem, especially in the Gaza Strip; the decreasing flow of immigrants; the reduction in American, and other, private financial support and contributions; economic difficulties and some unemployment. Topics of conversation in Israel in late September 1973 revolved around the Schonau Castle affair and the general election scheduled for 31 October. Considerable interest and feeling had been aroused in the domestic political sphere. Strong trends of dissatisfaction had developed with the policies and activities of the ruling Alignment Government led by Premier Golda Meir. This party had been in power for a long period and was thought by many to be trading on the 1967 victory. Many Israelis thought it was time for a change.

The Israeli Defence Force, the IDF, or the "Zahal" (Zwa Hanagah Le Israel) as the Israelis liked to call it, was highly trained, dedicated and efficient, and was probably at its peak in 1967. The three separate services—army, air force and navy—

were firmly under the control of the chief of staff, who headed the General Staff, a body of about forty senior officers. A census taken in 1969 indicated 1,385,000 Arabs living in Israel and the occupied territories (300,000 Muslims and 72,150 Christians in Israel proper) and 2,434,000 Jews. Conscription in Israel included both men and women, the men serving initially for thirty-six months and the women for twenty months, followed by varying periods of annual training according to age limits. Few exceptions to the conscription laws were allowed for the Jews. Also subject to conscription were the Druse in Israel; thirty thousand members of this religious sect had accepted Israeli policies and become integrated into the national life. Circassians, a small ethnic group whose ancestors came from Russia, also served normally in Israeli units. But the Arabs, even Christian Arabs, were not allowed to serve in the IDF.

The regular element in the IDF numbered about 25,000: 11,500 in the army, 2,000 in the navy and 11,500 in the air force. About 50,000 conscripts were in various stages of training at any one time, plus an unknown number, greater in the spring and autumn, of recalled reservists undergoing annual training. On full mobilisation, the Israelis expected to muster about 310,000 personnel within seventy-two hours, of whom approximately 275,000 were in the army. Thirty-five percent of this force were women, who were used in noncombatant jobs although they were taught elementary use of small arms. Women formed a high proportion of the administrative "tail," performing tasks that released soldiers for combat duty, which explains the high "teeth" to "tail" ratio in the IDF of about fifty-fifty.

The basic field formation was the brigade, or regimental combat team, which varied in size from about 3,000 to 4,500 men, depending upon its type. The Israelis normally mobilised up to fifteen brigades at a time, usually a mixture of armoured, mechanised and infantry, and including three artillery brigades. These were employed either on garrison duty on the Golan and Suez Canal fronts, on standby alert, in a training role, or absorbing reservists for annual training. On mobilisation this number could be increased to thirty-two or thirty-four brigades, and, in fact, by the end of the October War about forty brigades had been identified, some of which had been hastily formed to replace others depleted by casualties. These brigades were grouped together for operational needs into a "task force" (Ugdad), which was virtually a division. About ten "shadow" divisions were designated on paper, to be activated only in an emergency; and regular and reserve officers, whose normal jobs would be temporarily suspended during hostilities, were "nominated" to command them.

The Israelis had always planned for a short war of about one week, calculating that the United Nations or the superpowers would quickly step in to stop any Arab-Israeli hostilities. Israeli strategy was to rapidly thrust as far as possible into Arab territory so they would hold the most advantageous position when the cease-fire was suddenly imposed. To support this strategy, the Israelis always put "their best goods in the shop window," that is, their best formations entered the battle first and then progressively, as required, the lesser-equipped or lesser-trained troops were employed in order of capability. Certain regular and reserve formations were trained to fight in certain areas, such as on the Golan or the Suez Canal fronts.

Israeli battle tactics had, since 1956, utilized the "armoured punch" (concentrated, head-on assault by tanks and SP guns), deep penetration and the pincer movement. This concept remained, but since 1967 Fortress Israel required a broad defensive capability as well, Israeli defenses being limited to forward forts and positions. Pride of place in the Israeli army was given to the armoured corps, and other services and arms had a lesser priority. On 10 December 1972, when the national budget was being discussed in the Knesset, the Israeli parliament, one-third was allocated to defence and Minister of Defence Dayan asserted "that 80 percent of the military budget planned for the next five years is earmarked for the air force and the armoured corps."

Weapons available to the prestigious Israeli armoured corps, however, were a mishmash, having been obtained by any available means as not all arms-producing nations would supply Israel. In round figures the Israelis possessed 1,750 tanks: 450 M-48 Pattons (with 105mm gun), 700 Centurions, 250 "Ben Gurions" (being Centurions with the French 105mm gun), 250

Super Shermans (with 105mm gun), and small numbers of other types including 100 T-67s or "Tirans," which were T-54s and T-55s captured during the 1967 war and renovated. According to Luttwak, all Pattons had been brought up to M-60A standards and all Centurions up to Mark 10 standards. There were also 300 Shermans waiting conversion to gun or mortar carriers.

The armoured personnel carriers included at least 1,000 old American M-2 and M-3 half-tracks, American M-113s and some captured Soviet models. Other weapons included the 175mm SP gun, the 155mm gun mounted on a Sherman chassis, 120mm guns and howitzers, 120mm and 160mm mortars, 106mm jeep-mounted recoilless guns, and 20mm, 30mm and 40mm antiaircraft guns. The United States magazine *Armor* estimated that seventy-eight percent of the Israeli tanks were superior to the Soviet T-54s and T-55s. The IDF's small number of vehicles, sufficient for normal activities, was supplemented in an emergency or mobilisation by a large number of civilian buses and trucks that carried troops, ammunition and supplies. Numbers of the tanks, guns and special vehicles were in "moth balls," that is, "greased up" in stores or on vehicle parks waiting to be issued on mobilisation. Generally the Israeli soldiers had gained a sound reputation for good maintenance of vehicles and for skillful improvisation in repairs, as many were years old and subject to frequent mechanical failure.

The Israelis possessed antitank weapons such as the old American LAW, the French SS10 and SS11, and the 3.5-inch rocket launcher, the latter made in Israel but using American ammunition; but they placed little reliance on them. The accepted doctrine was that "the best antitank weapon is another tank." In fact, the Israelis had been given an opportunity to have the American TOW antitank missile prior to October 1973 but had refused it.

A small Israeli armaments industry produced some small arms, ammunition, spare parts and equipment, but not weapons such as aircraft, tanks and guns. An "arms show" in Israel on 27 March 1973 displayed certain new items, including the Galil assault automatic rifle and an air-to-air missile. However, the loudly hailed Israeli surface-to-surface missile, the Jericho, with a claimed range of over 180 miles, had not appeared before October 1973. Progress had been made in repairing and renovating captured Soviet vehicles and weapons, and one Israeli munitions factory was able to produce ammunition for most types of captured Soviet guns. In this field the Israeli aim was to produce seventy-five percent of all weaponry required by 1977, including missiles and small naval craft, mortars, machine-guns, sub-machine-guns and rifles, as well as spare parts for tanks and other armoured vehicles. Producing guns was still an unsolved problem because of the difficulty in obtaining sufficient suitable steel.

The team of generals and colonels who directed the Israeli Defence Force in October 1973 consisted of relatively new appointments. With the normal flow of promotion, the majority of names in the IDF that had become familiar to the outside world in 1967 had gradually passed from the military scene. In any case, most IDF personnel were unknown to the public as Israeli censorship allowed only the names of certain senior officers and commanders to be revealed and the press referred to most personnel by forename or sobriquet. With a few exceptions, the unknown brigade commanders of 1967 became the unknown divisional commanders of 1973; and the unknown battalion and company commanders of 1967 became the unknown brigade and battalion commanders of 1973.

Moshe Dayan remained defence minister, a position he had assumed on the eve of the 1967 conflict; however, most of the senior General Staff officers had changed. The current chief of staff, Lieutenant General David Elazar, was appointed in January 1972 as successor to Chaim Bar Lev, who had left the army to become minister of commerce and industry in Golda Meir's government. Elazar had been the GOC, Northern Command, in 1967 and previously had commanded both the Infantry and Armoured schools, and then a paratroop brigade. Chosen primarily for his managerial talents, he favoured maintaining defensive fortifications rather than placing reliance on mobile operations. The deputy chief of staff and director of operations was Major General Israel Tal, also appointed in 1972. As commander of the armoured corps from 1964 to 1969, he led an armoured column in the 1967 war. General Tal was against static defensive positions and favoured mobile warfare.

Another important senior appointment was GOC, Northern Command, assumed by Major General Yitzhak Hofi in May 1973. He had been director of training for four years and in 1967 had fought on the Golan Plateau. Major General Shmuel Gonen, commander of the famous 7th Armoured Brigade in the Sinai in 1967, had been appointed GOC, Southern Command, in July 1973. The commander of the armoured corps, a prestige appointment, had been held since 1969 by Major General Avraham Adan, previous commander of the armed forces in the Sinai. Adan had served under Major General Avraham Mandler, former commander of the armed forces; Mandler's tenure was due to expire on 7 October but he continued serving when war broke out. The important position of director of intelligence was assumed by Major General Eliahu Zeira in 1972, replacing Major General Aharon Yariv, who had served in this capacity for nine years. Zeira had previously been military attaché in Washington and held the opinion that the Arabs would never attack Israel.

A retired general, Ariel Sharon, was recalled and achieved notoriety during the October War. He had commanded the paratroops from 1954 to 1956, had been divisional commander in the Sinai in the 1967 war, and had assumed the post of GOC, Southern Command, in 1969. Sharon left the army in July 1973, reputedly disappointed because he was not selected to be chief of staff. He had entered politics, as had a few other retired generals, and as a member of the Liberal Party was active in organising the Likud, a right-wing group. He was not elected to the Knesset, however, until after the October War.

The first hint that the amused Israeli tolerance of Arab military capability might be misplaced came on 26 September, when Moshe Dayan, accompanied by the chief of staff, paid a routine visit to the Golan Plateau. The GOC, Northern Command, General Hofi, expressed concern, openly questioning the confidence the Israeli military intelligence placed in the early warning system. Hofi pointed out that the plateau was defended only by an understrength armoured brigade and an infantry brigade. He requested the return of the regular garrison formation, the 7th Armoured Brigade, which was still in the south near Beersheba having participated in a training exercise. Dayan, who generally had a nose for military danger, agreed with Hofi. The regular element of the army was placed on a "low state of alert," which meant only that no more leaves were granted to the soldiers. The Jewish New Year, Rosh Hashanah, 27 to 29 September, was a major holiday period in Israel and no newspapers were printed. It therefore attracted little attention when, during this period, Dayan persuaded the chief of staff to move the 7th Armoured Brigade back to the Golan Plateau.

In America, careful observers noticed ominous signs about the situation in the Middle East. On 24 September, the United States National Security Agency, which monitored international political and military radio traffic from a base in Iran, warned the Israelis that the Syrians were making warlike preparations. The Israelis did not take this seriously, and visits to the Golan Plateau by tourists were still allowed. During Rosh Hashanah over 20,000 Israelis and tourists visited the Mitla Pass in the Sinai to view the rusting tanks and vehicles by the roadside— relics of the 1967 war and cherished symbols of Israeli military supremacy. By the thirtieth, American anxiety heightened. United States intelligence services, however, relied heavily upon confirmation from Israeli sources, and, since the Israelis had a good reputation for opinions and deductions, their skepticism was accepted. The Israelis monitored sensors and other listening devices well forward on both the Egyptian and Syrian fronts and, although their air reconnaissances were not as frequent as in the past, they were aware of troop movements. The Arab activity was casually dismissed as the usual autumn manoeuvres.

On 1 October, the Israelis became aware of increased Egyptian activity behind the high sand ramparts—convoys of trucks being moved, stakes being driven into the ground near the canal by the new concrete slipways, and an increased number of soldiers manning the defences. But Israeli thoughts were elsewhere: Premier Meir was in Austria attending a meeting of the Council of Europe, and while there she also met with the chancellor in an unsuccessful attempt to change his decision regarding the closure of Schonau Castle. The news media focused on these diplomatic efforts and gave minimal coverage to the Arab activity. Only one Israeli newspaper reported Dayan's remarks that "a complete air defence system, based on SAM-2s and SAM-3s, had been installed on the Golan Heights," and that "Syrian guns and heavy tanks had been moved to the front line." On the second, another Israeli newspaper reported that Egypt had declared a "state of alert" in the Suez Canal Zone, but the following day other newspapers soothingly stated that there were no signs of an Egyptian alert.

General Gonen visited the Bar Lev Line on 2 October but did not express alarm. Although signs were becoming obvious, it seemed as if the Israelis did not want to recognize the approaching danger. Gonen then disappeared on a "private visit" and was still away from his general headquarters on the fourth when more disturbing aerial photographs were obtained. On the fifth, orders were given to hurry the construction of two pontoon bridges the Israelis were constructing for a potential canal crossing.

On 3 October, cabinet meetings were held in both Jerusalem and Cairo. In Cairo, the only subject on the agenda was the proposed merger of Egypt with Libya. In Jerusalem the Schonau Castle affair was discussed, Premier Meir having returned from Austria. However, Meir later wrote that on that day she met Dayan and certain senior staff officers (but not General Zeira as he was ill and unable to attend), who told her they were uneasy about Arab preparations to attack Israel. The consensus was that there was no danger of Egypt's launching an attack, and it was not thought that Syria would attack alone. In view of this, no decision was made to take any immediate action.

During the week before 6 October, United States Secretary of State Kissinger had called for American intelligence predictions and each time was given the opinion that hostilities would not break out in the Middle East. On the fourth, he again asked about the situation, and both Israeli and American military intelligence organisations gave the same forecast—war was unlikely.

Premier Meir had formed the habit of informally gathering a few ministers, and others, on an impromptu basis to discuss any particular matter of immediate importance. The press referred to these small meetings as her "Kitchen Cabinet." She was vaguely worried about the military situation and called an emergency meeting for noon, on 5 October, the day before Yom Kippur. The nine ministers who were in Tel Aviv attended as well as generals Elazar and Zeira. Reports were read of Russian families leaving Syria, but neither Dayan, Elazar nor Zeira attached any importance to this event. Mrs. Meir later commented: "No, it hadn't changed their assessment." During the morning of the fifth, Israeli reconnaissance planes had flown only over the Egyptian front. Had they flown over the Syrian front, they would have noticed the changed posture of the Syrian divisions near the cease-fire line. Because of the premier's anxiety, the ministers present passed a resolution that, if necessary over the coming holiday weekend, the premier and the defence minister could jointly order a "full scale call-up," the authority for which normally required a full cabinet decision. Later, Premier Meir wrote, "That Friday morning I should have listened to the warnings of my heart and ordered a call-up."

At approximately 4:00 A.M. (Israeli time) on 6 October, Premier Meir received a signal which Abba Eban, the Israeli foreign minister, then in New York, had dispatched at 9:00 P.M. (New York time) the previous day, there being a time difference of seven hours. The message reported that the Egyptians and Syrians would launch a joint attack on Israel late in the afternoon. General Zeira was also informed from America at the same time. He at once passed the information to Dayan and Elazar by telephone, and by 6:00 A.M. the three were in conference. Elazar proposed general mobilisation at once and a preemptive air strike against Syria, but Dayan disagreed. At about this time certain foreign diplomats in Israel, including United States Ambassador Kenneth Keating, were given this information.

Premier Meir met with Dayan and Elazar at 8:00 A.M. General Elazar still recommended a preemptive air strike and general mobilisation starting with the entire air force and four divisions of soldiers. If called up immediately, they would be ready to go into action at first light on the seventh; "But you must give me the green light now," he stated. Moshe Dayan was against this plan and instead favoured calling up the air force plus mobilising two extra divisions, one for the north and one for the south. He argued that full mobilisation before a shot had been fired would cause Israel to be branded as the aggressor. The premier, remembering that Elazar had called "wolf" once in May 1973 and had been proved wrong, would not agree to his suggestions and gave permission to mobilise only 100,000 men. Elazar, in fact, stretched this permission and activated many more.

At ten o'clock that morning, Ambassador Keating met with Premier Meir in her office and warned against making a preemptive strike against the Arabs as such a course would make it difficult for the United States to send military aid to Israel. Mrs. Meir gave him her assurance that this measure would not be taken.

At 7:00 A.M. on the sixth, a reconnaissance by Israeli aircraft over the Golan front showed clearly for the first time that three Syrian divisions had changed from a defensive to an offensive posture, while on the Egyptian front the bridging and other assault equipment were noticed. Little doubt remained that the Arabs were about to attack, but the Israelis expected it to be launched at dusk, about 6:00 P.M., and assumed they had several hours to prepare. By 9:00 A.M., senior officers and key personnel were being alerted and told to report to their mobilisation centres. The "logistic phase" of mobilisation began: briefings were prepared, weapons and equipment issued, and the men of various units progressively called to report to their centres by code words given over the radio, a different word or phrase being used for each unit and known only to the personnel of that unit.

Although it had become obvious to the General Staff that hostilities were imminent, the warning passed slowly through the chain of command. General Elazar later admitted that brigade commanders were not informed until the morning of the sixth (he did not say what time) while junior officers and many commanding officers were not informed at all. Many of them first realized the urgency of the situation either minutes before the Arab attack or when the first bombs or shells exploded. The one exception was the air force, with its large proportion of regulars, which was in a full state of alert. Air force reservists, who were less than one-third of its total strength, had been re-called on the fourth, seemingly without ministerial permission.

At the Commission of Enquiry after the war, General Elazar claimed that the Israeli army alert had begun ten days before 6 October and had reached its peak on the morning of the fifth as far as the "regular army was concerned." He was referring to the low state of alert that had come into force on 24 September and had been slightly upgraded although not extended to recall regulars and those on their initial or reserve training. In fact, on the fifth he had "called in," rather than "called up," certain commanders and staffs of the reserve divisions for briefing, and other senior officers were called in during the morning of the sixth for the same purpose. It was not until 11:00 A.M. on the sixth, however, that Elazar cancelled all leave and warned that a call-up of reservists was possible. Full mobilisation was never formally decreed: it just happened. When the war began, the "logistic phase" had been partially completed, the mobilisation machinery fell into gear, and code words were given by radio calling soldiers to their units.

On the governmental level the reluctance to order full mobili-sation continued even as late as the morning of the sixth. There had been three mobilisations since the 1967 war, all costly and disruptive to the Israeli economy—one in December 1971 when the Egyptians were about to bomb Sharm El-Sheikh, the second in December 1972 when the Egyptians were about to drop para-troops in the Sinai, and the last in May 1973. According to General Elazar, the last situation had seemed more serious than the present state of affairs and still there had been no war. Hesi-tation and indecision resulted. The opinion of the Israeli General Staff was that the real danger period for Arab attack should have been during the Jewish New Year holiday, Rosh Hashanah, when from a mobilisation point of view the Israelis would be at their weakest. Furthermore, it was thought that the Arabs would not launch a military operation during the month of Ramadan, which in 1973 was from 26 September to 26 October, when all Muslims should fast during the hours of daylight. It was not until noon on the sixth that the full Israeli cabinet met to dis-cuss the situation and to formulate a course of action. When the

Arabs struck at 2:00 P.M., the cabinet was still in session and Premier Meir later wrote, "The shock wasn't only over the way it started, but also the fact a number of our basic assumptions were proven wrong."

In America, on the fourth and fifth, the intelligence services had been working on a new evaluation of the situation in the Middle East. This updated information was not yet available at 6:00 A.M. (New York time) and 1:00 P.M. (Israeli time) on the sixth, when the Israeli ambassador telephoned Henry Kissinger to say the Arabs were about to attack Israel. Immediately after this telephone call, Kissinger checked with his intelligence organisation which confirmed the information and, at 6:07 A.M., he telephoned the news to President Nixon in Washington—just fifty-three minutes before the Arabs actually struck. The Americans had also been caught by surprise.

5

STORMING THE
BAR LEV LINE

*Each of us knew by heart what he was supposed
to do. We had been training for the mission for
quite a long time.*

Wounded Egyptian soldier on Cairo Television,
9 October 1973.

On the Suez Canal front, behind the Bar Lev Line, there were three main north-south roads. One, running roughly alongside the canal, was marked part of the way by a line of telegraph poles which formed a distinctive and useful landmark. Another, a metalled (paved) road, known as Artillery Road to the Israelis and designed for rapid deployment of artillery and tanks, lay between six and seven miles to the east of the canal. It was covered from the west by a 600-foot high ridge of small features that included Tasa Hill, Subha Hill, and Katib el Kheil, the last known to the Israelis as Triangle 100. Mounds and banks of sand had been added to this ridge to conceal tanks, stores and movement. It also provided the Israelis with excellent observation points not easily distinguishable against the higher background of the Khatmia Ridge farther to the east. The ground in general sloped gently upward from the canal eastward. Tasa, on Artillery Road, almost in line with Ishmailia, was a small mili-

65

tary complex with an underground command post, accommodation, stores, vehicle parks and a small airstrip.

Farther to the east, between eleven and thirteen miles from the canal, was the third metalled road, known as Supply Road. Overlooking it from the east lay the Khatmia Ridge, rising to a height of 2,500 feet above sea level, with its foothills at distances varying from twenty to forty miles from the canal. It is higher and broader in the south, where it merges into the mountainous mass that is southern Sinai, than it is in the centre and north. The Khatmia Ridge peters out in line with Kantara and gives way to soft sand which, in turn, going farther north, gives way to saltmarsh near the Mediterranean coast. The Canal, Artillery and Supply roads were linked by a network of smaller lateral ones. The elongated area between the Suez Canal and the Khatmia Ridge, reaching from just north of Kantara to just south of Port Tewfik, was suitable for armoured movement although it had patches of loose sand.

Lying some ten miles or so back from the canal, spaced out along the whole front, were six strongly constructed Israeli command posts, camouflaged and well protected against bombs and shellfire by concrete walls and roofs and further bolstered by mesh-wire crated stones. These CPs had sophisticated communication equipment with which to control their respective areas. Behind the Khatmia Ridge lay Bir Gifgafa, known as Redafin by the Israelis, a fairly large military complex which was the HQ of the Suez Canal front command.

Only four east-west roads crossed the Sinai Desert, although there were lateral ones and military road networks branching off from them. The northern Coastal Road went from Kantara East (to differentiate it from Kantara West on the west bank of the canal) through Romani eastward to El Arish. From Romani a causeway-type road ran westward toward the Suez Canal, through the saltmarsh to Port Fuad. The Israelis had built a small network of roads in the saltmarsh triangle. The other three roads went through the three vital passes in the Khatmia Ridge: the Central Road from Ismailia through the Khatmia Pass to Bir Gifgafa, Jebel Libni and Abu Ageila; the Southern Road from the shore of Great Bitter Lake through the Giddi Pass to

Bir Hasana and on to Kusseima; and the age-old Pilgrims Way, from Port Tewfik through the Mitla Pass to Nakhel, Thamada and Ras el-Nageb. These three passes were the only means of access for vehicles through the Khatmia Pass from the west into the open Sinai Desert beyond, because to the north of the ridge the sandsea and saltmarsh were formidable vehicle barriers.

On the sixth of October the forts in the Bar Lev Line were manned by a reserve brigade from the Jerusalem area identified as the 116th Infantry Brigade. Although Premier Meir later stated that there had been 600 troops holding the line, General Chaim Herzog, who became an official military commentator during the war, said in *The War of Atonement* that there were "436 men in 16 forts" supported by seven batteries of artillery. While the Egyptians do not flatly contradict this number of forts, they say the Israelis talk only of their main positions and omit mention of alternative ones or those they had been unable to reach and occupy in time because they had been caught by surprise. The Bar Lev Line held ammunition, food and supplies sufficient to last for one month at least; water had been piped through the desert from El Arish to each fort; electricity had been installed, and civilian telephones were available for the soldiers to ring their homes at cheap rates. Another independent infantry detachment covered the area of the northern triangle of saltmarsh.

The Israelis had three armoured brigades available for instant action: two between the canal and the Khatmia Ridge which had in total some 280 tanks and fifty SP guns, and the other just to the east of the ridge. The forward armoured brigade, with its nine companies scattered along the front, was in position just a couple of miles or so behind the Bar Lev Line, ready to rush forward within thirty minutes to knock back any invaders. Behind it was another armoured brigade, in the vicinity of Supply Road, prepared to strike at any major thrust within a reaction time of two hours. The third armoured brigade was positioned just to the east of the ridge near the passes and was ready to move through them quickly. There were also three other brigades to the east of Khatmia Ridge. These several formations were identified as the 7th, 14th, 401st and 460th Armoured Brigades, the 204th Mechanised and the 99th Infantry (paratroop) Brigades. The Israeli system of designation of their formations was deliberately confusing, and some designations were duplicated; for example, there was also a 7th Armoured Brigade on the Golan Plateau.

Normally there were about eight brigades of different types in the Sinai, either in garrison or in training. Their reaction time to reach the canal in an emergency was up to eight hours. Another three reserve brigades were earmarked to reinforce the area on mobilisation. There were also four NAHAL (initials of Hebrew words meaning "Pioneering Fighting Youth") battalions composed of soldier-workers establishing settlements in the Sinai and the Gaza Strip. The Egyptians estimated that on full mobilisation the Israelis would be able to muster twenty brigades in the Sinai, but they miscalculated as the number rose to twenty-seven by the time the October War ended. On 6 October they calculated there were about eight thousand Israeli troops in the Sinai with over 300 tanks and seventy SP guns.

On the Suez Canal front the Israeli troops manning the Bar Lev Line, and those in immediate support behind it, were unaware that war was about to descend heavily upon them; the atmosphere of urgency felt at higher level had not filtered down to them. On the west bank the usual off-duty activities went on —Egyptian soldiers fishing, swimming and lounging near the water's edge. One senior Egyptian officer told me that at 1200 hours he went to the sand rampart in the southern sector to look across at the terrain he was about to invade, only to find many reconnoitering commanders and officers from armoured, artillery, engineer and infantry formations there before him for the same purpose. They milled around on the top of the rampart, smoking, laughing and drinking coffee. Since the Egyptians did not carry arms, they were ignored by the Israeli sentry in his sixty-foot high watchtower. The sentry was shot by an Egyptian sniper in two hours' time.

One unit commander brought up his whole unit in trucks saying, "Let my men have a look before the battle." There seemed to have been other similar but smaller incidents along the length of the canal, but no suspicion was roused until about 1345 hours, when suddenly, on the Egyptian side, all went quiet. Off-duty soldiers disappeared, and the more observant Israeli sentries in their watchtowers noted that muzzle covers were being removed from guns and mortars on the west bank. About midday General Mandler, who commanded the three forward armoured brigades and the northern infantry one, was alerted that an Egyptian attack was expected that evening. Initially slow to implement the immediate counterattack plan, he had not commenced moving his tanks when the war began. About the same time the commanding officer of the 116th Infantry Brigade in the Bar Lev Line was also warned. He began telephoning each of the forts but had great difficulty in persuading his people that an attack was expected. Herzog asserted that "it took him at least five minutes in every single case to convince his officers he was talking about real war." A few Israeli commanders began to sense that something was wrong and took the precaution of alerting extra sentries, of recalling off-duty soldiers to the confines of the defensive positions, and of manning the outer defences. However, most of the Israeli soldiers, if they were religious, continued their devotions; if not, they carried on playing football, doing their chores, or just relaxing.

About 1400 hours 240 Egyptian aircraft in small groups flew over the canal eastward into the Sinai to drop bombs and fire rockets at a dozen or more Israeli targets. (The Iraqis claim that twelve of the planes were theirs, but the Egyptians deny that any were present.) Their objectives included Israeli HQ, communication and radar installations, three airfields, HAWK batteries, gun concentrations, and the Budapest fort on the Mediterranean. The object was to ensure that the bombs and rockets hit their targets precisely at S Hour, and the majority did. The Egyptians admit losing one plane, but they claim that a number of field guns, including a battery of long-range 175mm guns, and some radar and communication equipment were destroyed. A second Egyptian air strike was planned and ready; it was not carried out because it was thought that the first had caused sufficient damage.

On the previous night, during the hours of darkness, the Egyptians had brought their guns and mortars forward, immedi-

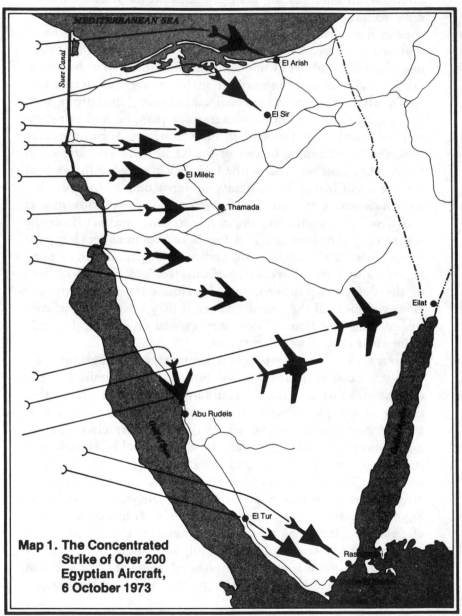

Map 1. The Concentrated Strike of Over 200 Egyptian Aircraft, 6 October 1973

MEDITERRANEAN SEA

Suez Canal

El Arish

El Sir

El Mileiz

Thamada

Eilat

Gulf of Suez

Abu Rudeis

El Tur

Ras

Source: Egyptian rendition.

ately behind the shielding sand rampart and had positioned their tanks on the pyramids. At S Hour, 1405 hours, about two thousand weapons opened up with a tremendous barrage; about half were fired directly at the Bar Lev Line. Rocket launchers were aimed so as to explode their rockets on the forward slopes in order to set off all mines and booby traps between the forts where the assaulting troops were to climb. The other half, mainly mortars and long-range artillery, used indirect fire on the targets behind the Bar Lev Line in four lifting phases which lasted for fifty-three minutes. In this barrage some 10,500 shells and bombs, interspersed with smoke shells, were fired at the rate of 175 a minute. In all, this amounted to over three thousand tons of high explosive (HE). The Egyptians had catered for a fifteen-minute extension of the barrage in the event of the Israeli secret weapon being used. This was to allow time for the blazing oil on the water to burn itself out, but this safeguard had not been necessary as all the oil pipes had been put out of action. At the same time a number of FROG missiles were fired at the various Israeli command posts in the Sinai from three sites on the west bank. The seventeen United Nations observation posts along the canal contained forty-two U.N. observer officers who were evacuated at the request of the Egyptians once S Hour had passed, but the news of this action was not released until the ninth, three days later.

The Egyptian artillery generally had six guns to a battery and three batteries to a regiment. It had changed from the British technique of "all-round fire" to the Soviet mode of massed guns all firing on the same arc, usually of not more than ninety degrees. The whole barrage was centrally controlled by Major General Said el-Mahi, commander of artillery. The Egyptian gunners told me the Russians were very good at handling artillery in mass on this principle, but, as the system was so rigid, its weakness was that it was not possible to switch quickly to fire to a flank or the rear in case of a surprise attack.

At 1405 hours, just as the artillery barrage began, the Egyptian tank hunting teams, armed with Sagger, Snapper, and RPG-7 weapons, lowered their inflatable rubber boats into the water and commenced crossing the canal. They were men in a

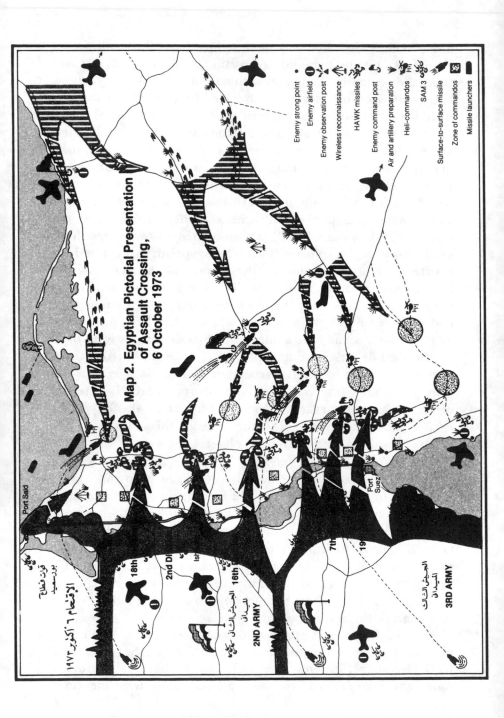

Map 2. Egyptian Pictorial Presentation of Assault Crossing, 6 October 1973

hurry. Their task was to scale the main sand rampart on the Israeli side and then race to the secondary one to take up positions to meet the anticipated Israeli armoured counterattacks. Heavily laden with weapons and ammunition, these soldiers wore boots with special soles designed to give some protection against mines. They also carried gas masks as it was anticipated the Israelis might use war gases, but the Egyptians insist they did not possess any war gas at all. As the soldiers scrambled over the rampart, it became a time and space race.

One of the first Israeli officer prisoners to be taken was Lieutenant Shimon Tal of the Engineer Corps. He had been inspecting the Israeli secret weapon. When the initial Egyptian barrage began he was near the Bar Lev Line fort, known to the Israelis as Hizayom, near El Ferdan. He took shelter and was captured.

It was the Israeli intention, once the alarm went, to get their tanks onto the positions on the secondary sand rampart, from which they could either use their guns for overhead fire or their machine guns to the flanks to catch any attackers between the two ramparts. The anticipated Israeli initial reaction time of thirty minutes was about right, but the Egyptian tank hunting teams seem to have won the time and space race, as they all claim that no Israeli tank pushed past them in this phase of the battle. Some of the soldiers said they had made it to the secondary rampart with only seconds to spare, and, as they were completely out of breath, they had difficulty in keeping their weapons steadily aimed at the approaching tanks. As anticipated, the Israelis made eight company-sized armoured attacks within a half hour. They charged headlong, at great speed, with hull down and sometimes firing on the move, into the barrage of Egyptian missiles and rockets, but all were halted with loss. The ninth company of the forward armoured brigade was in the north, supporting the static infantry brigade where it remained stationary watching the Port Fuad garrison.

The main weapon of the tank hunting teams was the Sagger, the "suitcase" missile, so-called because its carrying case forms the base plate for the weapon and is shaped and carried like a suitcase. Called the Maluka by the Egyptians, it has a maximum range of about 3,000 yards and a minimum of about 500. Its antitank missile, a guided type that rotates in flight, travels at a speed of 150 yards a second and is manually guided to its target by a "joy stick" device. Three months' training and continual practice are normally required to produce an efficient, accurate operator, as the guidance joy stick requires a very delicate touch. If the operator falls out of practice, he needs some retraining. The Egyptian operators had been training all through the summer and autumn of 1973 on the Sagger, on special ranges, firing up to twenty-five missiles a day.

The tank hunting teams also used the Snapper, an older antitank missile with a four-round launcher system. The Snapper, with its HEAT warhead, is guided by fins and does not rotate in flight. Its maximum range is about 2,000 yards, its minimum about 500 yards. Time is also required for the Snapper operator to become efficient and accurate. The shoulder-held RPG-7 fired a spin-stabilized rocket with a HEAT warhead. Its maximum range was about 450 yards, its minimum 100 yards or less.

At 1420 hours, just as the last of the Egyptian planes were overhead returning from their initial mission, the first wave of about 1,000 rubber assault boats began to cross the canal. Propelled manually by paddles, they carried in all about 8,000 soldiers. The majority of these boats contained infantry whose job was to leap ashore and secure a toe hold on the east bank, but some contained "beach parties" that were to put out markers on the bank, remain in position to control the arrival and departure of successive assault boats, and direct assaulting troops. By this time the canal, like the Bar Lev Line, was heavily wreathed in coloured smoke and visibility was spasmodically obscured. Cables were soon strung across the canal as guide and demarcation lines; different colours indicated different formation areas and sectors.

The second wave, in addition to carrying more infantry, brought over at least sixty detachments of engineers together with their pressure pumps and hoses. They immediately began to blast gaps in the huge sand rampart preparatory to erecting bridges which would enable vehicles to pass over to the east bank. Each of these detachments consisted of fourteen men,

Egyptian soldiers landing from rubber boats on the Suez Canal's East Bank to assault the Bar Lev Line.

with two pumps, each with two hoses, carried in four assault boats, two of which became floating platforms for the pumps. Two soldiers acted as sentries on the top of the rampart. Some of the gaps in the northern sector were made in under three hours.

There were twelve waves of a thousand assault craft each; very few were lost in crossing, and each wave successively landed on the east bank at fifteen-minute intervals. The third wave carried mainly soldiers of the five infantry divisions selected for the operation. In view of the derogatory criticism in 1967 that Egyptian officers ran away and left their men in battle, it was strictly laid down exactly where the officers should be. Platoon commanders were in the first wave, of course, company commanders in the second, and battalion commanders in the third. While brigade commanders, their equivalents and staffs, were in the fifth, the divisional commanders themselves crossed in the seventh wave, most setting foot on the east bank by about 1550 hours. The crossing seemed to run according to schedule.

The Egyptians, crossing in line abreast, used their five infantry divisions in this assault. They were divided into two corps, or "armies," the bounday between them being the Bitter Lakes. In the north the Second Army, commanded by Major General Mohammed Saad el-Din Maamun, contained three infantry divisions. From north to south these were the 18th, commanded by Brigadier Fuad Aziz Ghali; the 16th, commanded by Brigadier Abd Rah el-Nabi Hafez; and the 2nd, commanded by Brigadier Hassan Abu Saada. To the south was the smaller Third Army, commanded by Major General Abdel Moneim Mwassil, having two infantry divisions only: the 19th, commanded by Brigadier Tassef Afifi, and the 7th, commanded by Brigadier Ahmed Badawri. About 14,000 strong, the infantry divisions contained three infantry brigades and one mechanised brigade. The integral armoured element amounted to about ninety-five tanks in four units, one to each infantry brigade, the other being divisional reserve. The First Army lay in reserve, stripped of many of its tanks, weapons, and much of its equipment to ensure that the assaulting armies would be adequately equipped.

The assaulting infantry landed on the east bank between the

Bar Lev Line forts which, blinded by smoke and subjected to both direct fire from tanks on the pyramids and indirect mortar fire, were momentarily ignored as the soldiers rushed to the secondary sand rampart to form five initial bridgeheads. The infantry brought more antitank missiles and guns forward with them; the latter were carried in sections and assembled, once the first rampart had been surmounted. Small four-wheeled hand-carts, or trolleys, were used to transport the heavier items of equipment and ammunition and were hauled up the first rampart by ropes. The men used scaling ladders of both wood and rope and other aids to enable them to scramble quickly up through the soft sand of this steep obstacle. As the Egyptian platoons reached the top of the rampart, they raised their national flag. It was claimed that the first such flag appeared in the Third Army sector, opposite El Shatt, at 1430 hours; the Second Army's first flag went up at Kantara East at 1443 hours. The first Israeli artillery reaction came at 1445 hours.

In the north, of the four forts at Kantara East that the 18th Infantry Division attacked on that afternoon, it was reported that one fell within ten minutes, a second within fifteen minutes, and a third at 1550 hours. All the defenders of the last were found dead. In view of the actual distances the infantrymen had to cover, these claims tend to be rather exaggerated. The fourth fort still held out, and later that afternoon the Israelis bombarded all four of them, including the one they still held. In the Third Army sector, the southernmost of the two forts guarding the southern end of Little Bitter Lake fell at 1525 hours when taken by troops ferried across the lake by motor launch. Three others, one at kilometre 146 and the other two opposite El Shatt, fell or were entered at 1538 hours.

Generally, the Bar Lev Line forts were merely contained, or even ignored for the time being, to be dealt with later. Although most Egyptian assaults on these forts were successful, one notable failure was the attack on the fort at the southern end of the canal. An elongated, narrow position on a thin peninsula of land opposite Port Tewfik, known to the Israelis as the Quay (Melakh), was held by forty-two men and had five tanks within its compound; it was the only fort to have tanks. The initial

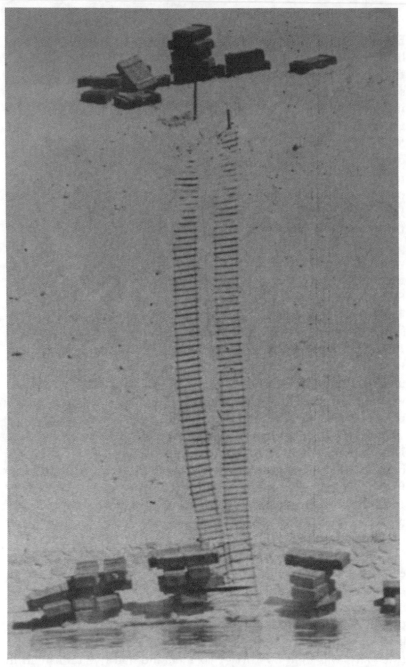

Egyptian ladders used to scale Israeli sand ramparts on the East Bank.

Egyptian frontal assault was beaten off, but a second attack on the other side of the peninsula cut the position in half. The half at the extreme southern tip of the peninsula was evacuated. One of the first Israeli armoured counterattacks to attempt to relieve this fort was beaten off by the Egyptians when most of the attacking tanks were destroyed. The neck of land leading to the position from landward was barely thirty yards wide. Later, I counted eleven destroyed or badly damaged Patton tanks scattered alongside the narrow roadway, most with their hulls completely detached from the body of the tank, the result of their ammunition exploding. Even though attacked again from the front, and then on all three sides, the main part of the Israeli position, that nearest the canal, continued to hold out. Another Egyptian attack that failed was one made on the southernmost of the two forts opposite El Ferdan; the northernmost of the two was taken at 1620 hours.

The Egyptian-held triangle of territory around Port Fuad on the northern tip of the east bank extended about six miles south along the canal and about eight miles east along the coast. The Egyptians had constructed a raised causeway eastward from Port Fuad as a deceptive measure. About two miles from the edge of Egyptian-held territory was an Israeli strong point, known to them as Budapest. They liked to include it as one of their Bar Lev Line forts, although it was well away from the canal and actually on the Mediterranean shore. It was constructed of rocks and girders in a somewhat primitive manner and was held by eighteen soldiers who manned its four 175mm guns. The guns used a special U.S. ammunition that increased their range to 45,000 yards. This gun position could easily cover the whole of the Port Said area on the west bank.

The Israeli guns at Budapest were knocked out of action in the initial barrage by marine-manned guns at Port Said and the air strike. The barrage lasted for two hours; shells were fired at the rate of thirty a minute. It was afterward admitted by the Israeli director of artillery in a lecture in France that they were not able to fire at all during the war, although the position had ample ammunition. Three Israelis were killed, and intercommunication equipment was put out of action. At 1600 hours an

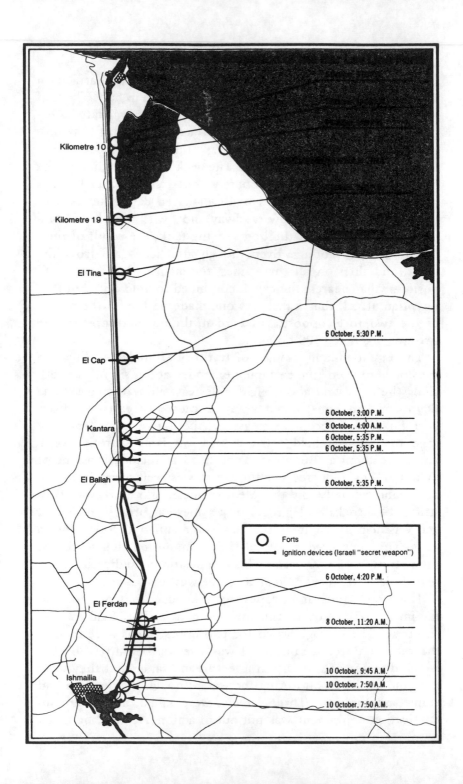

Kilometre 10

Kilometre 19

El Tina

6 October, 5:30 P.M.

El Cap

6 October, 3:00 P.M.
8 October, 4:00 A.M.
Kantara
6 October, 5:35 P.M.
6 October, 5:35 P.M.

El Ballah
6 October, 5:35 P.M.

○ Forts

━━► Ignition devices (Israeli "secret weapon")

6 October, 4:20 P.M.

El Ferdan

8 October, 11:20 A.M.

10 October, 9:45 A.M.
Ishmailia
10 October, 7:50 A.M.
10 October, 7:50 A.M.

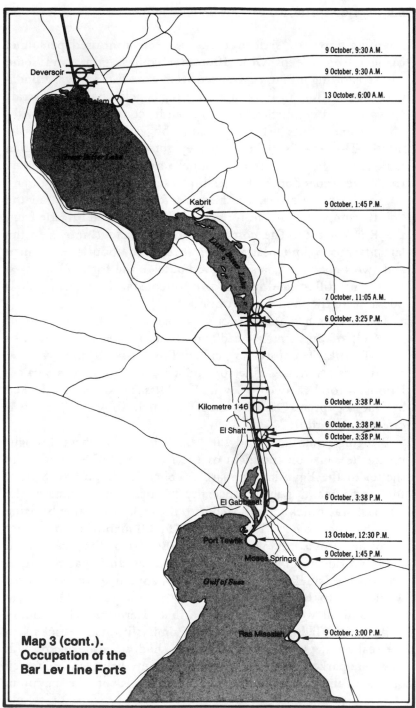

9 October, 9:30 A.M.

9 October, 9:30 A.M.

13 October, 6:00 A.M.

9 October, 1:45 P.M.

7 October, 11:05 A.M.

6 October, 3:25 P.M.

6 October, 3:38 P.M.

6 October, 3:38 P.M.

6 October, 3:38 P.M.

6 October, 3:38 P.M.

13 October, 12:30 P.M.

9 October, 1:45 P.M.

9 October, 3:00 P.M.

Deversoir

Matzmed

Great Bitter Lake

Kabrit

Little Bitter Lake

Kilometre 146

El Shatt

El Gabbanet

Port Tewfik

Moses Springs

Gulf of Suez

Ras Misalah

**Map 3 (cont.).
Occupation of the
Bar Lev Line Forts**

Source: Information provided to the author by the Egyptians.

Egyptian force of sixteen tanks, sixteen armoured personnel carriers, some jeeps with 106mm recoilless guns, and some trucks carrying infantry advanced from Port Fuad toward Budapest fort. After an exchange of fire, Israeli Phantom aircraft appeared and compelled the Egyptian force to scatter and withdraw; some of its vehicles became bogged down in the saltmarsh. The Israelis claim that they set on fire seven Egyptian tanks and eight armoured personnel carriers and that seventeen trucks were abandoned. This claim was denied by the Egyptians, who insisted the attack was merely a feint designed to draw the "ninth company" of the forward Israeli armoured brigade from the Romani area. The company did not, in fact, move. In the late afternoon Budapest was reinforced by about twenty men and two tanks; the tanks remained outside the fort and survived Egyptian artillery and mortar fire by constantly changing their positions in the sand dunes around it.

The Israelis had another fortress position on the east shore of the Gulf of Suez, on a headland about fifteen miles south of Port Tewfik. The fort was called Ras Missalah and was also counted as a Bar Lev Line fort, making, according to my calculations, a total of twenty-seven. Ras Missalah was not attacked by the Egyptians on the sixth although some shellfire was directed toward it.

Bridging equipment and the assault boats had been brought up to the canal on the night of the fifth and hidden under the shelter of the Egyptian rampart or concealed in pits. At S Hour the sand remaining in the specially thinned out sections of the rampart was quickly bulldozed into the canal to enable bridging to commence; by 1515 hours some 15,000 men of the Engineer Corps had crossed the waterway. The Egyptians first erected ten dummy bridges about ten miles apart; they anticipated that, as soon as the Israelis realised what was happening, their air force would try to bomb any bridges across the canal. They were right, and all were hit during the first afternoon. The dummy bridges were light and serviceable, similar in many respects to the real ones, especially in silhouette shadow; also, decoy vehicles were parked on them. When the dummy bridges were tested on one of the canals branching off from the River Nile, Egyptian pilots said that, from the air, they were unable to distinguish the false from the real ones. Later, these bridges were used either as footbridges or for empty supply vehicles on their return journeys. This created a circular traffic pattern, of which it was said that traffic control was far better than that in Cairo.

The Egyptians had sufficient material to construct eighteen or nineteen bridges across the canal, but the material was of different types. It included both the old and more modern British Bailey-type sections, as well as old World War II Soviet TPP bridging (Tyazheli Pontonnyi Park) which had cumbersome alloy pontoons that had to be manhandled into the water. The TPP bridge could be erected at the rate of four feet a minute, which meant that it took two and a half hours to span the canal. Its pontoons and other equipment required 150 vehicles to carry them. The Egyptians also had sections of the newer Soviet PMP bridge (Pontonno Mostovoy Park) which required only forty vehicles to transport it; it could be erected at the rate of 125 yards in twenty-five minutes. Each section opened into four pontoons after it had been mechanically lowered into the water. Thus it took only thirty to forty minutes to span the canal. An Israeli officer who watched one being erected later said, "It grew across the water like an extending arm." The Egyptians possessed only three such PMP bridges, and, to make up their requirements, they had obtained quantities of Uniflote bridging, a commercial product known as LPP (Leg Pontonnyi Park). To carry enough to span the canal required 190 vehicles, and this, too, had to be manhandled down to the water's edge.

All sections of the various types of bridging were modified so they were interchangeable with each other. The current Egyptian joke was that this was the first time they had been able to force the communists and the capitalists to work together. All bridges soon were of a mixed composition, as pontoon sections damaged by Israeli aerial activity and shelling were replaced by other types. The pontoons were filled with a foamlike substance to prevent their sinking if damaged, and they all had simple wooden planking trackway over them. The total length of the Egyptian bridging convoys was about 185 miles. The flexibility of the bridges allowed them to be floated to new sites or lashed to the bank. This mobility gave rise to later Israeli claims of sinking many bridges.

Excluding the dummy ones that were controlled by the Engineer Corps, each infantry divisional commander was allocated two bridges, and each commander had them erected across the canal as soon as possible. The one exception was the commander in the north who, for over twenty-four hours, used the pontoons of one of his bridges to float his divisional armour across; each pontoon generally was capable of carrying two tanks. In the plan a period of seven to nine hours was allowed for the construction of the bridges. While all five of those of the Second Army were across by 1800 hours, and thus well ahead of schedule, those of the Third Army were delayed.

By that hour the engineers had blasted about seventy-six gaps in the sand rampart on the east bank. This number was increased to eighty-two by midnight, the majority in the northern sector where about fifty ferries were working. The Egyptians possessed numbers of the new Soviet GPS ferry, as well as some older types. The GPS moved on land on tracks, in two parts; these were joined together in the water. The major part of the infantry divisions were on the east bank by 1930 hours, when commanders began moving their divisional armour across the bridges. By then the bridgeheads were up to two miles deep; the objective was for each division to expand to a width of five miles and penetrate to a depth of at least three miles before the artillery and armoured formations began moving to the east bank.

By 1700 hours it had become apparent that the Third Army had run into difficulty in bridging. The sand rampart on the east bank proved thicker than anticipated; it was up to 200 feet in width in places, and clay was mixed with the sand. Under jets of water from the pressure hoses, the mixture turned into sticky mud that did not quickly and easily wash away like loose sand. Troops and materiel were crossing by assault boats and ferries, but, as there was still no bridge across in the south, General Ismail sent Major General Ali Mohammed, together with his deputy, Brigadier Ahmed Hamadi, to the Third Army with orders to get the bridges across immediately and at all costs. The general had to select fresh crossing sites, which were some fif-

teen miles north of those previously chosen, and bring in bulldozers. It was not until about 0900 hours the following day, the
seventh, that he had his first bridge spanning the canal—about
twelve hours behind schedule.

For the Israelis on the east bank, the afternoon of the sixth
was one of great confusion that at times verged on panic. The
personnel in the Bar Lev Line, for example, who were relied
upon to pass back detailed information about the invasion force
and to direct the fire of the Israeli guns, lying back in positions
along Artillery Road, were unable to see what was happening
because of the dense smoke that had been deliberately put down
by the Egyptians. On several occasions Israeli guns and even aircraft fired upon their own positions, and for long periods the
Israeli guns shelled the empty desert. One Israeli brigade commander said, "The whole of the Sinai was on fire."

There was also confusion over code words, map coordinates
and recognition signals; no one seemed to know what others
were doing, and there were instances of Israeli tanks and guns
shooting at each other. The Israelis gave code names to practically every identifiable feature, landmark, road, track and junction on the ground, as a basis for target indication. The code
words were changed frequently, and the Israelis in the forts had
voluminous code books. Quick reference tended to be difficult
unless one were very familiar with them. From information
gained from talking to survivors, it appears that GHQ had been
slack, and there was the probability that GHQ, the armour, the
artillery, and the infantry in the Bar Lev Line forts were using
different sets of code words. If this is true, the confusion is understandable. In *Insight on the Middle East War,* one authority
wrote that "Avi's fort called for artillery support when attacked,
and HE landed on his fort, so Meyerke called to stop the artillery, but HQ took some persuading and the barrage continued
for a while. A northern fort was shelled by its own artillery, and
on at least three occasions the Israelis shelled their own positions."

Despite this, Israeli armoured assaults by small company-sized
groups of tanks continued to be launched in a similar reckless
manner by charging blindly forward at speed; the tactic only re-

sulted in the loss of more tanks to missiles and rockets fired by Egyptian infantrymen crouched in the open sand. At 1600 hours, for example, an Israeli armoured attack was made on the southernmost of the two forts at the south end of Little Bitter Lake. The fort had just been taken by the Egyptians at 1515 hours, and they repelled the attack and destroyed seven Israeli tanks. One Israeli officer later told me that "there was not one, but several Israeli armies" and that on the first two or three days "the various units were charging around the desert all 'doing their own thing' without any control or coordination." By 1600 hours one armoured brigade was moving up on two axes through the Giddi and Mitla passes. Another had reached the Baluza area, and Brigadier Kalman Magen, a regular officer, was put in charge of the northern sector down to Kantara. Yet, General Gonen had still not determined where the main threat was.

Both Egyptian and Israeli aircraft came into the battle. The strong Egyptian Air Defence Barrier on the west bank proved to be very effective in countering attacks by Israeli planes. In the course of the first afternoon it brought down at least ten Israeli aircraft; Israeli pilots were then ordered to keep fifteen kilometres away from it. At 0645 hours on the seventh, Israeli aircraft made a series of strikes against the Egyptian SAMs, after which they generally kept their distance for a few days. (The aerial aspect of the war is discussed in detail in chapter thirteen.)

On the afternoon of the sixth General Gonen left his GHQ, Southern Command, at Beersheba and moved to the command post at Baluza, where he remained until darkness. He then tried to move southward along Supply Road to the prepared advanced battle HQ for this front, at Khaseiba (sometimes spelled Kashiba, or Um Hashiba) near the western mouth of the Giddi Pass. Finding his way blocked by Egyptian rangers, he instead turned about and moved to the Israeli command post at Romani, where he stayed for a while.

The Egyptians say that at 1839 hours they intercepted a message from the Israeli General Staff in Tel Aviv, informing the commander at Romani that it had lost contact with the GOC (who was actually on the move at this particular moment) and ordering him to take command of the entire Suez Canal front until contact was restored. Some of Gonen's GHQ communication equipment and vehicles had been damaged by Egyptian aircraft in their initial raid. General Gonen finally arrived at Khaseiba, which is located twenty-three miles from the shore of Great Bitter Lake, at about 0100 hours on the seventh. During the afternoon the Israeli Sinai Air HQ also moved from Um Morgan, which was near Central Road, about fifty-three miles from the canal, to just north of Melize airfield, then to Baluza, and finally to El Arish, where it remained.

The Israelis had been conditioned to believe that the Bar Lev Line was a good defensive barrier, that it would take the Egyptians at least twenty-four hours to bring up the necessary bridging equipment to cross the canal, and up to forty-eight hours to erect bridges and to put a military force on the east bank. This schedule would allow ample warning time for the Israeli air force to be brought into action to deal with the situation. These had been bad miscalculations, for the Egyptians had crossed the canal in force in minutes rather than hours. Further, the Israeli air force as well as the Israeli armoured counterattacks had been repelled. The Israelis had been caught by surprise.

Mobilisation was hasty and chaotic; roads, so empty before 1400 hours, were suddenly jammed with vehicles, both military and civilian, trying to move to and from mobilisation centres or to one of the fronts. For example, at the armoured centre at Beersheba, tanks and vehicles on the mobilisation parks were not ready, and many weapons were still in their preservative grease, while fuel and ammunition were not readily available. Stocks of ammunition and spares had been reduced to a dangerously low level, according to E. Luttwak in *The Israeli Army*, "on the assumption that a war would require only a few days fighting, and not very intense fighting at that."

There was a shortage of tank transporters to lift the tanks and SP guns the 120 miles to the Suez Canal front, but such as there were worked ceaselessly for the next few days, moving along at a steady fifteen mph. Meanwhile, there was nothing else for it but to muster tank crews to collect their tanks and send them off westward across the Sinai Desert, churning along

Egyptian troops after having captured a fort of the Bar Lev Line.

Egyptian rangers landing for a raid against Israeli positions in the October 1973 war.

on their tracks at less than twelve mph. It was a long and tiring journey for the men and a very wearing one for the vehicles, many of which fell by the wayside. The newly mobilised tanks and guns did not begin arriving at the front until about noon the next day, the seventh, when they were thrown immediately into action. The Israelis later admitted that twenty percent of their mobilisation tanks and SP guns were "nonrunners," and one suspects the percentage was really much higher, for the figure of "only forty percent runners" was the one most commonly mentioned in Israeli circles. Most Western armies of reasonable efficiency would reckon to have at any given moment something like eighty percent runners, fifteen percent on the road within twenty-four hours, and five percent always off the road. To add to the uncertainty and confusion, wounded men were being brought back from the front to the hospital at Bir Gifgafa, and they told harrowing tales of Israeli setbacks.

The Israelis claim their mobilisation, planned to take place over a seventy-two-hour period, had to be telescoped into six hours. General Herzog says that "the mobilisation will go down in history with the taxicab mobilisation before the Battle of the Marne. It was incredible in its hasty, improvised character." The Israelis had another big advantage in 1967 because the army had mobilised days before the war commenced. This enabled units to shake down together and gave them time to carry out some refresher training. It also ensured that vehicles and weapons were in serviceable condition and that ample fuel and ammunition were available. In 1973 these conditions did not obtain.

As darkness fell the Egyptian rangers, who had been trained in sabotage and antitank ambush warfare, came into the picture. Egyptian infantry on the east bank would be weak in firepower for about twenty-four hours or so, until sufficient armour and guns came across to give support. The rangers' task was to delay Israeli reserves joining the battle, especially the armour from the main Israeli tank concentrations in the Sinai at Melize, Bir Gifgafa and Thamada. The rangers were to penetrate the Israeli lines on foot and by helicopter—the Soviet Mi-4 that could carry twenty-four men.

Formed in 1961 and modelled on the American Green Berets,

the rangers had platoons consisting of about twenty-four men, three platoons to a company, and three companies to a battalion; a "group" could consist of one or more battalions. Within their own zones the divisional commanders had complete freedom of action, not only of deciding where and how to bridge the canal and how the Israeli secret weapon should be neutralised, but also how to employ the rangers attached to them.

In small groups, beginning at 1800 hours, the rangers moved eastward on foot to slip through Israeli positions and set up vehicle ambushes along lateral approach roads. Their orders were to penetrate up to seven miles. Two platoons went from the El Ferdan area, two made their way toward the Khatmia Pass, a platoon penetrated toward Tasa, another toward the Giddi Pass, and yet another toward the Mitla Pass. Other ranger platoons with a similar mission, but with a deeper penetration role of up to twenty miles and directly under command of GHQ, were put down behind Israeli lines by helicopter after darkness. Of these, one platoon landed near Baluza, another near Bir Gifgafa and another near Subha Hill (in the central sector); two companies, totalling about 300 men, went into the Sudar Valley in the southeast to block it. Yet other detachments of rangers were given strategic tasks calling for an even deeper penetration into the Sinai Desert, southern Sinai, and along the coast of the Gulf of Suez. One company of rangers in assault boats moved by sea to a position on the causeway road to the east of the Israeli Budapest fort, on the Mediterranean coast, to set up an ambush position.

At 2300 hours, still on the sixth, the Israelis admitted that three rockets had been fired into a camp at Bir Gifgafa, causing damage; that Egyptian rangers had penetrated the Mitla Pass; and that the Egyptians had made several attempts to land rangers by helicopter. The Israelis claimed to have shot down twenty such helicopters. It was later added that ninety Egyptian rangers had been encountered and eighty had been killed. Other Israeli claims included shooting down eight Egyptian helicopters, each carrying thirty rangers (although the helicopters used for this purpose could carry only twenty-four men), and wiping out a fifty-man ranger unit near Abu Rodeis. At 0100 hours on the seventh the oil wells at Abu Zeina, Sudar, and Feeran had been set on fire by rangers. The Egyptians later admitted their greatest losses had occurred in the Khatmia Pass, but they would not give further details. General Herzog writes that the Egyptians used thirty-five helicopters, of which the Israelis claim to have shot down fourteen.

Throughout the first night the remaining elements of the five Egyptian infantry divisions were ferried across the canal, while armoured vehicles slowly trundled over the bridges. On the east bank the infantry began to creep slowly forward in an "inching war," keeping their antitank weapons well to the fore. Their armour, as it arrived, was kept at the rear. The Israelis had made liberal use of antitank and antipersonnel mines, which, according to the Egyptian engineers, were of a density of "nine to the metre." These had to be painstakingly prodded for, marked when located, or dealt with on the spot. Armoured attacks continued fierce and speedy, but piecemeal. The Israelis made fourteen such attacks during the night; each was of company strength at the Egyptian bridgeheads, and all were repulsed.

To summarise the fighting on the first day: by midnight on the sixth the Egyptians had crossed the canal, successfully breached the Bar Lev Line, had taken fourteen of its forts, put five bridges (and ten dummy ones) across the waterway, and had moved the bulk of five infantry divisions, with a loss of only 208 killed. It was a moment of triumph for the Egyptian armed forces and the Egyptian nation; everything had gone in their favour and against the Israelis. Their success had been largely due to hard training and calculated organisation, rather than to sheer luck. As one wounded Egyptian soldier said on television (on the ninth), "Each of us knew by heart what he was supposed to do. We had been training on the mission for quite a long time."

6

ISRAELI HESITATION
AND CONFUSION

*No matter how many [Egyptian soldiers] we
killed they kept coming.*

Israeli officer

After darkness on the sixth an Egyptian mechanised
brigade equipped with light, amphibious PT-76s and BTRs
moved by ferry across Great Bitter Lake and landed unopposed
on the eastern shore where there was no sand rampart. One of
its battalions made for the Giddi Pass and the other headed for
the Mitla Pass, a move that coincided with that of the Israeli
armoured brigade moving from the opposite direction. The confused Israeli two-way movement of combat and logistic vehicles
through the Giddi Pass was further complicated by Egyptian
ranger involvement. While part of the Egyptian unit got through,
the remainder was held and had to return to the canal early the
following morning. The Egyptians claim they intercepted an
Israeli message at 1010 hours on the seventh, stating that Egyptian tanks were advancing on Thamada which was some fifty
miles further east. Rockets were fired at the Israeli-held Thamada airfield and camps, and later a radar station was shelled by
this small Egyptian force, which remained to the east of the
Khatmia Ridge until the evening of the eighth. Then the raiders

93

again slipped through the confusion of the Giddi Pass to rejoin the bridgehead.

The other Egyptian mechanised battalion made for the Mitla Pass but clashed at about 2000 hours with an Israeli armoured battalion that had just come through the pass. The Israelis claim the battalion was driven back to the canal. The Israeli brigade commander himself arrived on the canal bank about 2200 hours and was able to shoot at Egyptian ferries crossing there. Fearing the Bar Lev forts were being outflanked, he recommended they be evacuated at once. Part of the Egyptian mechanised battalion had evaded the Israeli armour and continued through the Mitla Pass. At 0810 hours on the seventh the Egyptians claim to have intercepted an Israeli message from the Mitla Pass command post saying that it was "surrounded by Egyptian tanks." After shooting up some radar posts, the Egyptians returned to their bridgehead by 1350 hours.

When General Gonen arrived at his advance front HQ at Khaseiba in the early hours of the seventh, he was under the impression that his forward tank companies had succeeded in linking up with the Bar Lev Line forts and that there was no desperate urgency for the moment. When dawn came he was quickly disillusioned. General Mandler reported that he had lost two-thirds of his 300 tanks, that his northern brigade had only ten tanks left out of about a hundred, and that the armoured brigade that had moved through the passes in the night was down to only twenty-three tanks. Gonen had still not identified the main threat, and he also had to decide whether to continue to hit at the Egyptian landings or to rescue the garrisons besieged in the forts, two conflicting requirements. Although he had earlier refused to allow the garrisons of the forts in the southern sector to leave, later, at about 1100 hours, he gave permission for those in certain parts of the northern sector to be evacuated.

While the sixth had been a day of Israeli company-sized attacks, on the seventh the assaults were of battalion size, but they were no more successful. For example, at 0700 hours the Israelis launched an attack toward Kantara with the intention of trying to retake the three Kantara forts. In the fighting they lost at least another fifty tanks. Another battalion-sized attack,

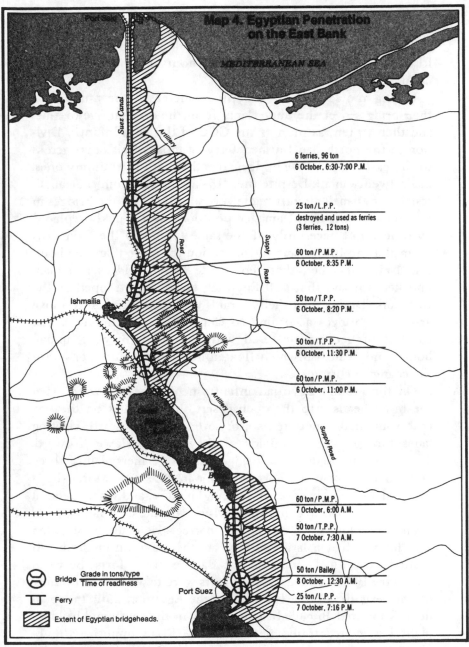

Map 4. Egyptian Penetration on the East Bank

MEDITERRANEAN SEA

Port Said

Suez Canal

Artillery

Road

Supply

Road

Ishmailia

Supply

Road

Artillery

Road

Port Suez

6 ferries, 96 ton
6 October, 6:30-7:00 P.M.

25 ton / L.P.P.
destroyed and used as ferries
(3 ferries, 12 tons)

60 ton / P.M.P.
6 October, 8:35 P.M.

50 ton / T.P.P.
6 October, 8:20 P.M.

50 ton / T.P.P.
6 October, 11:30 P.M.

60 ton / P.M.P.
6 October, 11:00 P.M.

60 ton / P.M.P.
7 October, 6:00 A.M.

50 ton / T.P.P.
7 October, 7:30 A.M.

50 ton / Bailey
8 October, 12:30 A.M.

25 ton / L.P.P.
7 October, 7:16 P.M.

Bridge — Grade in tons/type / Time of readiness

Ferry

Extent of Egyptian bridgeheads.

Source: Information provided to the author by the Egyptians.

developing into a two-pronged one, was aimed at the forts to the immediate north and south of Lake Timsah. Farther south still another, also two-pronged, was made toward the southern forts. Both commenced about 1000 hours and petered out by noon.

During the seventh the Egyptians increased the number of their bridges over the Suez Canal from the original five to nine, and then to ten, as soon as the GOC of the 18th Infantry Division in the north had finished ferrying most of his tanks across to the east bank. These bridges, together with the dummy ones, made twenty in all. Despite the "15 kilometres from the canal" restriction, Israeli aircraft made several attacks on the bridges in the course of the day. Damaged pontoons were quickly replaced by others, not necessarily of the same type, and the Egyptians claim that no bridge was out of action for more than one hour. The Israelis claimed that ten of the eleven bridges had been knocked out and that 400 Egyptian tanks were trapped on the east bank. During the Israeli air raids vehicles continued to move across the bridges according to General Shazli's directive. The canal itself became cluttered with the debris of war: human bodies and dead fish which floated in alternate directions with the changing currents.

On the ground Egyptian infantrymen seeped forward from the bridgeheads into the open desert, and by dusk on the seventh some had penetrated six or seven miles eastward, clearing lanes through the minefields as they moved slowly forward. Gradually the original five bridgeheads were merged into three larger ones, two in the north and one in the south. More troops and tanks were moved across during the day, and when General Ismail said he had five infantry divisions on the east bank within twenty-four hours, he was largely correct. He could have added that he also had a large part of another division in the north around Port Fuad, opposite the Bar Lev Line forts, between kilometre 10 and El Cap. All six forts were taken by the evening of the seventh. About 1600 hours the Egyptian 25th Independent Armoured Brigade began crossing in the south and by midnight had concentrated near Artillery Road opposite the El Shatt area. At about the same time the 2nd Independent Armoured Brigade crossed to the east bank opposite Ismailia.

The Egyptian tank hunting teams remained out in front and were often completely isolated in the open desert. The Israelis, continuing their gung ho tactics of charging blindly forward at speed, fully expected the teams to disappear when they rushed at them with tanks. However, the Egyptians stood firm and fired their weapons, three or four missiles being aimed at a single tank. By this time the Egyptians had artillery and mortars on the east bank to give close fire support. They also had both long-range guns and tanks on the pyramids which fired over the heads of their own troops at the attacking Israelis.

The Egyptian rangers were also active on the seventh, and they say they were involved in fights near Baluza (between 0500-0600 hours), near Kantara (0500-1600 hours), at Subha Hill (between 0600-2400 hours), opposite Ismailia (from 0300 hours onward), and opposite Deversoir (from 0500 hours onward). They claim they were also involved in action in the Gulf of Suez area at such places as El Tur, Abu Zeina, Feeran, Metulla and other places whose names do not appear on all maps, such as Baba, Rik el-Rates and Sird. Perhaps the most successful ranger operation was an ambush in the central sector which caught an Israeli armoured unit in the act of unloading its tanks from transporters. Also, the southern flanking route through the Sudar Pass was blocked at each end by rangers until the end of the war. The Israelis like to say these raids were generally of little consequence because most of the raiders were killed, captured, or failed to find their targets. In reality, these actions worried the Israelis considerably, especially in the first week of the war. Ranger attacks caused casualties and damage on supply routes, thereby affecting Israeli morale which was already under great strain.

On the canal front, Gonen and Mandler were the two regular commanders on the spot who initially had to cope with the invasion. General Gonen, as GOC Southern Command, was in overall command of the theatre of operations. Major General Avraham Mandler, who had been a brigade commander on the Golan front in 1967, was assigned as commander of the armoured forces in the Sinai. Two other generals had been de-

tailed to take command of reserve divisions as they were mobilised, and it was intended that Mandler should command the
third. One of the generals was Major General Avraham Adan, a
regular officer who had been commander of the armoured corps
since 1969 and before that had been commander of the armoured forces in the Sinai. He arrived on the canal front about
0800 hours on the seventh and was assigned to the northern
sector, where Brigadier Magen had been in temporary charge.

Major General Ariel Sharon arrived about 1300 hours and was
assigned to the central sector; Mandler took over in the south.
Neither Adan nor Sharon was very happy at being placed under
the command of Gonen, who had only recently been subordi-
nate to both of them. Sharon had, in fact, exchanged positions
with Gonen as GOC for the command of a reserve division.
Gonen was also comparatively new at his post and could not
possibly know the area, the job, or the problems as they thought
they did. Both considered themselves more experienced and
more worthy of overall command than the GOC, and their attitudes reflected their views. This did not make for a good command relationship on the Israeli Suez Canal front.

As Israeli reserves and reinforcements began to arrive about
noon on the seventh, they were bundled into these three formations, either as units or to replace casualties in decimated ones.
Most of the armour had travelled to the Sinai on its tracks. The
men were tired, but in many cases they had to go straight into
action. Because vehicles had broken down or been damaged,
huge logistic and repair problems arose. By the evening of the
seventh Adan had two armoured brigades, Sharon had three,
and Mandler had two; Gonen had a brigade of paratroops,
mounted in half-tracks, as his only reserve.

General Gonen's battle front HQ at Khaseiba was behind a
steep ridge which rises about two thousand feet above sea level.
The ridge is roughly two miles in length, runs parallel to the
canal, and is situated in the northwestern part of the mouth of
the Giddi Pass. The ridge had been prepared just after 1967, and
it bristled with radar, communication equipment, and sensors.
The actual front HQ, shelters, and vehicles were behind the
ridge. At times Gonen was able to get a good view of parts of

the battlefield spread out before him. He later spoke of "human waves" of infantry advancing toward his attacking tanks—an unbelievable sight of human flesh against hard steel; he likened them to the Chinese soldiers in the Korean War. General Gonen thought the Egyptian soldier was tougher than he had been in 1967 and had great staying power; at this stage he had not formed a very high opinion of the officer leadership. The Israelis claim there was a volume of Russian voice traffic over the Egyptian field radio networks. They felt this must indicate heavy involvement of Soviet personnel, but I can find no solid evidence to support this allegation.

Moshe Dayan, the defence minister, visited the Suez Canal front on the seventh, arriving at Khaseiba about 1140 hours. Gonen had advised him not to, according to Herzog, because of Egyptian commandos in the surrounding hills. Dayan was dismayed by what he saw. "This is war," he said. "Withdraw to the high ground. Leave the fortifications. Let whoever can evacuate. The wounded will have to remain as prisoners." On his return to Tel Aviv he saw Premier Meir and told her the situation was so bad that he thought the Israeli troops should pull back substantially to establish a new defence line along the small ridge shielding Artillery Road, abandon the Gulf of Suez, and retain only Sharm el-Sheikh at the southern tip of the Sinai Peninsula. General Elazar, the chief of staff, disagreed with the withdrawal suggestion and instead suggested going immediately to the Suez Canal front himself to decide on the spot what should be done. He flew to Khaseiba, arriving there about 1900 hours. Later that evening, in Jerusalem, Premier Meir called a cabinet meeting and gained the ministers' approval for a counterattack to be mounted against the Egyptians the following day, the eighth.

Seeing the Egyptians digging in around their slowly expanding bridgeheads, erecting obstacles and laying mines, and appreciating how stubborn they could be in defence, all three divisional commanders advocated that the best course would be to smash through them to reach the canal, seize some bridges, and cross to the west bank before defences could be strengthened and stabilised. The dissenting voice was that of Gonen. In view of the obviously large number of Egyptians on the east bank, he felt that he did not have sufficient force available to make such an offensive, and he wanted to wait until more reserves arrived. The divisional commanders were motivated largely by the plight of the remaining garrisons besieged in the forts on the canal.

General Sharon had spoken on the radio to the garrisons of the forts in his sector and asked permission of front HQ to make an effort to rescue them; Gonen hesitated. Sharon claimed he could destroy the Egyptians on the east bank within forty-eight hours, but Gonen would neither approve the plan nor let Sharon have the reserve paratroop brigade for it. Gonen's reasons were that the proposed operation was to be made at night and that he wanted "to straighten his line." About 1500 hours a battalion-strength attack was made for the second time that day toward the Kantara area; it was repulsed with loss. Later, in an article in *The New Yorker* of 11 February 1974, Sharon made the bitter and scathing statement that "nobody knew what was going on. Our GHQ didn't know the picture. They were conducting war from bunkers, not from the front. That day [the seventh] we lost 150 tanks, mainly to infantry carrying antitank weapons. That evening I established a defence line about six miles east of the canal."

When General Elazar arrived at Khaseiba, he was accompanied by General Yitzhak Rabin, a former chief of staff, and the two men were a calming influence on what had become a tense command situation. Elazar called a conference at which he evolved a plan of attack. Sharon was not able to attend because his helicopter had developed technical trouble. While Elazar's authority to mount an offensive pleased the majority, it did not please Gonen who felt he did not yet have sufficient reserves available to take such a course. The plan was to keep at least two miles from the eastern bank of the canal in order to avoid the effects of fire from the Egyptian weapons on the rampart and pyramids on the west bank and to make brigade-size sweeps laterally through the Egyptian bridgeheads to divorce the forward combat element from its logistic support. "We were in a bad situation that evening," Elazar said later. "It was after the initial success of the Egyptian force. We had to decide what were the alternatives. Should we retreat? Should we stay in the same

Map 5. Israeli Map Showing Plan for an Assault Crossing of the Canal

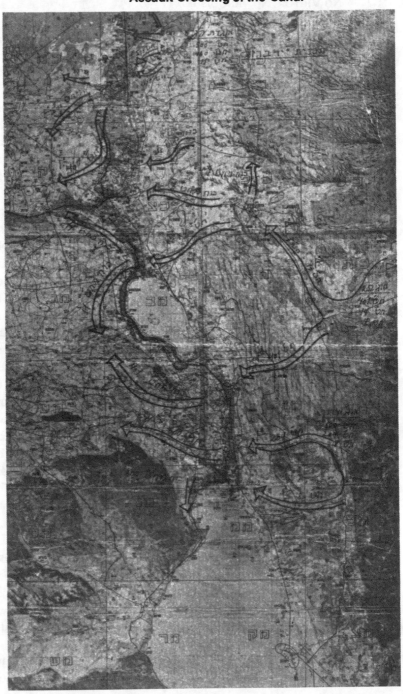

Source: Obtained by the Egyptians on 8 October from a captured Israeli tank in the central sector.

situation? Or should we attack? There was a consensus at that meeting that we must attack."

The details of the plan called for Adan's brigades to cut through the two Second Army bridgeheads. Sharon's division was to be in reserve in the centre, ready to reinforce and help Adan if he ran into difficulties. If Adan were successful, Sharon was to move south to cut through the Third Army bridgehead. Mandler's division was to make supporting and diversionary attacks. There was some argument as to whether the Israelis should actually cross the canal or not, a course many favoured, but Elazar insisted that this would be dependent upon their ability to capture Egyptian bridges intact. Commanders then began to prepare for this contingency, marking routes and objectives on their maps. Just before Elazar left Khaseiba, Sharon arrived with a plan for a night attack to rescue the garrisons of the forts. A decision on this proposal was left pending until after the outcome of operations on the eighth.

The seventh had been another good day for the Egyptians and a confused and costly one for the Israelis. By dusk three Egyptian bridgeheads had expanded to cover much, but not all, of the length of the east bank. In places, the forward infantry overlooked Artillery Road after having reached the first low ridge of sandhills. The Egyptians modestly claim to have destroyed 60 Israeli tanks and fifteen SP guns that day, but the true figure was much higher. Herzog states that by noon on the seventh the Israelis had only about 110 tanks left on the east bank, and even this estimate may have been overoptimistic. The chief rabbi to the Israeli armed forces hastily issued religious scrolls to boost flagging morale.

The third day of the war, the eighth of October, was a black day for the Israelis. On that day the film of the Egyptian crossing of the Suez Canal and the storming of the Bar Lev Line was shown to the Egyptian people on television. In the northern sector General Adan's three armoured brigades spread out along Supply Road between Tasa and Baluza and about 1800 hours began moving forward according to the Elazar Plan. Instead of moving to a point from which the brigades could turn south and cut a swath through the Egyptian bridgeheads, because of faulty

Israeli infantrymen in foxholes on the East Bank.

navigation they meandered off course in the desert, in places almost directly across the front of Egyptian guns. This error meant that the formations had to attack almost due east to get into their scheduled position, thus causing them to move into Egyptian ambushes.

The northernmost of Adan's brigades ran into Egyptian ambushes set by the 18th Infantry Division in the area of Kantara, but when Adan reported to Gonen that he had lost only six tanks in the skirmish, Gonen thought that all was going well. About 1100 hours Gonen ordered Sharon to move southward to carry out his part of the plan which was to cut laterally through the Third Army bridgehead. Adan's central brigade, trying to get back on course, ran into trouble opposite El Ferdan. At 0930 hours one company ran into a 2nd Infantry Division ambush and lost seven tanks. About a half hour later another company, probing south of the metalled road, also ran into ambush and lost four tanks; the remainder scattered and withdrew. Gung ho tactics had been used in both these attacks; the tanks charged at full speed.

About 1000 hours Adan was ordered to seize three Egyptian bridges: one just north of El Ballah, that at El Ferdan, and another opposite Ismailia. He ordered his northern brigade (the 14th Armoured Brigade, commanded by Colonel Amnon; there was also a 14th Brigade on the Golan Front), then in action at Kantara, to leave one of its battalions there and to bring the other south to help his central brigade at El Ferdan. He intended to make a two-pronged attack on this particular bridge. Just to the north of El Ferdan, the commanding officer of the detached battalion of the northern brigade (identified as the 190B Battalion, commanded by Lieutenant Colonel Asaf Yagouri) thought he had pinpointed the forward positions of the 2nd Infantry Division and mustered all his tanks and SP guns, over fifty in all. He then charged eastward toward El Ferdan through a 500-yard gap just to the south of the metalled roadway. While actually on the road, at about 1330 hours, the CO's tank was ambushed and hit by antitank artillery fire when only two miles from the canal. The CO and his crew of four jumped out and were taken prisoner. The CO was exhibited on Egyptian television the next day.

The CO's tank was set on fire by hits from missiles, while following tanks were ambushed from the flanks and rear. The Israeli CO had not discovered that another Egyptian company position had been established on a forward feature during the night. This company had remained concealed and quiet while the Israeli tanks carried out their reconnaissances and probes and entered the killing area. In this thrust the Israeli battalion lost all its tanks and SP guns. Thirty-five were still on the site of the battle when I visited it later, and I was told that seventeen others had been taken to Cairo for display purposes. This Israeli attack was given some air support because Adan did not yet have any divisional artillery of his own, and it should also have been supported by Sharon's guns.

Adan's southern armoured brigade advanced eastward on two

axes toward the Egyptian bridgehead opposite Ismailia. One battalion was aimed at a Bar Lev Line fort known to the Israelis as Purkan, in which the garrison was still holding out. The other battalion went south toward a fort known to the Israelis as Matzmed. This fort was on the northern tip of Great Bitter Lake, which was to be a crossing place if the Israeli attacks were successful. About 1400 hours this armoured brigade made contact with the Egyptian bridgehead and halted. After a pause the Egyptians advanced toward the Israelis, and by 1530 hours, after a half hour's fighting, had driven them from a feature, known to the Israelis as Hamutal, which overlooked Artillery Road. Another Egyptian attack began about 1630 hours and drove the Israelis from another adjacent, tactically valuable feature. In both instances the Israelis suffered heavy losses, but so did the Egyptians. It was in this fighting that one Israeli officer commented that "no matter how many we killed, they kept coming." About 1430 hours the southern prong of this southern brigade of Adan's had run into an Egyptian ambush and hastily withdrew with the loss of over twenty tanks.

By 1400 hours General Gonen realised that all was not well, but he did not yet know the full extent of the setbacks. He ordered Sharon to return to the central sector. When Gonen realised the gravity of the situation, he directed Sharon to attack to help Adan's southern brigade that was fighting opposite Ismailia. It would also help the central brigade that was fighting opposite El Ferdan. Both brigade commanders knew of the order and anticipated that the pressure on them would soon be relieved by Sharon's attacks. A few minutes later, according to Herzog, Sharon came on the air and said that he would not attack. When they learned of this and realised their adverse situation, "both [brigade commanders] asked permission to improve their positions to the rear." In the *New York Times* article of 11 February 1974 Sharon said of this battle, "I watched and saw his [Adan's] force slaughtered. The attack failed because of lack of tanks. If we had all gone together, we would have succeeded." However, Sharon seems to have been deaf to Adan's calls for help and his GOC's orders. Much later Sharon alleged he had been given "contradictory and confused orders"

and complained that his division had just arrived after hundreds of kilometres of travel across the desert on their own
tracks. At first they were sent south to attack the Third Army,
and then they were called north again. Sharon's refusal to help
caused a quarrel to develop between the two generals. The deep
suspicion arose that Sharon was determined to be the first Israeli
commander to cross the canal and penetrate into Africa and
that he was not disposed to help give that honour to anyone
else.

During the evening of the eighth the Sharon division was involved in rescuing survivors who had escaped from a Bar Lev
Line fort (Purkan). Some thirty-three of them were brought in
on one tank, but this gung ho action was criticised afterward because so many senior officers, including a brigadier, had rushed
forward to take part.

In the southern sector General Mandler's brigades made two
attacks. One of battalion strength, launched from the Mitla Pass
area, developed into a three-pronged assault against the southern
Egyptian bridgehead. In the other, a two-pronged attack, two
battalions struck from the southeast. Both were repulsed. The
total Israeli losses were over forty tanks. Of the day's fighting,
Herzog writes, "The plan was to counterattack in the area of
Ferdan bridge and Ismailia. But it was a failure, for the armoured forces were not concentrated." This is an understatement oversimplifying the reasons.

Disagreement between Adan and Gonen arose from this
battle. The latter insisted that he had ordered Adan to break
through and to cross the canal at Kantara; Adan emphatically
denied receiving such an order. There is no doubt that the
Israelis were working on a plan, even at this early stage of the
war, of somehow breaking through the Egyptian line and crossing the Suez Canal. Although this was later played down by the
Israelis, the Egyptians obtained a map from a captured Israeli
tank on the eighth in the central sector on which were marked
the routes to be taken and the designation of units. This leaves
little doubt as to the real intention of the Israelis.

The controversy between Adan and Gonen was further heightened and given a mysterious twist when the Agranat Commis-

sion enquired into the events of the early days of the war. It found that the relevant page in the war log of General Adan was missing and that another page had been "rewritten." Presumably, General Gonen's war log of that date is complete and confirms his order to Adan. When questioned on the matter, both men seemed to be holding something back, and neither appeared to be as frank as he should have been.

In Jerusalem in the evening of the eighth, General Elazar held a press conference at which he presented a bold, confident picture, talked of an "Israeli victory soon," and said, "We shall strike them, we shall beat them, we shall break their bones." His object was mainly to deter Jordan from joining the war against Israel. Elazar was not then in possession of the facts of the disastrous defeats and losses of the day. Clearly, had he known of them, he might have tempered his remarks accordingly.

The eighth had been a day of successes for the Egyptians, and by evening they claimed to be in possession of the whole of the east bank. Their claim was substantially correct. In fact, in some places they had reached their "first bound" which was Artillery Road. Egyptian communiqués specified east bank "liberated areas" that included Port Tewfik (which was not quite accurate for, although the position at the tip of the peninsula had been taken, the main fort position still held out), Ismailia East, El Ballah, El Shatt, Southern Lakes, and the area south of Port Fuad. Also, on the eighth, two more Bar Lev Line forts had fallen to them: the first at 0400 hours was the remaining one of the Kantara group; then at 1120 hours the second fort at El Ferdan was taken. During the daytime Egyptian tanks, men and supplies continued to pour onto the east bank, and by evening all the tanks and men of the five infantry divisions had crossed, together with two independent armoured brigades. Then the armour of five mechanised brigades (one for each infantry division) began to move over the bridges.

Shortly after his press conference, when he realised the full implication of how the battle had gone on the east bank, General Elazar gave the order to immediately stop the costly counterattacks. That evening fewer than 90 Israeli tanks remained facing the Egyptians, and later General Herzog stated that the

Israelis had lost 400 tanks in the first three days of the war. On the other hand, the Egyptians claim to have taken forty-five Israeli prisoners and destroyed 92 tanks in the first two days—another modest understatement.

At 0400 hours on the ninth, General Gonen gave permission to all personnel still holding out in the remaining Bar Lev Line forts either to surrender or try to break out to rejoin their own forces. In *The Israeli Army*, Luttwak writes of this painful decision that "when it was decided to leave the strongholds to their fate, the open radiotelephone network was still carrying desperate pleas of their men all over the front."

About midnight on the eighth, General Gonen relayed General Elazar's order to the three divisional commanders that all counterattacks should cease, but there were now sharp differences between Gonen and Sharon, and Sharon and Adan. Gonen did not trust Sharon, who was still insisting that he be allowed to attack to "make a quick crossing" of the canal, and so, suspecting that Sharon was intriguing behind his back, Gonen listened in on Sharon's radiotelephone conversations, some of which were with Moshe Dayan.

Despite these orders, on the ninth Sharon launched a two-brigade attack against two features opposite Ismailia (known to the Israelis as Machshir and Televizia) which had been lost the previous afternoon by one of Adan's brigades. Although part of one of the positions (Televizia) was retaken, the assault generally was a failure, and Sharon lost over twenty tanks.

Sharon claimed that Gonen had ordered him to attack the Egyptians at these two features and to continue the attack if they withdrew but not to maintain an attack if the Egyptians held fast. Gonen insisted that he had not authorised the attack at all, and that he ordered Sharon to stop it immediately. Sharon said that, as one of his brigades had held an Egyptian assault in the morning, and as there were many antitank missiles and Egyptian soldiers in the area, he was about to push them back toward the canal. Gonen flew by helicopter to Sharon's HQ and again ordered him to stop, but, after he had left, Sharon continued with the assault. When Gonen found out about this he was furious and sent a request to General Elazar for Sharon to be removed from his command. Sharon afterward complained (in *The New Yorker*, 11 February 1974) that "the GOC did not know what was happening in the field" and had failed to back him for personal reasons, and so the opportunity of reaching the canal was lost.

During this action Sharon's divisional reconnaissance unit probed southwest around the Egyptian-held Chinese Farm position, so-called because it was the site of a Japanese experimental farm, and when they entered it in 1967 they mistook the markings on crates for Chinese. The Egyptians called it Galan, or Evacuation Village, as there were over a hundred small, box-like houses that originally housed workers on the experimental farm. Sharon's unit reached the shore of Great Bitter Lake and the lakeside fort (known to the Israelis as Lakelan), where it remained through the hours of darkness. It was ordered to withdraw again the next morning, the tenth, but it had established the fact that there was a physical gap on the east bank between the two Egyptian armies.

On the ninth the Israelis organised a press visit to the canal front, which reached to within eighteen miles of the waterway. Reporters saw many damaged tanks, but also many others that had come to a halt merely through mechanical failures. They also saw long convoys of brightly coloured, civilian-impressed trucks carrying ammunition and supplies, "EGGED" (Hebrew initials for the National Bus Company) buses carrying soldiers forward, and the wreckage of a Soviet helicopter with a mass grave nearby. The newsmen noted that the Israeli crews were tired and irritable and that visitors were not welcome, a sure sign that things were not going well. They were told that the battle was now a defensive one as priority had been given to the Golan front. The real Israeli fear was of Egyptian commandos in the sand hills on either side of the roads, and helicopters flew overhead, continuously watching for them.

Although there was firing along the whole extent of the front throughout the ninth, action by the Israelis was distinctly limited. With the notable exception of the Sharon attack, they contented themselves with remaining at a distance from the Egyptians and merely answering shot for shot. The truth was they had suffered from losses and had organisational and logistical problems; they were exhausted and glad for the respite.

The Egyptians made several further gains during the day, and at 0930 hours they occupied the two Bar Lev Line forts opposite Deversoir. In the south they advanced toward the mouth of the Mitla Pass and, at 1345 hours, occupied the Israeli position at Moses Springs which guarded the southern part of the entrance. The Egyptians then occupied the 155mm gun position with its six French guns located some six thousand yards from Port Tewfik. The battery had initially held out against them and then was found to be abandoned. (These guns had been responsible for much of the damage done to the town of Port Tewfik.) Israeli positions on Bitter Hill, which dominated the oases of Moses Springs, and at the old Pilgrim's Quarantine Station on the coast were also found to be abandoned. Beginning at 1800 hours the Egyptians in the centre launched an attack against Adan's division at Katib el-Kheil, immediately to the west of Tasa. Six hours' fighting followed before the Egyptian infantry were in complete possession of the feature. This surprised the Israelis who were still under the impression that the Egyptians were of little use at night fighting.

At 1345 hours, after only a half hour of fighting, the fort at Kabrit was taken by a land force from the Third Army, assisted by a company from the 25th Independent Armoured Brigade. (The fort was on the east bank and the large village of Kabrit was on the west shore of the neck of water between the Great and Little Bitter Lakes. The Israelis called this fort Botzer.) Four Israeli tanks were defending the fort and two were destroyed. The other two escaped and then, as the garrison began to withdraw across the open sand, they were followed and fired upon by Egyptian tanks. A number of Israelis were killed. The Kabrit fort was occupied the following day by the Egyptians. This was rather unusual, as they tended to keep clear of the Bar Lev Line forts, partly because they still bristled with mines and booby traps and partly because they were accurately pinpointed on Israeli artillery maps.

On the evening of the ninth the Egyptians advanced into the mouth of the Mitla Pass to occupy the southernmost Israeli command post. This was the fifth of the six Israeli CPs to be taken, leaving only that at Baluza in the north in Israeli hands. It showed signs of being abandoned in a hurry. The Egyptians claim that marked maps, code books, copies of signal messages and instructions had been left behind which helped them identify Israeli formations and gave other valuable intelligence information. One valuable item was an Israeli code book for radio traffic; only nine copies were in existence. It was immediately translated into Arabic and issued to Egyptian formations. The code books, together with generally poor Israeli radio communication security, gave the Egyptians a great advantage for a few days until the Israelis changed their codes.

The bickering among the generals on the Suez Canal front became increasingly bitter and acrimonious, especially between Sharon and Gonen. When Dayan again flew down to Khaseiba on the ninth to see what was happening, he found a "crisis of confidence" at the front HQ. He saw that Gonen did not have a firm grip on his command, and on his return he suggested to Elazar that Sharon and Gonen change jobs. Elazar would not agree. After a cabinet meeting, General Elazar offered the position of GOC Southern Command to Lieutenant General Chaim Bar Lev who had been visiting the Golan front on the eighth on a fact-finding tour for the premier. Bar Lev initially accepted the appointment, only to have doubts when he heard that Gonen had objected to being superseded by him. A compromise solution was found, and Bar Lev was sent to the Suez Canal front as "representative of the general staff" under which facade he became the de facto commander. To save face, to preserve prestige, and to try to maintain confidence in the existing commanders for the sake of morale, Gonen remained nominally as GOC; all orders were issued in his name.

General Bar Lev was one of several senior officers who had been recalled for service at the outbreak of war, although the formal notification of this action was not made public until the ninth. As chief of staff from 1968 to 1971, he had guided the Israeli armed forces through the War of Attrition, had reorganised the army, planned its re-equipment programme, and, indeed, had given his name to the unfortunate Bar Lev Line.

Before leaving the army to enter politics (he eventually became minister of commerce and industry), he had held several important appointments, including that of commander of the armoured corps. Most important, he was a rank higher and had always been senior to the quarrelling generals on the canal front. Although firm, he was of a more conciliatory temperament than Gonen. When he arrived at Khaseiba early on the tenth, he brought with him Brigadier Uri Ben-Ari, also a recalled officer and one who had commanded brigades in the 1956 and 1967 wars. Ben-Ari had considerable administrative ability and was given the task of reorganising and running the front HQ, which was badly in need of such a chief of staff at that moment.

General Bar Lev had an immediate problem of discipline to solve, as Gonen wanted to relieve Sharon of his command for disobedience. Sharon's excuse again was that Gonen's order was contradictory and confused. To cool tempers and to persuade the team of generals to work together at this critical moment, Bar Lev let the matter ride, and so, for the time being, General Sharon, discontented and restless, remained in command of his division. The regular officers such as Gonen and Adan were irked. They suspected that both Dayan and Bar Lev, each a minister in the government, tended to favour Sharon because he had become involved in politics and was standing for the Knesset at the next general election.

Bar Lev then turned to the graver concerns of the moment. There were three courses the Israelis could take on the Suez Canal front: one was to launch a major attack against the two large Egyptian bridgeheads; another was to make a more concentrated effort to cross the canal at one single point; and the third was to wait until the Egyptians advanced to meet them in the open desert and beat them at mobile warfare. At a GHQ conference, which began at 1200 hours on the ninth, it was decided to take the last course. The Israeli troops on the east bank were ordered to stay where they were, to reorganise their shattered forces, and to resupply with tanks, guns, vehicles, materials, and men.

Despite this decision, the subject of the crossing of the canal remained a very lively one, and Sharon had many supporters in his pet project. An influential one was Brigadier Abrasha Tamir, a former commandant at the Command and Staff College who had written several military textbooks and was considered one of the brightest of the "back room boys" on the General Staff. He was of the opinion that the Egyptian troops were not interested in advancing any farther forward. By this time both Bar Lev and Gonen were firmly against a canal crossing. They pointed out that the Israeli air force had not been able to knock out the Egyptian bridges, that General Ismail had (they thought) still some eight hundred tanks on the west bank as yet uncommitted which could be brought into action against any Israeli force that reached the west bank, and that priority had been given to the Golan front. They argued that, if anything went wrong, no additional resources were available to help out, and much, or even all, might be lost. Dayan, Bar Lev, and Elazar now thought the gamble was too great and opted to wait; even Sharon and Tamir admitted it would be "a risky affair."

Meanwhile, on the ninth, despite the brave official facade, which was aided by censorship, the shock of the military disasters was beginning to hit an unbelieving Israeli nation with full force. That afternoon Dayan addressed a closed meeting of the Editor's Committee and gave them much of the bad news. (The speech was not made public until 15 February 1974.) After the meeting Dayan was due to speak to the nation on television, but someone told Premier Meir the gist of his speech and she forbade his appearance. Instead, a watered-down version of the war situation was given on television by Major General Yariv, another of the recalled officers, who told the people that "the war is going to be a long one"—a shattering statement to a nation steeped in the victorious traditions of the Hundred Hours War and the Six Day War. The confidence of the Israelis, civilian and military, was not improved by Yariv's speech.

So far the optimistic Israeli official statements, glowing with confidence and hinting of victories, had been accepted without question, but they began to be regarded dubiously by the people as wounded soldiers, back from the battle zones, told of disasters, defeats, Arab advances, and besieged Bar Lev Line forts. In the first three days on the canal front, the Israelis lost over 250

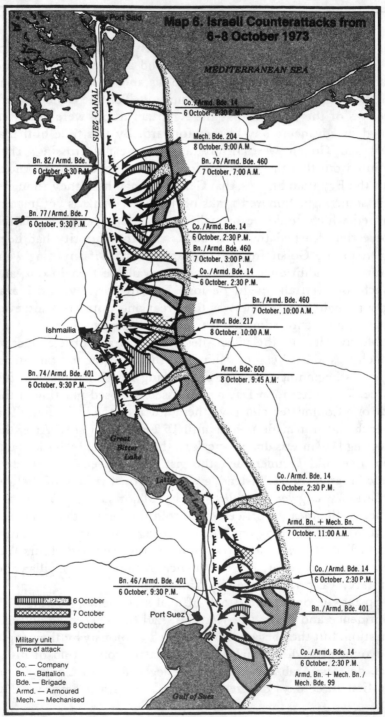

Map 6. Israeli Counterattacks from 6-8 October 1973

MEDITERRANEAN SEA

Port Said

SUEZ CANAL

Co. / Armd. Bde. 14
6 October, 2:30 P.M.

Mech. Bde. 204
8 October, 9:00 A.M.

Bn. 82 / Armd. Bde.
6 October, 9:30 P.M.

Bn. 76 / Armd. Bde. 460
7 October, 7:00 A.M.

Bn. 77 / Armd. Bde. 7
6 October, 9:30 P.M.

Co. / Armd. Bde. 14
6 October, 2:30 P.M.

Bn. / Armd. Bde. 460
7 October, 3:00 P.M.

Co. / Armd. Bde. 14
6 October, 2:30 P.M.

Bn. / Armd. Bde. 460
7 October, 10:00 A.M.

Armd. Bde. 217
8 October, 10:00 A.M.

Ishmailia

Armd. Bde. 600
8 October, 9:45 A.M.

Bn. 74 / Armd. Bde. 401
6 October, 9:30 P.M.

Great
Bitter
Lake

Little Bitter Lake

Co. / Armd. Bde. 14
6 October, 2:30 P.M.

Armd. Bn. + Mech. Bn.
7 October, 11:00 A.M.

Co. / Armd. Bde. 14
6 October, 2:30 P.M.

Bn. 46 / Armd. Bde. 401
6 October, 9:30 P.M.

Bn. / Armd. Bde. 401

6 October
7 October
8 October

Military unit
Time of attack

Co. — Company
Bn. — Battalion
Bde. — Brigade
Armd. — Armoured
Mech. — Mechanised

Port Suez

Gulf of Suez

Co. / Armd. Bde. 14
6 October, 2:30 P.M.

Armd. Bn. + Mech. Bn. /
Mech. Bde. 99

Source: Information provided to the author by the Egyptians.

killed. Israeli morale dropped rapidly, both at home and in the field. Psychiatrists had to be rushed to the field hospital at Bir Gifgafa to deal with war-shocked soldiers. It was later estimated in a study published in the Israeli Medical Association journal that of all the Israeli wounded (total figures still not released) nine percent were psychiatric cases.

The Elazar press conference on the eighth had helped to widen the growing credibility gap. While at this early stage Egyptian communiqués were models of restrained understatement, those of the Israelis were often blatantly misleading. For example, Israeli communiqués claimed that an Egyptian ranger unit had been surrounded at Sharm el-Sheikh. This statement enabled the Egyptians to reply blandly that they did not have any rangers in that area at the time; this seemed to be true. Yet another Israeli claim on the eighth was that, of a fifty-man Egyptian ranger unit that had landed near Abu Rodeis on its way to Sharm el-Sheikh, five men had been killed and forty-five taken prisoner. This was perhaps a modified or even amended claim, but it seemed to duplicate a similar one made on the seventh.

During the first three days of the fighting the Israelis had made twenty-three armoured attacks of battalion size or larger, and all had been repelled. The basic reasons for these failures were that the Israelis had blindly put all their faith in a mass of charging tanks, rather like the heavy cavalry of old, anticipating they would automatically crush all opposition and cause the Egyptians to run away. In addition, tanks were easy prey to the determination and capability of the tank hunting teams which went out in front of the infantry and solidly stood their ground.

The Israelis knew the Egyptians had ample antitank weapons, but they were contemptuous of them and depended upon their tank gunnery to beat them in battle. The Israelis had also ignored the principle of concentration of force at a vital point and, instead, made scattered uncoordinated attacks along the length of the front. They later estimated the Egyptian antitank weapons to be of a density of "55 to the kilometre." The Egyptian tank-hunting teams were easy to spot out in the open, and one Israeli tank commander explained that he at first thought they were tree stumps until they moved. Expecting to fight

tanks and not infantry, the Israelis had no HE shells for their
guns, which would have broken up the Egyptian infantry and
tank-hunting teams in open terrain. Then, too, in their tank formations they had no integral infantry or mortars which would
have helped to counter the teams.

The Sagger antitank missile proved to be very effective when
used in groups of three with all of them directed onto one tank.
The shorter range RPG-7s proved to be effective at ranges of a
hundred yards or more and also were fired in threes and fours,
all aimed at one tank. The Snapper was much less effective, and
one in four of its missiles was nullified by technical faults. General Herzog says that twenty-five percent of Israeli tank casualties were knocked out by antitank missiles, and the majority of
these must have been hit in this initial three-day period when
they were vulnerable because of faulty tactics. Corporal Abdul
A'ata, a student at an agricultural college before he was con-
scripted into the Egyptian army in 1969, was credited with
destroying twenty-three Israeli tanks on the sixth of October,
including eight M-60s within the first hour. Later, when the
Israelis changed their tactics, the antitank missiles became less
effective. The Egyptians claim that seventy percent of the Israeli
tanks left behind on the battlefield had been hit by antitank
missiles.

Speaking later of the Israeli armoured tactics during the first
three days, General Ismail said his aim was to inflict maximum
casualties on the Israelis with minimum loss to the Egyptians.
He said, "First they began to strike rashly, but their counterattacks were perplexed and confused. They attacked first by
companies, then by battalions, and then by brigades, and it was
only later they began to control their nerves." General Shazli
also told me there was a distinct lack of coordinated Israeli
armoured response during the first two days when it was a free-
for-all with every subunit commander and soldier seeking personal glory on the battlefield.

Since the 1967 War the accent in the Israeli army had been
heavily on the tank, and the old, loose "Ugdad," or task group,
had been formed into what were virtually tank divisions. Each
was made up of two armoured and one mechanised brigade, to-

gether with some mobile artillery such as SP guns. In each armoured brigade there were just two tank battalions, and they had been stripped of their organic infantry and mortars. The mechanised brigade had been reduced in size and allowed only a low priority for vehicles and weapons. Its task was merely to mop up in the wake of a tank spearhead advance. In 1967 the Israeli armoured brigades were in the minority, but, as more tanks were received and, together with those captured in 1967, were put into service, infantry brigades were progressively converted to armoured ones with an establishment of ninety-six tanks. By 1973 the armoured brigades were in the majority.

Most armoured brigades were equipped with rebuilt M-48 Pattons and Centurions which had a high-velocity 105mm gun and a diesel engine, and M-60s, but many of the mechanised battalions still had World War II half-tracks, the M-3. Numbers of the American M-113 armoured personnel carrier had been received, but they were less well armoured than the M-3, and when standing up in them the infantry had only partial armoured protection. The concept of an all-round combat team of armour, artillery, mortars, and infantry with antitank weapons, working and fighting together, had been abandoned. This was partly because the old M-3 could not keep up with the tanks and so was discarded by the armoured brigades. All hope and faith was placed in the tank alone; it became, in Israeli eyes, the omnipotent god of the battlefield. Later, in an interview printed in *Maariv* of 25 January 1974, General Sharon was to say of this initial phase that "the Army had ceased to be brilliant and had substituted for military thought, initiative, and intelligence, a blind belief in the qualities of steel." Sharon was a paratrooper.

7

THE SYRIANS ATTACK

> *Golda, I was wrong in everything ... we shall*
> *have to withdraw on the Golan Heights ... and*
> *hold on to the last bullet.*

Moshe Dayan

On the northern battlefield Israel faced Syria on the Golan plateau. It is an extremely valuable strategic piece of terrain, overlooking the Upper Jordan Valley and blocking the old route between Damascus and Palestine. The elongated plateau is roughly thirty-five miles long from north to south at its maximum and about seventeen miles wide from east to west. It is an undulating stretch of countryside, interspersed with volcanic outcrops. Some, such as Tel Faris (3,989 feet above sea level), rise from the plateau like huge mounds to become the dominating features of the landscape. The rest of the ground is characterized by basalt rock outcrops and patches of lava, with some vegetation and trees. There is some cultivation on small, stony fields, some of which are terraced, but the economy of the area is essentially pastoral.

On its western edge an escarpment drops steeply down to the Upper Jordan Valley. On the south another steep escarpment goes down to the Yarmuk Valley, forming the boundary with

119

Jordan, which to the east gives way to sand and lava fields. The north of the plateau is blocked by the huge Mount Hermon massif, called Jebel Sheikh by the Arabs, rising to 9,223 feet above sea level. It runs diagonally from northeast to southwest and is snowcapped throughout the year. The eastern side of the plateau, facing the Damascus Plain, is more open.

The Golan Plateau is inhabited by Druse, a heretical sect that broke away from Islam in the twelfth century. They are a nation of some 200,000 people scattered in the mountainous regions of Israeli-held territory, Syria, and the Lebanon. At the opening of hostilities about 10,500 Druse lived on the plateau, about half of them in Majdal Shams and the remainder in a dozen or more other villages. After the 1967 war they had elected to stay and live under the Israeli military administration. The Israelis had established sixteen settlements, mainly around Kuneitra where the ground was more favourable to cultivation. They had also organized one *moshav,* which consists of individual farms with a collective marketing arrangement. Called Ramat Magshimim, it was manned by personnel of the NAHAL, the soldier workers.

The Golan Plateau was not good tank country, and, although it was more passable in its southern part than in the north, areas of it were impassable to vehicles because of the huge basalt boulders and outcrops of rock; the many defiles provided ideal ambush sites. Several roads crossed the plateau, and there was a network of motorable tracks made by the army and the settlers. Two roads ran roughly from north to south. One, for a distance of 75 kilometres, followed parallel to and a little way back from the alignment of the 1967 Cease-fire Line and can be called the Cease-fire Road. It ran from Rafid in the south, through that town to Massada, a Druse village in the north. Along the Cease-fire Line there was a narrow strip of "neutral territory." It was less than a half mile wide on the average, and it was patrolled by U.N. personnel from the sixteen U.N. posts on either side of the line.

The other north-south road ran somewhat diagonally for about twenty miles alongside the Trans-Arabian pipeline (TAP), the oil pipeline from Saudi Arabia which came from Jordan across the Golan Plateau into the Lebanon. This oil pipeline was underground, and its course was marked by a high, expanded-metal, double fence, the area between which was free from mines. To the east of the pipeline was a narrow maintenance road, which can be called the TAP Road. A north-south road also ran alongside the River Jordan at the foot of the plateau.

Five lateral roads ran from west to east across the plateau with bridges over the River Jordan. The northernmost, the Massada Road, went from Dan and Banias (two of the three sources of the River Jordan) to Massada. After June 1967 the Israelis had continued this road to the ski lift they had erected near the Druse village of Majdal Shams at the foot of the Mount Hermon massif. There were no roads over Mount Hermon, only a few donkey tracks and footpaths which were impassable in winter.

To the south of Massada Road another lateral ran from Kibbutz Gonen, near the River Jordan, to Wazit and continued to the Cease-fire Road. In the centre was the Damascus Road, the age-old route from Haifa to Damascus. It crossed the River Jordan (which was about twenty feet wide at this point) by the Benot Yacov Bridge, then wound up the escarpment and on through Naffak and Kuneitra to Damascus. The Benot Yacov Bridge was a strong one, built of stone. The others over the river were lighter, either Bailey-type bridging or of sectional girder construction.

A fourth lateral was the Yehudia Road from the Arik Bridge at the head of Lake Tiberias. It climbed the steep slope and passed just north of Barak to join the TAP Road, just south of Khusniye. The fifth, the El Al Road, went up the Yarmuk escarpment from Ein Gev and Ma'agan (both on the shore of Lake Tiberias) to El Al, and then on through Ramat Magshimim to join the TAP Road at Juhader. Thus there were at least five good bridges over the River Jordan.

The forward static Israeli defences were held by two infantry battalions and four batteries of artillery, each having six SP guns. They were based on a line of seventeen defensive positions on volcanic hills or huge mounds. Each of these was held by an infantry platoon supported by three tanks, in bunkerlike positions with good fields of fire and protected by wire and mines.

Along most of the length of the Cease-fire Line a large antitank ditch had been dug to a depth of about fifteen feet, with a twelve-foot high bank of spoil on its Syrian side. Other tank obstacles had been constructed and mines laid to channel any attacking vehicles into selected killing grounds. The infantry was armed with antitank weapons, including the French SS-10 and SS-11. Positioned about two thousand yards or more farther back were four tank battalions and eleven batteries composed mainly of 155mm guns. Their primary task was to block roads and tracks and also to cover the killing grounds. Special ramps, or pads, had been constructed on higher ground so that the tanks and guns could shoot down on any invaders, giving a tactical advantage.

The Golan front HQ was at Naffak, on the Damscus Road, where there was a small army camp on a small mound with some underground bunkers. The town itself had been in ruins since the 1967 war. The Israeli garrison amounted to about twenty-five hundred men in all and consisted of three brigades, two armoured and one infantry. The infantry brigade was distributed to man the static forward defences and certain other key points. One armoured brigade, the Barak Brigade, had three tank battalions, one spread out to support the infantry defences and the other two deployed in the rear. The Barak Brigade, commanded by Colonel Shoam, possessed about seventy-five tanks, mainly Centurions, and had its HQ at Naffak.

On the fifth the front HQ moved from Nazareth to Naffak forts were increased to about twenty men each. The 7th Armoured Brigade (the other "garrison" one) had returned from exercises in the south and was concentrating around Naffak. This brigade, commanded by Colonel Avigdor, also had three tank battalions, which were equipped with Shermans. One battalion was placed under the command of Barak Brigade and sent forward to the northern sector. Another was stationed at the Wazit crossroads and the third at Sindiana, which was about two miles southeast of Naffak on the TAP Road. There were also elements of the Golani Infantry Brigade on the Golan Plateau.

On the fifth the front HQ moved from Nazareth to Naffak. Herzog estimates that by the next day the Israelis had 177 tanks and eleven batteries of artillery on the Golan Plateau. While Major General Hofi, as GOC Northern Command, had the over-all responsibility for the Golan Plateau, the commander on the spot was Brigadier Rafel Eytan, who also had his HQ at Naffak. Hofi, Eytan, Shoam, and Avigdor were regular officers. In an emergency, according to Herzog, it was planned to reinforce the Golan Plateau with up to an extra seven reserve brigades.

Perhaps the most valuable position the Israelis held was that on the southwestern tip of the Mount Hermon range. A strong fort and observation post had been built at a height of about 6,600 feet on part of a ridge, the remainder of which was in Syrian and Lebanese hands. This observation post, which over-looked the whole of the Golan Plateau and some miles of Syrian territory to the east of it, contained sensory and communication equipment. It was manned by a detachment of the Golani Bri-gade and some technicians, amounting to fifty-five men in all. Syria also had an observation post higher up on the ridge, over-looking that of the Israelis.

Between the Golan Plateau and Damascus the Syrians had three linear defence complexes running at right angles across the Damascus Road. All were constructed on the Soviet pattern, having concrete gun and tank emplacements and bunker posi-tions. The first, and weakest, was between 1,000 and 2,000 yards to the east of the Cease-fire Line. The second, and strong-er, was based on the Sasa Ridge—an uneven stretch of hills, rocky outcrops, and lava beds. The Damascus Road wound through this area some twelve miles or so farther east. Both the first and second defence lines contained static T-34s, over 200 in all, used as artillery. (On the morning of the sixth the Israelis noted the second Syrian defence line was not manned, which caused them to be suspicious.) The third, and strongest, line was another ten miles or so farther back and was just to the west of the road from Katana to Kiswe—both garrison towns. The Syri-ans also had a strong Air Defence Barrier just to the west of the road that ran from Damascus through Kiswe to Sheikh Miskin.

The Syrian aim was to recapture the whole of the Golan Pla-teau within thirty hours, as they thought the Israelis would need twice that amount of time to mobilise their reserves. The plan was that there would be an air strike at S Hour on targets on the plateau, which would include the Benot Yacov Bridge. It was to be seized and held by helicopter-borne troops immediately after the strike, and at the same time the Israeli OP on Mount Hermon was to be taken to deprive the Israelis of their vision over the battlefield. The Israeli forward defences at several points on a wide front were to be breached by three infantry divisions, after which the two waiting armoured divisions would sweep through the gaps down to the River Jordan. No time was to be wasted on the individual defensive positions; they were to be bypassed and left to be dealt with later.

The main weight of the Syrian attack and initial thrust was to be made through the Rafid Gap (an opening in the jumble of hills and uneven ground that made vehicular movement easier) and then on to the TAP Road from the southeast. Moving along this road, brigades or battalions would branch off westward down to the River Jordan as the lateral roads were reached. There was to be a penetration through the Kudne Gap, about ten miles south of Kuneitra, and another about six miles north of that town, which itself was to be initially bypassed. Yet another thrust farther north would diagonally hit the Wazit Road; another, aimed at Massada, was to reach Dan and Banias, the last to be completed by 2359 hours on the sixth. The overall operation was directed by General Shakkour from a field GHQ at Katana. The Israelis thought the main Syrian attack would come down the Damascus Road toward the Benot Yacov Bridge, with lesser or even feint attacks at the Rafid Gap and other points to divert attention and cause dispersion.

The Syrian divisions lined up to make the initial breakthrough were, from north to south, the 7th Infantry Division, commanded by Brigadier Omah Abrash, whose task was to break through just north of Kuneitra opposite a feature which the Israelis called Booster and to cut through to the Wazit Road; the 5th Infantry Division, commanded by Brigadier Ali Asslam, which was to break through the Kudne Gap to take Khusniye and then Naffak and to eventually link up with the commandos at the Benot Yacov Bridge; and the 9th Infantry Division, commanded by Brigadier Jelal Jehan, which was to break through the Rafid Gap and move along the TAP Road, its brigades advancing westward down the El Al and Yehudia Roads to Lake Tiberias and the River Jordan.

These Syrian "infantry" divisions were really "mechanised" ones, despite their name. Each had four brigades—one tank, two mechanised and only one infantry, and even the last had about thirty tanks. The mechanised brigades each had an integral tank battalion of T-62s, the remainder being either T-54s or T-55s. Each of these divisions had about 180 tanks, making a total of 540 in the leading assaults. The tanks were backed up by many batteries of 130mm guns (which had a range of 27,000 yards) and 152mm (with a range of 18,000 yards). Syrian brigades of all types had a troop of four PT-76 reconnaissance tanks per company and another for each battalion and brigade HQ. (The PT-76 weighed about fifteen tons and could move at twenty-five mph.)

At S Hour (1400 hours), the Syrians, using about a hundred aircraft, made an air strike at targets on the Golan Plateau. They did not include the Jordan River bridges, as was expected by the Egyptians, because, for political reasons, the original plan had been modified at the last moment. Also at S Hour Syrian guns began laying down a creeping barrage that lasted for fifty minutes; under it the forward brigades of the three divisions crashed through the Cease-fire Line wire fence at the selected places and bypassed the U.N. observer posts. All the U.N. observer posts along this Cease-fire Line held out throughout the war, except four which were evacuated, one from the Syrian side and three from the Israeli side. The observer officers in them remained in contact with the U.N. HQ in Jerusalem. One U.N. observer officer later described the initial part of the Syrian advance: "It was not like an attack, it was like a parade ground demonstration." The Syrians had been training for months, using tactics based upon wave after wave of assaulting tanks advancing, regardless of casualties or of whether or not the wave in front had been brought to a halt.

The Syrian columns moved on a broad front with three or four vehicles abreast on either side of the road or track, using "flail" tanks to explode mines. Bulldozers and SU-100 guns

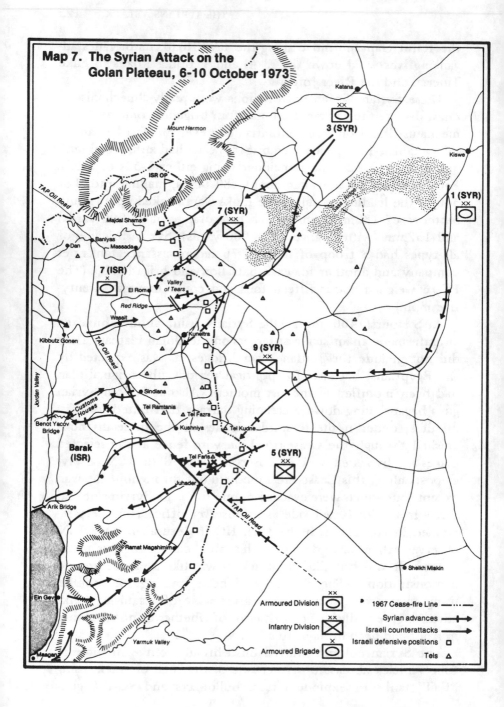

Map 7. The Syrian Attack on the Golan Plateau, 6-10 October 1973

were interspersed well forward, with infantry armed with Saggers, Snappers, and RPG-7s travelling in armoured personnel
carriers. Bulldozers soon filled in parts of the antitank ditch,
nullifying this obstacle and enabling vehicles to cross it and bypass the forward Israeli static defences. Nonetheless, several
tanks were knocked out in the process. As the Syrians advanced,
the Israeli tanks supporting their forward defences withdrew to
prepared positions in the hills overlooking the approaches.

Although the Israelis were taken by surprise, they rallied
quickly and were soon shooting back at the invaders, opening
up at ranges of 2,000 yards or more as soon as the Syrians
crossed the Cease-fire Line. This was exceedingly long range for
accurate shooting, causing the Syrians to allege that the Israelis
had been supplied by the Americans with a type of "laser fire
control." The Israelis deny this, saying they knew the ground
and the exact distances, and this precise knowledge was the
reason for their success in knocking out so many Syrian tanks.
Regardless of casualties, the Syrian armour surged forward, and
the Israeli tanks and guns in many cases had to abandon their
prepared positions and withdraw to prevent being overrun. They
simply withdrew off the main routes into the broken ground in
an attempt to hit the Syrians on the flanks. When the Syrian
tanks were knocked out or ground to a stop through some
mechanical fault, as was frequent, they often caused traffic jams,
especially when their routes were funnelled through uneven
ground. At times on the roads there were traffic blocks, which
were good targets for the Israelis' guns.

The town of Kuneitra was initially bypassed, and a Syrian
brigade from the 7th Infantry Division attempted to penetrate
at a point about four miles north of the town, opposite Booster.
Elements of a battalion from the 7th Armoured Brigade had
positions on the ridge, known to the Syrians as Red Ridge,
about two thousand yards from the antitank ditch. The ridge
shielded Cease-fire Road, which ran to its west. The Syrians
bridged the antitank ditch and attempted to advance across an
open stretch of terrain which the Israelis had planned as a killing
area, only to be picked off two or three at a time. After an hour
the Syrians withdrew to the ditch. The Israelis claim the Syrians

left over sixty destroyed or disabled tanks behind them.

About ten miles south of Kuneitra a brigade of the 5th Infantry Division bypassed one of the Israeli infantry forts to the south and swept through the Kudne Gap, an opening opposite Tel Kudne, toward Khusniye, which is about six miles from the Cease-fire Line. The Israeli tanks gave way before them, and the Israeli infantry fort was evacuated. Another ten miles or so farther south two brigades of the 9th Infantry Division forced their way through the wide Rafid Gap and began moving along the TAP Road from the south toward Juhader, at the junction with the El Al Road. The three Israeli infantry forts blocking the gap were evacuated in the afternoon. Overhead, the Israeli air force, upon which the Israelis relied so heavily for ground support and interdiction in such a situation, was having a disastrous time. It hit up against the Syrian Air Defence Barrier and lost some thirty aircraft that first afternoon.

The Syrians intended that the Israeli OP on Mount Hermon should be dealt with at S Hour, but there was a delay in briefing and organising the assault force, which was the 500-strong ranger group, the only one the Syrians had. Not receiving their orders until about 1200 hours, the rangers did not reach the foot of the massif in position to commence scaling until 1400 hours. At 1445 hours they arrived within some 200 yards of the Israeli position. During the first part of the climb no shots were fired by either side, nor was any covering fire given by either aircraft or artillery, but it must be remembered that a full scale battle was in progress below, and already sections of the Golan Plateau were covered with black and coloured smoke. Contrary to many reports, the Syrian rangers did not arrive by helicopter but climbed the mountain on foot, although other Syrian paratroops were lifted by helicopter at about the same time to be put into blocking positions lower down in the foothills to cover the Massada Road. The Syrian rangers were armed with Kalashnikov rifles and grenades and wore normal camouflaged battledress, unlike the Israeli defenders who wore white to blend with the snowy background.

The Israeli position was a strong one of concrete construction, surrounded by a number of firing positions connected to

it by underground tunnels. The Syrians had gained precise information of the layout of the position from espionage sources,
from observation from their OP higher up on Mount Hermon,
and from the Druse inhabitants of Majdal Shams. The rangers
were individually briefed so that each section knew exactly
what to attack and how to attack it. When they had recovered
their breath, they charged the position frontally, hoping to overcome it by sheer firepower and numbers, but the attackers were
brought to a halt less than a hundred yards from their objective.
It was in this unsuccessful assault that the Syrians received most
of their casualties, which exceeded fifty.

The Syrians then reorganised and adopted different tactics,
sniping at the Israeli outer positions while they worked their
way forward from rock to rock. The Israelis were in a state of
alarm, and, as Herzog says, "Some of the service personnel, for
whom this was the first exposure to fire, clustered in the rooms
of the bunker, frozen by fear, and the pleas of those fighting to
come and give a hand were unanswered." The Syrians made
their second assault about 1700 hours. They charged in suddenly from the west without any preliminary covering fire, when
the sun was shining in the eyes of the defenders. They were
successful in taking all the outer positions. The Israeli defenders
then withdrew into the main central position, which was protected by a high wall. The rangers scaled the wall, using grap-
pling hooks and ropes. Once inside there was fierce hand-to-hand
fighting, which the Syrians won by sheer weight of numbers.
About eleven Israelis managed to escape and scramble down the
mountainside to regain their own lines, and about twenty were
taken prisoner.

The Syrians cleared the underground passages but were
baulked at the main sensory and communications centre, which
was protected by a huge, locked steel door. An Israeli prisoner
was brought back and was compelled to show the Syrians how
to open the door. According to David Nicholle, writing in the
RUSI Journal of July 1975, the Israeli prisoner, who at first
refused to help the Syrians, was severely beaten until his resistance broke. "The Israeli then put his hand on all five buttons
and pressed them all at once. Behind the door was a handful of

men operating a communications centre, who surrendered immediately." It was at this stage the Israelis allege these prisoners were shot, causing the Israeli government to later make a formal complaint that, contrary to the Geneva Convention, five prisoners were killed. On the morning of the seventh General Hofi gave orders for a counterattack to be mounted to retake the OP. Then, due to the adverse situation on the plateau, he cancelled it, only to reactivate the order when he heard (wrongly) that some Israelis were still holding out in the OP. On the morning of the seventh a detachment of the Golani Brigade began an attack, moving up the normal road to the OP. They were ambushed by the Syrians and had to withdraw, losing twenty-two killed and about fifty wounded. Taken by surprise, the Israelis had no chance to reinforce the OP in sufficient time or to make diversionary moves.

The Syrian ranger group stayed to garrison this vital OP for the remainder of the war. It was anticipated that the Israelis would attempt to retake it because of its immense value, but, apart from later attention by Israeli aircraft and artillery fire, the captured OP had a fairly quiet time. The Israelis were preoccupied on the plateau below. The sensory and communications equipment, which was of Japanese origin, was removed by the Syrians and given to the Soviet Union; for over two years the Russians had been unsuccessful in trying to persuade the Japanese government to sell it similar equipment.

By 1630 hours General Hofi realised that the main Syrian threat was from the south, by way of the Rafid and Kudne Gaps, and not along the Damascus Road as had been expected. He thought the attack on the Booster position had probably been a feint but was not sure. Instead of moving the remainder of the 7th Armoured Brigade south, he gave it the responsibility for the northern part of the plateau, including the Damascus Road. Command of the plateau was given to Brigadier Eytan, who remained at Naffak. During the afternoon Eytan ordered the women and children to be evacuated from the settlements, and the following morning the men were ordered to leave. Many of them did so under protest as they wanted to stay to defend their own settlements, but all had to go, some to serve on the

Suez Canal front. Also that afternoon Palestinian Fedayeen fired rockets at Kiryat Shimona. In riposte, at 1440 hours, the Israelis fired shells into the Lebanese village of Blida, from which it was thought the guerrillas were operating. During the night more rockets were fired from Lebanese soil.

When it was reported at about 1700 hours that the Syrians were moving in strength through the Rafid Gap toward Juhader, Colonel Shoam, who was now in command of the southern part of the plateau, moved there as well. He thought he could direct the battle from Juhader, but, when he reached it, he found that the village was under heavy shellfire and that the Syrians were infiltrating past it. Unable to return directly to Naffak, he had to make a circular detour by way of Lake Tiberias during the hours of darkness. However, about 2200 hours a few tanks of a reserve brigade, the 79th Armoured, reached TAP Road and were the first reinforcements to join in the battle. Being widely dispersed, the Barak Brigade had suffered heavily in the fighting and, by Herzog's estimate "numbered [only] fifteen tanks by the late hours of Saturday night [the sixth]."

About 2200 hours on the sixth a Syrian brigade of the 7th Infantry Division made another attack on the Booster position just to the north of Kuneitra. Once again it was held by the Israelis from their commanding positions, and the Syrians retired with loss about three hours later. In the south, during the night of the sixth/seventh, one Syrian brigade turned southwest along the El Al Road, while yet another reached and turned down the Yehudia Road. Much to the surprise of the Israelis, Syrian forces, especially their infantry who moved out on foot with their antitank weapons, were continually active throughout the night. According to Herzog, their probing columns continued to advance "using coloured lights and flags to distinguish the various units." The Israelis were at a disadvantage because they did not have "adequate optical equipment for night fighting" and had been led to believe the Syrians were not trained for night movement and fighting.

During the night the tanks of the 5th Infantry Division flooded through the Rafid Gap, and the Syrians moved their two armoured divisions forward to the Cease-fire Line. Most of

the Syrian tanks had infrared apparatus, which winked and reflected in the flashes of gunfire and illuminating flares that lit
up the battlefield. According to Herzog, "The attack by night
by the Syrians was described by men on the Golan Heights as
being like hundreds of cats' eyes coming across the plain."

As Israeli reserves arrived on the shore of Lake Tiberias and
the west bank of the River Jordan, they were immediately sent
forward in small groups into battle. By 0230 hours on the seventh elements of the 19th Armoured Brigade had reached El Al,
and those of the 17th Armoured Brigade were moving eastward
along the Yehudia Road; both were reserve formations. By dawn
on the seventh the Syrians had made a large indentation through
the Kudne Gap and were approaching Khusniye, while farther
south one Syrian brigade had reached and occupied Ramat Magshimim on the El Al Road. Realising their success and wishing
to exploit it, the Syrians ordered the 1st Armoured Division,
commanded by Brigadier Tewfig Jehne, to move through the
Rafid Gap to seize the TAP Road, and a brigade from the 3rd
Armoured Division, commanded by Brigadier Mustafa Sharba,
to move through the Kudne Gap. Battered, bewildered, and outnumbered, the Israelis fell back before the Syrian advances, and
Herzog states that "pressure was growing at all points, and ammunition was beginning to run short because in the initial heat
of battle many of the crews had been rather wasteful."

Soon after dawn on the seventh a brigade from the Syrian
7th Infantry Division penetrated the Cease-fire Line in the
northern sector toward the Hermonit position. This was about
five thousand yards to the northwest of the Booster position;
between them lay an open, elongated valley, an ideal killing
ground. It became known to the Israelis as the Valley of Tears.
The brigade advanced without infantry support and, after fighting all morning, had to withdraw after suffering heavy losses. It
had been making for the Wazit Road to get behind the Israeli
defences at Booster and Hermonit. Beginning at 0800 hours
another Syrian brigade attack was mounted on the Booster position. The advance was on a wide front, but again, without infantry support, it was beaten back with loss. Later in the morning
a brigade of the 3rd Armoured Division attempted to force its

way to the Wazit Road, but it also was held before the Hermonit position and eventually had to break off the action at about 1300 hours. A few miles still farther north that same morning yet another brigade of the 7th Infantry Division, also without infantry support, pushed toward the Massada Road in the vicinity of Majdal Shams. It also had to withdraw.

While the Syrian armoured and mechanised units moved and attacked according to the plan, they were badly let down by their infantry on the morning of the seventh. This was especially so in the north where infantry elements in the area of the foothills of Mount Hermon should have moved forward to support the armoured thrusts toward Massada and the Wazit Road and to plug a vulnerable gap in the area of Majdal Shams. A Moroccan infantry brigade, about eighteen hundred strong, which had been in Syria since June 1973, was in position in the Mount Hermon foothills. When the Syrian order came to advance, the Moroccans declined to move. There was also a Druse infantry formation, commanded by Lieutenant Colonel Omah Abu Shalash, in the same area. It too was ordered to move forward, but the colonel failed to "raise two of his companies on the radio," because they simply did not reply to his orders. The third company responded but flatly refused to budge. A Syrian infantry brigade in the same area also refused to advance. This was sheer mutiny, and has never been satisfactorily explained. Being deprived of infantry support contributed considerably to the Syrian armoured failures. A Syrian staff officer later told me that the Moroccans "were not well disciplined, or trained for conventional war, and so were of little use." They remained in the battle area for political reasons, but they were not used again in the fighting, and the Druse unit was withdrawn. Luttwak writes, "Unkindly, it was suggested that . . . King Hassan of Morocco sent two battalions of troublemakers to fight and die."

Back at his HQ at Naffak on the morning of the seventh Colonel Shoam, realising that the main Syrian thrust was coming toward him along the TAP Road, knew he must organise a defence against it. He again moved southward to Juhader where he intended to establish his forward HQ, but on arrival there found that Syrian and Israeli tanks were almost intermixed. As his losses were heavier than he feared, he returned to Naffak. When within about three hundred yards of the HQ bunkers, standing up in the turret of his tank, he was machine-gunned and killed by a burst of fire from a disabled Syrian tank by the roadside.

By noon in the Kudne area the Syrians were occupying Khusniye, merely a collection of battered and derelict buildings from the 1967 War; only a solitary minaret stood intact and aloof. A brigade from the 1st Armoured Division pushed north along the TAP Road, reaching Naffak about one hour after Colonel Shoam had been killed. Its forward elements attacked the camp area, and Brigadier Eytan evacuated just in time, moving his HQ about three miles north on the TAP Road. The Syrian formation was soon engaged by the leading troops of the Israeli 79th Armoured Brigade. This reserve brigade had just reached the area. By afternoon one Syrian brigade had stopped just 800 yards from El Al, and another on the Yehudia Road was less than six miles from Lake Tiberias. The Barak Brigade was almost wiped out; the senior remaining officer was a captain. Ammunition was critically short, and the Israelis sent jeeps from one disabled tank and gun to another to collect the unused ammunition. About noon a brigade from the Syrian 9th Infantry Division attacked westward just south of Kuneitra but was held in the afternoon by elements of the Israeli 7th Armoured Brigade. Kuneitra was now invested, and only a small Israeli garrison held out in one part of the town.

But Syrian casualties had been heavy too, especially as the Israeli air force was able to come into action when the Syrians advanced beyond the cover given by their Air Defence Barrier and gave close ground support. Syrian tanks and vehicles seemed to remain on or near the roadways, making no attempt to camouflage or to dig in, and by 1700 hours the Israelis reckoned they had knocked out over 400 Syrian tanks.

The Israelis were giving priority to the Golan Front, and by noon of the seventh helicopters were flying in replacement tank crews and returning with wounded. The previous evening Major General Laner, detailed to command a reserve division on the Golan Plateau, had arrived and set up a temporary divisional HQ at the Arik Bridge. From there he directed reinforcements, as they appeared, up the Yehudia Road and the two roads that led to El Al Road to block the Syrian advance. General Hofi divided the Golan Plateau between Eytan and Laner, with the Damascus Road being the boundary. One unit had moved forward only a couple of miles or so when it reported back that it was being attacked by Syrian infantry. General Laner, a reserve officer who had formerly commanded the armoured forces in the Sinai, ordered it to stand fast, which it did, only to find, as described by Herzog, that "the attacking forces were in fact infantry units of the Golani Brigade, retreating before the massed Syrian armoured attack." That Israeli morale was uncertain can be deduced from the comments Herzog attributes to Lieutenant Colonel Pinie, the deputy commander of the Golan District, who, on the seventh when moving up from the Jordan Valley to Naffak, "saw sights that horrified him. . . . Could this be the IDF? Here before him straggled units of a defeated army. He stopped one fleeing unit by standing in the middle of the road and pointedly reminding the officer in charge what the penalty for cowardice in the face of the enemy was, even in the IDF. It was clear to him that the Israeli Army was at a loss when withdrawing."

Meanwhile, elements of Major General Peled's reserve division, originally intended to be used on the Suez Canal front, had arrived from southern Israel. (General Moshe Peled, a regular officer, had just recently relinquished his post as commandant of the Command and General Staff College.) This newly formed division was not well equipped; it had been given Sherman tanks, some of which still had the old 75mm guns. Its leading formation, the 19th Armoured Brigade, pushed straight up the El Al Road from Ein Gev and Ma'agan, and the 14th Armoured Brigade was soon following. The Israeli roads leading to the Golan Plateau were choked with loaded tank transporters, buses and civilian cars (some daubed with mud as camouflage) filled with reservists desperately trying to reach their units or just get to the front somehow. Generally, there was confusion, and, while many volunteers were rushing toward the battle, the majority were slow to arrive.

On the seventh Moshe Dayan visited the Golan Front, and the briefing he received caused him to return to Tel Aviv in a despondent mood. He recommended to Premier Meir that Israeli troops be withdrawn from the plateau to form a defensive line just to the east of the crest of the River Jordan escarpment and that a stronger defensive line be formed on the river itself. Before leaving the front he had given orders for the escarpment roads to be blocked and the Jordan bridges prepared for demolition.

About 1700 hours Premier Meir sent for General Bar Lev to come to her office in Tel Aviv. She recounted Dayan's recommendations and sent the general to the Golan to see what could be done. Dayan had said, according to Herzog, "Golda, I was wrong in everything. We are heading towards a catastrophe. We shall have to withdraw on the Golan Heights to the edge of the escarpment overlooking the valley, and in the south in Sinai to the passes and hold on to the last bullet." Bar Lev arrived at the River Jordan about 2000 hours, toured the area, spoke to commanders and men, breathed confidence into them, and issued orders for a counterattack to commence the next day. His calm and firm action did much to stabilise morale. General Laner was put in charge of the defences of the Upper Jordan Valley.

Meanwhile, on the Syrian side in the afternoon of the seventh, a top-level conference was held at Katana, the Syrian field GHQ. It was attended by Generals Tlas, Shakkour, and Naji Jamil (commander of the air force) and other senior officers. It was decided to halt the advance of the Syrian troops in the southern part of the plateau—one of the most intriguing and surprising decisions of the war. With this unnecessary halt the momentum of the advance was lost and was difficult to restart. Had the Syrian columns not stopped at about 1700 hours, with still one hour of daylight left, they could have reached the rim of the escarpment and, perhaps, even the River Jordan. The Syrian pause lasted all night; during this time more Israeli tanks, guns and soldiers arrived. (The Israelis had been short of ammunition, tanks and guns, and had lost over 250 killed.) The Syrians decided to advance again, but they had missed their initial opportunity.

General Tlas admitted to me that such an order had been given, but would not elaborate, saying, "The time is not yet ready to discuss the reasons for this decision." It is unlikely it was caused by any of the reasons ascribed to it by the Israelis, such as loss of control, excessive casualties, shortage of fuel, or cracking morale. Despite the heavy losses, the Syrian field radio networks functioned well, maintaining radio silence except for code words, reporting "bounds," indicating enemy positions, and issuing orders; a good, aggressive spirit was maintained. A possible explanation may be that they had advanced beyond the cover of their Air Defence Barrier, and the Israeli air force had begun to intervene. Even had the Syrians reached the River Jordan they would have been at the mercy of the superior Israeli air force. Also, there may have been a desire to straighten the line, as some columns were racing ahead of the others and rendering themselves vulnerable to flank attacks. Additionally, due to the failure of the infantry, there was a gap in the northern foothills which the air force commander said he could not block to prevent an Israeli counterattack from that direction. There may also have been some second thoughts and faint hearts in high positions. It may have been a combination of these reasons. Whatever the explanation, it cost the Syrians the Golan Plateau, which they probably could have taken within thirty hours. Whether they could have held it is another matter.

Not all the Syrian units obeyed the order to halt, but the 1st Armoured Division did, settling in the area of Khusniye together with elements of the 5th Infantry Division. The brigade of the 1st Armoured Division, which had taken Naffak, slackened off, and by darkness it had been driven from the area by the Israeli 79th Armoured Brigade moving up from the Benot Yacov Bridge. Another following brigade of the 1st Armoured Division had sheared off slightly westward to bypass Naffak and the Israeli 79th Armoured Brigade. One of its battalions reached the customs houses on the Damascus Road, four miles from the Benot Yacov Bridge, only to be marooned there as Israeli reinforcements came up from the Jordan Valley and smothered it.

To the north of Kuneitra the battle continued between the Syrian 7th Infantry Division and the Israeli 7th Armoured Brigade holding the Booster position. About 2200 hours the Syrians attacked again, but they had to give up after three hours of fierce fighting. Undaunted by their losses, the Syrians attacked the Booster position again about 0400 hours the next day, the eighth, just before it was light, but with the same result. During this night fighting the Syrian infantry dismounted from their vehicles and roamed the battlefields, their RPG-7s taking a toll of Israeli tanks.

On the evening of the seventh General Hofi had told General Peled to launch an attack on the eighth and to push to the TAP Road, but the Israelis were not ready. Many of their tanks and vehicles had broken down because of mechanical failures on their way to the Golan. The Syrian 1st Armoured and 5th Infantry Divisions had settled in the area of Khusniye which was being turned into their major administrative and refuelling centre. There was confused fighting there but no major push. On the Yehudia Road, in one afternoon's fighting, the 79th Armoured Brigade had a hard time, losing three battalion commanders and five out of the nine company commanders without gaining any territory.

In the north, during the night of the seventh/eighth, the Syrians again attacked along the route toward Wazit. With two infantry battalions, they still could not break through. Even so, at daylight on the eighth they tried again. A Syrian armoured brigade and the Assad Republican Guard made a determined assault in the same direction, only to be halted before the Hermonit position. On the eighth the Israeli 17th Armoured Brigade still battled heavily along the Yehudia Road, while to its south the Israeli 19th Armoured Brigade had begun an advance at 0830 hours along the El Al Road. It was of this fighting that an Israeli officer remarked, "They shot and missed. We shot and hit." Still, no progress was made, so the Israeli 20th Armoured Brigade was sent along its southern flank with slightly more success. The same morning General Peled's 14th Armoured Brigade came into action, clearing the Syrians from Ramat Magshimim. It reached the TAP Road, pushed along it, and arrived at Juhader by 1300 hours. It was halted by Syrians armed with Saggers and RPG-7s.

In the afternoon of the eighth three Syrian armoured groups again attacked the Booster position, moving on a broad front along the valley to the Hermonit position. Again the Israelis held the attack, although with loss to themselves. That night the Syrian 7th Infantry Division launched yet another attack, spread over a six-mile-wide front and lasting several hours, but the Syrians were simply walking into a tank killing area. The remnants of the three battalions of the Israeli 7th Armoured Brigade kept to the high ground, remaining in favourable positions, but they were nearing exhaustion. Despite promises, reinforcements of tanks, guns, and men were still not arriving.

Journalist Gerald Seymour, describing a visit to the Golan Plateau on the eighth, said that every other vehicle on the road to the Golan was a civilian car, packed solid with young Israeli soldiers joining their units. This indicated that the Israeli mobilisation was still not complete, although priority had been given to that front. Seymour went on to say that the Israeli line appeared to have stabilised just south of Naffak, where he saw an Israeli battery of 155mm SP guns laying down barrages on Syrian vehicles attempting to supply their troops in Kuneitra. Syrian guns soon replied, causing the Israeli battery to hastily change position. The shells set fire to the grass, and the smoke drifted in clouds toward the east over the heads of the Syrians. General Hofi's claim, on the evening of the eighth, that "we have launched a breakthrough," was premature. Though the Syrians had not advanced far on that day, the Israelis, with one minor exception in the south, had also been checked whenever they tried to advance.

On the morning of the ninth, the period of high-level Syrian indecision over, the Syrians moved out to attack Sindiana but were held by the Israeli 79th Armoured Brigade which prevented them from reinforcing or rescuing the Syrian unit at the customs houses. During the afternoon the Syrians fell back, and only four Syrian tanks returned from the customs houses. The Israeli brigade advanced southward to Ramtania on the TAP Road.

In the south the Israelis began closing in on the Khusniye area where the Syrians had been concentrating. Moving more troops along the El Al and Yehudia roads to the TAP Road, the Israelis caused the Syrian 9th Infantry Division to ease itself southward to avoid being trapped. By 1100 hours the Israeli 19th Armoured Brigade had reached the high ground to the southeast

Knocked-out Syrian tanks in and around the Israeli antitank ditch near Red Ridge.

Israeli repairmen putting damaged tanks back into action on the Golan Plateau on October 11, 1973.

of Khusniye, while the Israeli 20th Armoured Brigade unsuccessfully stormed Tel Faris, which dominated the Rafid Gap.

On the ninth the Israeli air force came into the battle, enabling the 14th Armoured Brigade to reach Cease-fire Road. Once again the 20th Armoured Brigade failed to take the vital feature, Tel Faris. (It was later taken in the rear by infantry on foot.) The first attacks by the 17th and 19th Armoured Brigades, made before noon on Khusniye, failed. The Syrians had made the area into a strong defensive locality by skillfully using their antitank weapons. At 1600 hours the 19th Armoured Brigade was ordered to make another attack on Khusniye. This time, with more artillery and some air support, and by encircling from the rear, it was able to block a Syrian brigade advancing from the southeast. By evening part of the Syrian 1st Armoured and 5th Infantry Divisions were in a trap at Khusniye; only one of their brigades had been withdrawn eastward in time to escape. As darkness fell the Israeli 79th Armoured Brigade was closing in from the northwest to take Tel Ramtania, which overlooked Khusniye; the 17th Armoured Brigade was on the TAP Road blocking it; and General Peled's 14th, 19th, and 20th Armoured Brigades were approaching from the south. Eventually, the 19th Armoured Brigade broke through the Syrian defences into the Khusniye area, but the Syrians held out in parts of it.

In the north, at dawn on the ninth, seven Syrian helicopters appeared over the Red Ridge battlefield, and four of them put down commandos near Bukata, behind the Red Ridge. This action worried the Israelis more than they cared to admit. At 0600 hours the Syrians again attacked the Booster and Hermonit positions and the Red Ridge between them. From the north the Assad Republican Guard tried to push past the Hermonit position to get to El Rom behind the Red Ridge position, and, in the fighting, Israeli and Syrian tanks became intermixed. In the assault, according to Herzog, "Avi's battalion destroyed the Assad force, which proved to be very mediocre on the field of battle." At the height of the Red Ridge battle on the ninth Brigadier Omah Abrash, GOC 7th Infantry Division, sent back a message to his field GHQ at Katana saying he had only seven tanks left. The reply was "regroup and charge." Eventually

Abrash returned with only four tanks, out of some 230 that he had taken into the battle. He was recalled and later committed suicide.

According to Herzog, the Israeli 7th Armoured Brigade had been "fighting for four days and three nights, without a moment's rest or respite, under constant fire. On average each tank was left with three to four shells." The brigade commander wanted to withdraw but was persuaded to hold on. Shortly afterward an officer with eleven tanks of the Barak Brigade came into the battle, arriving "just as the 7th Brigade, left with seven running tanks out of an original total of approximately 100, was on the verge of collapse. Both sides had fought to a standstill." The Syrians then commenced to withdraw and the Israelis cautiously followed down the valley, the Vale of Tears. The Israelis claim there were 260 tanks and hundreds of other armoured vehicles and guns lying destroyed or abandoned. At that critical juncture, such was the luck of battle. By nightfall the Israelis had crossed the Cease-fire Line. Immediately to the south the Israeli pocket in Kuneitra was still invested. Thus ended the battle of Red Ridge, so nearly won by the Syrians, so poorly directed by them, but fought by them with a ferocity and bravery that has probably not been equalled in Syrian military history.

On the tenth Israeli pressure on the Syrians increased. In the battle for Kuneitra, after a small artillery barrage, the Israeli tanks, back to their gung ho tactics again, charged straight up the Damascus Road into the centre of the town. It fell to them after an hour's fighting, and the Israelis trapped within its buildings were released. The Israelis had the advantage that their tanks could manoeuvre freely in the fields around Kuneitra, as they were free from mines. Thus they could bring their mobile warfare skills into play against the Syrians. By midday of the tenth the Israelis were across the Cease-fire Line in several places.

In the south, at 0300 hours, the Israeli 20th Armoured Brigade held the Kuneitra-Rafid crossroads, while their 19th Armoured Brigade was still fighting near Khusniye, baulked before Tel Kudne. At 0400 hours the 19th Brigade moved out to attack, moving through Tel Fazra to Tel Kudne, but by this time the Syrians had been ordered to withdraw, and many of their tanks and guns slipped out from the Israeli trap. By evening on the tenth the Golan Plateau was clear of Syrian troops except for a few pockets still holding out such as one on Tel Faris. Of the original seventeen Israeli forward infantry forts, all except four had managed to hold out. The Israelis claim the Syrians left behind 867 tanks destroyed or abandoned. For example, only fourteen Syrian tanks returned from the thrust down the El Al Road.

Journalists reported that, during the fighting for Khusniye, the Israeli medical evacuation was good, their helicopters going quickly forward to pick up casualties, but that there were too many wounded for the ambulances to take; ordinary trucks had to be used to evacuate them. There was the continual noise of exploding shells as Syrian guns fired at the Israeli columns, and the wailing of ambulance sirens. As no official Israeli casualty figures had yet been released, these seemingly heavy losses caused wild, unsettling rumours. The journalists saw few Syrian prisoners.

In the fighting on the ninth and tenth the Israeli tanks had a rough time from the Syrian tank-hunting teams, which fired their missiles with great accuracy from dug-in positions. Journalists visiting the battlefields reported that they saw many burnt-out Centurions, with a small hole drilled in the turret by the missile, and draped with missile guidance wires. Even so, the Israelis were full of praise for the Centurions but did not think much of the ability of the Syrian tank crews or their gunnery.

So far the Syrians had been operating completely independently, ignoring their Soviet advisers. It was not until sometime on the tenth that the Russians were allowed into the field GHQ operations room to see the battle map. A group of senior Soviet officers under a Soviet general was working in the GHQ, and, when they saw the situation, they at once persuaded the Syrians to change their objective from that of the River Jordan to Kuneitra, which had just been retaken by the Israelis, and to withdraw their forces to the Sasa Defence Line to stabilise the situation. In view of the failures and heavy losses, the fact that the Israelis seemed to be pushing out to the flanks, and, further, that the Syrian force in the south was in danger of being encircled, General Shakkour agreed. The order to withdraw was given sometime in the early afternoon.

However, in the early morning of the eleventh the Syrians made one last attempt to retake Kuneitra. They were unsuccessful, and so the withdrawal, which was in progress elsewhere along the front, continued. In this last-fling battle for Kuneitra, the crossroads to its east was under heavy and continuous Syrian shellfire, and the Israelis lost many trucks taking ammunition and supplies to their forward tanks. An Israeli air strike caught the Syrians withdrawing down the road about two miles east of Kuneitra. The road was soon littered with destroyed or abandoned T-62s, many in groups of fours—two burnt out and two abandoned, some with their engines still running.

One Israeli brigade swung south around Kuneitra toward the Damascus Road to try to catch the withdrawing Syrians in the rear, but they escaped. By evening this formation was some four miles over the Cease-fire Line. Generally, the Syrian withdrawal on the night of the tenth and on the eleventh was reasonably orderly, and reports that it was a rout cannot be substantiated, although many vehicles were abandoned. Herzog writes, "The withdrawal which they [the Syrians] carried out into Syria was orderly and controlled." On the eleventh Defence Minister Dayan, in a far different mood from that of the seventh, visited the Golan Plateau by helicopter to announce, "The Syrian Army is broken." A senior Syrian intelligence officer told me that an Israeli officer prisoner he had interrogated said that on the eighth Dayan had said to him and other officers with him at the time that he would have lunch with them in the Damascus Officers' Club on the eleventh; he was a little premature. Priority was then switched to the Egyptian Front.

On this Israeli-northern front also, during the first three days of the war, the Syrians fired about twenty FROG rockets into the Jezreel and Huleh valleys, causing some casualties and some damage. On the night of the ninth/tenth Palestinian Fedayeen operating from Lebanese territory fired about thirty rockets at targets just over the Israeli border.

Initially, like the Israelis, the Syrians were overconfident, feeling that not only did they have numerical superiority over the Israelis of the order of ten to one in infantry, twenty to one in artillery, and twelve to one in armour, but that they were individually superior in battle. Middle grade and junior officers and their soldiers certainly fought with great bravery and doggedness, but the flair for battle seemed to be lacking in senior ranks. The faults of the defeated are usually overemphasised and their good qualities overlooked; such was the case of the Syrian soldier, whose valour was of a high order. Especially praiseworthy were those who repeatedly attacked the Red Ridge positions. It should be remembered that they nearly broke through the Israeli 7th Armoured Brigade, which was slow to be reinforced. The Israelis were about to withdraw on the fourth day of the fighting, staying only when a few reinforcement tanks reached them; a few minutes more might have meant a Syrian breakthrough instead.

It should not be automatically assumed that once the Israelis got into their stride they were unstoppable. Reinforcements were slow to arrive, and they were generally at a loss when deprived of their expected air-ground support. There were many instances of panic and hesitation on their part, but fortune was always with them at the last moment. Unfortunately for the Syrians, courage alone is not sufficient to win battles. An element of luck is essential.

The original Syrian deception plan caused General Hofi to think the main Syrian attack would be made down the Damascus Road, instead of through the Kudne and Rafid gaps. Accordingly, he initially disposed his available forces wrongly. It is of interest to note that the Soviet advice had been for the Syrians to crash across the Cease-fire Line with their armoured formations in the lead and then to penetrate the gaps with their infantry divisions. General Tlas did it the other way round, with costly results.

In common with so many other Middle East states, the Syrians were afflicted by the current "tank madness." They pinned their faith on armour, which was at a great disadvantage on the Golan Plateau, much of which was almost impassable. Also, in that rough country tanks were vulnerable to ambush tactics. It was terrain in which the infantry should have had a far greater role. The infantry mutiny was a handicap to the Syrians.

Casting a shadow over the Syrian high command was the haunting spectre of the 1967 defeat. This may have been a significant psychological factor in the decision to halt on the seventh, when just a little extra push was needed to reach the River Jordan. General Tlas told me that he considered the River Jordan to be "the natural Syrian boundary." Syrian determination was not lacking, and the Soviet advice to fall back to the Sasa Line to save the army at the expense of terrain and equipment was strongly opposed by the military section. It was agreed to only with the greatest reluctance by the political element in the high command; again the spectre of 1967 must have influenced this decision.

Another psychological aspect was that all transmitter radios were taken from the troops. Unlike the Israelis, the Syrians were not able to listen to foreign broadcasts to learn how things were going. Also, HQs and field units had "political guidance officers" (on the Soviet pattern), who were mainly there to watch for subversion of any sort.

In the Israeli view one of the main reasons for the Syrian failure was that they used their armoured forces piecemeal instead of concentrating them, when they would have initially made gains. The Israelis spoke highly of the skill of the Syrian gunners and the toughness of the infantry. The big surprise to the Israelis was the Syrians' capacity to move and fight at night with their antitank weapons. In their opinion the Syrian soldier had come a long way since 1967—he had certainly given them a shaking.

8

THE EGYPTIANS ATTACK

> *The Egyptian fire was very heavy and many Israeli tanks became bonfires.*
>
> An Israeli Armoured Corps colonel

In the south on the Suez Canal front the first five days of the October War had been ones of tremendous achievement for the Egyptians, but these were followed by another five days of caution and hesitation. It was as though the Egyptian momentum had run down, and their soldiers stood with leaden feet on the east bank, unable to move any farther forward. This "military pause," a new expression brought into the military vocabulary, became increasingly embarrassing to the Egyptians after their initial successes. By the tenth of October General Ismail had some 80,000 men and 700 tanks on the east bank, and, with the exception of the eastern shore of Great Bitter Lake, occupied a strip more than ten miles deep along practically the whole length of the canal. His forces lay snugly under the Air Defence Barrier and were covered by long-range artillery in static positions on the west bank. Ismail considered his two armies to be in good, strong defensive positions, with the infantry and their antitank weapons still out in front and the armour remaining in the rear; he was content for them to be "the rocks upon which the Israeli waves would be shattered."

On the other hand, General Shazli, the chief of staff, wanted to push eastward quickly to seize the three main passes while the Israelis were still shocked, confused, and disorganised. He had advocated this move from the beginning, and a sharp difference of opinion arose between the two generals. Shazli wanted to make an armoured thrust along the coastal road, to activate another round of helicopter-borne ranger raids and ambushes, and to advance to the three passes using armoured brigades. General Ismail would not agree, saying he was not ready, that there was much more logistic work to be done first, and that he did not have enough equipment, supplies, or ammunition on the east bank for such an operation.

It was true that Egyptian fire control, in their overenthusiasm, had been poor at times, and ammunition of all types and missiles needed replenishing, but the logistic confusion was not nearly as bad as some writers would have it. Egyptian officers who were there at the time, when I questioned them on this point, insisted they were never really short of ammunition, food, or other supplies. The only exception was water; during the first twenty-four hours soldiers had to carry it in plastic containers across the dummy bridges until the gaps in the sand rampart had been made passable for the wheeled water tankers. By the third day water pipes had been laid under water from the west to the east side of the canal.

The cautious General Ismail was also reluctant to move out into the open desert beyond the cover of his Air Defence Barrier, where his tanks and men would be at the mercy of Israeli aircraft. The Egyptian air force was being deliberately held back and not committed to battle to keep it as intact as possible. Also, the Arabs were of the belief that the Israelis had only two days' supply of ammunition left, which Ismail hoped they would soon exhaust; then their guns would become impotent.

General Ismail was later criticised for his military pause which lasted from the tenth to the thirteenth of October, during which there was hardly any Egyptian forward movement, but he insisted that it was a necessary period of consolidation in which to prepare properly for the next stage. One suspects that Ismail, like the Israelis, thought the war would be a short one, perhaps only of one week's duration, before the superpowers, or the United Nations, would enforce a cease-fire. Had this happened, the Egyptians would have found themselves in a very sound and satisfying position that would have stood them in good stead at the negotiating table; instead the war dragged on. General Ismail told me later that he fully intended to have a military pause after he had reached his first bound, which was to encompass Artillery Road, and he reckoned he had roughly achieved this by the ninth. He would not elaborate any further.

Although a static picture is given in the strategic sense, in the tactical one the front was by no means quiet. In the northern part, on the night of the ninth, the Egyptians claim that a unit of rangers, on foot, infiltrated into the Baluza area and succeeded in destroying fuel, ammunition, and supply dumps. Still in the north, on the tenth, the Israelis made contact with their Budapest fort on the Mediterranean shore after the two companies of rangers, which had been in a blocking position to its east for four days, had been withdrawn the previous night. The same day the three Bar Lev Line forts opposite Ismailia were occupied by the Egyptians, two at 0750 hours and the other at 0945 hours.

On the tenth the Egyptians made several attacks on Adan's division. In one, launched in the afternoon, they claim to have destroyed twelve Israeli tanks and three other armoured vehicles. In the centre Sharon's division tried to retake Katib el-Kheil, but the first attack on the morning of the tenth was unsuccessful. A second assault launched later in the day also failed when Israeli tanks and half-tracks carrying infantry ran into a minefield, causing the Israelis to lose most of their vehicles. In darkness, about 2100 hours, a third Israeli attack, a three-pronged one, was made on the Katib el-Kheil feature. In this attack some Israeli troops were landed by helicopter behind the Egyptian position and immediately tried to surround it. The assault developed into a fiasco as Israeli vehicles ran into minefields and prepared ambushes and were also pounded by artillery and mortar fire. In this battle the Egyptians claim that the Israelis abandoned their vehicles and were pursued by Egyptian infantry on foot. The Egyptians also say that they had not even one soldier

Egyptian armour crossing bridge to exploit success on the East Bank.

View of Quay (Melakh) fort after its surrender, with captured Israeli tank.

wounded in this engagement, and that they destroyed twenty-five Israeli tanks. The Israeli account differs, and Herzog writes that, when the Egyptian 21st Armoured Division attacked Sharon's division, it was driven off, with the Egyptians leaving fifty tanks on the battlefield, a story the Egyptians deny.

In the south the Israelis claim that Mandler's division, reinforced with an extra armoured brigade, was harassing the Third Army; there certainly was skirmishing along its front. Still farther south an Egyptian mechanised brigade moved out southward parallel to the shore of the Gulf of Suez but was halted by one of Major General Gavish's armoured brigades; the Egyptians say this was just a reconnaissance in force. General Gavish, who had been recalled from the reserve, had taken command of the southern part of the Sinai when the Southern Command was split into two parts shortly after the war began. His area included the Ras Sudar Valley but not the Mitla Pass. In the same area another Egyptian tank brigade moved toward the Ras Sudar Valley, which was blocked at both ends by Egyptian rangers. The tank brigade, being outside the cover of the Air Defence Barrier, was attacked by Israeli aircraft, which the Israelis claim destroyed fifty tanks.

It was on the tenth that the Egyptians took their first press party, containing several foreign journalists, on a visit to the east bank, crossing over one of the Third Army's bridges. The journalists confirmed that the Egyptians had reached a point some ten miles from the canal in the south and that Egyptian claims seemed to be substantially correct. They reported that the Egyptians were still moving tanks and supplies to the east bank, that an Israeli 155mm gun was shooting at the bridges from a distance of about fifteen miles, that the Egyptian bridges seemed to have been hit several times, and that an Israeli aircraft flew overhead on one occasion but at such a height it could hardly be seen. The journalists, who heard sounds of battle to the north, reported that the Egyptians claimed their bridges were out of range of all Israeli artillery except for their long-range 155mm guns.

On the same day General Shazli visited the east bank and, during the course of his tour, spoke to the journalists. He modestly commented that "the crossing went off in a very satisfactory way. The operations are taking place according to plans drawn up by the Egyptian command." The following day, the eleventh, on television, he assured the Egyptian people that "the Egyptian Army will not bite off more than it can chew."

On the tenth the first Soviet supplies arrived by air in Egypt and Syria, and, although they consisted only of ammunition and spares for the SAMs and other missiles, they encouraged the Arabs. This Russian support caused General Shazli to again try to persuade General Ismail to advance to the three passes, pointing out that five of the six Israeli CPs had been taken, and that the time to strike was before they could regain full control over the whole front. Ismail had over 700 tanks on the east bank, and, although he was to move over another 200 in the following two days, he still planned to retain the remainder on the west bank because he anticipated the Israelis might make an airborne assault on that side of the canal. In short, he did not feel he had enough armour on the east bank to cope successfully with the Israelis in an all-out offensive.

The eleventh was the Jewish Succoth, the Feast of Tabernacles, commemorating Moses leading the Jews from their Egyptian bondage some three thousand years before. The holiday had a strong religious connotation, and the religious soldiers erected small booths, the Succah, under which all meals should be taken for several days. On this day there was spasmodic firing and fighting along the front, but its intensity tended to dwindle, mainly because of exhaustion and the shortage of ammunition.

As more Israeli tanks and reinforcements arrived, they were pressed hastily into new brigades; some were given the designations of those already scattered or decimated. Practically all of General Adan's brigades had been wiped out, and his division was reconstituted with four newly formed armoured brigades. Sharon's division was brought up to five brigades and Mandler's to four. Adan's division was designated the 131st Operational Group, Sharon's the 45th Operational Group, and Mandler's the 252nd Operational Group; likewise the designations of the brigades were deliberately made random and confusing. A fourth armoured division had also been formed and was kept under the direct command of General Gonen; another was formed under the command of Major General Israel Tal.

In Israeli senior military circles discussion continued as to whether Israeli forces should be allowed to attempt a crossing of the Suez Canal. One of the principal protagonists of this course was General Sharon, who wanted to lead such an operation. He became more insistent, claiming that, if given sufficient troops, within forty-eight hours he could make a gap in the Egyptian Air Defence Barrier and "punch a hole in the sky." Sharon was a paratrooper and not basically a tankman, and his idea was decried by the armoured generals such as Adan (commander of the Armoured Corps with whom Sharon was now openly quarrelling), Mandler, and of course Gonen, Sharon's GOC. Sharon was supported only by the distant Brigadier Tamir, who urged that Sharon be allowed to activate Operation Gazelle immediately while General Ismail was in the process of moving his armoured forces across to the east bank.

An Israeli plan to counterattack across the canal had been in existence since 1968, even before Sharon became GOC Southern Command. Known as Operation Gazelle, it envisaged crossing at one of three points—near Kantara, near Deversoir, or just north of Port Suez. Roman-straight roads or tracks had been constructed from these points to Supply Road, along which the necessary bridging could be towed to a "park," some 150 yards by 700 yards, carved under the shelter of the primary sand rampart. The rampart had been deliberately thinned out so that its remaining spoil could be quickly bulldozed into the canal. The Israelis had not taken this plan very seriously, and their bridging preparations were not far advanced, although they had collected sufficient equipment to form two bridges, one of the Uniflote material and the other of ordinary Bailey-bridge type. On the night of the ninth/tenth the pontoon bridging was brought forward from the Tasa area to the shadow of a hill feature, known to the Israelis as Yukon, some six miles to the southwest where it was assembled and put on bogies ready for towing.

On the eleventh the crossing plan was discussed at General Gonen's front HQ, and he proposed crossing the Suez Canal at the prepared point near Deversoir. Sharon and Adan objected to this; they wanted to cross elsewhere to gain surprise. They both stated that there were many gaps made by the Egyptians in the primary sand rampart which could be used for the purpose, but Gonen pointed out that this would mean first fighting a battle. The prepared point at Kantara, which was favoured by Adan because it connected with a good road system on the west bank, was overruled because of the number of irrigation canals and the belt of dense cultivation in this area. At this time the Israelis reckoned that the Egyptians had about 900 tanks on the east bank. These, apart from the ones integral to the infantry formations, included many from the two armoured divisions—the 4th in the south, and the 21st in the centre—and the two independent tank brigades—the 25th in the south and the 2nd in the centre. The Israelis were almost certain that the northeastern shore of Great Bitter Lake, the point of division between the two Egyptian armies, was not physically occupied.

On the twelfth General Bar Lev went to GHQ with a proposal to cross the canal near Deversoir. To the General Staff there seemed to be three alternatives: the first, to make a major attack on the Egyptian bridgeheads, which it was not yet prepared to do until a more decisive stage had been reached on the Golan front; the second, to cross the canal and take out sections of the Egyptian Air Defence Barrier in the centre between the two Egyptian armies; and the third, to wait for the anticipated Egyptian advance, which, according to Soviet doctrine, should occur either on the eleventh or the twelfth, and then to meet it and defeat it in mobile warfare, after which the crossing could be made against less resistance.

At this meeting Moshe Dayan and General Elazar became bogged down in a futile and rather obscure argument as to who should make the decision. Both seemed to want to put the onus on the other. Dayan did not like Bar Lev's idea at all; he thought it could not be a deciding factor nor would it bring about a cease-fire. He left it to Elazar to decide. Elazar insisted that the decision should be made by Dayan, a somewhat strange attitude for a chief of staff. Herzog tries to explain the impasse: "He [Dayan] was of the opinion that it was not for Elazar to make decisions on the basis of political considerations, pointing out that if, from a military point of view, Elazar thought it was a desirable move he had to make his decision and act accordingly."

This indecision caused Dayan to bring the matter before the premier and the small group of ministers who formed the War Cabinet. There was an impromptu meeting of ministers and generals that evening, at which time General Bar Lev presented his proposed plan to cross near Deversoir. While this meeting was in progress, information came through that General Ismail had begun moving his remaining armour to the east bank. It was agreed that the proposed operation should wait until after the expected battle had been resolved, but that preparations could be made for it. Adan's division was detailed to make the crossing, and that evening part of it was withdrawn from the battle zone to make ready.

From the eleventh onward General Ismail was under heavy political pressure to mount an offensive against the Israelis to relieve pressure on the Syrian front. Reluctantly, on the twelfth and the thirteenth, he began to prepare, bringing over to the east bank the bulk of his remaining tanks, some 300 in all. The Israelis thought, not altogether incorrectly, that these were from the three armoured and mechanised divisions that constituted Ismail's strategic reserve. Heikal writes, rather confusingly, that by the thirteenth "the 21st Armoured Division, behind the Second Army, had crossed the canal, and so had one brigade of the 4th Armoured Division, behind the Third Army." By the evening of the thirteenth the Egyptian tanks on the east bank probably numbered about 1,300. According to the Egyptian order of battle, this left some 400 or more tanks unaccounted for on the west side of the canal. While some of these formed the cadres of the armoured and mechanised divisions which had been held back for the defence of the capital and the delta, a number would be nonrunners for normal reasons of breakdown. Also, a number had been sent forward to replace casualties and breakdowns on the east bank. In fact, the west bank was pretty well denuded of armour.

On the twelfth the Russians brought down their second reconnaissance satellite (COSMOS 597), which they had launched on the sixth, after only half its normal time in orbit. It gave good information of the battles of the tenth and eleventh, indicating where the bulk of the armour was located. Shazli later told me that he then thought "the Israelis had mustered an estimated 1,000 tanks in the Sinai Peninsula, of which 800 had already been committed to battle, of which about 400 had been destroyed." His information was not far wrong.

As the Egyptian armour arrived on the east bank some of it became involved in small tank battles that swirled and eddied along the front, but generally the Israeli probes were dealt with by the infantry with their antitank weapons, thus forcing the Israelis to keep their distance. On the twelfth Sharon's division made yet another attempt to take Katib el-Kheil. At 1000 hours a company of about fourteen tanks and armoured personnel carriers moved against the feature, only, according to the Egyptians, to be completely destroyed. The same day there was a tank clash in the region of Kantara in which the Egyptians claim to have knocked out thirteen Israeli tanks and nineteen other armoured vehicles and inflicted over 200 casualties, mainly by artillery fire, infantry-manned antitank weapons, and minefields.

On the thirteenth the Egyptians made several probing attacks all along the front in preparation for their main thrust, which basically was to be a wide pincer movement on to Bir Gifgafa. At the end of the day the Israelis claimed they had knocked out between fifty and sixty Egyptian tanks, but at this stage the Israeli war communiqués were still suspect. On the other hand, until this date the Egyptians had adopted a "deliberate policy of restraint" in their communiqués, and, in keeping with this low-key attitude, they had made no mention of the liberal Israeli use of napalm and the number of Egyptian casualties caused by it.

At 0600 hours the Bar Lev Line fort at the north end of Great Bitter Lake, known as Tel Salam to the Egyptians and Matzmed to the Israelis, fell to the Egyptians. This left just one fort holding out, that opposite Port Tewfik, known to the Israelis as the Pier. It, too, surrendered, at 1230 hours the same day, in the presence of representatives of the International Red Cross and the press. The garrison, originally of forty-two, consisted of five officers and thirty-two soldiers; fifteen were wounded and five died. Within the fort perimeter were three Patton tanks, and it was seen that the defenders had plenty of ammunition left. The press representatives reported that they heard sounds of battle some twenty miles to the north and that an Egyptian SAM-6 shot down an Israeli aircraft during the evacuation.

On the thirteenth General Gonen, accompanied by Major General Weizman, a recalled officer who had formerly been commander of the air force, flew to Sharon's HQ near Tasa for a conference on how to deal with the anticipated Egyptian attack. The proposal was that, if it were a frontal attack, Sharon and Mandler should hold it; if the Egyptians forced their way toward Bir Gifgafa, Adan's division should hit them in the flanks. Consequently, one of Adan's brigades was moved down to the western entrance to the Khatmia Pass. Any Egyptian advances along either the Mediterranean coast or south along the shore of the Gulf of Suez, both being outside the cover of the Egyptian Air Defence Barrier, would be dealt with by the Israeli air force. Sharon still wanted to attack the Egyptians first and cross the canal, but he was overruled. Gonen said that, regardless of whether the Egyptians attacked or not, they would prepare for a crossing to be carried out on the night of the fourteenth. The previous day, the twelfth, General Bar Lev recommended that Sharon be relieved of his command for his indiscipline on the ninth, and Elazar said he would consult Dayan, who replied that to do so would create political problems; the matter was tabled.

On his way to this conference at Sharon's HQ, General Mandler, commanding the armoured division in the south, landed his helicopter as far forward as he could, descended from it, entered one of the vehicles of his advance HQ, and had just moved off at about 1100 hours when an Egyptian missile hit the vehicle he was in and he was killed. Mandler had unwisely brought his helicopter down in view of the Egyptians and on moving off had given his position over the radio "in clear"; thirty seconds later he was dead. The debate continues as to whether it was a chance shot or whether the Egyptians had heard him on the radio and had made a deliberate attack on him.

The command of his division was given to Brigadier Kalman
Magen, who had been in the northern part of the front until the
twelfth.

While the Israelis lost a general in battle, on the same day, the
thirteenth, the Egyptians also had a casualty of general rank
when at about 0730 hours General Saad Maamun, GOC Second
Army, suffered a heart attack and had to be evacuated. His
chief of staff took over and carried on until the new commander, Major General Abdul Khalil, who had been commanding the
Cairo Military District, arrived on the fifteenth.

On the night of the thirteenth, the Egyptian rangers claim to
have mounted a successful ambush just south of Tasa. These
ranger raids worried the Israelis, and, while the Egyptians are
still vaguely silent about these activities, the Israelis were loud
in their claims to have inflicted casualties on them. Herzog says
that in the first week of the war the Israelis killed forty-five
Egyptian commandos and captured 155. The Egyptians dispute
these figures but do not correct them.

The quality of the Egyptian aggressive spirit is illustrated by
Israeli officers who say that during this period, from the ninth
to the thirteenth, they held, on an average, five Egyptian attacks
daily. The favourite Egyptian method was to crawl forward
during the night to the high ground overlooking Artillery Road,
to be ready for a dawn attack. This would take place after a
half-hour's artillery barrage. Then, under cover of the artillery
and a hail of Katushya rockets, the tanks would follow the
infantry. Herzog writes that:

> Sometimes, as the line of infantry approached, having sus-
> tained a large number of casualties from small arms and artil-
> lery fire, it would stop, and a fresh line, which had dug itself
> into the sand overnight, would emerge and continue the attack.
> . . . All these Egyptian attacks were broken with heavy losses,
> both in armour and infantry, but, nevertheless, time and again
> the Egyptian infantry would surge forward in attack, only to
> be mowed down by the waiting armour and artillery.

This was high praise indeed for the courage and determination
of the Egyptian officer and soldier in battle. Herzog describes

these assaults as "senseless infantry attacks," while, later, General Magen stated that "until the eleventh the Egyptian attacks had been of great determination, with waves of Egyptian soldiers following each other regardless." Magen had been facing the Egyptian Second Army.

At 0615 hours on the fourteenth Egyptian aircraft hit targets in the Sinai; these included HAWK missile batteries and electronic jamming stations. At the same time an artillery barrage of over 500 medium and heavy guns fired over the heads of the thin Israeli armoured screen positioned some five thousand yards or so from the forward Egyptian infantry. At 0630 hours the barrage ceased and the Egyptian main attack began. It consisted of three main thrusts and a number of subsidiary ones. In the north, two armoured brigades, one with T-62 tanks, advanced from Kantara toward Romani, and in conjunction with this a number of ranger units were put down by helicopter in the saltmarsh area to cover the flanks. In the centre, four armoured brigades moved along the road from Ismailia toward the Khatmia Pass, making for Bir Gifgafa. In the south, two tank brigades moved toward the Mitla Pass. Of the subsidiary thrusts, one mechanised brigade made for the Giddi Pass, while farther south three more tank and mechanised brigades moved toward the Ras Sudar Valley. A total of about twelve brigades advanced to battle, and they were faced by four Israeli armoured divisions. Over two thousand tanks were about to clash in the largest tank battle since World War II. (The biggest tank battle in history was at Kursk, on 12 July 1943, in which 6,300 tanks and SP guns were involved; in the battle at Alamein, which began on 23 October 1942, the Allies had 1,029 tanks and 2,311 guns, and the Axis Powers had 489 tanks and 1,219 guns.) About 0800 hours Moshe Dayan arrived at the front HQ at Khaseiba; he was doubtful whether this was the anticipated main attack, but the generals on the ground, Bar Lev and Gonen, were certain that it was.

Meanwhile, in the extreme north, a battle developed when a detachment from Port Fuad moved out about 0300 hours to attack the Israeli fort on the Mediterranean coast, Budapest, and was able to get past it to block the road to its east. This was an Egyptian penetration that seemed to disconcert the Israelis as well as surprise them. The fort continued to hold out, and an Israeli force moved against the Egyptians. The battle lasted until about 1000 hours when the Egyptians withdrew. They claimed that this movement had been merely a feint. The Israelis were supported by their aircraft and after the battle claimed to have recovered twenty-eight Egyptian armoured vehicles from the saltmarsh and the minefields around the fort. By this time Port Said was cut off, as the two bridges connecting it to the causeway to the south had been damaged by Israeli air action.

The Egyptian thrust toward Baluza was held by the Israelis, while in the centre there were two big clashes. One was in the area of Galan (Chinese Farm) where the Israelis claim the Egyptians left ninety-three tanks on the field, against a loss of only three Israeli tanks hit by missiles. The other was between two armoured brigades nearby, wherein the Israelis claim the Egyptian 21st Armoured Division lost 110 tanks, more than its complement, in fact. The two armoured thrusts, one toward the Mitla and the other toward the Giddi Pass, also ran into Israeli armoured formations and were halted; the latter reached Jebel Shaifa, halfway between the Giddi Pass and the canal. The Egyptian armoured force in the extreme south, making a wide flanking movement, suddenly swung round northward in an attempt to enter the wide mouth of the Mitla Pass by way of Moses Springs, but it ran into an Israeli armoured brigade which caught it in the flank. The Israeli air force intervened and claimed to have destroyed sixty Egyptian tanks and guns.

By this time the Israelis had completely abandoned their gung ho tactics and switched to more conventional ones. It was Gonen's plan to allow the Egyptian armour to roll forward, to tempt it to advance beyond the cover of the Air Defence Barrier, and to draw it into ambush. In the initial Egyptian advances many of the outlying Israeli positions on and near Artillery Road were overrun. The Israeli armour lay concealed in ambush positions, hull down, and, when the Egyptians came within range, the tanks opened fire with a few rounds and then moved to alternative positions to fire again, and so on. Relying largely upon tank gunnery, the Israelis also made liberal use of antitank missiles—the SS-10, SS-11, and also the American TOWs, which had been issued to the divisions the previous day. The Egyptian tanks ran into ambush after ambush, and, when they stopped, the Israeli armour attacked them in the flanks.

Instead of fighting individually, or in threes or fours as formerly, the Israeli tanks fought as companies. The company commander would indicate the targets and rigidly control the fire; all guns were directed against one target at a time. The Israeli fire control and accuracy were good, and in particular they singled out the Sagger-carrying BRDMs and BMPs.

The Egyptian armour had gone into action without full infantry support but had taken with them the Soviet BRDM, an improved BTR-40, formed into platoons of four. Of these, three carried racks of Saggers, which could be elevated from the vehicle for firing or lowered down into the vehicle again for cover or travelling. Each vehicle carried fourteen missiles but could fire only one at a time; this restricted them to salvoes of three missiles. The fourth BRDM in the platoon was the command vehicle; it was armed with machine guns. The Egyptians also brought into action the new Soviet tracked BMP, an armoured personnel carrier; it carried four Saggers, which could be fired one at a time. The BMP, with a crew of three, had a smoothbore 76mm gun. It also carried twelve infantrymen, who could fire through the side slits in the armour, which was itself rather poor. Alternate controls enabled either the Sagger or the self-loading gun, which used antitank ammunition, to be fired; a trap-door arrangement enabled a man to fire either the Sagger or the RPG-7. The Egyptians afterward said the BMP performed well in the October War. The integral infantry with the armoured brigades carried the suitcase version of the Sagger. The Israelis later said that after this battle one of their Centurions had fourteen pairs of thin, twin-guidance wires draped over it.

On the fourteenth the Israelis had their mechanised infantry, mortars, and antitank weapons forward with their leading tanks. There was a mechanised company of between fourteen and sixteen U.S. M-113s, each armed with four or five machine guns; the soldiers were able to fire over the sides of the vehicle, having a good, clear, all-round field of vision. The Israeli machine guns opened up at long ranges against the Egyptian tank-hunting teams when the latter set up their Saggers on the ground, spraying them with bullets to divert the aimer's attention. The BRDMs and BMPs had to be momentarily stationary while they were firing missiles. In flight the Sagger missile takes about ten seconds to cover a thousand yards, perhaps the maximum battle range, and it is a brave and determined soldier who can keep his missile target in his sights all this time in the face of small arms fire. Not many Egyptians were killed by these tactics, but they tended to nullify the antitank missile salvoes. Also, the Israelis now had HE shells for their tank guns, which helped to break up infantry formations.

The Israelis denied they had TOWs at this stage, but later General Sharon admitted his division had been issued them the previous day, the thirteenth, when he had taught his men to use them. Only four hours' practice was required to attain reasonable proficiency in their use. The TOW was a tube-launched, optically tracked, wire-guided antitank missile. It was man-portable, handled by a two-man crew. In Vietnam the TOW had proved to be a very accurate and effective guidance system. It is now clear that the Israelis had ample numbers of the TOW and used them. In fact, they used and relied upon their missiles far more than they cared to admit. Heikal writes that the "accurate fire from a variety of French SS antitank missiles, and also from newly arrived TOW missiles . . . stopped the Egyptian armour about twelve to fifteen kilometres from its starting point."

During the battles on the fourteenth the Egyptians claim they came up against new American Patton tanks that had only "180 kilometres on the clock," the approximate distance from El Arish to the battlefield. If so, there could not have been many. It was later revealed that only one plane-load of tanks arrived from the United States, to land at Lod airport, not El Arish, carrying a few (estimates vary from four to ten) Pattons. However, the commander of the Egyptian air force told me that at this stage El Arish was heavily protected by air "at all levels," and he went on to say, "We suspected that Patton tanks were being landed there by helicopters of the U.S. Sixth Fleet, having been taken from European NATO stockpiles."

Egyptian infantry advancing with armour into the Sinai on October 14, 1973.

Israeli armour advancing under air cover during the battle for the breakthrough across the Suez Canal, October 16, 1973.

Heikal writes that General Ismail's "instructions were that the armour of the two Egyptian armies was to penetrate into the three passes, and in particular to capture the lateral Supply Road, to neutralise the Israeli reserves which were being deployed around it." It should be added that this would also prevent the Israelis regaining control of that road. About 1800 hours General Ismail realised that he was not going to achieve his objectives, so he ordered his forces to return to their bridgeheads and the shelter of the Air Defence Barrier.

Israeli priority had been switched from the Golan to the Suez Canal front on the thirteenth. Thus the Israeli air force was able to give more attention to the Egyptian battlefield on the fourteenth, although its aircraft generally kept clear of the Air Defence Barrier. The Israeli air force claims to have "destroyed one mechanised brigade in the south" near the Ras Sudar Valley. It had also been active in the north against Port Said and in support of the Budapest fort, both outside the reach of the Air Defence Barrier.

Israeli aircraft had hovered overhead during the battles of the fourteenth but had not been able to intervene effectively because most of the time Egyptian and Israeli tanks were close to each other and sometimes even intermixed. The Egyptian air force was still held back, being used mainly in a strategic role rather than for ground support or interception. The Egyptians had managed to move a few SAM-6s to the east bank, but there were problems of calibrating them in. However, when the Egyptians broke off their actions and began to withdraw, the Israeli air force came into action and harassed them until they came up against the Air Defence Barrier. The Israelis claim to have destroyed fifty tanks in this phase. The Egyptians claim that the Israeli Phantoms were dropping Smart bombs (being guided ones, rather than free fall) which the U.S. government did not admit supplying until the nineteenth.

The Israeli armoured divisions slowly followed the withdrawing Egyptian columns and remained just out of range of their antitank weapons. This tactic enabled the Israelis to bring their artillery farther forward until it was able to bombard the bridges and Air Defence Barrier installations on the west bank. Movement stopped shortly after darkness fell, but firing by both sides continued throughout the hours of darkness. It was during this bombardment of the bridges that Brigadier Ahmed Hamadi, deputy commander of the Egyptian Engineer Corps, was killed by shellfire while supervising the reconstruction of one of the Third Army's bridges.

The Israelis claim that in the fighting on the fourteenth the Egyptians left 264 tanks on the battlefield, as against an admitted Israeli loss of only 6 tanks, while the Egyptians claim to have destroyed 150 Israeli tanks and 44 aircraft. So far Israeli claims had been overinflated, and the figure of only 6 tanks lost cannot be considered to be correct. For example, one Israeli colonel in the Armoured Corps, who took part in the battle, told me that "the Egyptian fire was very heavy and many Israeli tanks also became 'bonfires.'" On the other hand, although Egyptian claims had been modest so far, from this date onward they began to get out of hand and overoptimistic. This day marked a change in both Israeli and Egyptian war communiqués, the former becoming more accurate and the latter less so.

The truth seems to be that the Egyptians probably lost about 200 tanks in the fighting (with perhaps as many other armoured vehicles and guns) and another 50 in the withdrawal. Israeli losses must have exceeded 60 tanks and as many other armoured vehicles and guns. The farthest extent of the Egyptian advance had been between 18 and 20 kilometres into the mouth of the Mitla Pass, but elsewhere, while all their columns crossed Artillery Road, they failed to reach Supply Road, their first objective.

Later, I discussed this battle at length with General Ismail, and he was firmly of the opinion that the Israelis had been warned by the United States that the Egyptians were about to attack, and so the Israelis were fully prepared. He confirmed that he was under political pressure to attack because of Syrian reverses, and that, contrary to popular rumour, he had enough ammunition for his limited aims. He pointed out that Egypt possessed munitions factories capable of filling shells and manufacturing small arms ammunition. He said that his main object was to enlarge the bridgehead and to inflict more losses on the Israelis but admitted that his soldiers, who advanced beyond the cover of the Air Defence Barrier, did not gain their planned objectives. As there were heavy losses on both sides, he ordered his men to withdraw to the bridgeheads, anticipating a big Israeli attack the following day. General Ismail declared it was a "drawn battle," but claimed that it had eased Israeli pressure on the Golan front. Later, General Shazli, addressing his soldiers, was reported to have admitted that they were surprised on all axes by Israeli tanks and missiles, which blocked all Egyptian advances and caused losses. The fact that the Second Army had no commander during this battle was not considered by Ismail to be important as, unlike the Israelis, all senior officers cooperated with the chief of staff and supported him in his responsibility. However, it was later deduced that the commander's absence had stopped the flow of infantry across the canal.

The Israelis were convinced that they had won a great armoured battle against the Egyptians, and that their armoured forces had again proved dominant and victorious. Israeli morale rose. Credit should go to General Gonen, a good tactician who restrained his "hot-head" commanders, drew the Egyptians from the cover of their Air Defence Barrier, then rode and held their attack. He did not allow any westward movement until he was sure the Egyptians were withdrawing. At the end of the day the Egyptians still held all the territory they had taken by the thirteenth. Thus the Israelis can be credited merely with having won an armoured battle on ground of their own choosing and then of closing up behind the withdrawing Egyptians, whereas before, in many instances, they had remained at distances of a few thousand yards. The Israelis were of the opinion that the Egyptian armoured forces were poorly led in mobile warfare, and that their tactics were unimaginative.

As General Ismail anticipated, on the morning of the fifteenth the Israelis attacked, with nine brigades along the whole front, and the Great Tank Battle, or rather series of battles, continued. The Egyptians repulsed all Israeli attacks until the evening of the seventeenth; the Israelis merely filtered forward into unoccupied stretches of desert terrain. The Israelis claim that by the seventeenth they had destroyed another 100 Egyptian tanks, and there was no doubt they had suddenly become plentifully equipped with U.S. TOWs, which took a heavy toll.

Alarming rumours of heavy Israeli casualties were circulating in Israel, which the Israeli government did nothing to allay until the fourteenth. Then it issued its first casualty figure, admitting to 656 dead so far, which hardly stemmed the mounting anxiety within the country, especially as no figures of wounded were given. This figure obviously did not include the casualties of the battles of the fourteenth. The Israelis also stated that they had taken 414 Arab prisoners but did not specify how many were Egyptians, Syrians, or other nationalities. The Egyptians say that, until the fourteenth, only 60 to 70 of their soldiers had been taken prisoner.

9

GENERAL REACTION

This is the end of the Third Temple.

Moshe Dayan to Golda Meir

Arab reaction to the outbreak of the October war was one of wild enthusiasm, while that of Israel was one of shock and dismay. Both sides were taken by surprise, as were, to a degree, the governments of the United States and the Soviet Union. President Nixon was involved in the Watergate affair and had little time for foreign affairs, leaving them mainly to his secretary of state, Henry Kissinger. The latter had brought about a cease-fire in the war in Vietnam, eased tension with the Soviet Union, and had made a tentative breakthrough in this direction with China. Kissinger, busy solving world problems, had not paid any special attention to the Middle East. He felt, as did many others, that the state of No War No Peace had crystalised for the time being and could be dealt with in due course. Kissinger did not want a war in the Middle East as he thought it would imperil detente with the Soviet Union. When the signs of imminent war became obvious, he had to hurriedly call for the "Middle East file" to "hastily read himself in." On a later visit to Cairo, Kissinger admitted, "I had not opened the Middle East file before. I had imagined it could wait its turn."

169

The United States had been further caught off balance, because it was thought the Arabs would not attack on the sixth until 1800 hours, instead of 1400 hours. The U.S. Sixth Fleet in the Mediterranean, consisting of some fifty ships and 20,000 men, was placed on special alert, and all shore leave was cancelled. Yet, putting into motion the secret supplying of ECMs, missiles, and vital spare parts to Israel (this seems to have been a prearranged agreement), was about all that happened immediately. The Soviet Union did not want a war in the Middle East either, as it thought the Arabs would be quickly defeated and cause the U.S.S.R. to lose influence and prestige in that part of the world.

In Egypt the Cairo International Airport was closed. The Egyptian government declared certain areas of the eastern Mediterranean to be "areas of military operations," and warned all shipping to keep clear of them. That evening in Cairo there was a "blue-out" for car headlights and lighted windows, and President Sadat spoke to the nation on television. In Syria the immediate reaction was much the same; the Damascus Airport was closed and President Assad spoke on television.

Although there was considerable excitement in Jordan, there was also more than a trace of caution and reluctance to enter the fight spontaneously, as bitter memories of the events of 1967 caused doubts and hesitation. Although privy in part to Operation Badr, King Hussein had not been told in advance when Y Day was to be, so he too was taken completely by surprise. As he was expected to form a third "threatening" front, he telephoned both President Sadat and President Assad, who told him the war had begun and asked him to take immediate action. Hussein, hesitant and cautious, ordered a full alert of his standing forces but took no further action, waiting to see how events unfolded. The bridges across the River Jordan remained open to individuals crossing to and from the west bank.

In Iraq President Ahmed al-Bakr had not been taken into the confidence of President Sadat. Although the Iraqi president may have suspected something was about to happen, he too was taken by surprise, as were other Arab rulers and governments that heard the news from foreign broadcasts. The two neighbouring countries of Iraq and Syria had many differences with each other; their main political dispute was that each espoused a rival schism of the Baath party. This rivalry produced defections from both sides, together with consequent bitter recriminations. There were differences over the waters of the River Euphrates, which, rising in Turkey, flowed through Syria before entering Iraq. With Soviet assistance, the Syrians had built the Tabqa Dam on the Euphrates, and the Iraqis complained that the Syrians were holding back too much water and so depriving Iraqi farmers. When Iraq nationalised part of its oil industry in 1972, Syria raised the tariff on oil passing through the TAP oil pipeline that ran across Syrian territory from Iraq to the port of Sidon.

Iraq had a problem with its other neighbour, Iran, over navigation in the Shatt el-Arab. Political problems also arose as the power and influence of the shah extended, tending to overshadow that of Iraq. At times the major part of the Iraqi army was watching its frontier with Iran. Iraq also had a huge internal security problem, a heritage of the civil war with the Kurds in the mountains. It had dragged on from 1961 until 1972.

Iraq, with a population of about 9.25 million, had just over 100,000 men serving in the armed forces, with as many more reservists available for mobilisation. There was a two-year period of conscription followed by a ten-year reserve liability. The army was formed into six divisions—two armoured, two mechanised, and two infantry—with two groups of mountain troops and a brigade of special forces. Its weapons and equipment were mainly of Soviet origin—T-54s, T-55s, PT-76s, BTR-152s, and 120mm and 130mm guns. The remaining weaponry was of British manufacture.

On the sixth President al-Bakr spoke by telephone to President Assad, but relations between the two were poor. Assad hoped to be able to finish his fight with the Israelis quickly and successfully, and he did not want the Iraqis brought into the battle to share any credit. Hence, the initial conversation was not fruitful. However, the Iraqi government wanted to take a full share in the "Arab responsibility" against Israel and on the seventh gave a warning order to the 3rd Armoured Division, based at Hadhar some 200 miles north of Baghdad, to move to Syria. The next day President al-Bakr announced he was placing the Iraqi armed forces at the disposal of the joint Egyptian-Syrian Revolutionary Command Council. He sent three squadrons of aircraft to Syria, renewed diplomatic relations with Iran (which enabled him to move some army formations away from the region of the Iranian frontier), and nationalised certain American oil holdings in Iraq. Syria had been persuaded to accept the limited political goal of simply recovering the lost territories, thus differing from Iraq which pursued the more comprehensive objective of "liberating all Arab territory." This, of course, implied the destruction of the state of Israel. There were strategical, tactical, and organisational military differences as well.

Syrian setbacks early in the war caused Assad to lose his self-confidence, and on the eighth he sent his deputy premier to Baghdad to ask for help. The following day an Iraqi staff general went to Damascus to see what was required, and the Syrians asked for as many tanks and troops as possible, as quickly as possible. This request presented problems as not all Iraqi formations were armoured, and they were scattered over a wide area. Portions were on the Iranian frontier, and all were up to a thousand miles away from the Syrian-Israeli front. As the Golan Plateau and Iraq were separated by such a huge expanse of desert terrain, the Israelis had not reckoned on more than token Iraqi participation in this war.

Meanwhile, on the seventh, news of the Arab attacks, that ran like wildfire through the Arab world, created an immense surge of enthusiasm and hope in people who had been fed for so long on a diet of defeat. That night two Israeli pilots who had been taken prisoner were shown on Egyptian television, together with some film of the air fighting and the wreckage of Israeli aircraft; it was claimed the Egyptians had already captured seven Israeli pilots.

On the eighth Gaddafi of Libya openly criticised Sadat's battle plan. He said, "We continue to disagree over plans and objectives. We call for the liberation of Palestine, and for transferring the battle into Palestine in its early hours, by means of tactics which differ from those by which the battle is now fought." The statement annoyed Sadat, but Gaddafi agreed to provide oil, aircraft, and money to help the war effort. Libya, according to Pajak, provided $500 million to support the war effort; this included the financing of seventy replacement MiG-21s and other equipment for both Egypt and Syria. Gaddafi also tactlessly called King Hussein a coward for not joining in the fight. That day a British Boeing airliner, on its way from London to Nairobi, was forced down in South Yemen. This action showed how, for once, the mood of the moment was affecting even the more backward Arab states. Promises of military and other help came rolling in from Arab sources, and on the eighth the first Algerian aircraft, a token one, arrived in Egypt. Colonel Abdul Ghani, head of the Algerian special mission, talked to Sadat about possible additional aid from Algeria. The Moroccan government announced it would reinforce its brigade in Syria, and on the ninth the Sudanese government promised to send a detachment of troops to fight alongside the Egyptians.

On the tenth reports were current of small units of Kuwaitis, Sudanese, Tunisians, and Algerians fighting on the Suez Canal front, but these were not true. Although promised, no units had yet reached the battle area. That day President Bourgiba of Tunisia reviewed an armoured unit of about nine hundred men before it set off on the 1,800-mile journey to the Suez Canal. General Ismail later told me, "They didn't bring any administrative backing with them, unfortunately, so they were more of a military nuisance than of any value, but they did have some political value."

In Israel there was no enthusiasm for the war. It came as a deep shock to the people, whose radios suddenly opened up at 1400 hours on the sixth, Yom Kippur, giving brief news of imminent danger and warning the people to keep off the streets. At 1402 hours air raid sirens sounded in Tel Aviv, but it was not until 1445 hours that code words began to be broadcast, indicating that mobilisation was underway. When darkness fell there was a blackout in Tel Aviv, Jerusalem, and other main cities, but journalists observed that several neon signs were left on in Tel Aviv, thus causing local anxiety. Lod Airport, due to reopen at 2000 hours, remained closed.

At 1815 hours Premier Meir addressed the nation on television, telling the people that the Arabs had attacked them, but she added confidently that "our forces are deployed according to the plan to meet the impending danger." Later, at 2100 hours, Defence Minister Dayan also spoke to the Israelis on television. The national mood was one of anxiety, not one of depression, as all expected the war to be a short, victorious one that would once again, as in 1967, teach the Arabs a lesson and put them firmly in their place for their temerity. To appeal to world opinion, Israeli Foreign Minister Abba Eban, in New York, declared that the Arab attack was a "second Pearl Harbour, plus blasphemy and sacrilege." This contrasted sharply with his statement made immediately after the Israeli pre-emptive attack in June 1967 in which he gave as an excuse for Israel's attacking without warning "that in any case, Arab shells crossed our frontier first."

During the first part of the war the Israeli people were sheltered by censorship from the full knowledge of the gravity of the situation. The premier, defence minister, and other officials and senior IDF officers were aware of the situation, and to say they were extremely anxious was an understatement. It had long been suspected that Israel had a nuclear potential. This had never been confirmed but, according to a report in *Time* magazine of 12 April 1976, Israel was prepared to use nuclear weapons in dire extremity. At 2200 hours on the eighth General Hofi, GOC Northern Command, told General Elazar, chief of staff, that "I am not sure we can hold out any longer"—an opinion quickly passed on to Dayan, who at 0005 hours on the ninth went to the premier to ask permission to "activate the Israeli nuclear bombs." He said to her, "This is the end of the Third Temple." The first Jewish Temple was destroyed by the Babylonians in BC 586, and the second by the Romans in AD 70. Golda Meir gave the necessary permission.

It has since been revealed, in April 1977, that the Israelis probably had at least 200 tons of uranium, enough to make about twenty nuclear bombs of the type (twenty kilotons) dropped at Nagasaki. In October 1968 a consignment of 560 cannisters, marked "Plumblatt: natural uranium oxide," was loaded on the tramp steamer, *Scheersberg,* at Hamburg, West Germany, destined for Genoa, Italy. After leaving Hamburg the ship called at Antwerp, and the following day changed its name, and later changed its crew and name yet again.

Euratom, the European nuclear authority, which had been informed of the shipment as a matter of course, made its usual routine check, only to find the uranium had not reached its destination. Euratom made enquiries but came up against a wall of silence from the espionage services of America, West Germany, Italy, and Israel. After about a year the Euratom enquiry was "closed inconclusively." The inference was, and such evidence as was available indicated, that the uranium had ended up in Israel.

According to the *Time* article, Israel possessed thirteen atomic bombs "which were hastily assembled at a secret underground tunnel during a seventy-eight-hour period at the start of the October War." As each bomb was assembled, it was rushed off to waiting air force units. Before "any triggers were set" the tide of battle turned for the Israelis, and the assembled atomic bombs were sent to desert arsenals, presumably somewhere in the Negev not far from Dimona. They were of the twenty-kiloton yield and were to be dropped from specially equipped Phantoms, and, for reasons of national prestige, from the Israeli-assembled Kfir fighters. They were also to be used as warheads on the Israeli Jericho missiles, a weapon that was not yet in production. The Israelis have still not tested their nuclear armoury.

A follow-up of the nuclear preparation was that on the thirteenth U.S. intelligence sources reported that the Russians, from their naval base at Odessa, had dispatched nuclear warheads to Alexandria for their SCUDs, based in Egypt under Soviet control. Carried on Soviet ships, they passed through the Bosphorus on the fifteenth. The Israelis were convinced the Russians had learned of their (the Israelis') possession of atomic weapons through the COSMOS reconnaissance satellite.

Meanwhile, the would-be peacemakers of the world were at work, albeit some with axes to grind. The Soviet Union mistakenly believed that, once President Sadat had demonstrated his military capability, he would want a cease-fire at once. Consequently, at 2000 hours on the sixth Vladimir Vinogradov, the Soviet ambassador to Egypt, visited Sadat and told him that Syria had asked for a cease-fire, which was quite false, causing Sadat to suspect the Soviet government of trying to "trick him into giving up the fight." President Assad was also angry when he heard of this ploy and was annoyed that his name had been used in this way without his consent. Vinogradov visited Sadat on the seventh, and repeated his suggestion, to which Sadat later said, "My reply to him was violent." At midday on the seventh Sir Philip Adams, British ambassador to Egypt, went to Sadat to ask him if he was interested in a cease-fire. Sadat angrily rejected the suggestion but added that it would be considered if linked to a long-term settlement.

On the eighth Kissinger, the U.S. secretary of state, was advocating a cease-fire on the basis of a return to the positions held before the sixth of October. He said in an interview that the United States had "stated its principles," but that he had not submitted them to a formal vote in the United Nations "because we realised that no majority was available." It is not often a secretary of state is so frankly partisan. On the eighth, when it had become clear the Arabs were doing unexpectedly well, the Soviet Union suddenly changed its tack and began to urge other Arab states, such as Iraq, to join in the fight against Israel.

On the eleventh, the day the Israelis put a captured T-62 tank on show in Tel Aviv, Kissinger tried a new line. He suggested that the Syrian losses of territory on the Golan front be exchanged for Egyptian gains in the Sinai, a proposal which would have been distinctly to the advantage of the Israelis. Until that moment he had been insisting on an Arab withdrawal to the 1967 boundaries. The Americans had suddenly become suspicious of Israeli capability, partly because of the squabbling generals, and for the first time had doubts as to whether they could in fact eject the Egyptian force from the east bank. On the twelfth Kissinger pressured Premier Meir to accept harsher terms for a cease-fire: that both sides halt where they had been on the night of the tenth/eleventh. The Soviet Union, without even consulting the Egyptian government, said that Egypt would never agree to this. Kissinger was trying, unsuccessfully, to exclude the Soviet presence from the cease-fire negotiations.

Kissinger wanted Britain to propose a cease-fire on this basis in the United Nations, but the British prime minister was suspicious and ordered his ambassador in Cairo to confirm that the Egyptian government was in full agreement. Sir Philip Adams visited Sadat at 0400 hours on the morning of the thirteenth, and the Egyptian president sharply rejected the terms proposed by Kissinger. Sadat's rejection upset Kissinger and caused some Anglo-American friction. Adams returned to Sadat again at 1600 hours but still was not able to persuade him to accept the Kissinger proposal. Meanwhile, on the same day, Premier Meir said on television that Israel would be willing to hold talks for a cease-fire if the Arabs were, but she did not mention that she had already accepted one on fairly humiliating terms.

At the beginning of the war neither side was absolutely sure it would be able to obtain immediate supplies of vital arms, ammunition, and spares; certainly neither had stocked up sufficiently for a twenty-three-day war. On the contrary, Israeli supplies had been run down, and they were, for example, desperately short of 105mm HE shells. Luttwak writes that Israeli "ammunition and spare parts stocks were reduced on the assumption that a war would require only a few days of actual fighting, and not very intense fighting at that."

From the first day of the war, despite lack of formal authority by the U.S. government, there seemed to be ample evidence that Israel had been quietly told it could have whatever military items it wanted if it could collect them, and so the entire El Al fleet of eleven Boeing 707s and five Boeing 747s was diverted for this purpose. Most urgently needed were the latest ECM pods for their aircraft to counter the more advanced Soviet SAMs. On the tenth, for example, an El Al Boeing, its markings masked, was seen at Ocean Naval Air Station, Virginia Beach, Virginia. It was being loaded with U.S. Sidewinder and Sparrow missiles and other unidentifiable items.

However, on the seventh Kissinger refused an Israeli request for large quantities of arms and ammunition, as he thought the Israelis would certainly win quickly and felt that a minor setback would bring the Israelis to heel—his heel. Heikal writes that Kissinger told him that "the Americans thought that within forty-eight hours of the opening of hostilities the Israelis would be in a position to deliver a devastating counterattack against the Egyptian forces in the Sinai." On the tenth Britain announced an embargo on all arms to the Middle East, which hit the Israelis hardest as spares and ammunition for their Centurion tanks were withheld. The French also placed an embargo on the shipment of arms to the Middle East.

On the ninth the Russians, who were now supporting the Arabs in the war against the Israelis, brought down their first COSMOS reconnaissance satellite after six days in orbit, only half its normal time. (They had launched another one on the sixth.) The information it produced indicated the staggering material losses incurred by both sides. The next day a Soviet air lift of military material began to both Syria and Egypt. The Arabs referred to it as their "air bridge." In this project the Soviet Union had no "overflying problem." Its aircraft were given permission to fly over Yugoslavia by Marshal Tito, not because of any Soviet pressure, but because he had been a personal friend of President Nasser. Also, much to Kissinger's annoyance, permission was given to fly over Turkey, a NATO country.

The Soviet air lift was soon in operation, with its Anatov-12 transport aircraft landing at airfields near Palmyra, in Syria, and the longer range Anatov-22s landing near Cairo. The Israelis alleged that initially the cargoes consisted mainly of SAM-6s and missiles. The Americans greatly exaggerated the number of Soviet flights made, claiming that there were up to seventy on the tenth and that this number rose to a hundred by the twelfth. It was later ascertained that they averaged between twenty-five and thirty daily for the first fortnight or so. Considering the Syrian "turn-around" time of three hours to be too slow, the Soviet Union flew in its own ground controllers, load masters, and mechanics, who reduced it to a half hour.

The Soviet Union also mounted a sea lift for heavier items to both Syria and Egypt. A Soviet ship from Odessa, laden with military material, arrived at Latakia on the eleventh, causing the Israelis to allege that the resupply programme had been commenced before the sixth. A ship could not have been loaded and make a journey of that distance in that short time, they claimed, inferring the Soviet Union must have had prior knowledge of the Arab attack. The Syrians told me that was not so, that the vessel was a normal military supply ship. They reminded me that the Soviet Union had been supplying Syria with arms and vehicles on a regular basis for some time.

Meanwhile, the Israelis were urgently requesting ammunition and military supplies from America in far greater quantities than the El Al fleet could transport. Also, pressure was being put on President Nixon by the Jewish lobby to accede to this request. On the tenth, the day the Arabs calculated the Israelis had only two days' supply remaining of certain types of ammunition, President Nixon was about to agree but on Kissinger's advice did not do so. There was some friction between Kissinger and James Schlesinger, the U.S. defense secretary, and in *Kissinger* Marvin and Bernard Kalb allege that Kissinger wanted the Arabs and the Israelis to "bleed each other white," while Kissinger arranged a scenario that would make the Pentagon look like "bad guys." Kissinger was later to try to blame the U.S. Department of Defense for the delay in sending supplies to Israel. The Kalbs also say that when Britain placed an embargo on arms shipments to the Middle East, Israel was on the brink of defeat through shortage of ammunition, and U.S. planes taking ammunition to the Middle East were refused permission to land and refuel at Cyprus.

Once convinced of the magnitude of the Soviet air lift to the Arabs, Kissinger tried to charter civilian aircraft to send the vitally needed material and ammunition to Israel. He had no intention of allowing the Israelis to be defeated, once his ploy of trying to persuade Britain to pressure Sadat into accepting a cease-fire had failed. Now he ran up against the Department of Defense and other departments, and could not get this project under way. According to the Kalbs, Kissinger alleged that the Pentagon was not cooperative and added that Kissinger's request to charter twenty civilian aircraft to supplement the El Al fleet was refused; when ordered to use military aircraft, Schlesinger would not let them fly to the Azores. It was only after Premier

Meir had spoken to President Nixon by telephone, urgently asking for military supplies, that late on the thirteenth the president agreed to the request. He was under the impression that the Israelis were on the brink of defeat owing to a shortage of ammunition; the round-the-clock air lift to Israel began, and the first supplies reached Lod Airport on the fourteenth. There is some evidence that Kissinger wanted the air lift to be a covert operation, and that Schlesinger disagreed and insisted that it be carried out openly.

Unlike the Soviet Union, the United States did not find this an easy operation to mount because of the vast distance, some seven thousand miles each way, mainly over ocean and sea. Existing U.S. midair refuelling techniques and facilities were insufficient to service on a nonstop basis the large air armada that would be required. None of the NATO allies would grant landing or refuelling facilities for this air lift. Spain and Italy openly refused, Turkey and Greece quietly refused, as did others, while neither Britain nor France was asked, it being assumed they too would refuse. The Americans had to stage their large aircraft, mainly the gigantic C-5s, at the Lajes air base in the Azores, and then refuel them in midair by tanker aircraft from the U.S. Sixth Fleet over the Mediterranean.

The Lajes air base had been leased to the United States since 1943, a lease that was due to lapse in February 1974. The Americans had begun using the base for the air lift without formally asking permission of the Portuguese government, which did not want to get involved, and it was only when the Portuguese realised the volume of material that was being carried to Israel that they protested. Use of Lajes for transshipment of material to Israel was allowed to continue only on the condition that the United States support Portugal in the United Nations on an unpopular colonial issue. The air lift flew from Dover Air Force Base in Nantucket across the Atlantic Ocean to the Azores. There were difficulties. In *Aviation Week and Space Technology* of 10 December 1973 one authority wrote that "when the air lift was ordered on the twelfth [but not approved by the president] Military Airlift Command had only nineteen pilots qualified in air-to-air refuelling." Other preliminary steps had been taken, and in the same article it was stated that "prior to the start of flights to Israel, maintenance equipment and personnel were moved to Lajes Field."

The cargo carried by this air lift included laser-guided Smart bombs such as the Walleye, which had a television camera in its nose, and the Rockeye, which dropped clusters of bomblets for use against small groups of infantry, tanks, guns, or vehicles. Some Skylark fighter aircraft were flown directly from America by U.S. pilots. They were refuelled over the Atlantic by KC-135 tankers and then, after a stopover at Lajes, were again refuelled over the Mediterranean by tankers of the U.S. Sixth Fleet. The air route avoided flying over land after leaving Lajes.

The shorter-range C-130s were used mainly to bring supplies from Europe. The United States took quantities of material from NATO stockpiles there, especially from Holland and Germany, without informing the host country. This practice later caused diplomatic friction. Items shipped included tanks, helicopters, antitank missiles, ammunition, and spares. It has been variously estimated that within a few days over two thousand TOW antitank missiles were air-lifted to Israel. This was a weapon once rejected scornfully by the Israelis; now they urgently demanded them. The air lift was mounted only just in time. The Israelis were extremely short of ammunition and missiles of all types, as well as vehicles, spares, and aircraft.

The United States was far less advanced in satellite surveillance than the Soviet Union, and complaints had been voiced by U.S. intelligence-gathering organisations that, after a cost-cutting exercise, satellite observation in the Middle East had practically been suspended. It was said that, while the United States had detailed observation of every single Soviet emplacement and vehicle in the Soviet Union and Eastern Europe, the Middle East was a blank map.

The next brush of friction between the United States and Great Britain occurred over an American request for the use of the British air base at Cyprus. The United States wanted to station two SR-71 Lockheed (Blackbirds) long-range reconnaissance aircraft there and use them for surveillance of the Middle East battlefields. When this request was made to the British government on the tenth, the British prime minister, Edward Heath, demurred. In *Insight on the Middle East War* one authority alleges that Heath said he would agree only if "the United States could come up with a cover story that would stand up and not be blown in a matter of days." It was reported that Kissinger, in a fit of anger, cancelled his request and then, despite lateral agreements, withheld from the British certain intelligence that was normally pooled on a NATO basis. However, a later, somewhat conflicting report in the *Daily Telegraph* of 16 February 1974 indicated the British government had not placed any restrictions on the Blackbirds being flown from British Middle East bases. In any case the Blackbirds, with an operating range of over four thousand miles, could easily have flown from either Alconbury or Mildenhall, U.S. air bases in the United Kingdom, to the Middle East and back without refuelling.

Whatever the precise truth might have been, and relations between America and Britain at this stage were certainly touchy, Kissinger made other arrangements to have the two Blackbirds stationed in Iran. They did not make their one and only reconnaissance flight until the thirteenth, thus causing Kissinger to blame the British government for holding up his battlefield information for three days. About 1300 hours on the thirteenth the two Blackbirds made a twenty-five-minute flight over the Middle East at altitudes of 65,000 to 70,000 feet and a speed of over 2,000 mph. They took a route from near Greece to Port Said, along the Suez Canal to Dag Hamadi, then back northward over Cairo, then east across the canal again and into the Sinai before returning to base. Based on the information gained, U.S. intelligence sources estimated Israeli losses to be 400 tanks, 3,000 killed, 1,000 taken prisoner, of whom 43 were pilots, and 15,000 wounded. The aerial photographs show amazingly minute detail. The estimated Israeli tank loss was about correct, but the other estimates were high. It was suspected they were deliberately inflated, and deliberately leaked, to sway American public opinion in favour of the U.S. round-the-clock air lift to Israel. News of the air lift was not made public until the fifteenth.

A gigantic problem that loomed larger as the war progressed was that of world oil. By 1972 the United States had suddenly become aware that there would be an energy shortage, that is, an oil shortage, by 1978. The Middle East produced about 35 percent of the world's oil output, while Saudi Arabia produced about 60 percent of that amount. Although the United States imported only about 5 percent of the total Middle East output, it was worried about the continuing supply. The Middle East oil-producing states had more income from oil than they could absorb in their own economies, and furthermore their reserves of cash had been eaten into by inflation and devaluation. There was talk of cutting back production (to conserve natural reserves) and of raising the price. In 1972 Kuwait was the first Middle East state to reduce its oil production to three million barrels a day. This action was a shock to the U.S. oil cartels, which for years had succeeded in keeping oil and politics apart in the Middle East.

Among the oil-producing states of the Middle East, Saudi Arabia was the only firm friend the West had. In early 1973 the Saudis were producing six and a half million barrels of oil a day; they had agreed to increase production to ten million barrels by 1974, and then to twenty million by 1983. But Saudi Arabia was not happy about U.S. policies and had privately warned the United States to modify its extreme support of Zionism. When President Sadat expelled Soviet personnel in July 1972, King Feisal had expected in return that America would bring pressure to bear on Israel to negotiate with the Arabs over the occupied territories, and he was disappointed when this did not happen. The Teheran Agreement of 1971, made by six OPEC (Organisation of Petroleum Exporting Countries) members, fixed the price of oil at three dollars a barrel for five years. This arrangement had not worked well; for example, Iran was demanding six dollars a barrel. On 3 September 1973 Libya raised the price of its oil to six dollars a barrel. In August President Sadat secretly visited King Feisal and persuaded him to promise to restrict oil production by 10 percent a year. This meant that for the first time the Arabs had used the pressure of oil diplomacy to achieve their political objectives as well as their economic ones. On the tenth of September ten oil ministers of OPEC countries met to discuss oil as a weapon.

Great though the need for oil was in time of peace, it was multiplied many times in war. This point was brought home forcibly to Israel, which basically had no natural oil wealth, but, paradoxically, was an oil-exporting country. Its domestic needs were estimated to be between seven and nine million tons annually. Up to six million tons came from their oil wells in the Sinai, in occupied territory. In addition, up to eighteen million tons were imported from Iran by the backdoor method—ships, flying flags-of-convenience, coming into Eilat. The Israelis had constructed a forty-two-inch oil pipeline, which could take up to thirty million tons a year. It ran from Eilat to Ashdod, on the Mediterranean, and there were storage tanks at both terminals. The surplus oil was exported, principally to Rumania and adjacent countries.

On the sixth of October Egypt imposed a sea blockade on Israel to ensure that no oil or other supplies reached that country. This was a serious enough matter for the Israelis, but the Arab use of oil as a weapon hit other countries as well. America felt its edge only marginally, but West Europe and Japan relied upon Middle East oil to keep their industries going. On the ninth delegates of some twenty oil companies met representatives of the OPEC to express their concern. On the same day it was announced that there would be an OPEC meeting to discuss the role of oil in the current conflict.

On the tenth there were talks between Egyptian and Saudi Arabian representatives, and the following day, in a last-chance effort to persuade the American government to modify its stand toward Israel, King Feisal sent his foreign minister, Omar Saqqaf, to Washington with an urgent note to President Nixon. On the fifteenth there was a crucial meeting in Riyadh, and the next day, OPEC announced price increases ranging from five dollars to twelve dollars a barrel. That day Omar Saqqaf and some other Arab foreign ministers arrived in Washington, where they were given a poor reception. Saqqaf gave Feisal's letter to Nixon; it stated that, if the United States did not alter its policy toward Israel, there would be an oil embargo in two days. President Nixon said that America was committed to supporting Israel and that the Senate had voted by a two-thirds majority to send aid.

On the seventeenth OPEC agreed to cut oil production pro-gressively by 5 percent a month until Israel withdrew from the occupied territories. The next day, when President Nixon asked Congress for $2.2 billion in "emergency aid for Israel," King Feisal took this as almost a personal slight. He had already announced, on the seventeenth, a 10 percent cutback in oil sup-plies to the West, double that agreed to by the OPEC representa-tives. Then, after a cabinet meeting on the twentieth in Riyadh, it was announced that, because of continuing military aid by America to Israel, all Saudi Arabian oil exports to the United States would cease.

On the twenty-first Algeria suspended its oil shipments to Holland, a country that was accused of previously offering tran-sit facilities to Russian Jews on their way to Israel and of cur-rently "transforming herself into a bridgehead of assistance sent to the enemy." It was alleged that KLM airline "made continu-ous flights to transport mercenaries to Israel," and also that Holland was "transshipping crude oil to Israel." The Arabs accused the Dutch defence minister of Zionist bias because he had taken part in a demonstration in support of Israel. Kissinger was largely, and generally, blamed for the international oil crisis. It was said that he did not understand the attitude of Western Europe, which obtained 80 percent of its oil from the Middle East, or that of Japan, which obtained 90 percent of its oil from the same source.

Inside Israel, on the tenth, Arab guerrillas sabotaged the Eilat-to-Ascalon oil pipeline and put it briefly out of action. It is also of interest to note that throughout the war oil continued to flow through the TAP oil pipeline where it passed underground across the Golan Plateau on its way to Sidon. The flow was reduced to half pressure so that there would be less oil wasted in case the pipeline was fractured owing to an act of war.

One of the lighter episodes of the October War was the odys-sey of Idi Amin, the rather eccentric Muslim president of Ugan-da. Uninvited, unwanted, and unrewarded, he flew around in his own aircraft to visit several Arab capitals (including Riyadh, Baghdad, and Damascus) to offer his advice. At one stage he advised Premier Meir to "pack up her knickers and run to Washington." On the fourteenth he was at Amman, encamped on the edge of the airfield; from there he flew out through Syrian air space, escorted by Syrian MiG fighters.

An equally bizarre figure was the Israeli, "Abie" Nathan, and his coastal vessel, "Shalom" (Peace), which he had fitted out as a floating radio transmitting station. He had cruised around the eastern Mediterranean since February 1973, urging Arabs and Israelis to make peace. On the sixth he was ordered to keep away from the Arab and Israeli coastal areas, but he sailed determinedly toward Port Said, broadcasting a mixture of pop songs and peace propaganda and reproaching both Arabs and Israelis for their "senseless killings." On the fifteenth he was sighted some forty miles north of Port Said. He then sailed for Beirut, where he anchored but was not allowed to land.

On the afternoon of the sixteenth President Sadat made a major speech to the People's Assembly. He said he would accept a cease-fire provided that the Israelis, under international supervision, withdrew behind their pre-1967 boundaries. The Israelis were then to attend a U.N. peace conference. Sadat also boasted that he had missiles that could reach any part of Israel. Many thought he meant the Egyptian-made rockets which had not come into production because of directional faults, and so the threat was not taken seriously by the Israelis. In fact, Sadat was referring to twenty Soviet SCUDs, which had a range of over 140 miles.

Also on the afternoon of the sixteenth Soviet Premier Kosygin arrived suddenly in Cairo to confer with President Sadat. This was the first real contact between Egyptian and Soviet leaders since the war began, a fact which tended to confirm that Sadat began hostilities without first obtaining Soviet approval. Kosygin's real task was to persuade Sadat to accept a cease-fire, to which Sadat agreed, saying he had only wanted to break the No Peace No War stalemate. Kosygin also wanted an assurance that Sadat would not use the SCUDs against Israeli population centres, and again Sadat agreed, but only on the condition that the Israelis did not first attack his cities from the air. Now that the Soviet Union was actively backing the Arabs, it did not want them to be defeated. The Russians were accurately informed through their satellite reconnaissance. They knew the exact amounts of material losses suffered by the combatants and could follow the course of the war. Understandably, they were anxious. As a first measure, about 300 Russian personnel were immediately flown to Egypt to stiffen the Air Defence Barrier, as the Russians feared the Israelis might make aerial attacks on Egypt.

10

STALEMATE ON THE EASTERN FRONT

Go forward and fight.

Syrian advice to the Iraqis

By the tenth it was fairly obvious the Syrians were withdrawing, or about to withdraw, back across the 1967 Cease-fire Line. The Israelis had yet to deal with the Egyptian Front and that evening called a high-level military conference to decide whether to consolidate on the 1967 Cease-fire Line or to advance into Syria. General Elazar wanted to penetrate up to twelve miles, to be within shelling range of Damascus, and to consolidate on the eastern edge of the Sasa Ridge. Dayan was hesitant and the matter was put before Premier Meir, who opted to advance into Syria.

A plan was made in which Eytan's division, consisting of the 7th Armoured, the Barak, the Golani, and the 131st Paratroop brigades, would move along the foothills of Mount Hermon. Laner's division, consisting of the 17th, 19th, and 79th Armoured brigades, was to attack and take Tel Shams, preparatory to forcing its way along the Damascus Road to Sasa and then beyond. Peled's division was to remain in the area of the Rafid Gap and reorganise. H Hour was to be at 1100 hours on the eleventh, when the sun would be in the eyes of the Syrians.

Israeli armour starting the breakthrough of Syrian lines on the Golan Heights, October 9, 1973.

Long-range artillery giving supporting fire to Israeli armour in Syrian-front operations, October 11, 1973.

Meanwhile, the Israelis concentrated on bringing up more tanks, guns, ammunition, and fuel, and more reservists were drafted to fill gaps in the ranks. Some of the Israeli formations had been badly knocked about; for example, Herzog writes, about the 7th Armoured Brigade, that "they left Avigdor with some twenty tanks."

One of Eytan's armoured brigades, the 7th, moved up to the area of Majdal Shams and then began to move eastward along the foothills of Mount Hermon to take the village of Mazrat Beit Jann. The area was held by a Syrian armoured brigade with about thirty-five tanks. Eytan's brigade soon ran into opposition at the Hader crossroads, where it was held. Darkness fell, and the Israelis still had not been able to enter Hader village. At dawn the next day, the twelfth, the Golani Brigade was sent to take the village and succeeded in occupying it. Almost at once, however, it was faced with a Syrian counterattack, which was beaten off. Other Syrian counterattacks took place during the day until about 1700 hours, when the Syrian brigade withdrew from this area. Herzog writes that the commander of this Syrian armoured brigade, Colonel Rafiq Hilawi, a Druse, was later tried by court-martial and shot for withdrawing without orders. This is emphatically denied by the Syrians.

The southern prong of Eytan's division, led by the Barak Brigade, was ordered to capture the village of Jaba. It soon ran into opposition near Tel Ahmar, which overlooks Khan Arnaba, and by the evening of the eleventh had reached only the small Druse village of Horfa. The next morning the Israeli paratroops were pushed forward to rescue one of Laner's brigades that had managed to reach the crossroads at Maatz, and then had been cut off during the night by Syrian infantry.

General Hofi was anxious to break quickly through the Sasa Ridge defences, and he ordered Eytan to move his northern armoured brigade diagonally across the Syrian front to attack and take Tel Shams. This huge feature dominated the area to the east, particularly the Damascus Road where it went through the Sasa defile. Elements of the 7th, 5th, and 9th Syrian Infantry divisions (from north to south) held the Syrian defence line and scattered outlying positions; although they had lost or abandoned their vehicles, they had ample artillery and infantry weapons. The two armoured divisions had been taken to the rear, where they were being re-equipped with tanks and guns.

The Israelis made three separate attacks against Tel Shams on the twelfth. The first was made early in the day when one Israeli tank battalion, coming from the Massada Road, moved into the low ground to the northwest of Sasa village and raced across the open terrain toward the objective. It was broken up by Syrian artillery fire from the northern part of the Sasa Ridge; the remnants of the Israeli unit withdrew back to the shelter of the low ground. During the morning of the twelfth the Syrians intended to put down some paratroops on either flank of the Tel Shams area, but by mistake they put them down in the centre of the battlefield, where both helicopters and men were lost.

The second Israeli attack began about noon and also failed. By this time the Syrians claim to have destroyed forty Israeli tanks and twenty other armoured vehicles. About 1630 hours yet another futile Israeli armoured attack began in which the Syrians claim to have destroyed an additional eighteen Israeli tanks. During the day the Israelis on this front used their new TOW missiles in quantity, having received a batch from a NATO stockpile in Holland. Despite these two setbacks, Israeli morale had recovered considerably, and many Israeli vehicles were daubed with such slogans as "The Haifa-Damascus Express" and "Visit Sunny Syria."

The following day, the thirteenth, the Israelis made another frontal assault on Tel Shams, which soon faded out, but by this time they realised they were using the wrong tactics. They had been attacking with tanks over open, rocky, and stony ground—the commander of the 7th Armoured Brigade himself declared it was "a misuse of armour." Also, the Syrians had settled down in defence and were by no means a rabble on the run, which, in view of their huge losses and casualties, some of the Israeli commanders thought they should be. That night, without any preliminary artillery barrage or any other supporting fire, men of the Israeli 131st Paratroop Brigade, on foot, quietly moved in from the rear and took the massive Tel Shams feature at a cost of only four wounded. At dawn on the fourteenth Israeli ar-

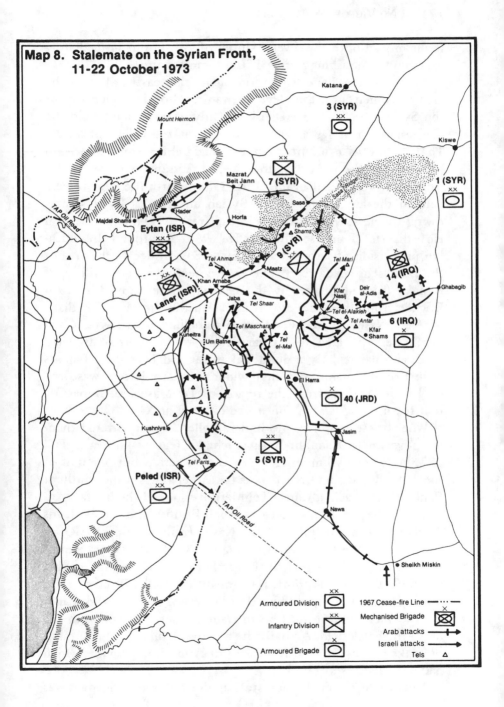

Map 8. Stalemate on the Syrian Front, 11-22 October 1973

mour moved onto the reverse slopes of the tel but immediately came under punishing Syrian 160mm mortar fire.

To the south, Laner's division, advancing eastward from the area of Kuneitra on the eleventh, ran head-on into elements of the Syrian 9th Infantry Division. Only with difficulty did the division reach as far as the crossroads at the village of Maatz. That night Syrian infantry cut the road behind Laner's forward brigade, and the next day, the twelfth, Eytan's paratroops had to be used to clear it again. During the twelfth the Israelis were held in the area of Maatz by Syrian air attacks. By this time, owing to the strong resistance in the area of Tel Shams, General Hofi diverted Laner southward. He was to go around the southern protrusion of lava outcrop of the Sasa Ridge to the area of the Damascus-Deraa road. The first objective was the village of Kanakh (spelled Knaker by the Israelis). Laner moved his 19th Brigade from the Maatz crossroads southward to take the village of Kfar Nasij, where he set up a refuelling point. Kfar Nasij dominated the area to its east down to the Damascus-Deraa road, and particularly around Tel Antar and Tel el-Mal. Laner's 17th Brigade, making a rather wider southern detour, was fired on by the Syrians from the region of Tel Maschara. Bypassing that feature, the Israelis continued on to Kfar Nasij.

When these two brigades had refuelled, Laner ordered them to move on to Kanakh. Both reached a feature known as Hill 127, just over two miles short of the objective, but one unit of the 19th Brigade had reached as far as Tel Mari on the southern flank of the Israeli advance. Tel Mari overlooked the lateral road from Ghabaghib (referred to as Abab by the Israelis). With his 79th Brigade refuelling at Kfar Nasij, Laner set up his HQ on Tel Shaar. In the afternoon, looking eastward, he saw two groups of tanks, which he estimated to number up to 150 in all, moving northward across his front. He thought it was the Peled division moving up, but Hofi told him that Peled was still at Rafid. Laner then deduced that it must be an Iraqi armoured division moving on to the battlefield. Actually, he had overestimated the number of tanks he saw; it was the Iraqi 6th Armoured Brigade, which had only about sixty tanks.

Meanwhile, a small Iraqi staff under an Iraqi brigadier was

being set up in Damascus to administer the Iraqi troops in Syria, who were to be under command of the Syrian GHQ. Cooperation of a sort between Syrians and Iraqis was jarringly forced into gear. The Iraqi staff general, Major General Ahmed el-Alneami, was to be the representative of the Iraqi chief of staff with full authority to act in Syria. The alerted Iraqi armoured division, the 3rd, was moving toward Syria, but the general realised it would be insufficient. Consequently, he made plans for two more divisions and a brigade of special forces (commandos) to be moved to the battle front as well.

Iraqi troops came into Syria piecemeal. The first formation to arrive was the 8th Mechanised Infantry Brigade (of the 3rd Armoured Division), commanded by Colonel Mahmoud Wahabi, which crossed the border on the ninth. The next day it was overtaken by the 6th Armoured Brigade, commanded by Colonel Imami; he had arrived the previous evening at Shamarat, near the Syrian border. Colonel Imami arrived in Damascus about 1900 hours to find he was not expected and that neither instructions nor information were available. He was simply told to "go forward and fight," the direction of the front being vaguely pointed out to him. The 6th Brigade eventually arrived just north of Ghabaghib about 1000 hours on the eleventh.

The following day Major General Mohammed Ameen, the Iraqi commander of the 3rd Armoured Division, reported to General Shakkour, the Syrian chief of staff, in Damascus. Shakkour also directed him to "go forward and fight," but told him little else of any value. General Ameen saw only confusion and chaos, coupled with a distinct lack of information about the current battle situation. The Iraquis had only the maps they brought with them; none were issued by the Syrians. They were given no codes, call signs, radio frequencies, or recognition signals nor were any Syrian liaison officers allocated to them.

Within the first twenty-four hours the orders given to the Iraqi 6th Armoured Brigade were frequently changed; for example, it was first put under command of the 9th and then the 5th Syrian Infantry Division. At 0500 hours on the twelfth the brigade commander was ordered to attack the Israelis in the area of Kfar Nasij and to move out from Tel el-Mal, but this plan was soon changed. Colonel Imami later commented to me that this was "a wasted morning."

At 1300 hours the colonel was told to move his brigade to a start line between Kfar Nasij and Tel el-Mal, and that S Hour was to be at 1400 hours. Just before that time, however, a new start line was given. It was to be between Deir el-Adas, farther to the east, and Tel el-Mal. It was from his position on Tel Shaar, some six miles from Kfar Nasij, that General Laner saw these Iraqi troops manoeuvring into position. The 6th Brigade moved from Tel Antar in two groups, one along the axis of the lateral roadway westward and the other slightly northwestward toward Tel Shams.

The Israelis and the Iraqis give conflicting accounts of what followed in their actions against each other; in particular, it is difficult to reconcile the alleged timings and movements. The Israelis say that, once Laner realised what was happening, he ordered his 79th Brigade, refuelling at Kfar Nasij, to deploy southward. He ordered his 17th and 19th Brigades to pull back from Hill 127 and sent the 20th Armoured Brigade, which had just joined him, to deploy between Tel Maschara and Tel el-Mal. The Israelis say the Iraqis moved slowly into the mouth of the "ambush box" that Laner was preparing for them but stopped just short of it at 2100 hours on the twelfth.

During the night of the twelfth/thirteenth Laner further strengthened his ambush box by deploying the 19th Brigade on the road that ran past the foot of Tel Shaar, the 17th south along the road to Kfar Nasij, and the 79th northward to the Maatz crossroads. This formed a strong "horseshoe" position, based on Tel Maschara, Jaba, Maatz, and Kfar Nasij, with a four-mile-wide opening between Tel Maschara and Kfar Nasij. The Israelis say the Iraqis resumed their advance at 0300 hours on the thirteenth, and that they (the Israelis) waited until the Iraqi tanks were 300 yards away before opening fire. They claim that by dawn their guns and missiles had destroyed or hit seventeen Iraqi tanks, and that the Iraqis were forced to withdraw.

The Iraqi account differs. They say that, when they were moving off from their start line on the afternoon of the twelfth, Israeli aircraft came into action against them, that they continued the advance, and that about 1630 hours they came under fire from Israeli guns and TOW missiles. They say that firing continued until about 1800 hours, after which there was a comparative pause until 0200 hours on the thirteenth. The Israelis strongly deny there was any initial exchange of fire on the twelfth.

The commander of the Iraqi 6th Armoured Brigade told me that he did not resume his advance on the thirteenth until 0720 hours, when his "right group" was ordered to take Kfar Nasij. His brigade was divided into two task forces, right and left, because he had only two tank battalions. After about an hour's fighting he succeeded in taking only a part of the village. The Israelis counterattacked, and the Iraqis withdrew into the Tel Antar area again. On the afternoon of the thirteenth the Iraqis assaulted again and this time succeeded in occupying Kfar Nasij without any resistance at 1630 hours.

When the "left group" of the brigade advanced, it was also ambushed and badly knocked about, causing it to withdraw in some confusion. At one stage both Iraqi and Israeli tanks were intermixed in a melee in the area between Tel Antar and Kfar Nasij. The Israelis claim another thirty Iraqi tanks destroyed in the left group. That group was then withdrawn and sent south of the Deir el-Adas road to hold Kfar Shams. The commander of the 6th Brigade, who received another tank battalion as a reinforcement during the day, told me that he received good Syrian artillery support during this fighting, the Iraqi artillery not yet having arrived.

Although the Iraqi 6th Armoured Brigade had walked into an ambush, suffered casualties, and had withdrawn to its start line, it had succeeded in bringing the Israeli southern flanking movement to a halt. The Iraqis stood by waiting for an Israeli night attack, which did not materialise. Herzog writes that on the thirteenth the Israelis had "destroyed one armoured brigade and scattered another," an overstatement, as they had put only part of the armoured brigade out of action. The other Iraqi formation, the 8th Mechanised Infantry Brigade, was hardly in action that day. On the fourteenth, the day a Jordanian armoured brigade entered Syria to join the Iraqis, Laner was ordered to stay where he was and to block the Iraqi advance. Laner was by this time short of ammunition, and his men were exhausted.

The Israelis claim that on the thirteenth their commandos, in a heliborne raid, destroyed a bridge sixty miles northeast of Damascus on the road from Palmyra, near Kasr el-Hayr. This was the route along which Iraqi troops were moving into Syria by way of Abu Haditha and Abu Kemel. Herzog writes that they "blew up a bridge on the Iraqi line of advance, and, when the Iraqi army stopped, the Israelis opened fire from ambush positions, setting fire to trucks and blowing up tanks." The Iraqis deny all knowledge of this incident, saying that in any case a damaged bridge in that area would have been no obstacle in the dry season.

Meanwhile, illustrative of the situation in Syria was the reception accorded to the 8th Mechanised Infantry Brigade (part of the 3rd Armoured Brigade), which arrived on the outskirts of Damascus at 0400 hours on the eleventh. The commander, Colonel Wahabi, told me there was no one there to meet him and that no one expected him or seemed to know anything about Iraqi intervention. He said that when dawn broke he saw Israeli aircraft bombing Damascus and for the first time in his life saw SAM missiles in action. He then went into the city to search for someone to whom to report and who would give him orders; he noticed that the shops were closed and people were hiding. He met some soldiers of "Tlas's bodyguard" who took him to GHQ, which was "inside the mountain." Presumably this was the Dourouz Mountain that dominates Damascus from the north. Once inside, he "walked for ten minutes" to reach the operations room, where he found President Assad.

Assad was pleased to see him, told him that the Israelis had "made a small penetration" in the Sasa area, and said to him, "A small regimental combat group from Iraq will change the situation." The Iraqi colonel, who still had not been given any maps, was directed to the southern part of the front and told to protect a SAM site just to the south of Deir el-Adas. Taking the road south from Damascus, the Iraqi brigade commander turned west at Ghabaghib, where he was directed by some local militiamen to "go forward and fight," a phrase that became almost a

Syrian catch phrase to the Iraqis during this critical time.

As Colonel Wahabi approached Deir el-Adas, he realised there was no front line and that all was in fluid confusion. To the northwest he saw Centurion tanks and 155mm SP guns. Knowing they must be Israeli, he placed his formation in defensive positions along the roadway. The Israelis he saw were part of Laner's division approaching Kanakh. An Iraqi staff officer appeared and indicated that Wahabi was to defend the length of roadway from Ghabaghib to Deir el-Adas, a front of twenty kilometres which he held for the remainder of the war. Wahabi made contact with the commander of the 43rd Syrian Armoured Brigade, which was nearby, who told him, "We are finished. Now it is your job."

Although given a "threatening role" in Operation Badr, Jordan had remained inactive during the first days of the war, and only three Israeli brigades were covering the Jordanian front. Rumours abounded of a secret nonaggression agreement between King Hussein and Premier Meir, with the French as the reputed go-between. However, information that the Iraqis were sending an armoured division into Syria clearly worried Hussein, who had unwillingly allowed an Iraqi division to be stationed in Jordan at the time of his civil war against the Fedayeen in 1970 and 1971. Eventually, and only with difficulty, had it been persuaded to leave. Relations between Jordan and Iraq were distinctly poor. In the *Daily Mail* of 4 January 1974 King Hussein was quoted as saying that "after the war broke out I had an agreement with President Sadat and Syrian President Assad that Jordan would enter the war and mount an offensive across the River Jordan, once the Syrians had completely liberated the Golan Heights and the Egyptians overran the major desert passes that control Sinai."

On the tenth King Hussein called up his reservists, and, as a gesture of Arab solidarity, he released a number of Fedayeen prisoners he had been holding. On the eleventh he decided to send troops into Syria, the reason given being to "protect the southern flank of the Iraqi division," but most read political implications into his decision. Orders were given for his 40th Armoured Brigade to prepare to move. It was probably his best

Jordanian soldiers preparing a position for their armoured equipment on the Golan Plateau.

Jordanian brigade commander sharing a meal with his headquarters staff on the Golan Plateau.

formation; barely three years before it had been in action against Syrian armour when the Syrians invaded Jordan. This brigade, commanded by Brigadier Khalid Hujul al-Majali, had about ninety Centurion tanks and was composed of two tank and one mechanised infantry battalions with supporting subunits. It crossed the frontier into Syria at Ramtha about 1200 hours on the thirteenth and moved first to Nawa and then to Jasim, arriving there about midnight. It was first given a general counter-attack role, and then, early on the fourteenth, was placed under command of the Iraqi 3rd Armoured Division.

On the fifteenth, the day the Syrians showed thirty-four Israeli prisoners to the press in an orchard near Damascus, the Jordanian brigade received orders to take part in a combined Iraqi-Jordanian attack on the following day. The Iraqis were to retake Tel Antar and then push northward; the Jordanians, on the Iraqi left, were to take Jaba and then cut the road between Jaba and Tel Antar. To the left of the Jordanians, as a thin screen against the Israelis now in the area between Rafid and Kuneitra, were a number of Syrian defensive positions on tels. The Israelis held a series of commanding features that included Tel Shipton, overlooking Kuneitra; Tel Faris, overlooking the pass from the Rafid Gap; Tel Shams, which overlooked the Damascus Road near Sasa; and Tel Maschara, Tel el-Mal, and Tel Antar, guarding the southern flank. The Israelis generally had the advantage of being on slightly higher ground which fell away to the east to merge with the Damascus Plain and which was open, dry, and dusty. On the southern flank the Israelis had developed a bulge that extended almost to Deir el-Adas.

On the fourteenth Saudi Arabia entered the war, air-lifting a detachment of troops in six Iranian C-130 transport aircraft from Saudi Arabia to Syria. The Saudi Arabian formation was a lorried infantry brigade of about 2,000 men. It had some French Panhard armoured cars and was given the task of guarding the Damascus to Deraa road. The Saudi Arabian army was about 38,000 strong, and one of its brigades had been stationed in south Jordan since 1967. The same day, Kuwait sent an artillery battery to Syria, and on the seventeenth the Kuwaiti government resumed payment of the annual subsidy of about £40 million sterling which had been suspended in 1970.

At 0500 hours on the fourteenth Iraqi artillery, which had just arrived, put down a barrage on certain Israeli formations, but at 0520 hours the Israelis counterattacked, using both tanks and TOWs mounted on vehicles. They forced the Iraqis to withdraw from Kfar Nasij. The officer commanding the Iraqi right task force was wounded. The brigade commander immediately sent a small force of four tanks to try to help the element of the right task force still pinned down near Kfar Nasij. Laner thought it was another Iraqi armoured unit arriving. The Iraqi brigade commander told me, "Immediate reaction with a small force gives a better result than waiting for a larger one later on. It was shock action, and it worked." That evening he sent another small tank group to reinforce his troops near Kfar Nasij. Another tank battalion, which had been left behind owing to shortage of tank transporters, arrived that day to join the 6th Armoured Brigade, thus making four tank battalions in that formation.

In the early morning of the fifteenth there were exchanges of artillery fire between the Israelis and the Iraqis, and Israeli columns moving eastward between Tel Shams and Tel Antar were shelled. At 1100 hours a particularly heavy Israeli barrage, lasting seventy minutes, was put down on Tel Antar where the HQ of the 6th Iraqi brigade was located. Later that day the Israelis captured and held Tel Antar. On the fifteenth the GOC of the Iraqi division arrived, together with another armoured brigade, the 12th, and set up his HQ some three kilometres back from Tel Antar near Kaita. The commander of the 6th Iraqi Armoured Brigade told me he was surprised at the speed with which the Iraqi troops were arriving on the battlefield. At this point the Iraqis did not realise the superior strength of the Israelis, who now had on the Golan Plateau six armoured and three infantry brigades, and nine companies of Tirans, which were converted and reconditioned Soviet T-54s, T-55s, and SP guns. They also had eighteen artillery batteries, equipped mainly with 155mm SP guns. These were distributed at two batteries per brigade, making a total of 106 guns. The bulk of these forces was grouped into two divisions, Laner's and Eytan's, and in addition there was Peled's division, which consisted of four brigades in the Khusniye and Rafid area. The Israelis were also surprised by the Iraqi attacks.

During the period from the twelfth to the sixteenth the Israelis made many small attacks during the daytime on both the Iraqis and the Jordanians, but the Iraqis claim the Israelis stayed in their defensive positions at night and seldom ventured out. The Iraqis claim that their own special forces made good use of the hours of darkness, making several small infantry assaults on the night of the twelfth/thirteenth. On the thirteenth the first battalion of their three-battalion Special Brigade arrived to be used in action that night and the following; it was claimed that they put several Israeli tanks and vehicles out of action.

The Iraqi plan for the combined attack on the sixteenth was that it should be led by the 6th Armoured Brigade, which was to take Kfar Nasij and Tel el-Mal. The newly arrived 12th Armoured Brigade was to remain in the area of the start line as a "stop." Herzog says the Iraqis "moved in an uncoordinated manner," and the Israelis say they caught them with artillery fire while they were deploying on the start line and then ambushed them as they advanced. When many of their tanks were destroyed the Iraqis were unable to carry out that part of their task, which was to protect the Jordanian right flank. The Iraqi GOC told me that the 6th Brigade penetrated through Israeli opposition "for ten kilometres," reached their objectives (Kfar Nasij and Tel el-Mal) and then were faced with strong Israeli counterattacks and aerial bombing in which TOW missiles were used liberally. The Iraqi formation was withdrawn to the start line. The Israelis say the Iraqis moved from Kfar Shams toward Tel Antar and Tel el-Alakieh held, respectively, by the Israeli 19th and 20th Brigades. The 17th Brigade, after hitting the Jordanians, made a wide outflanking movement to the south to join battle with the Iraqis. Herzog says that when the Iraqis withdrew "they left sixty tanks on the field burning." On the other hand, the Iraqis claim to have destroyed thirty Israeli tanks.

The Jordanian 40th Armoured Brigade, which was divided into two task forces of roughly equal composition, moved out early on the sixteenth to its start line, which was just north of

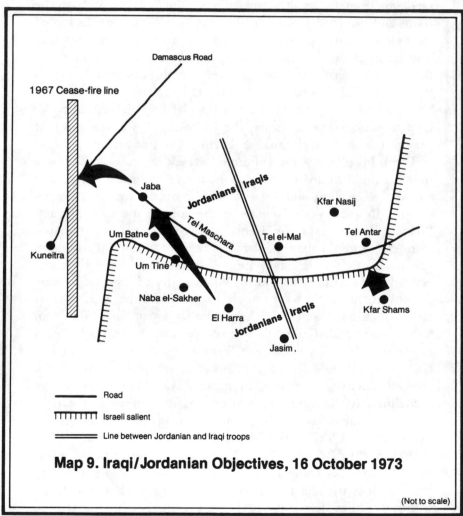

Damascus Road

1967 Cease-fire line

Jaba

Jordanians Iraqis

Kfar Nasij

Tel Maschara

Tel el-Mal

Tel Antar

Um Batne

Kuneitra

Um Tine

Naba el-Sakher

El Harra

Jordanians Iraqis

Kfar Shams

Jasim

Road

Israeli salient

Line between Jordanian and Iraqi troops

Map 9. Iraqi/Jordanian Objectives, 16 October 1973

(Not to scale)

Source: Hand-drawn map by Jordanian senior officer.

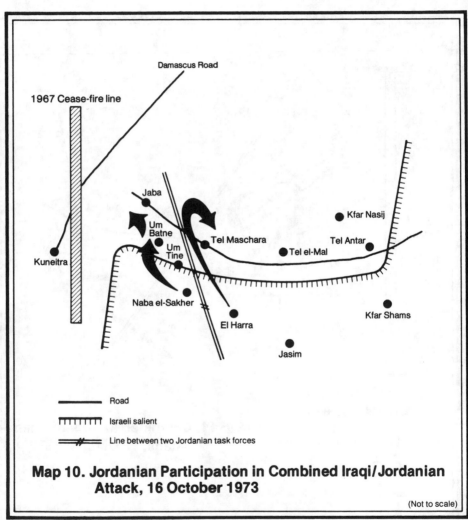

Damascus Road

1967 Cease-fire line

Jaba

Kfar Nasij

Um
Batne

Tel Maschara

Tel Antar

Um
Tine

Tel el-Mal

Kuneitra

Naba el-Sakher

Kfar Shams

El Harra

Jasim

——— Road

┬┬┬┬┬┬┬ Israeli salient

═══╫═══ Line between two Jordanian task forces

Map 10. Jordanian Participation in Combined Iraqi/Jordanian Attack, 16 October 1973

(Not to scale)

Source: Hand-drawn map by Jordanian senior officer.

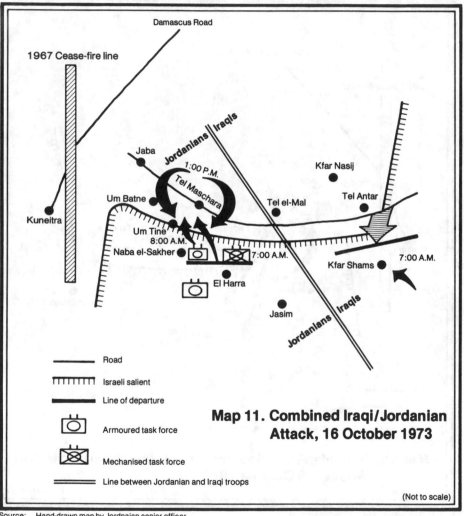

Damascus Road

1967 Cease-fire line

Jordanians | Iraqis

Jaba

Kfar Nasij

1:00 P.M.

Tel Maschara

Um Batne

Tel el-Mal

Tel Antar

Kuneitra

Um Tine

8:00 A.M.

Naba el-Sakher

7:00 A.M.

Kfar Shams

7:00 A.M.

El Harra

Jasim

Jordanians | Iraqis

Road

Israeli salient

Line of departure

Armoured task force

Mechanised task force

Line between Jordanian and Iraqi troops

Map 11. Combined Iraqi/Jordanian Attack, 16 October 1973

(Not to scale)

Source: Hand-drawn map by Jordnaian senior officer.

el-Harra. S Hour was to have been 0500 hours, when both Iraqi
and Jordanian forces were to advance, but, as there was no sign
of the Iraqi troops on the right flank, the brigade commander
postponed the advance to wait for them. There was still no sign
of the Iraqis by 0600 hours, and he decided to carry on without
them "as I felt there was a lack in the combat readiness of the
Iraqi forces."

Under cover of their own artillery barrage, the Jordanians
moved forward toward Tel Maschara and then turned eastward
toward Tel el-Mal. The tank commanders, wearing their red and
white kafiyas, rode with their heads out of their turrets. The
waiting 17th Brigade caught them in ambush, and the Jordanians admit losing ten tanks and two armoured personnel carriers
in an hour's fighting. The Israelis say they destroyed twenty-
eight tanks before the Jordanians withdrew.

At 0700 hours the other Jordanian task force moved in to
attack Tel Maschara from the southwest, and, although the Jordanians came under Israeli fire from 155mm guns and TOWs,
this time it proved less effective and the Jordanians claim to
have destroyed five Israeli tanks. The Israelis admit that by this
time they were all very tired. The Iraqis took Tel Maschara and
held it until about 1300 hours, when the task force was pulled
back to el-Harra because "Israeli formations were outflanking it."

It was a day of confusion for the Jordanians and the Iraqis,
owing to lack of coordination. For example, when the first Jordanian task force advanced, it was shelled by Iraqi artillery with
a barrage that fell short of its actual target. Later, Syrian aircraft, called in to give ground support, strafed Iraqi armour by
mistake. At midday the Syrian officer in charge of the sector
called off the operation. For the next two days the 40th Armoured Brigade remained in the area of el-Harra with the mission of holding the original start line. Although there were
exchanges of fire, the Jordanians spent most of their time reorganising and refuelling.

Farther north on the sixteenth, under cover of an artillery
barrage, with Syrian 160mm mortars falling heavily on Kuneitra
and the surrounding area, the Syrians made a strong thrust westward along the Damascus Road. The object was to knock the

Israelis from Tel Shams and enter Kuneitra, still the main Syrian objective. The attack hit up against two Israeli brigades, which had some 200 tanks in all; one brigade was on Tel Shams and the other was on a feature to its north. The fight for Tel Shams was particularly fierce; an Israeli deputy brigade commander was killed. By afternoon the Israelis had held the attacks and claim to have inflicted many Syrian casualties. The Syrians claim to have knocked out forty-five Israeli tanks on Tel Shams alone. On the sixteenth the Israeli government for the first time released news of the fall, on the sixth, of its Mount Hermon position.

On the seventeenth new recognition codes, signs, and signals were issued by the Syrians to the Iraqis and Jordanians. Apart from some shelling, both sides spent most of the day resting, replenishing, and reorganising. The Israelis later claimed "they had the day off." During the seventeenth Peled's divisional HQ took over from Laner's, but most of the brigades remained in the same position, simply transferring their allegiance.

There was an exception to the general inaction. General Hofi ordered Peled to capture the village of Um Batne, held by the Syrians and located some three miles east of Kuneitra; it dominated the Kuneitra opening. Paratroops from Eytan's division, who had previously taken Tel Shams in a night attack, were used to seize this objective. They succeeded in doing so, incurring few casualties; they claim to have destroyed six Syrian tanks.

As the village of Um Batne came under Syrian artillery fire, the Israeli paratroops continued, in the early hours of the eighteenth, to take some high ground to its south. At first light a mechanised infantry brigade, sent to hold the positions just taken, was hit by a Syrian counterattack and also came under heavy Syrian artillery fire. (This Israeli force has been identified by Herzog as the 14th Mechanised Infantry Brigade, commanded by Lieutenant Colonel Moshe Meler. After the war Meler became a prominent protester against the way it had been conducted.) This battle continued throughout the day and night until the morning of the nineteenth. In the north on the eighteenth an Israeli infantry battalion had captured the village of Mazrat Beit Jann, reputedly held by Colonel Rafat Assad and his Republican Guard. Also on the eighteenth the Iraqis wanted to mount another combined attack on the Israelis, but the Syrian GHQ would not agree, instead issuing orders for an attack to be mounted on the following day.

The nineteenth was the day of the second combined Arab attack on the Israelis on the Golan front. The Jordanian brigade, being on the left of the Iraqis, was still divided into two task forces. One of them moved off at dawn from a position to the southeast of el-Harra but was beaten back by the Israelis, who had a tank battalion located nearby. The Jordanian Centurions were shot at, not only by the Israelis, but also, mistakenly, by the Iraqis and the Syrians. The Jordanians, who had twelve men killed, withdrew, leaving two destroyed tanks behind them.

At 0700 hours the Jordanian formation was ordered to retake Um Batne and, leaving Naba el-Sakher, moved northward. Although the Israelis saw one group of Jordanian tanks moving toward them, they did not see another, hull down, covering them in a static position. The latter opened fire on the Israelis at 1,500 yards and claim to have hit and destroyed ten Israeli tanks with their first shots. The Israeli mechanised brigade then withdrew back to Jaba. The pursuing Jordanian armour was ambushed by the Israelis just to the southwest of Jaba and lost at least four tanks hit by TOWs.

At 0730 hours the other Jordanian task force was ordered to move to cut the Jaba-Maschara road, and the Israelis sent a group of seven tanks from Jaba out to meet them. In the fighting, the Jordanians destroyed three tanks, after which the Israelis withdrew. The Jordanians cut the road and remained in position until about noon, when they withdrew. About 1530 hours the Jordanians were attacked by two Phantom aircraft. This was somewhat unusual as there was little direct air activity by the Israelis in this area about this time. The Jordanians told me they did not fire back with their antiaircraft guns.

At 1730 hours the two Jordanian task forces began to move forward again. When each received several hits from Israeli guns and TOWs, both commanders of the task forces were told to "act on their own judgement and initiative." The Jordanians put down smoke on Jaba and the nearby Tel el-Kroum, but by this time, as daylight was fading and visibility poor, the Jordanians were ordered to pull back to el-Harra.

The Israeli account of the fighting against the Jordanians on the nineteenth differs in many respects. They say that at about 1000 hours a Jordanian task force moved out from el-Harra to hit at the west flank of Peled's division, between Tel el-Mal and Tel Maschara. The Jordanians, advancing in a wide formation against Tel Maschara, were slow to move forward, taking over an hour to reach their objective. By that time the Israeli artillery came into action. It was noon before the Jordanians gained the high ground surrounding Tel Maschara, but then they were held by the Israelis on the tel itself. About 1300 hours an Israeli mechanised unit from the hills to the west of Um Batne launched an attack on the Jordanian flank and forced the Jordanians to withdraw. They left some twelve tanks burning on the hillsides, and by 1500 hours the Jordanians had returned to the area of el-Harra. The Israelis claim to have destroyed thirty tanks that day.

The Iraqi and Israeli official versions of their fighting against each other on the nineteenth also differ. The Iraqis say their 12th Armoured Brigade advanced at about 0900 hours with its tanks leading, followed by infantry in armoured personnel carriers. The Iraqi GOC told me that they "advanced for about six kilometres, but by 1500 hours were pushed back again by air bombing and TOW missiles, which had a greater range than our tank guns."

The Israelis say that at first light on the nineteenth the Iraqis, centering on Kfar Shams, moved forward under a heavy artillery barrage put down on Tel Antar and Tel el-Alakieh (two strategic heights dominating the Great Leja, an expanse of limestone and volcanic rock to the southeast on the other side of the Damascus-Deraa road). These two heights were held by the Israeli 20th and 19th Armoured Brigades respectively. The first attack was against the 20th Brigade on Tel Antar, during which the 19th Brigade was pinned down by heavy fire. The 19th managed to break away and then make a broad sweep toward the Iraqi southern flank, a move that caused the Iraqi attack to falter.

The second Iraqi attack began about midday, and this time infantry in armoured personnel carriers led the way with tanks following in close support. The infantry dismounted some 3,000 yards from the Israeli positions and made an infantry assault which was beaten back. The third Iraqi attack was launched in the afternoon, when wave after wave of armour led the way, this time with the infantry following on foot. So began a seven-hour battle in which the Israelis used ample artillery support but no close support aircraft. At times the Iraqi and Israeli tanks were intermixed on the two features. The 20th Brigade came into action from the north, from the area of Tel el-Alakieh, at a critical moment in the battle. This surprised the Iraqis as they were under the impression that the Tel el-Alakieh foothills were held by the Syrians. The Iraqis eventually withdrew, leaving, Herzog says, "sixty tanks burning behind on the field, plain, and slopes of Tel Antar and Tel el-Alakieh, and about the same number of armoured personnel carriers." Herzog goes on to admit that this battle had been "touch and go," and that the Israelis suffered many casualties and lost many vehicles.

On the night of the nineteenth the Iraqi special forces, now a complete brigade of three battalions, were active against Israeli positions. At dawn on the twentieth a group of them were caught in the area between Tel Antar and Tel el-Alakieh as Israeli tanks were moving forward to take up their forward day-time positions. The Israeli tanks rushed at them and many men were crushed. The Israelis claim that thirty-five bodies were left behind; the rest escaped. On the nights of the twentieth and twenty-first Iraqi special forces infiltrated Israeli lines at night, destroying and damaging vehicles and guns.

During the period from the twentieth until the twenty-second there was little change in basic positions on the Golan front, but in the daytime there were frequent exchanges of shellfire, patrol clashes, and occasional aircraft activity. The Iraqis claim the Israelis made no moves at night, but remained huddled in their defensive positions; the Israelis say this was not so. The Israelis also say that a pattern of action began to emerge, and that every morning between 1000 and 1100 hours the Iraqis and Jordanians ventured an attack on the Israeli southern flank. The Arabs say the Israeli pattern was that the Israelis carried out harassing fire with guns and mortars between 0300 and 0700 hours but remained silent during the night.

The Israelis were hoping to advance along the axis of the Damascus Road, but the Iraqis and the Jordanians hit them in their southern flank. This forced General Hofi to stop his main thrust and attempt to deviate southward. General Laner had overestimated the numbers pitted against him. In view of the priority given to the Suez Canal front, the Israelis had tacitly come to accept the virtual stalemate of not being able to advance through, nor around, the Sasa Ridge Line. However, with talk in the air of an early anticipated cease-fire, the Israelis were anxious, for prestige purposes, to regain their Mount Hermon observation post, which had been lost on the first day of the war.

On the twentieth a battalion of the Golani Brigade was detailed to retake the position, and it advanced frontally up the roadway that wound up the slope from Majdal Shams near the ski lift. They had not gone very far when they ran into sniper fire from the Syrian special forces, who were in stone hangar-type positions on either side of the roadway. All of the snipers had rifles with telescopic sights that enabled them to pick off the attackers. The Syrians also rained down mortar fire on the Israelis, and, of the four Centurion tanks that led the advance, one was destroyed almost immediately by antitank gunfire and another was burnt out, as were several half-tracks. When the battalion commander was killed and it was seen how strong the opposition was, the Israeli attack was called off. The penalty for such a poor appreciation of Syrian morale was thirty Israeli dead and many wounded.

Piqued at such a humiliating setback, the Israelis planned a large combined operation to recover their prestige position. It involved the use of armour, artillery, paratroops, infantry, and aircraft. This attack began about 1400 hours on the twenty-first. Tanks and other armoured vehicles remained near the ski lift, while infantrymen of the Golani Brigade began to scramble up the mountainside in the face of sniper and mortar fire. At one point both the brigade commander and his deputy were wounded, causing the impetus to fail and the assault to come to a halt. There was a pause until the brigade operations officer, a major, came forward and started it off again. During this day-light advance up the mountainside the Israelis lost forty killed in the afternoon. One battalion commander was killed and another wounded.

About 1500 hours four Israeli helicopters landed around the objective, disgorged paratroops, and quickly took off again. The paratroops commenced sniping at the Syrian-held position, moving from rock to rock as they tried to manoeuvre closer. About the same time the Israelis landed at least ten more helicopter-loads of soldiers at points lower down the mountainside, farther to the northeast. Although these soldiers climbed some way up the slopes, they remained below the crest of the main ridge and so were largely immune to the sniper and mortar fire of the defenders. Yet other helicopters dropped ammunition and supplies to them.

The colonel in command of the Syrian special forces holding the observation post had taken the ridge initially (and remained holding it throughout the war). At this particular moment he was in another position farther along the mountain but ordered his men in the observation post to "resist to the death." About 1600 hours the Syrians rushed reinforcements to their Mount Hermon positions, and an air battle raged intermittently overhead between 1600 and 1700 hours as both sides attempted to give their own troops close ground support. The Israelis claim that by the end of the day they had destroyed fifteen Syrian aircraft and three helicopters, "mainly over Mount Hermon."

However, at the Syrian GHQ, which was involved in planning a gigantic combined operation for the twenty-third, there were second thoughts about the advisability of allowing its only special forces unit to fight to the last and be destroyed. All its expertise would be lost, leaving nothing on which to rebuild or expand. Partly due to Russian persuasion, partly because of the success claimed by the Iraqi special forces in their night operations, but generally because it appeared the Israelis had stopped moving and fighting by night, the order to remain was counter-manded, and the highly-trained Syrian commandos were ordered to evacuate Mount Hermon during the night of the twenty-first and to make their way back to their own lines.

After darkness fell the Syrian commandos, in small groups, left the observation post and other positions they had been holding on the Mount Hermon massif. Fewer than a dozen were caught by the Israelis. Those Syrian special forces who were stopped by Lebanese troops when they came to the sector of the mountain that was part of the Lebanon were interrogated and allowed to rejoin their own troops farther along to the north. They were given no food, water, or any help at all, even for the wounded; this made the Syrian commandos rather bitter toward the Lebanese. The 500-strong special forces unit suffered about a hundred casualties during the war.

Farther along to the northeast of the Mount Hermon ridge, the Israeli paratroops, who had spread out just below the crest-line, climbed forward sometime after darkness fell and occupied two Syrian positions and the actual peak of Mount Hermon. Luttwak writes that "in the entire operation the paratroops lost only one man wounded." It was a walk-over; the Syrian defenders had gone.

The Israeli accounts of the occupation of the Mount Hermon massif on the twenty-second tend to vary somewhat, but they generally assert that at 0600 hours fighting was resumed as their troops continued to force their way up the road from Majdal Shams to their former observation post. They claim they again raised the Israeli flag over the post at 1058 hours. They also mention sniper fire and even some hand-to-hand fighting. The Syrians insist they had withdrawn their troops from the mountain the previous evening. Israeli officers admit they encountered Syrian soldiers coming down the mountainside during the night, but perhaps a few Syrian snipers remained behind to the last moment.

Using helicopters to put down more troops and guns, the Israelis cautiously advanced along the crest of the massif. They occupied three more empty Syrian positions before the cease-fire at 1852 hours brought ground movement to a halt. Firing in the area, and indeed along the whole front, continued until about 2300 hours or perhaps even later. Unofficial estimates by Israeli officers are that the Golani Brigade lost over 70 killed and up to 250 wounded in the latter three days of action against the Syrians on the Mount Hermon positions. Elsewhere on the Golan front on the twenty-second another Jordanian armoured brigade, the 90th, arrived just south of el-Harra, and on occasion the Israelis shelled Fedayeen targets in Lebanese territory.

Meanwhile, more reinforcements arrived in Syria and brought the Iraqi contingent up to three divisions, including their special forces brigade. By the twenty-second, the independent Iraqi line of supply had been completed, and some 35,000 to 40,000 tons of material, fuel, and food were dumped inside Syria. There were about 22,000 Iraqi soldiers in that country as well. The 90th Jordanian Armoured Brigade had joined the 40th, while the two Syrian armoured divisions, the 1st and the 3rd, had been re-equipped with Soviet tanks and were ready for action again. Seventy tanks had been sent from Yugoslavia, ninety from Iraq, and nearly six hundred from the Soviet Union (not all the latter going to these two divisions).

The Syrian GHQ planned a five-division attack in two phases, the first to consist of the two re-equipped Syrian armoured divisions, two Iraqi armoured divisions, one Jordanian division (made up with one Syrian armoured brigade), plus Syrian and Iraqi special forces. S Hour was to be at 0300 hours on the twenty-third, and during the evening of the twenty-second these formations began to move to their forming-up places and start lines. At 0005 hours Syrian GHQ ordered the operation to halt. When General Tlas informed General el-Alneami, the Iraqi staff general urged him, unsuccessfully, to reconsider and to carry on the fight. It was pointed out that the Israeli troops were tired and weak and had lost a degree of confidence on the Golan front. Further, they had no reserves available to help in an emergency as Israel was extremely stretched on both fronts as far as logistics were concerned.

The cease-fire was called for under U.N. Resolution 338, but it caused discontent and controversy. The Jordanians accepted it, but the Iraqis refused to do so. At first the Syrians, who were planning an offensive, said they would study the proposal. They later announced they would accept it unconditionally, even though they had not been a party to the earlier U.N. Resolution 242 to which the present one was linked. The Syrians then cancelled their offensive. The cease-fire was not popular with either the Syrian or the Iraqi forces and caused tension and discontent. The Iraqi contingent withdrew from Syria on the twenty-seventh. They scornfully rejected the Syrian request that they "sell their tanks" to the Syrians, even though the Soviet Union promised to replace them. The Jordanian 40th Armoured Brigade returned to Jordan in December 1973, and the 90th a month later.

The Israelis had gained about three hundred square miles of Syrian territory, mainly in the northern part of the battle area near the foothills of the Mount Hermon massif, but had been unable to break through the Sasa Ridge Line or to outflank it from the south. On this front the Israelis admit losing 772 killed, 2,453 wounded, and 65 prisoners, but they claim the Syrians lost over 3,500 killed and some 370 taken prisoner. The Syrians have since unofficially admitted their casualties were between 10,000 and 12,000, but have given no breakdown. According to Herzog, the Israelis lost about 250 tanks, of which about a hundred were complete "write-offs," the others being repairable. The Israelis are silent as to their other material losses such as guns and vehicles. They claim to have destroyed or immobilised over 1,200 Syrian tanks, of which 867 were abandoned when the Syrians withdrew from the Golan Plateau. If it is to be accepted, this figure must be taken to include SP guns, as the Syrians possessed only about that number in total at the outbreak of war, although during the fighting the Soviet Union supplied probably another 600 and a few others arrived from both Yugoslavia and Iraq. The Iraqi losses have not been officially declared, but it is generally accepted that they lost over a hundred tanks, SP guns, and other armoured vehicles, and the Israelis claim to have captured seventeen Iraqi prisoners. The Jordanians were more forthcoming and admit losing twenty-eight men killed and twenty-nine wounded, but they say that none were lost as prisoners. They admit also having eighteen tanks destroyed and twenty-nine armoured vehicles damaged but repairable, while other sources, such as the Soviet Union, say they lost at least fifty tanks.

On the twenty-second a Saudi Arabian communiqué was issued, saying that in eight hours of fighting they had destroyed five Israeli tanks and damaged five others; that they had lost four of their own Panhard armoured cars, four 106mm recoilless guns and one jeep; and that their casualties were two killed, six wounded and one missing. No one I spoke to in Syria knew anything of this action, and, as the Saudi Arabian soldiers were on line-of-communication duties on the Damascus-Deraa Road, it is suspected any losses they had may have been sustained from Israeli aerial action. The Israelis, however, claim to have captured a Panhard armoured car, used only by the Saudi Arabians, so the latter may have been on the fringe of the fighting in the area of Kanakh.

Although not publicly revealed, the Syrian losses in the second half of the war were by no means as great as in the first part, and the Syrians seem to have been able to hold the Sasa Ridge Line without difficulty. One tends to see the guiding hand of the Russian advisers, who insisted the Syrians sacrifice their vehicles and weapons, withdraw safely to the Sasa Ridge Line, and rely upon defence to hold the Israelis. However, the Israelis, in the form of Laner's division, then would have been able to outflank the Syrian line and to cut the Damascus-Deraa road, and from there they would have been within shelling range of Damascus. It was only the arrival of the Iraqis, and then the Jordanian troops, that prevented this. Although both fell into Israeli ambushes and had to withdraw again whenever they advanced, they stopped the Israelis. The Arab five-division attack, due to start at 0300 hours on the twenty-third, would have heavily taxed the Israelis.

The Israeli view of the Iraqis was not high. The Israelis thought that generally the Iraqis had a low standard of competence and fell back at once when hit. On the other hand, an Iraqi general told me that the most important fact that emerged from this war was that the Iraqi soldiers discovered that the Israelis were not the military supermen they had been led by propaganda to believe. The Iraqi chief of staff, Lieutenant General Abdul Jabar Shenshell, told me that in his view the main lesson of the war was that of surprise, which it is still possible to obtain despite modern sophisticated aids, and he insisted that Laner's division was surprised by the Iraqi 6th Armoured Brigade and thrown off balance by it. His other comments included the need for good training, especially in night fighting, and the need for greater cooperation between the infantry and the tanks. He was of the opinion there was still a place for the tank on the modern battlefield and spoke of the still unresolved duel between the tank and the antitank missile and of the U.S. TOWs that had a greater range than any tank gun in service in the world today.

The Syrian defence minister, General Tlas, told me that he thought the Syrian rangers were much better than the Israeli paratroops or commandos. He commented that "in 1967, when Syria was not prepared for war, then Israel was considered to be superior to Syria, but now we regard Israel as inferior." General Shakkour, the Syrian chief of staff, being a political rather than a military officer, did not come up to expectations in battle. Brigadier Habeisi, the deputy director of operations, a Christian and, therefore, nonpolitical, proved to be more efficient, but, on the whole, Syrian senior officers did not come out of the war very well. All the Israelis I spoke to who had been in action on the Golan front agreed that the Syrian infantry fought with great courage and determination, being better equipped and trained than ever before, but none had a high opinion of the Syrian armoured personnel. Moroccan and Druse troops failed in battle and little more was heard of them. Lieutenant Colonel Omah Abu Shalash, in command of the Druse elements, was later promoted to colonel—obviously a political officer.

Views on the performance of the Jordanians varied, but the general opinion was that they fought well, although "their heart was not in the battle." Luttwak was scathing, writing that "the Jordanians, including the 40th Armoured Brigade of 1967 fame, did not try very hard to seek combat." However, Herzog writes that "they as usual fought well. I have never known the Arab Legion not to fight well." He adds that "the Jordanians suffered because they received no support from the Syrians or the Iraqis on their flanks." Certainly, cooperation between the Syrians, Iraqis, and Jordanians hardly existed. They had never worked together before, had fought each other in the recent past, and seemed prepared to turn their guns on each other once again if necessary. Old suspicions lingered, and they each remained exclusive entities, each very much on guard.

On the Israeli side, after the hard knocks taken at Tel Shams and the rebuff by the Iraqis and Jordanians, there was a reluctance to surge eagerly into battle. The Israelis seemed content with what they had taken, and it was not they but the Arabs who attacked on the sixteenth and again on the nineteenth. It was only when the cease-fire deadline drew near that, from a prestige point of view, the Israelis made efforts to retake their Mount Hermon OP.

Contrary opinions were expressed in the "missile versus tank" controversy. The Israelis say that TOWs were little used by them as they took time to absorb. This was flatly contradicted by the Syrians and Iraqis who say the Israelis used them extensively. Although Syrian tank gunnery was not up to the standard of that of the Israelis, Herzog writes that "all the Israeli tanks fighting in this operation [on the Golan front] had been hit at one time or another." This causes one to wonder why the Israelis held such a low opinion of Syrian armoured personnel—perhaps they were all infantry hits.

The Israelis admit the Soviet T-62 tank was a good one, but say it was not handled properly by the Syrians and the Iraqis. The Syrians say they captured forty Israeli Centurions and the Iraqis eleven; both countries eventually handed them over to Jordan.

11

ON THE
WEST BANK

Look at this valley of death.

Israeli brigade commander to Dayan

In the afternoon of the fifteenth the Israelis decided to cross the Suez Canal and exploit on the west bank, but there had been considerable hesitation, not to say trepidation, about launching such an operation. Both Elazar and Bar Lev had come round to the idea, and they had discussed the matter with Dayan. The latter was not very enthusiastic, as he did not think it would bring about a military decision or force the Egyptians to ask for a cease-fire.

The project had been discussed at a meeting presided over by Premier Meir on the twelfth. All present felt that first of all it would be best to think about and deal with the major attack it was expected the Egyptians, for political reasons alone, would be forced to launch. While the meeting was in progress, news was received that the Egyptians had begun to move their strategic armoured reserve to the east bank. General Bar Lev at once suggested that Southern Command, that is, he and Gonen, prepare a plan to defeat the Egyptian offensive. This suggestion was approved, and the meeting ended with the agreement that the Israelis would consider their next move after the coming battle had been decided. Moshe Dayan left the future decision, and its timing, to General Elazar, but Elazar wanted Dayan to make the decision to cross the canal—something Dayan was reluctant to do—so the responsibility fell on Elazar.

A number of factors led to the Israeli decision to cross the Suez Canal. The major considerations were that the Israelis reckoned they had won the gigantic armoured battles on the fourteenth, had driven the Egyptians back to their bridgeheads, and had inflicted heavy tank losses. Also, that day the United States openly admitted that it was mounting air and sea lifts of military materiel for Israel, which gave the Israelis a terrific morale boost. As well, information gained by the American SR-71 reconnaissance aircraft on the thirteenth confirmed that on both sides of the canal south of Ismailia and on the shores of Great Bitter Lake, there was a large area about forty kilometres in width that was almost empty of troops. This gap between the two Egyptian armies was held by an extremely thin screen of foreign troops: in the north, the Ain Jalloud Brigade of the Palestine Liberation Army; in the south, the Kuwait Yarmuk Brigade.

From the twelfth onward a number of groups, each composed of two or three men of the Mektal (the Israeli Intelligence Service), had crossed to the west bank in this area. They went either by boat or by infiltrating through the Egyptian lines, presumably across the Egyptian bridges, some wearing Egyptian uniforms. Yet others were put down by helicopter. (The first Israeli use of a helicopter for this purpose was on the thirteenth.) These Mektal personnel were Israelis who spoke Arabic with local accents and so they could mix with local Arabs and gather intelligence without arousing suspicion. They had been sending back reports by radio, which confirmed how few troops were in this sector.

The formidable Egyptian Air Defence Barrier, developed in the War of Attrition, had been considerably strengthened in the latter weeks before the cease-fire of 7 August 1970. It had unexpectedly brought down a number of Israeli aircraft. This prompted the Israelis to devise a plan and make preparations to cross the canal with an armoured raiding party whose mission was to destroy SAMs and ZSUs on the west bank, to "punch a hole in the sky" through which Israeli aircraft could penetrate. A number of potential crossing points were selected; some reports mention three and Herzog says "several." At each the large sand rampart alongside the canal was thinned out so a gap could be quickly bulldozed through it to allow rafts and vehicles to pass. Near each selected crossing site a small vehicle park was established in the shadow of the sand rampart, protected by lesser sand banks. Certainly one of the crossing places earmarked was opposite the airfield at Deversoir; one of the brigades of the 21st Armoured Division had been there until the twelfth, before it had moved to the east bank. This plan was known as Operation Gazelle. It was probably General Sharon who originated it, because, as is now known, he had been deeply involved in its formation and preparation.

Probably because of his knowledge of the area and the plan, Sharon was allowed to spearhead the operation; indeed, he was told on the twelfth to prepare for it. The following day one of his armoured units was detached to tow the prefabricated Israeli bridge that was being put together in the area of Tasa. Self-propelled (SP) pontoons and rafts were also being concentrated there. The Israeli plan called for Sharon's division to move down the road from Tasa to a point opposite Deversoir, there to open and hold open a corridor, form a bridgehead on the east bank, cross the canal, erect the bridge, and form another bridgehead of four kilometres in width on the west bank. This would allow Adan's division to cross the waterway the following morning, his task being to move south to destroy SAMs. Sharon was to capture an Egyptian position, known to the Israelis as Chinese Farm, on the northern flank of the corridor and another one adjacent to it, known to the Israelis as Missouri, or Missouri Ridge. He would then hold open the corridor with his armour while his paratroop brigade, in half-tracks and carrying inflatable rubber assault boats, went through to cross the canal. Tanks were to be ferried over on SP pontoons. Two Israeli bridges were to be erected across the canal. If there was difficulty in clearing the fifteen-mile long corridor, Adan was to cross the canal, while Sharon was to stay on the east bank to complete the job.

The metalled Tasa-Deversoir road ran diagonally across the right flank of the Egyptian 16th Infantry Division, the southernmost of the Second Army. The area from there south as far as Kabrit (the Bar Lev Line fort now occupied by the Egyptians) was devoid of troops. Meanwhile, Magen's division, which had moved south into the mouth of the Mitla Pass, was to exert diverting pressure on the Egyptian Third Army. Another new division in the north, commanded by Brigadier Sassoon, which had been formed to contain the Egyptian garrison at Port Fuad, was to apply similar pressure against the Second Army. A fifth division, to be commanded by Major General Israel Tal, was forming in the southern part of the canal zone.

The Israelis had been experimenting with bridging equipment for Operation Gazelle for some time, but they had not hurried and could not match the Egyptians for expertise or quantity. They had two bridges, each about 200 yards in length, one of the Uniflote type and the other of cumbersome U.S. pontoons filled with polyurethane. They began to assemble this pontoon bridge on the fifteenth, near Tasa. They had not yet devised a satisfactory method of linking the sections together, and so they were joined by wire and improvised fittings, the whole being placed on bogy-wheels and trailers. There were difficulties and delays.

Sharon made a highly complicated plan to reach the canal, detailing one of his armoured brigades to make a feint attack on the front of the 16th Infantry Division while another made a detour in the sand to the south of the Tasa-Deversoir road. This latter brigade was to turn northward when it reached Canal Road and divide into three groups. One was to move as far north as possible on Canal Road and hold the Egyptian flank. Another was to turn westward at the Y junction to reach the canal and make the initial bridgehead. The third one was to turn eastward at the T junction onto Tasa Road to clear it from the reverse direction and allow the waiting paratroop and armoured brigades, and the mobile pontoon bridge and SP pontoons, to move through the corridor.

The decision to launch this operation was delayed. The Israeli general staff hoped the Egyptian armour would launch another big attack on the fifteenth, and it was only when there were no signs of this happening that the decision was made. Sharon admits he did not receive permission to go ahead until the afternoon of the fifteenth. Then there were delays in movement to start lines and in making the bridge mobile. General Bar Lev proposed that H Hour be postponed from 1700 hours to midnight. Sharon, although he knew it was unlikely he would be able to meet the deadline, decided to carry on according to schedule and deal with the situation as it developed. At 1700 hours Israeli artillery opened up all along the front, and in daylight one of Sharon's armoured brigades made its feint attack to draw the 16th Infantry and the 21st Armoured divisions. Then at 1900 hours, already an hour late, another armoured brigade, together with Sharon and his small battle HQ, began to make the detour to the south of the Tasa-Deversoir road. They arrived at the northern tip of the shore of Great Bitter Lake about 0100 hours on the sixteenth. The tanks had only been able to grind slowly through the sand, and Sharon was now two hours behind schedule. The bridge should have arrived at the canal by 2300 hours, so it could be put into position at midnight. Adan's tanks were scheduled to cross it in the early hours of the morning.

According to his plan, Sharon immediately sent his armoured brigade northward. One group, moving northeastward to the T junction over a thousand yards north, ran into some opposition but cleared it. The next group went another thousand yards or so farther on to the Y junction, where it turned west. Still another group carried on northward until it bumped into the outlying Egyptian position about eight hundred yards further on, in the area of the Missouri Ridge, where it was held. By this time the Egyptians had been alerted to the fact that there was Israeli movement along the Tasa-Deversoir road, and they had been shelling the road since about 2000 hours on the fifteenth. This shelling increased during the night and extended to the T and Y junctions and surrounding area.

Once the armoured group reached Tasa, it turned around again and led the paratroop brigade back along the road toward the canal. It was followed by the mobile pontoon bridge and the SP pontoons and rafts. As it moved through the corridor this long column was fired upon, especially from the Chinese Farm position. Two Egyptian infantry units with antitank weapons moved toward the roadway and managed to close the road behind the paratroops, thus cutting off the mobile pontoon bridge and SP pontoons and rafts. Damaged by shellfire, the bridge broke down, as did several of the SP pontoons and rafts.

Meanwhile, Sharon and his HQ had moved away from the junctions, which had come under heavy fire, back toward Great Bitter Lake. The tank formation leading the paratroop brigade ran into opposition near the junctions but broke through, losing several tanks in the process, to bring the paratroops to the canal bank. As they reached the canal, the paratroops jumped from their half-tracks, and, carrying their rubber assault boats, marched on foot to join Sharon on the shore of Great Bitter Lake. Their empty half-tracks, trying to return to Tasa, ran into Egyptian fire and were scattered in the sand. It was 0300 hours on the sixteenth before the paratroops started crossing the canal in their assault boats. They were later joined by ten tanks that had managed to break through and were ferried over on the SP pontoons. Contrary to many reports, it should be pointed out that this initial crossing was made over the northern tip of Great Bitter Lake where there were no defensive sand ramparts, and not across the canal itself. The area where the Israelis landed on the west shore of the lake had been heavily shelled to clear it of mines, but no hostile forces were encountered at all. Sharon had some SP guns, bulldozers, and tank-dozers, and also a "cherry picker" device, which was an elevated OP mounted on a Sherman chassis. Most of these arrived after daylight.

By dawn on the sixteenth, when an Egyptian artillery barrage was put down on the east bank, Sharon insists he had two battalions (one tank and one paratroop) on the west bank. This is a doubtful claim because the SP pontoons did not arrive at the canal until daylight, by which time Egyptian infantry had infiltrated near the T junction. As daylight came Sharon moved his vehicles and men into the ample cover provided by the trees and bushes around the fringe of the Deversoir airfield. The Egyptian barrage on the east bank ceased after about a half hour, after which there was a pause in the artillery fire. The Israelis took

Israeli portable observation post ("cherry picker") mounted on Sherman tank chassis.

Israeli armour moving through thicket near Deversoir on West Bank operations, October 16, 1973.

full advantage of it, and they say that by 0900 hours they had thirty tanks and 2,000 men on the west bank. This must have been largely correct.

There was only one small attack against Sharon's force in the morning. It was made by a group of rangers who claim to have destroyed some Israeli tanks and caused others to withdraw into the swamps near Deversoir. The local Egyptian commander thought he had eliminated a small Israeli reconnaissance party. During the morning Sharon received a signal informing him that the pontoon bridge had been damaged and would take all day to repair. He decided to move quickly northward to try to seize the nearest Egyptian bridge, some six miles away. His paratroops moved slowly along the sand rampart for about three miles until they ran into opposition. According to Herzog, the Israelis claim to have killed some thirty Egyptians and taken some prisoners, and also that the paratroops had seized the four main crossings of the inland Sweet Water Canal. When Egyptian aircraft came over about noon they saw no signs of the Sharon force on the west bank. It should have been forming a bridgehead but instead was under cover away from the canal.

Meanwhile, Sharon's guns shelled the antennas of the SAM radars, putting several out of action and causing others to move to alternative positions or even to withdraw to prevent capture. Sharon claims he put four SAMs out of action on the sixteenth, but seven or even more may have been a more accurate figure. This Israeli presence on the west bank caused the Egyptians to call the penetration a "bulge" and not a "gap."

Sharon's troops continued to cross the lake during the day, seemingly without being observed. Later the PLA Brigade insisted it had reported, and continued to report, the operation, but that no notice was taken of it by the Egyptian GHQ. By the end of the day Sharon, this time more accurately, insists he had two complete brigades on the west bank, hidden away in the trees, together with over thirty tanks and a dozen or more M-113s. However, Sharon had failed in his mission to seize and hold a bridgehead on both banks. Conversely, had he done so, the bridgeheads would have been heavily shelled, and the Egyptians would have had clear warning of the scope of the operation. As it was, the Egyptians shelled the east bank, where they suspected an Israeli force might be concentrating. Herzog writes that "the Sharon Plan of May 1973 to cross the canal *north* of Deversoir had been discovered by the Egyptians, which caused them to heavily fortify the vulnerable area, and to virtually ignore the sector south of Deversoir, which was only lightly held.

In the afternoon of the sixteenth Sharon sent a small armoured force northward along Canal Road toward Ismailia, but about 1800 hours about ten miles south of the village of Abu Atna it was ambushed by rangers and scattered. This action prompted Radio Cairo later to announce that the Israeli "penetration had been wiped out." This group had penetrated into the agricultural belt of small farms, mud-hut villages, date plantations, orchards, and fields of maize and vegetation in which wandered water buffalos and donkeys. The multiplicity of irrigation systems that lay south of Ismailia between the Suez Canal and the Sweet Water Canal came to be referred to by the Israelis as the "jungle" or "Vietnam." It was most unsuitable for vehicles. Sharon put his TOW missiles on the ground while the aimer and firer climbed up trees for a better view, but this was not a success because the dense vegetation interfered with the weapons' trailing guidance wires.

Also on the sixteenth a small Israeli force of twenty-seven tanks and seven armoured vehicles moved out on a reconnaissance sortie westward and then southward to the shore of Great Bitter Lake near the village of Sakronut, a distance of fifteen miles. During the course of this drive the Israelis destroyed four SAMs, twelve tanks, and twenty other armoured vehicles with the loss of only one man. They reported that the area was wide open and empty of Arab troops. However, at 0200 hours on the seventeenth the force was ordered to withdraw to the east side of Sweet Water Canal.

Meanwhile, when Moshe Dayan received the information that the pontoon bridge had failed to reach the canal, he became pessimistic and suggested pulling back the paratroops from the west bank. Herzog quotes Dayan as saying, "We tried, and it has been no go. . . . In the morning they will slaughter them on the other side." Dayan wanted to abandon the operation. General

Gonen, although not too confident himself, wanted it to continue, since it had been started. General Bar Lev was most emphatic that it must continue.

On the east bank at dawn on the sixteenth it was clear the Tasa-Deversoir Road was firmly blocked by the Egyptians. Their infantry with antitank weapons covered the major part of it. The main blocking position was at Chinese Farm; it was held by an infantry battalion, supported by a brigade of the 21st Armoured Division on a good, commanding feature. The area was crisscrossed by several irrigation canals—some dry and some with water in them—derelict sluice gates, a pumping house, and several other buildings. Nearby was a village of about a hundred small houses, known to the Egyptians as Evacuation Village or Galan.

As the morning mists lifted, Gonen ordered Adan to clear the eastern sector of the Tasa-Deversoir Road and gave him the responsibility of getting the mobile bridge to the canal. The Egyptians claim they monitored an Israeli message in which Adan's brigade commanders asked permission to put off their attack because heavy Egyptian artillery fire blocked the road. Nonetheless, Adan was ordered to go ahead and clear it.

About noon on the sixteenth Gonen spoke to Sharon on the radiotelephone and ordered him to capture Chinese Farm and the adjacent Missouri Ridge position. Sharon ignored the order on the score that his tanks were almost out of ammunition. He said that he would wait until Adan had cleared his sector before he replenished them. Gonen and Sharon also argued about the damaged pontoon bridge and how long it would take to get it moving again. Dayan met Gonen at Khaseiba at 1630 hours when it was decided that, if neither the stranded pontoon bridge nor the remainder of the SP pontoons reached the canal that night, the force on the west bank must be withdrawn. If the SP pontoons reached the canal, the force could remain, but Adan was not to cross the canal unless it was bridged.

Meanwhile, one of Adan's armoured brigades launched an attack on the Chinese Farm position and the fighting continued through the sixteenth. At one stage the tanks of the opposing forces were intermixed. Adan also had to cope with counter-

attacks from the 16th Infantry Division. In the evening reinforcements arrived, including a battalion of paratroops brought
in by helicopter, and at 2330 hours Adan began a fresh drive to
clear the corridor. The paratroops led the way, fighting a four-
teen-hour battle in which, by Herzog's count, they lost 40 killed
and 100 wounded. At 0330 hours on the seventeenth the paratroops were surrounded, but they held out while Adan, with
three armoured brigades, pushed heavily forward. By 1100 hours
he had reached and rescued the beleaguered soldiers.

The battle for Chinese Farm lasted a day and a night, when
the defenders were ordered to withdraw northward about six
miles or so to the next line of Egyptian-defended localities.
They withdrew after dawn on the seventeenth, but elements of
the 21st Armoured Division remained active in the area. The
Egyptians say that this was the only really successful Israeli
attack on the east bank during the war, but both sides suffered
many casualties. At one stage of the fighting Israeli tanks un-
knowingly entered the Egyptian divisional HQ area.

There was fighting all along the Tasa corridor on the seventeenth. The Egyptian 14th Infantry Brigade, to the west of
Chinese Farm, destroyed an Israeli tank unit, and the Egyptians
mounted at least two major attacks against the Israelis. About
noon Dayan arrived with Generals Bar Lev and Elazar at Adan's
forward HQ; it was located in the hills near Kishaf overlooking
the entrance to the Tasa corridor. They were joined by Sharon,
who came by helicopter. Sharon proposed that Adan should
clear the whole of the corridor while the remainder of his division crossed to the west bank, but Adan objected to this. He
wanted to adhere to the original plan. General Elazar agreed
with Adan and issued orders to Sharon to carry on and clear his
part of the corridor. When the news arrived of the advance of
the Egyptian 25th Independent Armoured Brigade from the
south this council of war was adjourned.

At dawn on the seventeenth the Egyptians began shelling the
SP pontoons ferrying vehicles across the canal, and among several that were sunk was one with four tanks and crews on it.
During the morning the Israeli pontoon bridge had been patched
up and made mobile again, and it was towed slowly and majesti-

cally alongside Tasa Road by ten Centurion tanks. This trackway had been made deliberately for this purpose, and it was
quite straight and direct. The bridge slowly trundled through
the Tasa corridor while the battles were actually being fought
above it by Adan's men trying to reopen the route. Although it
arrived at the water's edge about noon, it was 1600 hours before
it spanned the canal. The fact that it arrived at all, let alone
relatively unscathed from the frequently heavy shell and mortar
fire, was one of the miracles of the war. The Egyptians insist the
pontoon bridge had been so badly damaged that it could not be
repaired or made mobile and that the second, the Uniflote, was
brought forward instead. Although the Israelis deny this, Luttwak confirms that the original bridge was so damaged that it
could not be used and that the other had to be brought up and
used first.

Some reports state that the Israeli engineers with the bridge
looked for the "red bricks" that Sharon claims had marked the
projected crossing places where the sand rampart had been
thinned out. This is loudly discounted by the Egyptians, who
insist the Israelis used one of the several gaps the Egyptians had
blasted with their water cannon in this section on the first afternoon. It should be made clear that the bridge was erected at a
point where the canal almost entered Great Bitter Lake; it was
just under the shelter of the sand ramparts on both sides. Its
erection had been made possible by Adan's division, which was
engaged in pushing back the 16th Infantry Division from the
northern edge of the corridor. Adan's division had done so sufficiently to allow the bridge to pass through, as well as the SP
pontoons and some supply vehicles loaded with ammunition,
fuel, and food for Sharon's division. It was partly on the west
bank and partly scattered on the east bank. Sharon's eyes were
looking westward.

On the morning of the seventeenth the Egyptian 25th Independent Armoured Brigade was concentrated around a junction
on Artillery Road, about fifteen miles to the east of the canal,
covering the northern flank of the Third Army. This brigade had
three battalions, each of about thirty T-62 tanks. One unit was
left behind at Kabrit Fort. About 0630 hours, the other two,

with brigade HQ and support elements, began to move northward and were almost immediately confronted by ten Israeli
tanks. The leading Egyptian company claims to have destroyed
four of them and caused the remainder to withdraw. This Egyptian force, which was supported by artillery from both the 7th
and the 19th Infantry Divisions until it had advanced beyond
their range, soon came under continuous artillery fire from the
northeast. During the course of the morning the Egyptians were
also frequently attacked by Israeli aircraft.

As the Egyptian brigade began moving northward a small
group of Israeli tanks began to move in the same direction on a
parallel course—from the Mitla Pass to the Giddi Pass along the
axis of Supply Road. The Israelis were partly obscured by the
low, intervening ridge but, being generally on higher ground,
were able at times to look down on the Egyptian force. The
Egyptians claim to have intercepted an Israeli message the previous night ordering "sixty-six Israeli tanks" to make this move
on the seventeenth, but the Israelis say there were only thirty
tanks in this formation. The Egyptians also claim that, as their
armoured brigade advanced from feature to feature, with a flank
guard to the right covering the Israeli tanks, they intercepted
another Israeli message to the commander of these tanks ordering him to turn west and attack the Egyptian formation, but
that he refused to do so. He did fire his guns at the Egyptians,
who fired back, but he did not mount a formal attack.

By about 1600 hours the Egyptian brigade had covered a distance of about twenty-seven kilometres when it came up against
an east-west irrigation canal, part of which was a continuation
of the Wadi Giddi. The canal was mostly dry but it did contain
water in some places. It was about six miles south of the Chinese
Farm position, where the Israelis had established a screen of
TOW missiles. Until this moment the Egyptian brigade had lost
only five tanks. The operations officer, who took part in the
battle, told me that after about 1000 hours there had been "a
rush of helicopters" transporting what turned out to be numbers
of TOW missiles and their teams to the area of Kitab el-Habashi,
a feature to the west of the Giddi Pass near the ambush line, on
a ridge 300 feet high overlooking the irrigation canal.

As the 25th Independent Armoured Brigade neared this ambush line, the Israelis sent out seven tanks from Sharon's division against them, and the Egyptians claim that all were destroyed by their tank guns, "each with one shot"; the Israelis admit the loss of only four.

As the Egyptian tanks took hull-down positions to probe for a breakthrough point, they were suddenly bombarded with TOW missiles, and an Egyptian officer present said to me, "The skies were suddenly full of red balls coming towards our tanks, and many were hit and set on fire." After standing its ground and taking heavy losses for about an hour, the Egyptian force was ordered to withdraw to the Kabrit Fort area. Once they began withdrawing, Israeli tanks were launched against them, and there was a running battle back to the fort. The Egyptian counterattack on the Tasa corridor, a fierce and determined one, had been blocked by TOW missiles in a good ambush position along an irrigation barrier. The Israeli bridgehead on the east bank had been saved from encirclement—perhaps at a critical moment. The forward Egyptian tanks had reached within three kilometres of Kalah Salam, a deserted village on the shore of Great Bitter Lake which was held by Sharon's men. As darkness fell Egyptian artillery used flares to illuminate the battlefield around Kabrit Fort.

As seems inevitable in this war, there are conflicting reports and claims. The Israelis say that the whole of the attacking force was destroyed and its commander killed. The Egyptians admit to "30 percent tank losses" from the whole brigade, which would mean just over thirty tanks. Most of these came from the leading battalion whose remnants were brought back to Kabrit Fort by a lieutenant. The Israelis claim that they destroyed eighty-six T-62s and many other armoured vehicles and fuel trucks and that only four tanks escaped back into Kabrit Fort. They say their losses were only four tanks, which ran into a minefield when chasing the Egyptians. The Israelis say they had only about thirty tanks available to support their ambush line (a battalion hastily brought from confronting the 16th Infantry Division in the east), but the Egyptians allege they must have had about 120 there. This battle, the first one in which TOW missiles had been brought into action in number, demonstrated the missile's lethal capability against tanks. Its range of over 3,250 yards was greater than that of the Soviet 120mm gun in the T-62 tanks, or, indeed, of the guns in the Pattons and Centurions—a problem that still gives tankmen a headache.

For Adan the seventeenth had been a good day. He had opened the Tasa corridor in the morning and then in the afternoon had beaten back an Egyptian armoured brigade. He admitted losing only six tanks, three of which were from missile fire. The Israeli bridge across the canal had been ready since 1600 hours, but, being busily engaged in reorganising his division, Adan was not able to take the opportunity to cross it before the order came for him to wait. Despite Sharon's pleas for Adan's division to join him on the west bank, the crossing was delayed for another two days.

Commencing on the morning of the seventeenth, an Egyptian force, identified by Heikal as the 182nd Paratroop Brigade, moved in just south of Ismailia to the sand rampart by the canal. As he moved southward the brigade commander dropped off detachments who were to hold certain points. By the time he reached the lake he had used up most of his men and had to retire again for some distance when Sharon pressed northward to enlarge his bridgehead on the west bank, as he had been urgently ordered to do. As soon as the Israeli bridge was across the canal, Sharon demanded that Adan's division be sent quickly across as, in defiance of orders, he wanted to exploit westward himself. He attempted to do so but did not penetrate very far owing to the nature of the terrain: bushes, trees, and uneven ground. Even before the Israeli bridge appeared, Sharon had been demanding reinforcements, but Bar Lev's reply had been "not until there is a bridge across."

As soon as the Israeli bridge was identified by the Egyptians early on the morning of the seventeenth, artillery from both the Second and Third Armies was directed onto it, scoring several hits. The bridge was further bombed and damaged by Egyptian aircraft. The HQ of the Israeli Paratroop Brigade, which was near the bridge, received a direct hit, wounding both the commander and his deputy. Herzog writes that "from this moment until the cease-fire, the bridgehead and the area of the bridge were under constant heavy artillery fire and guns, mortars and katushyas combined to pour tens of thousands of shells into the area of the crossing. Planes attempted to bomb every afternoon . . . . Egyptian helicopters came in on suicide missions to drop barrels of napalm on the bridge and the bridgehead."

The Egyptian paratroop brigade with a small detachment of frogmen moved toward the bridge to blow it up. Sharon claimed that in this morning attack on his bridgehead the Egyptians left ten tanks on the field when they were beaten off. According to Herzog, it was later admitted that Sharon had lost over 100 killed and 300 wounded in the fighting on the west bank up to that day. At about 1700 hours the astonished Egyptian commander received an order to withdraw to his former positions "to avoid creating a salient." He double-checked only to find, according to Heikal, that the order came directly "from Number Ten." The artillery which had moved forward with him was also ordered to return to its former positions.

During the night the bridge was repaired, but only a small trickle of Israeli troops crossed. The force of the Egyptian counterattacks along the Tasa corridor had surprised General Bar Lev, who now had considerable doubts about the west bank venture. Consequently, even when Adan's division had reorganised after the battle for the corridor, Bar Lev refused to allow it to cross to the far side to join Sharon. Bar Lev felt that his fuel tankers and impressed civilian trucks carrying ammunition would not be able to survive the shelling, and so supplies could not be guaranteed. According to Herzog, "The last of Haim's forces crossed at 1130 hours on the seventeenth, and then for thirty-seven hours no more tanks crossed."

Earlier, at noon on the sixteenth when President Sadat, accompanied by General Ismail, went to the People's Assembly to make his important speech, he was not in possession of information about the Israeli landing on the west bank. Neither was General Ismail because it had not yet been passed back to GHQ. On leaving the People's Assembly building, Ismail was given the news and he in turn informed the president that "three Israeli reconnaissance tanks" had been landed on the west bank but were being dealt with. Later, in an interview in the Beirut magazine, *Al Hawadess,* of 24 April 1974, Sadat said, "When the Israeli forces made their counterthrust on October sixteenth, I ordered General Shazli to go personally to Ismailia within ninety minutes to hold the Israelis within the limits we had already defined around Deversoir Lake." He told Shazli to lay siege around the Israeli bridgehead, to allow Israelis to enter it, but to let none leave it. Ismail said he had warned the general staff on the eleventh that the Israelis might try to raid the west bank, and he also told me he thought the Israelis had "swum" their tanks across the canal.

In Israel, Premier Meir was also due to address her nation at noon, but presumably, hearing the timing clashed with Sadat's, she postponed her speech until 1600 hours to be able to reply. She thought that Sadat was aware of the Israeli landing on the west bank but had deliberately kept the fact from the Egyptians in order not to alarm them or to spoil the rosy picture he painted. Against military opposition, Premier Meir told the world that Israeli soldiers had "landed in Africa." When Sadat heard of this, he formed the opinion that it was a psychological trick designed to alarm him and did not pay a great deal of attention to the matter, nor did anyone else in authority.

The PLA warning of the "three Israeli tanks" on the west bank had been treated as an alarmist rumour, and such other information as was received at the Egyptian GHQ on the sixteenth and seventeenth merely indicated a small Israeli force of a few armoured vehicles. Reports that it had been dealt with locally were believed. As accounts of an Israeli presence persisted during these two days, small Egyptian units were pushed toward the Sharon force in a haphazard and piecemeal way— first of company strength and then of increasingly larger-sized formations, in an almost irritable manner.

On the evening of the seventeenth Moshe Dayan visited the west bank by helicopter to meet Sharon and suggested to him that he move southward in conjunction with Adan's division, which could move down the east bank. Gonen was pressing for the Missouri Ridge to be taken so as to push Egyptian artillery out of range of the Israeli bridge. Sharon wanted his other armoured brigade transferred to the west bank, but Gonen would not agree. Sharon appealed to General Bar Lev, who counter-manded Gonen's decision (perhaps an indication, if one were needed, of who was in command at Southern Command). Then Sharon suggested to Bar Lev that the plan should be changed and that, instead of his division pushing south, he should advance northward to take Ismailia. Bar Lev agreed. This meant that Adan's division would cross and move south along the west bank and that Magen's division should move parallel with it on the east bank.

About 2100 hours on the seventeenth Adan's division began moving to the west bank to concentrate on the Deversoir airfield. The crossing was difficult and dangerous. The Israeli bridge, under artillery fire all the time, was blocked for a time by a damaged tank. The tanks were floated over on the SP pontoons, the first of which was hit and sank with two tanks and their crews. By 0400 hours on the eighteenth two of Adan's brigades were on the west bank.

In the morning of the eighteenth, on the west bank, Sharon began slowly pushing the Egyptian paratroop brigade on the sand rampart northward to enlarge the precarious Israeli bridge-head in that direction. Also, some of his units attempted to move westward, but they were held at the crossroads in the village of Nefalia, where they were brought to a halt by both military action and the fact that civilians had blocked the narrow roadways. One detachment of paratroops, under Captain Asa Kadmouni had to take refuge in a large house, where it was cut off throughout the day, finally being relieved in the evening when more reinforcements arrived. (Kadmouni, who was awarded the highest Israeli decoration for his action, the Medal of Valour, in August 1975 returned his yellow-ribboned medal as a protest against the defence policy of his government.) The paratroops eventually were evacuated after the loss of eleven killed and twenty-seven wounded. During the day an Egyptian mechanised brigade was thrown against the Sharon force and cut into the area diagonally from the direction of Ismailia in an attempt to get behind what was thought to be a small Israeli armoured force.

Also on the morning of the eighteenth Adan's other armoured brigade mounted an attack from the rear on the Chinese Farm position, only to find it had been evacuated twenty-four hours beforehand. It then turned and engaged elements of the Egyptian 21st Armoured Division. That afternoon Moshe Dayan arrived at the Tasa corridor, and Herzog tells us that a brigade commander said to him, "Look at this valley of death."

The situation on the east bank was that the Egyptian armoured attacks from both the Second and Third Armies had been beaten back, the Chinese Farm position had been evacuated, and, even though the Tasa corridor was now in Israeli hands, it was subjected to periodic Egyptian shellfire. The Missouri Ridge, dangerously near the Israeli bridgehead, was still held by the Egyptians, and there was another strong 16th Infantry Division position about four miles to the north of Chinese Farm. During the day a large armoured battle took place in the hollow between these two latter positions; it involved a brigade of Magen's division and one of the 21st Armoured Division. Both sides suffered heavy casualties. There were conflicting reports of exactly how many, but over fifty destroyed tanks and SP guns, mainly Egyptian, were still lying derelict in the open sand when I walked over the battlefield some weeks later. The Egyptians claim the Israelis hastily towed away nearly twice as many as soon as the first cease-fire was observed in this area. By this time the Israelis were receiving, and using, U.S. TOWs in number. It was estimated that they had been sent some 2,000 by the eighteenth, and many more were delivered after that date.

On the west bank on the morning of the eighteenth Adan with his two armoured brigades moved out from the Deversoir airfield. One brigade went due west to a position the Israelis called Orel but failed to take it. The other brigade turned southward to run into trouble immediately at "Uri," a large feature near the northern tip of Great Bitter Lake. The first assault failed with the loss of several tanks. The brigade made a second armoured attack on Uri, and it too failed. Later a company of paratroops moved in to try to bypass the position, but they were ambushed in the undergrowth and trees by a detachment of Egyptian rangers with RPGs. At this point an Egyptian tank

Israeli soldiers standing at the Sweet Water Canal on the West Bank, October 18, 1973.

Smoke billowing from the town of Suez after an Israeli bombardment.

battalion advanced from the south against this Israeli brigade, but the Egyptian tanks bogged down in some muddy fields near the Sweet Water Canal road where the Israelis claim to have wiped them out. The armoured brigade that had failed to take Orel had become stuck at a crossroads west of Uri while another element of Adan's division, making for a crossroads east of Orcha, ran into fire from an Egyptian artillery brigade. Blocked off from the south and unable to advance, Adan sent out small parties to destroy SAMs.

The original Israeli pontoon bridge was again hit and damaged on the eighteenth by artillery fire and aircraft action, but in the evening it was repaired again. The Egyptian rangers made their third attack on the bridgehead, and the Israelis claim to have repulsed it. The rangers claim to have ambushed Israeli vehicles in the area of Abu Sultan, Sera Phaeon (Pharoaic ruins), and on the high ground near Atakia. The rangers also claim to have ambushed Israeli vehicles south of Adabiya, right at the southern end of the canal, south of Port Suez, but this incident is not mentioned by the Israelis at all, on their principle of not discussing details of Arab commando raids. During this fighting the rangers say they found the RPGs to be very effective. Meanwhile, the Israeli second bridge (a Uniflote according to the Israelis, but disputed by the Egyptians), assembled and placed on rollers and bogies, was brought forward along the Tasa corridor to reach the canal by evening, but it attracted shelling and was not put across the waterway until midnight. Herzog writes of the shelling that "in one night over 100 Israelis were killed and many hundreds wounded."

Premier Kosygin had secretly arrived in Cairo on the sixteenth and stayed there for three days. Owing to intelligence gained from Soviet satellite reconnaissance, he was much better informed on the battlefield situation than Arab ministers and senior generals. When it became obvious to him that the Egyptians did not appreciate the scope of the Israeli penetration, he had photographic evidence, together with expert interpreters, sent to him in Cairo. He pointed out to Sadat that there were at least 270 Israeli armoured vehicles in the gap on the west bank. The Israelis say there were almost twice as many by the time the Egyptian president was viewing the satellite photographs. At last the seriousness dawned on the Egyptian high command, and the following day General Shazli was again sent forward to assess the situation. By that time the Israelis probably had five brigades on the west bank: two armoured and one paratroop of the Sharon division and two armoured of the Adan division. The Israelis were using radio broadcasts to call upon the Egyptians to surrender.

According to Heikal, the Egyptians had a plan to deal with Israeli penetration on the west bank. Known as "Plan 200," it mentioned three probable crossing places, one being that near Deversoir. One may ask what went wrong. The main fault seems to have been that on the west bank no major formation was given the responsibility for covering the gap, and its defence was left to the foreign troops who were only lightly armed. Neither the Second nor the Third Army felt compelled to act upon its own initiative and rush forward to restore the situation. On the east bank, where such tasks were more clearly defined, there had been a better and more instant response, as witness the armoured counterattacks on the Tasa corridor, from both north and south, which held up the Israeli bridging for two days. The fact that the Sharon force remained hidden in the trees and bushes and did not overtly form a conventional defensive bridgehead on the canal bank as ordered, helped to deceive the Egyptians. It was not until the second Israeli bridge was seen to be across the canal early on the eighteenth that Egyptian interest was aroused and then supplemented by the Soviet satellite photographs.

On the west bank on the nineteenth one of Sharon's brigades continued to push the Egyptian paratroops northward along the sand rampart until the Israelis were within five or six miles of Ismailia, which was held by an Egyptian infantry brigade. Being so close to the southernmost Egyptian bridge of the Second Army, the paratroop commander broke down sections of the banks of the Sweet Water Canal and other irrigation canals to flood the area near the village of Toussoum and make it impassable for Israeli tanks.

Sharon's other brigade, which had so far remained on the east bank, began to cross on the nineteenth, leaving just one battalion to contain the Missouri Ridge which was still held by the Egyptians. The brigade's forward elements moved to Abu Sultan Camp, and from there they were ordered to move north and take Orcha. It was some four miles away to the west of Sera Phaeon, where an Israeli unit had been pinned down by Egyptian artillery. The Israeli brigade commander decided first to use an infantry company to eliminate a small Egyptian outpost, but it hit stubborn defences. Eventually all the Egyptian defenders were killed. One soldier, as described by Herzog, kept "leapfrogging backwards, firing as he went, fighting until he was killed at the summit of the hill." Extra units were brought against the main Orcha position and heavy fighting, including some hand-to-hand combat in trenches, continued until darkness fell. The fall of the Orcha position caused the collapse of this Egyptian defence line, enabling more Israeli troops to get onto the sand rampart. From there they were able to fire across the canal to support their own troops facing the Missouri Ridge. The Israelis claim that the next day they counted over 300 Egyptian dead for sixteen of their own soldiers killed.

Gaps in the Egyptian Air Defence Barrier enabled the Israeli air force to give close ground support which allowed Adan's division to complete its concentration at Deversoir airfield and to occupy another airstrip to its north. Then one of Adan's brigades moved slowly westward through scattered Egyptian, Palestinian, and Kuwait troops toward the Genifa Hills where it clashed with an Egyptian armoured unit at Mitznefet. A brigade of Magen's division began moving to the west bank, passing westward through Adan's division to reach a point claimed to be seventeen miles from the canal. Conversely, an Egyptian armoured brigade from the 6th Mechanised Division moved from the east to the west bank. During the day the Israeli bridges came under frequent attack and both were put out of action by noon. When darkness fell they were repaired, and during the night a footbridge was also erected across the canal, mainly as a decoy.

On the nineteenth Moshe Dayan was again on the west bank to visit General Sharon. While there he had a narrow escape.

Four Egyptian helicopters flew low and dropped napalm, aiming for the small Bailey-type bridges across the Sweet Water Canal and other irrigation canals. None hit their targets on this occasion, but they did disrupt the nearby Sharon HQ. The helicopters were brought down by ground fire and Herzog claims one was shot down by an antitank gun.

The invested Kabrit Fort, held by elements of the 25th Independent Armoured Brigade and an infantry unit, was attacked unsuccessfully by an Israeli force for the first time on the nineteenth. From that date it was subjected to frequent assaults and continuous pressure from the Israelis from the land side.

On the nineteenth the Israelis allowed press representatives to visit the east bank in the area of the bridgehead. They reported that the Tasa corridor was still under occasional Egyptian artillery fire and that the roadway itself was littered with burnt-out tanks and vehicles, including a battery of six Israeli SP guns and many civilian-impressed ammunition trucks. One correspondent, Gerald Seymour, reported that he saw three Israeli bridges across the canal and that a MiG aircraft attacked the middle one with rocket and cannon fire, only to be shot down by a Mirage that swooped on it. He saw many dead bodies floating on the canal, a wrecked Egyptian tank on the west bank, SAM sites on the east bank destroyed by U.S. laser bombs, and also several realistic wooden dummies of SAMs and guns. The Israelis complained that the U.S. equipment, which formed their "main bridge" (presumably the pontoon one), was cumbersome and unwieldy. The Israelis also claim that the gap on the west bank was twelve miles wide, but the journalists could see only a scant presence on that side of the canal.

General Shazli, who had been given the task of containing the Israeli penetration on the sixteenth, must have been primarily engaged with it, although not very successfully, for the following three days, but there is a veil of silence over what he actually did. Neither General Ismail nor General Shazli would talk to me about this period. It is known the two men differed as to what course should be taken. Shazli recommended that some armour, presumably three of four brigades of the strategic reserve, which had been pushed over to the east bank on the twelfth and thirteenth, be withdrawn to the west bank and used to encircle and crush the Israeli penetration. If this were not done, Shazli declared, the Third Army was in danger of being encircled. Shazli was overruled by Ismail, who said that to move any forces westward would be bad for morale, and in this he was backed by President Sadat. Obviously, both Sadat and Ismail were expecting an early cease-fire, and, in the meantime, they hoped to be able to prevent the Israelis taking any more Egyptian-held territory.

On the nineteenth Shazli was again sent forward to assess the situation and to report back to "Number Ten." He returned late that evening. President Sadat continues the story in the *Al Hawadess* interview by saying that "on the nineteenth the war minister, General Ahmed Ismail, called me just after midnight. I went to the command headquarters to find General Shazli collapsed. He was saying the war was over, a disaster had struck and that we had to withdraw entirely from the Sinai. I studied the situation and found that the Israeli thrust was not frightening . . . but I was afraid Shazli's despair might demoralise other commanders in the operations room, which was Israel's main purpose of the operation. So I relieved General Shazli and appointed Lieutenant General Abdel Ghani Gamasy in his place."

This dismissal was not made public, but Shazli quickly and quietly disappeared from the scene. All reports of his alleged activities in the following days, such as leading the 21st Armoured Division in desperate counterattacks, are foggy mythology. General Ismail refused to discuss the incident with me, saying it "affected Shazli's good name." In the same interview, when asked why he later appointed General Shazli an ambassador, President Sadat replied, "The man had crossed the canal and stormed the Bar Lev Line. I shall never forget that foreign correspondents wrote that traffic on the front was better than traffic in Cairo. This was Shazli's achievement and the collapse he suffered later was only human."

During the twentieth the Israeli bridges were damaged but repaired again at night. The traffic across them was not heavy, being mainly vehicles carrying ammunition, fuel, and supplies. Israeli aircraft were operating even more extensively over the gap in a widening arc as SAMs were eliminated. Attention was also given to trying to knock out the Egyptian bridges, but the most damage was done to them by the Israeli long-range 155mm guns situated some fifteen miles to the east. By this time exhaustion was setting in along the fronts on the east bank where the Israelis and Egyptians faced each other at distances between 1,000 and 3,000 yards. Magen's division, in the north, was pressed against the Second Army. In the south, in the area of the Mitla Pass where the ground was less favourable to armoured warfare because of its stony nature and undulations, Tal's division crept closer to the Third Army. On the west bank one Israeli brigade moved to the area of Jebel Um Katif, where it remained facing Egyptian armour for the next three days while elements of the Egyptian 4th Armoured Division had moved up to try to block Adan's advance southward.

It was only on the twentieth, after President Sadat had visited "Number Ten" and relieved Shazli of his appointment, that General Ismail and the general staff took the Israeli penetration of the west bank seriously. They began to move formations to contain it, but it was too late. The Egyptians were neither prepared nor ready for mobile warfare. There was speculation as to what course the Israelis would take, and some Egyptian commanders thought the intention was to make an amphibious crossing of Lake Timsah to bypass Ismailia. Sadat was of the opinion that the Israelis would try to land on the west coast of the Gulf of Suez.

On the twentieth Sharon wanted to move northward to encircle the Second Army, but Gonen would not allow this. Gonen then accused Sharon of disobeying orders and moving westward from the bridgehead. In fact, Sharon did move in that direction for up to 25 miles before turning northward but he never seriously attacked the Second Army positions. Sharon replied that he was "simply carrying out orders" and boasted that he could have engaged the Second Army "as planned" and encircled it if Gonen had not hesitated for so long in sending reinforcements over the bridges.

It was on the twentieth that General Gonen ordered Sharon, who still had one armoured unit on the east bank, to attack and eliminate the Missouri Ridge position. Sharon ignored the order and began moving southward, allegedly saying that the operation "was not necessary." Gonen wanted to immediately remove Sharon from his command and ordered him to remain where he was, but Sharon went over Gonen's head, and appealed directly to Dayan who countermanded the order. Sharon and Dayan were reputed to have had frequent conversations with each other over the radiotelephone link, bypassing Gonen, who was alleged to have had them monitored.

On the twenty-first one of Sharon's brigades was held on the outskirts of Ismailia by Egyptian paratroops and rangers, and in the morning Israeli soldiers on the sand rampart looked northward and saw Egyptian troops moving to the west bank in the area south of Lake Timsah. This caused Sharon to press again to be allowed to make a wide flanking movement behind the Second Army to contain it. However, Gonen wanted Missouri Ridge taken and ordered Sharon to transfer one of his brigades to the east bank for that purpose.

The attack on Missouri Ridge was begun at 1500 hours by Sharon's unit that had remained on the east bank, but the attack soon petered out, and only about one-third of the ridge was occupied by the Israelis. Gonen heard the operation was not going well, and, when Gonen's deputy tried to contact Sharon, he was told that Sharon "was too busy." In the evening General Gonen again ordered Sharon to attack the Missouri Ridge, but there appeared to be communication problems between the two commanders, whether deliberate or not is uncertain. Sharon replied that he did not have sufficient force to undertake the operation. General Bar Lev then came into the picture and spoke to Sharon, ordering him to move a brigade to the east bank and carry out the attack. Sharon had transferred only five of his tanks to the east bank when, some fifteen minutes later, General Tal transmitted an order from Dayan to Gonen calling off the attack on Missouri Ridge; Sharon had just spoken to Dayan.

On the west bank on the twenty-first a brigade of Magen's moved southwestward on paths through the hills and dunes. By dusk it had reached within range of the Cairo-Suez road, which caused the Israelis to claim prematurely that the Third Army was cut off. The same day Sharon tried to infiltrate the agricultural belt with only moderate success. His men did manage to put several SAMs and ZSUs out of action by hitting their radar antennas with shellfire. In the morning there was a twenty-plane Egyptian raid on the Israeli bridges which succeeded in breaking the main bridge and sinking several pontoons while six tanks were in the act of crossing. Tanks and crews sank to the bottom of the canal. The guns of the Egyptian Third Army then switched their fire to the Israeli bridgehead. The Israelis had a high regard for the capabilities of Egyptian gunners who now daily shelled their bridges and ground concentrations.

By this time the Israeli air force was active against the Egyptian SAMs and radar. This caused General Ismail to withdraw much of this equipment to prevent its being damaged or captured, which accordingly widened the gap in the Air Defence Barrier. Israeli aircraft were thus able to operate to give both overhead cover and ground support to Israeli troops on the west bank—two immense advantages. It meant in effect that the Air Defence Barrier over the Third Army was removed, and its vehicles began to move with some 300 yards between them, instead of 50 yards, as previously.

The Israelis claim that by the end of the twenty-first they had destroyed 850 Egyptian tanks in all, of which 60 had been accounted for that day, and that the bridgehead was twenty-five miles wide and twenty miles deep. The latter was a rather over-optimistic statement perhaps. Egyptian and Israeli views as to its precise size conflict sharply.

During the day the Israelis allege that Katushya rockets were fired from the U.S. freighter *African Glen,* one of the ships marooned in Great Bitter Lake since the 1967 War. Israeli aircraft appeared and attacked the ship with bombs and rockets, causing it to sink and the skeleton crew to abandon it.

On the twenty-second Sharon became piqued because Adan had been given the task of exploiting southward. He alleged that Adan had been chosen in preference to himself for "political reasons." Sharon moved northward again but ran into heavy resistance and lost many men. He was held along the Sweet Water Canal by Egyptian rangers, who foiled his attempt to get behind Ismailia. One of his battalions quickly lost three tanks in the sewerage farm area. Israeli political feelings certainly obtruded into this war, and Sharon was reported at times to have encouraged his men with the words, "The secretary of the Likud party is here with you." In the afternoon the Egyptian rangers launched an attack on Sharon's division and pushed some of his forward troops back to the Sweet Water Canal.

In the morning Dayan visited Adan on the west bank to urge him to make for the Lituf fort, at the southern end of Little Bitter Lake, giving him a target of "twenty kilometres for the day's advance." Adan's three armoured brigades fanned out, one moving through the Genifa Hills, another along a parallel road south of them, while the third moved toward Mina. The Israelis now had the freedom of the skies, and on the ground their small patrols probed forward everywhere, avoiding the main roadways and Egyptian positions. One Israeli press report stated that the Egyptians used Yak trainers over Adan's divisional area and that a witness saw "five of the nine shot down" in one raid.

One Israeli officer in Adan's division told me that the Egyptian armour seemed to have been withdrawn westward onto the higher ground of Jebel Shabrawat, the massif to the southwest of Fayid, where he could see tanks manoeuvring, but they did not fire at the Israelis moving southward. This officer told me the Israelis did not think much of the capabilities of Egyptian tank crews, who, it was said, had to get too close to their targets before they opened fire. Perhaps it was the Israeli armoured superiority complex showing through.

In the afternoon Adan's three brigades were ordered to break through to the canal, but they were held along a line of military camps and installations. By nightfall Adan's HQ reached a point just south of Fayid on Great Bitter Lake. One of his forward detachments got through to the tip of the sand rampart at the southern end of Little Bitter Lake, only to be knocked back again during the night, losing nine tanks. At one stage Adan's tanks were intermixed with the Egyptians', and at times he was harassed by the Egyptian air force. Egyptian positions were bypassed where possible; one at the southeast corner of the Deversoir airfield held out until 17 March 1974. On the twenty-second another of Magen's armoured brigades passed across to the west bank, as conversely did one of the Egyptian 19th Infantry Division in the south.

In the north the garrison of Port Said fought its own defensive battle against the Israelis. It was successfully reinforced by a 900-strong Tunisian unit that had been flown to Egypt in Algerian aircraft. The Tunisian soldiers entered Port Said on the eighteenth by the Damietta road, the causeway road to the south having been severed by Israeli bombing.

The cease-fire came into effect on both the Egyptian and Syrian fronts at 1852 hours. One Egyptian officer told me that when the news came through on the transistor sets the Israelis on the west bank all cheered and fired their rifles into the air like desert Arabs, so glad were they that the war was finishing— or so they thought. Although conversely both the Arabs and the Israelis were unhappy about the timing of the cease-fire, the Arabs generally respected it.

That evening a press conference was given by the Egyptian military spokesman, Major General Izz ad-Din Mukhtar. He claimed the Israelis had lost 600 tanks, 400 armoured vehicles, 25 helicopters, 303 aircraft, and 23 ships. At 1800 hours the same day the Israelis also held a press conference in which Major General Shlomo Gazit claimed the Israelis held about "1,200 square kilometres" of the west bank and "600 square kilometres" of Syrian territory. He further stated that Egypt had lost 240 planes and 1,000 tanks, and Syria had lost 212 aircraft and 1,000 tanks.

The ranger battalion that had been in the Sudar Pass area since the sixth had denied that route to the Israelis, blocking an armoured flanking threat to the Egyptian Third Army. On the twenty-second the rangers moved back into the Third Army perimeter. In the Mitla Pass area the Israeli division commanded by General Tal remained 8,000 to 10,000 yards from the Egyptian army while the Egyptian-held Kabrit Fort still held out against the Israelis investing it.

I later asked General Ismail whether he had considered that the Israelis might make a penetration of the west bank, and he replied that he had earmarked a brigade (presumably the 182nd

Paratroop Brigade) to deal with any such attempt. He further said that the fault was that of the local commander, who had attacked piecemeal, first thinking it was merely a tiny reconnaissance force. He also added that "information was interrupted due to a change of responsibilities which we had made in some commands in the emergency situation," referring no doubt to General Maamun's heart attack. Later the Israeli chief of staff, General Elazar, in an interview in *The New Yorker* of 11 February 1974 said, "The crossing came neither too early nor too late. Had it taken place earlier, the Egyptian armoured reserves would have still been on the western bank, constituting a threat to the Israeli forces once they crossed."

12

THE RUPTURED
CEASE-FIRES

> *Most of the material that we are furnishing Israel*
> *is being drawn from Department of Defense*
> *stocks and in some cases from the inventories*
> *of active and reserve units.*

> William P. Clements,
> U.S. deputy secretary of defense

Premier Kosygin had one meeting with President Sadat in
Cairo on the sixteenth, two on the seventeenth, and another
two on the eighteenth, and he realised that the Egyptian position had worsened considerably after the fourteenth. On the
seventeenth Kosygin produced satellite evidence of the extent
of the Israeli penetration of the west bank, but, despite this,
Sadat and his advisers were anxious to continue the war unless
it could be terminated by the withdrawal of all Israelis from the
occupied territories. By this time the Soviet Union and the
United States were anxious to stop the war for their own diverse
reasons and on their own conditions. They persuaded Sadat,
who admitted he had only wanted to break the No Peace No
War stalemate, to agree to a cease-fire.

On the eighteenth Anatoly Dobrynin, Soviet ambassador to
the United States, met Secretary Kissinger and suggested a cease-

fire with the condition that Israeli troops withdraw to their 1967 boundaries. Kissinger would not agree. He saw that the Israeli military forces were doing well and did not yet want them halted. On the nineteenth Kosygin had returned to Moscow and reported the results of his Middle East visit. There was an emergency Politburo meeting at which it was decided that something must be done immediately to prevent an Arab defeat. The "hot line" from Moscow to Washington, actually a teleprinter machine, was used for the first time in this war when First Secretary Brezhnev spoke to President Nixon, asking urgently that Kissinger come to Moscow for consultations. Nixon agreed. The next day, after General Shazli's collapse, President Sadat at last realised the full seriousness of the Egyptian position, and he too urged the Soviet Union to press for an immediate cease-fire.

On the twentieth, the day Saudi Arabia banned all oil exports to the United States, Kissinger, accompanied by Assistant Secretary of State Joseph Sisco, and Dobrynin, the Soviet ambassador to the United States, arrived in Moscow, where Kissinger had talks lasting for two days with both Brezhnev and Gromyko. Moscow wanted a quick cease-fire, and, while the United States wanted it to be linked to mediation between Arabs and Israelis, the Soviet government wanted it to be conditional on Israeli withdrawal from most of the occupied territories. Kissinger agreed to the first but demurred on the second, saying there should be "a minimum of conditions." The Soviet Union wanted both Soviet and American troops to police the cease-fire, but Kissinger, having no desire to see Soviet soldiers openly in the Middle East, wanted this done by a U.N. force. Kissinger was later to say to a group of American Jewish intellectuals, as reported in the *New York Times* of 26 October 1973, that he gave the Israelis an extra four days' fighting time by delaying the conclusion of the Israeli-Egyptian cease-fire.

A compromise was reached and it was agreed by both superpowers that there should be an immediate cease-fire and that it was Kissinger's job to persuade the Israelis to accept it. On the evening of the twenty-first a stormy Israeli cabinet was still in session. At 0200 hours on the twenty-second Premier Meir re-

ceived an urgent message requesting the acceptance of an immediate cease-fire, as the proposal was to be put to the United
Nations that day. The Israeli cabinet, which wanted "secure
boundaries and a negotiated settlement," agreed with great reluctance but requested that Kissinger come to Israel to discuss
the matter, which he did on his way back from Moscow to
America.

On the twenty-first Saudi Arabia had announced an oil cutback of 10 percent on supplies to the West and a complete embargo on oil to the United States and Holland. This was perhaps
the final bombshell that caused President Nixon to put pressure
on the Israeli government to accept an immediate cease-fire.
The following day, when Saudi Arabia announced a 20 percent
cutback of oil to the West, both the United States and the
Soviet Union openly called for a Middle East cease-fire, and the
Security Council approved Resolution 338. This called for the
cease-fire to come into effect no later than twelve hours after
the moment of adoption (which was 0852 hours local time) and
for all parties concerned to immediately implement Resolution
242 in all its parts. U.N. Resolution 338 was accepted by Egypt,
Jordan, and Israel; while not a party to Resolution 242, Syria
also reluctantly accepted it provisionally.

On the twentieth President Sadat had told President Assad of
Syria that he was going to accept the cease-fire because "he
could not fight the U.S. army" and had no intention of risking
a repetition of the destruction of the Egyptian armed forces as
in 1967. Sadat was under the impression that the Soviet Union,
the United States, and the United Nations would jointly guaran-
tee an Israeli withdrawal from the occupied territories and the
convening of a peace conference to settle the Middle East problem once and for all. Later, at a press conference on the thirty-
first, Sadat admitted his armed forces were reluctant to stop
fighting.

President Assad said on the twenty-ninth that he had not
been consulted about Egypt's acceptance of the cease-fire, but
on the twentieth the Soviet ambassador to Syria had told Assad
that in the future he would be supplied only with ammunition
and that no more heavy weapons would be sent owing to the

risk of their capture by the Israelis. Once Egypt agreed to accept the cease-fire, the ambassador told Assad, he would receive no further military supplies unless Syria too accepted it. He further threatened to withdraw the Soviet technicians working with the Air Defence Barrier. Assad was forced to agree to the cease-fire.

On the evening of the twenty-second ground movement ceased on the Golan front, and the countdown for the large combined operation about to start, involving Syrian, Iraqi, and Jordanian formations, stopped. However, shelling and aerial activity continued fitfully, and the following day the Syrian "82-day War of Attrition" began and continued with almost daily incidents.

The Iraqi government refused to accept Resolution 338, and Iraqi troops left Syria on the twenty-seventh, despite protests from the Syrian government. They refused to leave their tanks behind for the Syrians even though the Soviet government promised to provide replacements for them later. The Iraqis also criticised the Syrian conduct of the war. The two Jordanian brigades remained in Syria a few weeks longer, but all had left by 3 January 1974. Emergency restrictions in Jordan were relaxed on 25 October. On the twenty-ninth the Lebanese government asked the Palestinians not to launch any more attacks on Israel from the Lebanon.

Early in November 1973 Soviet technicians, variously reported as eventually numbering over 3,000 in all, began arriving in Syria to repair weapons and equipment. On 31 March 1974 Moshe Dayan, speaking in Washington, alleged that there was a brigade of Cubans in Syria with 110 tanks, as well as some North Koreans and other troops of an "Arab foreign legion." The Syrian disengagement agreement was not signed until June 1974, reputedly being delayed over the question of repatriation of Israeli prisoners who were alleged to have been subjected to a truth drug.

While the Egyptians seemed determined to honour the cease-fire (for example, the Cairo International Airport was briefly opened again), the Israelis, on the contrary, rushed troops across their three bridges throughout the night of the twenty-second/twenty-third. It seemed they had no intention of observing the cease-fire but were set upon exploiting their position on the west bank. Adan's division was ordered to move quickly south to take Suez while Magen's division was ordered to continue to block the Cairo-Suez road. On the twenty-third Adan tried to force his way forward from the airfield at Fayid. He managed only to reach the area of Genifa, at the southern end of Little Bitter Lake, where part of his force was held for two days. Adan then turned westward into the high ground and pushed through camel tracks to make a detour which brought him to the northern outskirts of Suez by about 1700 hours. His leading company made a weak attack, which was held, and so the Israeli first attempt to enter Suez was baulked.

To the west Magen's division was also moving along camel tracks in the area of undulating ground between Jebel Genifa and Jebel Shabrawat, making for the Cairo-Suez road, a somewhat shorter distance. The Israelis claim that Magen reached the road near kilometre 101 (about sixty-three miles from Cairo) on the evening of the twenty-third, and that he left a small group of tanks near that point; they admit that his division was reduced to only fifty tanks. The Egyptians do not agree and insist Magen did not reach that road until the following day. The area of the Jebels consists of stony ground generally unsuitable for armoured movement, so the Egyptian armour lay in a defile to their west, using indirect fire from their guns against the Israelis. In the Jebels themselves Egyptian infantry used short-range anti-tank weapons.

In the north Sharon was ordered to push northwestward to try to get behind Ismailia and to cut the Ismailia-Cairo road. He was unsuccessful, not being able to break through the close country. The Egyptians claim that at night the Israeli tanks and vehicles clustered together in villages and abandoned barrack areas, keeping their engines running all the time. The Israelis made no night moves and seemingly did not carry out any night patrolling either.

On the twenty-third U.N. Resolution 339 was approved by a fourteen-to-zero vote in the Security Council. It authorised the establishment of a U.N. peace-keeping force, which was to exclude both American and Soviet troops, and demanded the implementation of the cease-fire. The fact that the Israelis broke the cease-fire and went on to encircle the Egyptian Third Army led the Soviet Union to think the United States had deliberately outwitted it. They accused the U.S. government of "allowing Israel to violate the cease-fire on the twenty-second and make territorial gains." But Kissinger was also dismayed when he heard of the breach, and he contacted Premier Meir to urge an instant stop to the fighting, only to receive an evasive answer. The second cease-fire was due to come into effect at 0700 hours on the twenty-fourth, although the United Nations had asked for it to become effective at 0510 hours, which was daybreak.

On the twenty-fourth Magen's division, now on the Cairo-Suez road, began pushing westward but was held at kilometre 101, and so a part of it commenced moving eastward to try to cut off the Third Army. Suez was held by elements of the 19th Infantry Division, and in the morning Adan asked permission to attack that city again. He was told by General Gonen that "if it is to be a Benghazi, yes; but if it is to be a Stalingrad, no."

Adan chose to attack, using a tank unit and a paratroop battalion. They openly advanced along the wide main boulevard into the city, only to be fired upon suddenly from the buildings on either side of the roadway. One Egyptian officer who was there told me that "within twenty minutes twenty of the twenty-four Israeli tank commanders of the column, who were exposed in their turrets, were killed or wounded." The Israelis had not expected such stiff resistance, but, although surprised, the tanks still charged forward, mostly to take cover behind buildings.

Following in half-tracks, the paratroops also suffered casualties, but, dismounting rapidly, they took cover. Eventually, such Israeli tanks as were able withdrew from the city, but two groups of paratroops, cut off in the centre of the city, held out during the day. When darkness fell most of them managed to escape to their own lines. The Israelis admit to suffering eighty casualties in this abortive battle and to losing eleven tanks, seventeen armoured personnel carriers, and some trucks. The Egyptians say the Israelis left sixteen tanks and fourteen trucks behind in the city. Having failed to occupy the centre of Suez, the Israelis now began to surround it while elements of Magen's division approached toward Adabiya, an oil terminal on the south side

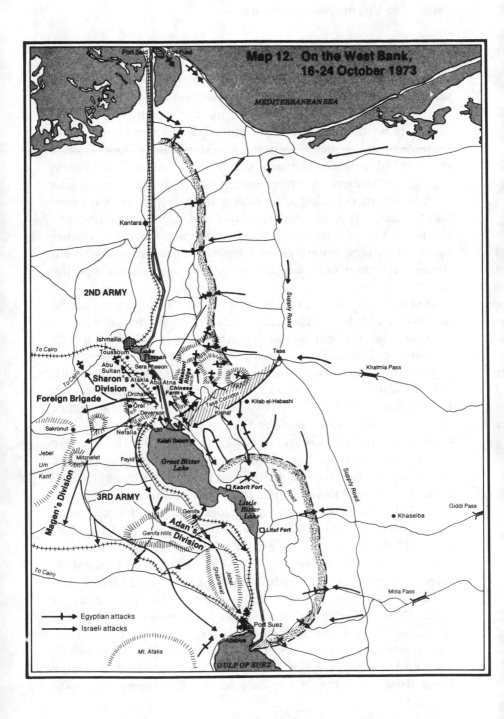

Map 12. On the West Bank,
16-24 October 1973

MEDITERRANEAN SEA

Port Said
Port Fuad

Kantara

2ND ARMY

Supply Road

To Cairo

Ishmailia
Toussoum
Lake Timsah
Abu Sultan
Sera Phaeon
Sharon's Division
Atakia
Abu Atna
Chinese Farm
Foreign Brigade
Orchard
Orel
Deversoir
Um
Nefalia
Sakronut
Kalah Salem
Mitznefet
Fayid
Great Bitter Lake
3RD ARMY
Jebel Um Katif
Genifa
Adan's Division
Genifa Hills
To Cairo

Magen's Division

Tasa

Khatmia Pass

Missuri Ridge
Tasa Corridor
Kitab el-Habashi
Kishaf

Supply Road

Artillery Road

Kabrit Fort
Little Bitter Lake
Lituf Fort

Giddi Pass
Khaseiba

Jebel Shabrawa

Mitla Pass

Port Suez
Adabiya
Mt. Ataka

GULF OF SUEZ

Egyptian attacks
Israeli attacks

of the bay, about eight miles from Suez.

On the east bank on the twenty-fourth General Tal's division encircled the Egyptian Third Army and also more tightly invested Kabrit Fort, which was physically separated from it. The Cairo-Suez road was now blocked by the Israelis, who would not even let through the International Red Cross (IRC) representatives and vehicles carrying blood plasma. Their aircraft commenced dropping thousands of leaflets on the Third Army, urging the soldiers to either surrender or desert. The Israelis were now concentrating upon taking as many prisoners as possible; the majority were administrative and logistic personnel left behind in the withdrawal of the Air Defence Barrier and other units. Also, U.N. observers were brought forward to try to enforce the second cease-fire but were not allowed through the Israeli roadblock.

On the twenty-fourth President Sadat sent a message to Brezhnev asking him to send a special force to help the Third Army. Brezhnev in turn got in touch with President Nixon through Ambassador Dobrynin and Kissinger, suggesting the employment of an "American-Soviet force" as a "unilateral institution of suitable measure." Nixon rejected this suggestion as he had no wish to have Soviet soldiers in the Middle East. In return, as Brezhnev was not prepared to let the Third Army be defeated or be forced to surrender, he sent his "tough note" to Nixon which said, "We strongly urge that we both send forces to enforce the cease-fire and, if you do not, we may be obliged to consider acting alone." Kissinger received this note at 2240 hours Washington time.

At 2300 hours Kissinger and Schlesinger, the defense secretary, agreed to put the U.S. forces worldwide on "Defense Condition 3" (in the jargon "DEFCON 3", more generally known as "Red Alert." There are five U.S. "defense conditions." U.S. forces are normally at "two." The last time DEFCON 3 was declared was after the assassination of President Kennedy in 1963. During the Cuban missile crisis the defense condition was raised to "five.") The order was passed on to the U.S. service chiefs and came into effect at 0230 hours on the twenty-fifth. The NATO allies had not been consulted, and at 0100 hours Great Britain was the first to be told. At 0200 hours the NATO council in Brussels was informed. At 0230 hours Kissinger replied to the Brezhnev note, saying that the United States would not tolerate unilateral movement of troops into the war zone and called for joint action through the United Nations. At 0300 hours Kissinger told President Nixon what had happened, and the president formalised his secretary of state's action.

The general reaction to this red alert was either that President Nixon had overreacted to the Russian tough note or that it was a deliberate diversion to take attention away from his domestic difficulties, which included the Watergate affair. At that time the U.S. intelligence agencies were of the opinion that the Soviet Union had sent nuclear warheads to Egypt during this war. Kalb states that the nuclear material reached Port Said on the morning of the twenty-fifth, immediately following the U.S. DEFCON 3 announcement. Electronic surveillance and other intelligence sources had indicated on the twenty-fourth that seven of the twelve Soviet airborne divisions in East Germany and Poland, some 42,000 men, had been put on a state of alert, that transport aircraft of the Soviet air lift to Syria and Egypt had been diverted toward them, and that Soviet ships with helicopters and landing craft were sailing near the Egyptian coast. However, Defense Secretary Schlesinger, quoted in the *New York Times* of 27 October 1973, stated that the Soviet airborne troops were placed on alert some five or six days before the U.S. DEFCON 3 alert.

On the morning of the twenty-fifth there was to have been a cease-fire at 0700 hours, but at 0650 hours, as U.N. observers approached an Israeli tank battalion standing near Adabiya, south of Suez, instead of waiting to meet them, the Israeli tanks suddenly raced forward and entered Adabiya. The Egyptians claim this was an unfair trick. About a hundred Egyptian servicemen collected on a rocky protrusion just south of Adabiya, where they held out against the Israelis until the thirty-first but were not allowed by the U.N. observers to hoist their own national flag.

On the twenty-fifth the Israelis made their third attack on Suez at about 0800 hours. This time they used one of their Soviet squadrons of some fifteen Tiran tanks supported by infantry in civilian-impressed trucks. Although the fighting continued until about 1550 hours, the Israelis could not break through into the centre of the city and had to withdraw with the loss of ten tanks. The fighting in this area died down about 1700 hours when four U.N. observers came on the scene. Later an Israeli spokesman gave the Israeli casualties for the battle for Suez as being 68 officers, 23 pilots, 373 soldiers, and one civilian killed. Port Suez, formerly a city of some 200,000, was now partitioned down the main street; the Egyptians held the centre of the city while the Israelis controlled the outskirts, the port installations, and the oil refinery, thus hemming in the Egyptians. The Egyptians admit that by this time the road was blocked at kilometre 101 where the Israelis again stopped an IRC convoy but did allow the blood plasma through. The Egyptian Third Army of some 20,000 men and some 250 tanks was surrounded. The tanks were integral ones to the two infantry divisions. The armoured formations except that at Kabrit Fort, together with one infantry brigade, had been withdrawn westward.

The Israelis claim that on the twenty-sixth, the day that marked the end of Ramadan, they had completely encircled the Third Army, scattered leaflets over it, and called on it to surrender. On the other hand, the Egyptians claim that their "army, local militia, and civilians" were "besieging [the] Israeli pocket" on the west bank. Certainly civilians were blocking roads and tracks with vehicles and obstacles and preventing Sharon from reaching the Ismailia-Cairo road to the west of Ismailia. On the canal side, after flooding certain areas adjacent to the sand rampart, Egyptian rangers regained a pyramid while paratroops pushed Sharon's men backward along the sand rampart. During the day there was considerable Israeli aerial activity over the Egyptian forces in this sector, but the northern part of the Suez Canal area, that of the Second Army, remained quieter, the cease-fire being generally observed by both sides.

To prevent the Israelis expanding northward and westward General Ismail ordered forward the reserves of the Second Army; he told me he also committed a part of the "general command reserve," that is, the First Army. Herzog, however, claims that 80 percent of the Egyptian army was on the Suez Canal front.

The Egyptian infantry had taken up positions on a secondary defensive line on the high ground west of the canal, some 5,000 yards away from the Sweet Water Canal. The Third Army made several unsuccessful attempts to improve its position by trying to take possession of the damaged pontoon bridges south of Little Bitter Lake, which had been made inoperative by Israeli ground fire, and to erect another one near Suez. The Israelis claim to have taken a few prisoners from the Third Army and also a few deserters.

In Washington on the twenty-sixth Ambassador Dobrynin met Kissinger and asked for a lessening of tension. Dobrynin was under the impression that the fate of the Third Army rested in American hands and that the Americans had been in collusion with the Israelis to break the cease-fire. Slightly alarmed because of the existence of the red alert, Kissinger made telephone contact with Premier Meir and demanded that the Israelis allow supplies through to the Third Army.

The next day the Soviet Union again demanded that the United States put pressure on the Israelis to observe the cease-fire, and the guns almost fell silent on both sides in this sector for the first time since the war began. But the Egyptians claim that for the fourth day running the Israelis had prevented IRC supplies reaching the Third Army. The Israelis' almost total dependence had enabled the United States to exert some pressure on them, and there was a hurried meeting at kilometre 101 between Israeli and Egyptian military representatives. On the twenty-seventh the Israelis began building a bridge across the canal just north of Great Bitter Lake, exactly twenty-seven kilometres south of Ismailia. It was constructed of huge, rectangular blocks of stone, with pipes inserted to allow the tidal canal water to flow through them. The blocks of stone were later recovered by the Egyptians and made into a pyramidlike monument on the west bank at the exact spot where the bridge had been. It had a small boat perched on the top and overlooked the Chinese Farm and Missouri Ridge positions in the middle distance.

Egyptian ranger groups began returning from their forays into the Sinai, and six such groups came back between the twenty-second and the twenty-seventh to be personally met and congratulated by General Ismail. Egyptian rangers claimed many successes during the war including taking a Port Tewfik fort, clearing Kantara East, ambushing all roads into the Sinai, causing the Israelis to assign a brigade to Southern Sinai, taking the first Israeli prisoner (and the last two as well), killing over a thousand Israelis and capturing sixty, and destroying over a hundred Israeli armoured vehicles. Some ranger groups returned from the Sinai as long as ten months after the war ended.

On the twenty-eighth, despite the second cease-fire and the comparative lull the previous day, the Israelis made their fourth, and last, attack on Suez. Starting at 0600 hours, it lasted for only an hour and was also unsuccessful. At the same time they tried to push southward to outflank the small Egyptian Adabiya pocket but were halted by Egyptian frontier troops and a detachment of Sudanese that had just arrived there. U.N. observers, most of whom from the twenty-fifth onward had been prevented by the Israelis from reaching the battle area, now began to arrive and were in position by 1230 hours. Shelling had caused the Israelis to postpone handing over some Arab prisoners to the U.N. detachment, a 200-strong company of Swedish soldiers that had just entered Suez, but by this time it had died down.

The U.S. government persuaded the Israeli Cabinet to allow supplies through to the Third Army, but the Israelis would not agree to any other concessions until a list of Israeli prisoners was produced. Herzog in *The War of Attrition* writes that "I understand Kissinger had said, 'If you don't do it, there will be nothing to stop the Russians taking supplies through.'" In a speech made on 19 December 1973 Dayan confirmed that "the United States threatened to supply the encircled Egyptian Third Army if Israel continued the siege." A supply convoy under U.N. supervision, said by the Israelis to consist of 100 trucks and by the Egyptians to consist of only 25 vehicles, was allowed through the Israeli checkpoint. The supplies were then loaded onto rafts to be floated across to the east bank. All the Egyptian bridges by this time had been put out of action by Israeli artillery fire and bombing.

During the period from the twenty-fifth to the twenty-eighth

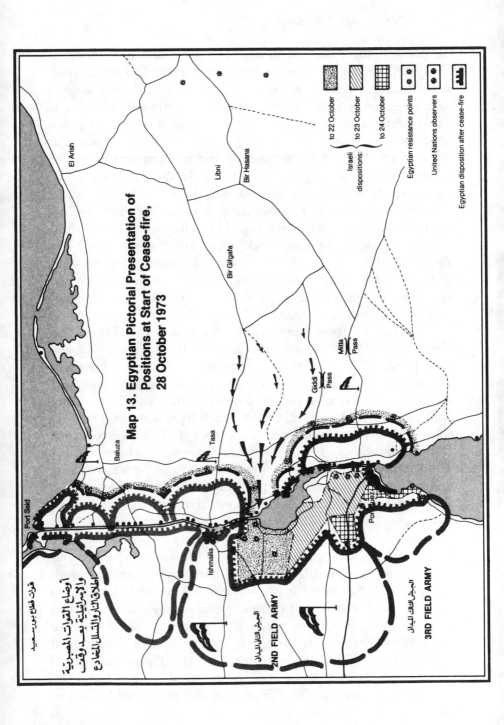

Map 13. Egyptian Pictorial Presentation of Positions at Start of Cease-fire, 28 October 1973

Israeli dispositions:
to 22 October
to 23 October
to 24 October

Egyptian resistance points
United Nations observers
Egyptian disposition after cease-fire

Port Said

El Arish

Baluza

Libni

Bir Hasana

Bir Gifgafa

Tasa

Giddi Pass

Mitla Pass

Ishmailia

Port Suez

2ND FIELD ARMY

3RD FIELD ARMY

قوات قطاع بورسعيد

أوضاع القوات المصرية والإسرائيلية بـوقـف إطلاق النار والانتشار بعده

الجيش الثاني الميدان

الجيش الثالث الميدان

on the west bank the Israelis attacked the many small pockets of Egyptian troops within the area they claimed to hold. Some were overrun, while in other instances Egyptian soldiers managed to escape into Suez, and yet others continued to hold out. The Egyptians say that on the twenty-eighth the Israeli brigades were well extended along a seventy-five kilometre front in a thin screen. They claim the Israelis did not physically occupy all the terrain they encompassed but only the dominating features, which enabled the Egyptians to pinpoint their positions and forced the Israelis to move daily to avoid Egyptian shelling. Egyptian rangers and other troops in small sections were in and among the Israelis, passing back information about them. The Egyptians claim the Israeli pocket was surrounded by three tank and two mechanised divisions, but these formations were not immediately available to close in battle because of slow Egyptian reaction and movement.

Regarding territory taken or lost on the Suez Canal front, the Israelis claimed they had gained about 500 square miles on the west bank, although they admitted there were many Egyptian pockets within that area. The Egyptians had gained and held about 300 square miles on the east bank, but their Third Army was surrounded. However, at the Israeli Symposium on the October War held in Jerusalem in October 1975 Colonel Trevor Dupuy stated that "it was clear that Brigadier Badawri and his Third Army were not on the verge of collapse." Further, Drew Middleton, military editor of the *New York Times,* wrote, "The Egyptian armies did not break. They were outmanoeuvred, not outfought. They were still in being."

Casualty figures are either blurred, incomplete, or absent. The first Israeli estimate, on 6 November 1973, was 1,854 killed and 1,800 wounded and still in hospital. The Israelis gave an amended figure of 2,522 killed and 2,500 seriously wounded, but their total number of wounded is clearly incomplete and is doubted in some quarters. On the normally accepted ratios of killed to wounded in battle of either one to five or one to six, their total casualties must have exceeded 12,000. The Egyptians, for example, estimate the number of Israeli dead at 8,000 and the wounded at over 20,000, figures that are supported by Soviet estimates. Neither Egypt nor Syria has yet issued official casualty figures, but U.S. estimates indicate the Egyptians suffered over 13,000, while a consensus of other sources shows the Egyptians had about 5,000 killed, a figure later hinted at by President Sadat, and about 11,000 wounded. Similar sources indicate the Syrians lost about 8,000 killed and had 12,000 wounded. When these figures are seen in relation to the populations of the countries mentioned, the impact of their losses on the Israelis can be appreciated. At the Israeli Symposium it was stated that the Egyptians had lost eighteen to twenty brigades out of a total of seventy-five brigades of all types.

Material losses were staggering, especially in tanks. At the time, for example, France was producing only about 300 a year and the United States about 360. The Israelis say the Egyptians lost 1,000 medium tanks out of 2,450; 400 amphibious armoured personnel carriers out of 1,875; 50 out of 1,050 other types of armoured personnel carriers; and 300 artillery units out of 2,220. They also claim that Syria lost 1,100 medium tanks out of 2,000; 400 armoured personnel carriers out of 1,500; and 250 artillery units out of 1,200; and that Jordan lost 13 tanks. In an interview with the editor of *The Times* published on 4 July 1976 President Sadat stated that "in the seventeen days of the war in October 1973 the casualties were 3,000 tanks from the three sides, mine, Israel, and Syria. I lost 500, 2,500 were lost by the Israelis and the Syrians, most of them by the Syrians because in one day in their retreat they lost 1,200. They said so officially. Israel lost more than 1,000. I lost 500 only." Correspondent Ronald Payne in the *Sunday Telegraph* of 6 October 1974 wrote that "to save the Israelis America had to send 1,000 tanks, and quantities of those came from the stores in Germany," and Glassman wrote, "In the war Syria received some 850 replacement tanks, of which 700 were T-62s." He added that "Syrian tank losses were at first believed to be 800 or 900 tanks. These numbers were later revised to under 500." Official estimates of tank losses vary dependent upon which country issued them. Figures of the losses and destruction of guns, vehicles, and other equipment can only be guessed at.

With U.N. personnel in position between the two opposing

forces, the guns at last fell silent. With the exception of an incident on the twenty-ninth, when the Israelis claim the Egyptians tried to build a footbridge across the canal some five miles north of Suez, a cease-fire came into effect but lasted only three days. On that day the Israeli general, Yariv, met the Egyptian general, Bashir Sherif, at kilometre 101 where a tent had been erected for the purpose, and Premier Meir visited Israeli troops on both the west and the east banks.

Egypt's second War of Attrition with Israel began on 1 November 1973 and lasted until 17 March 1974. During these months there were almost daily incidents of shelling, minor attacks, and patrol raids in the Third Army sector. There was frequent Israeli aircraft action against the besieged army, the Israelis trying desperately, for prestige reasons alone, to force it to surrender. For example, the Egyptians say there were over 1,500 such incidents from 1 November 1973 until 18 January 1974; they included four major clashes and eighty-nine others in November, 312 in December, and 133 in January. These are selective figures, perhaps, but they give an indication of how raw and abrasive the front was. Egyptian planes also intervened, and the first aerial dogfight took place over the Third Army on 6 December. The situation was as much a stalemate as a siege, although the Israelis did not like to see it that way. Some supplies were flown in at night to the Third Army by helicopter or brought across by boat, and water was obtained from the Ein Musa Springs. On 1 November the 7th and 19th Infantry Divisions were unified under the command of Brigadier Ahmed Badawri and became known as Badr Force.

Also, holding out on the east bank during this period was the besieged Kabrit Fort, which the Israelis also tried hard to force to surrender, subjecting it to constant artillery fire and bombing. The water at this point was particularly full of debris, including human bodies, which floated in each direction twice in every twenty-four hours. Some of the defenders swam out at night and caught a floating motor launch and then three SP pontoons which they used to ferry supplies across the narrow neck of water. The west bank was only 2,500 to 3,000 yards from the fort. The first supply run was made on the moonless night of the third/fourth of November; in all thirty such runs were made, carrying some thirty tons of supplies, mainly on the darker nights. The Egyptians consider the defence of Kabrit Fort, "taken in thirty minutes and defended for three months," to be one of their war epics in which the water shortage was overcome by boiling and vapourising salt water from the canal. The commander of the Kabrit Fort garrison, Colonel Ibrahim Abdul Tawab, was killed on 14 January 1974.

On the west bank the Israelis, probably with twelve brigades, settled themselves in defensive positions and surrounded themselves with mines. Later the Egyptian Engineer Corps claimed to have lifted three-quarters of a million mines, mainly of U.S. origin, which had been laid in the gap. On 9 December the Egyptians announced that the Israeli pocket was only three miles deep and not ten as claimed by the Israelis, and that there was a plan prepared to crush the pocket using five divisions and twenty ranger units. That month an Israeli Phantom was brought down over the Third Army area.

On 2 November President Sadat announced plans for reopening the Suez Canal. On the twelfth a six-point cease-fire agreement was signed at kilometre 101 by General Aharon Yariv and General Mohammed el-Gamasy, after which the Israeli blockade was lifted. On 15 November there was an exchange of prisoners, 8,301 Egyptian for 241 Israeli. On 24 January 1974 the tent at kilometre 101 was struck, and on 21 February Israeli troops withdrew from the west bank after a 129-day operation. By this time about 3,000 Soviet technicians had arrived in Egypt. The Israelis, on 31 October 1973, had stated that they held 5,467 Egyptian prisoners, 368 Syrians, 17 Iraqis, and 6 Moroccans, making a total of 5,858; no Jordanian prisoners had been taken.

The twelfth of November 1973 was a day of rewards and disappointments for many Egyptian officers and soldiers. The cautious Ismail was promoted to field marshal. Gamasy was promoted to lieutenant general and confirmed in the appointment of chief of staff. The two commanders of the Egyptian Second and Third Armies, Khalil and Mwassil, were removed and Major General Fuad Ghali was given command of the former, and Brigadier Badawri, the latter. Lieutenant General Shazli was absent from the glittering military gathering before the People's Assembly, where decorations, insignia, and medals were presented to many. Blamed for failing to liquidate the Israeli pocket and formally dismissed from his appointment, he was later appointed Egyptian ambassador in London. In April 1974 Ismail (who died on 25 December 1975) ordered an enquiry into how the Israelis crossed to the west bank, but no findings have so far been made public.

There was acute tension and suspicion between the Israelis and the Syrians, and it was exacerbated over the lack of information about Israeli prisoners held by the Syrians. The Israelis listed 113 of their military personnel missing on this front. The tardiness of these prisoner exchanges caused the disengagement agreement between the two countries to be held up, and it was not signed until 5 June 1974 in Geneva, when the last of the Israeli prisoners had been repatriated.

Apart from the two main Arab combatants, Egypt and Syria, and the latecomers, Iraq and Jordan, a number of other Arab states sent token contingents to show solidarity; one Muslim, non-Arab country, Pakistan, sent a field ambulance unit to both Egypt and Syria. A Moroccan infantry brigade had been on the Syrian front since June 1973, and during the war Iraq sent three squadrons of aircraft and at least a division. Jordan sent two armoured brigades to Syria, and they were eventually joined by a Saudi Arabian infantry detachment and a Kuwaiti artillery battery. The Iraqis also sent three squadrons of aircraft to Egypt. The Egyptians now deny this, but the Iraqi chief of staff insisted to me that this was so, mentioning "twenty-eight planes." These, together with a PLA brigade and a Kuwaiti infantry detachment, were already serving on the canal zone when the war broke out. A Tunisian infantry battalion joined the Port Said garrison on the eighteenth to take an active part in the defence of that city.

On the twenty-fourth, just too late to take part in the fighting, an Algerian armoured brigade with some 200 tanks arrived near the Suez Canal, exhausted after ten days' travel by road. A Sudanese infantry battalion arrived at Adabiya on the twenty-eighth, just in time to go into action briefly to help block Adan's attempted probe southward that day. The Moroccan detachment sent to Egypt did not arrive until after the war ended, although its commander visited the canal area on the twentieth. On the Egyptian front these foreign detachments all came without any logistic backing at all, expecting to be fed and fuelled by the Egyptians, but on the Syrian front, the Iraqis and the Jordanians developed their own supply lines. The Palestinian guerrillas stated on the eighteenth that they had requested King Hussein's permission to use Jordanian territory to fight the Israelis, but he had refused. A PLO spokesman in Beirut on 9 March 1974 claimed the PLA had suffered 256 casualties in the October War.

The Wars of Attrition between Israel and both Egypt and Syria dragged on, but land movement ceased. Although much was hidden from the Israeli nation by military censorship, the shock of being caught by surprise, the huge, but as yet unknown, casualty figures, and the lack of information about missing soldiers and prisoners caused the people to devolve into bitter recrimination as anger overtook fear.

In Israel there were the usual military rewards and disappointments for generals and others. On 30 October Eytan was promoted to major general. General Bar Lev, one of the first of the senior officers to be recalled, was released from the army on the thirty-first. General Adan briefly became military attache in Washington, only to be quickly brought home again on 14 January 1974 to become GOC Southern Command. Disappointed at not being selected as chief of staff, General Tal resigned on 19 March. Differences were reported between the general and both Dayan and Elazar, and it was said that Tal had refused Dayan's order to fire on Egyptian troops during the cease-fire period. On 14 April General Mordechai Gur, who had been military attache in Washington during the war, was appointed GOC Northern Command, while on 3 September General Hofi was appointed chief of staff.

In early November 1973 General Sharon, while still serving, gave an interview to correspondent Charles Mohr of the *New York Times*, in which he was highly critical of Israeli conduct of the war. Mohr flew out from Israel with his copy to avoid the censor. The interview was published on 11 November and caused some acid comment in Israel. Dayan ordered an immediate enquiry into the incident, which prompted General Bar Lev to accuse Sharon of claiming personal credit for the Israeli breakthrough on the west bank. Bar Lev insisted that documentary evidence could prove otherwise. On the thirteenth General Gonen applied to the chief of staff to appoint an investigating officer, with a view to having Sharon brought before a court-martial; Gonen resubmitted the request on the twentieth. Two days later Gonen was removed by Dayan and replaced temporarily by General Tal as GOC Southern Command.

On 18 November the Israeli government ordered a five-man judicial enquiry under Doctor Shimon Agranat, president of the Supreme Court of Israel, which became known as the Agranat Commission, to look into and to apportion the blame for the disasters of the first three days only.

The deferred general election in Israel was held on 31 December 1973. Sharon, as a member of the Likud party, was elected to the Knesset for the first time. He was demobilized from the army on 20 January 1974 in time to take his seat in the new Knesset the following day. In his farewell order of the day Sharon said that "in spite of the failures and mistakes, the loss of nerve and control, we emerged victorious." He criticised Israeli conduct of the war and called for the removal of General Elazar. Dayan refused requests to have Sharon tried by court-martial for insubordination, but Sharon's reserve appointment of command of a division was changed to a noncombatant one. It was alleged that, while still serving, Sharon telephoned members of the Likud party and asked them not to attack Dayan.

On 2 April 1974 the Agranat Commission issued its first, twenty-five-page, interim report, which was limited to examining the intelligence factors and the state of Israeli preparedness. It said, "One of the main mistakes was a misjudgement of available information due to the blind belief that enemy deployments on the Suez front were manoeuvres." It completely absolved Moshe Dayan, the defence minister, from all blame but laid it instead on Generals Elazar and Zeira. It also recommended that General Gonen be suspended from active duty pending the full report being issued.

Already unpopular, Dayan now faced a further outcry against him, but he still refused to resign although Gonen was dismissed the next day, the third. There were demonstrations against Dayan, including one led by Captain Motti Ashkenazi, who had commanded the Budapest fort on the Mediterranean for the first few days, urging that Dayan be removed from his post as defence minister. The intensity of feeling against Dayan eventually was instrumental in forcing Premier Meir to step down, bringing her government with her. Mrs. Meir left office on 4 June 1974, after which followed a period of some nine weeks of coalition bargaining while a caretaker government, led by Meir, held power. Eventually, in August General Rabin became premier, and he chose Shimon Peres as his defence minister.

Dayan's unpopularity continued. On 19 December at the Bar Ilyan University in Tel Aviv demonstrations by parents and relatives of casualties prevented him from giving a public speech, and he had to content himself with talking to members of the faculty. On this occasion he disclosed the fact that the United States had threatened to supply the Third Army by helicopter if the Israelis maintained their siege. This was yet another shock to the Israelis, who were convinced that, although the whole world seemed to be against them at this moment, the United States was their firm and steady friend. On 5 July 1974 it was announced that General Sharon, who had resigned his seat in the Knesset, at the instigation of Peres, was to return to the army to be adviser to the chief of staff.

On 10 July the Agranat Commission issued its second report, a 423-page document, but only a few extracts from it were made public. It commented upon the absence of clearly defined division of responsibility between the premier, the defence minister, and the chief of staff, and recommended the dismissal of General Elazar. General Gonen alleged that records had been falsified or erased, and that Adan's war logbook had been rewritten and edited. Peres asked the Agranat Commission to investigate these allegations, and on 9 December it reported there was no substance to them. On 27 October two Israeli sergeants had been sentenced to seven years' imprisonment by a court-martial for disobeying orders in the October War. Both were mechanics who had been sent to a Bar Lev Line fort on the morning of 6 October to repair vehicles and were there when the Egyptians attacked. For two days the sergeants refused to take an active part in the defence of the fort or to move ammunition, but eventually they did so on the third day, when the fort surrendered. Both men were taken prisoner. In view of the fact that senior military commanders seemed to be escaping all responsibility and blame for the initial setbacks in the war, these sentences caused an outcry in Israel, where emotion, anger, and chagrin were clashing with the normal processes of discipline.

The air lifts of military material from both the United States and the Soviet Union, vital to both sides, continued for several days after the last cease-fire came into effect. The American air lift began on 13 October and ended on 14 November. It carried over 22,395 tons, of which 10,763 tons were lifted in C-5s in 145 missions and 11,600 tons in C-141s in 421 missions, with round trips of about 14,000 miles. This amount was in addition to some 5,500 tons carried in eight 707s and three 747s of the El Al airline. The C-5s had large cargo doors, a "drive on, drive off" capability, and carried M-48 and M-60 tanks, 155mm howitzers, 175mm guns, CH-53 helicopters, and A-4E Skyhawk fuselages—items probably no other aircraft in the world could take.

For shorter runs, that is, from Europe, the Americans used C-130s, flying from such bases as that at Ramstein, in Germany. They carried missiles and ammunition, practically denuding NATO stockpiles of certain weapons such as the TOW. A report in *Aviation Week* stated that the U.S. stockpiles of TOW missiles were depleted by 90 percent during the October War, and that "the Israelis, who also received up to 50 percent of U.S. stockpiles of other types of ammunition, now say stocks in Israel were not as low as first thought. A computer error in the pipeline inventory from domestic supplies is blamed for the miscalculation." Other items carried by the air lift included ECMs and Smart bombs, which were mainly taken into either El Arish or Haifa.

According to Glassman, the Israelis had a "shortfall of 105mm tank gun ammunition, 175mm artillery rounds, air-to-air and air-to-surface missiles." He wrote that the "U.S. resupply reached full dimensions on October 14. After the fourteenth the United States supplied not only consumables, but also aircraft and other weapons."

The Israelis made a great propaganda splash when a U.S. planeload of tanks, about four, landed at Lod Airport, but it was the only occasion, and these tanks probably never got into action. Most tanks were landed by helicopter from ships of the U.S. Sixth Fleet at El Arish. Some still had their old 85mm or 90mm guns. Some also came direct from Europe, and these were the ones that drove straight into battle with only "175 kilometres on the clock." In all, at least 600 U.S. tanks, valued at some $950 million, came into Israel during the October War.

The Americans established an Air Lift Control Element of about fifty men at Lod Airport, which supplied some unloading equipment the Israelis did not possess and which claimed a turn-around time of two hours for a C-5 and under one hour for a C-141. Between twenty and thirty U.S. Skyhawks were ferried by American pilots to the Azores, refuelling from the carrier, the U.S.S. *John F Kennedy,* near Gibraltar by tanker aircraft, and then flying on to Israel. For example, the U.S. government admitted it had sent "forty-nine A4-E fighters" (Skyhawks) to Israel from its "inventory, in other words, out of stock." Heikal writes that "when the air lifts were finally halted, it was found the amounts of arms which America had supplied to Israel almost exactly balanced, ton for ton, the amount the Soviet Union had supplied to Syria and Egypt."

The Soviet air lift, which began on the ninth, used Anatov-12s, having a payload of 44,000-lbs, and Anatov-22s, with a payload of 176,000-lbs. They made some 943 round trips, carrying some 15,000 tons of material from bases in Hungary, but by late October 1973 the Soviet Union was relying heavily on sea transport. The distance was much shorter than that of the American sea supply line. Most of the Soviet air lifts were from Kiev, Russia (they overflew Turkey) and from Budapest, Hungary, where arms and ammunition had been collected from Warsaw Pact stockpiles and formations (they overflew Yugoslavia). None of the Soviet flights overflew Rumania; it was said that the required permission was not forthcoming.

The bulk of the material supplied to the Arabs and the Israelis by the Russians and the Americans was carried by sea, but no figures are yet available as to precise amounts. It is known that tanks, guns, missiles, and ammunition went in quantity to Syria and that lesser quantities, mainly of ammunition and spare parts, went to Egypt.

However, Glassman reports that "during the resupply operation Egypt reputedly received about 100 fighter aircraft, 600 tanks, and equipment for 30 SAM batteries." Soviet MiGs were flown to Syria by Soviet pilots, and, according to the *Washington Post* of 24 November 1973, "Because of the shortage of tank crews in Syria, Soviet personnel drove tanks unloaded from Russian ships from Latakia and Tartous to Damascus."

13

WAR IN
THE AIR

An ounce of ECM is worth a pound of additional aircraft.

Major General Hod

During the 1967 War the best weapon in the Israeli armoury had been its air force—the key to its success—and it had been kept sharp and bright to provide the great deterrent to aggression from surrounding Arab states. In that war the Egyptian air force had been largely destroyed, and that of Syria had been badly battered. Since then both had at intervals received batches of modern Soviet aircraft. Yet by October 1973 neither country's air force was considered to be a match for that of Israel. Since it took about four years to train a pilot up to combat standard, and training had to be graduated and progressive, it would be over six years before Egypt and Syria had sufficient pilots. Even then they would be at a disadvantage, as the Russians did not have a plane able to counter the U.S. Phantoms possessed by the Israelis. Jordan, whose small air force had been completely destroyed in 1967, was even less fortunate.

The Israeli assessment was that the Egyptians, whom they rated to be more advanced and skillful than the Syrians, would not attack Israel until they had achieved the capability of striking at all the Israeli airfields simultaneously, such as the Israelis had done in 1967. The Israelis estimated the Egyptians would require not only numbers of modern aircraft, such as MiG-21s, MiG-23s, and Sukhoi-7s, but also pilots skilled and experienced in handling them. Thus they did not feel there was any real danger of an Egyptian attack until at least 1975. The Egyptians and Syrians must have agreed with this calculation, as both made the decision to rely primarily upon a strong air defence system.

The Egyptians had learned the lessons of 1967 well, and they formed a new command structure, established alternative communications, and commenced intensive training of pilots, technicians, and ground staff. The Engineer Corps constructed an extra twenty airfields, bringing the number to about thirty-five in all, and added an extra runway to some of the existing ones in order to increase capacity. To avoid destruction by another Israeli pre-emptive strike, which in 1967 had destroyed so many Egyptian aircraft standing in the open, the Engineer Corps produced a concrete shelter, with sliding steel doors and a blast wall, for every aircraft. The aircraft remained in the shelter unless actually flying. The shelter is now in use by other Arab states and some Warsaw Pact countries. To repair airfields damaged by Israeli action, the Engineer Corps formed teams which stockpiled equipment and material in positions convenient for instant use. They claimed to be able to repair any bomb damage within three hours as a normal task. After experimenting, they devised an iron plate to put over craters. The engineers also provided teams for bomb-disposal purposes.

Air Vice Marshal Mohammed Mubarak took over from Major General Ali Baghdadi as commander of the air force in April 1972, and carefully selected officers were placed in key appointments. The strength of the air force was gradually increased; pilots and some technicians were sent to the Soviet Union for advanced training. Also, valuable experience had been gained during the 1968-70 War of Attrition. The period from 1970 to 1973 was one of familiarisation with other arms and services, especially the Air Defence Command, and training concentrated upon individual and task training, maintenance of equipment, air

cooperation with mobile radar units, and the combined operations system. The programme went so well that in March 1973,
when President Sadat asked Vice Marshal Mubarak if he needed
anything more, Mubarak was able to say he had everything he
required for war. Actually, he needed more time to train more
pilots to form an experienced reserve as he had barely enough
for his available aircraft.

A programme of mass pilot training had been put into operation in which, at first, there were many casualties due to accidents, but the proportion grew less each year as more experience
was gained. The Egyptians admitted that, initially, results were
poor, but their pilots gradually reached an accepted norm. Operational training included low flying and practicing the landing
and take-off of fighter aircraft on roadways in moonlight so
they would have this capability in the Sinai one day. Taking a
leaf from the pre-June 1967 Israeli book, dummy airfields and
installations—complete with dummy missiles, gun and infantry
positions, shelters, and communications—were built in the desert
at the exact distance from the Egyptian air base to the potential
target to enable a strike operation to be rehearsed in its entirety,
including exact timings.

There was frequent practice with live rockets and ammunition and dummy targets, and the pilots were briefed as for real
active-service missions. Immediately after the strike the air force
commander, Vice Marshal Mubarak, flew into the dummy target area to assess the effectiveness of the attack. He told me he
was never content with verbal reports but insisted on seeing
the results for himself. The pilots said this on-the-spot examination was harder than real war. Despite this crash training programme, the Egyptian air force did not really have enough
pilots, and a percentage of them were only partially trained.

The Egyptian air force consisted of about 25,000 men, mainly
regulars or those, such as pilots and technicians, on a fixed
engagement. There was also an element of deferred conscripts,
especially for maintenance and ground duties. The Egyptians
possessed about 768 Soviet-manufactured aircraft, all of which
were modern types. About 150 were still in storage owing to
lack of pilots. This left about 620 operational, on which the

standard of maintenance was higher than Israeli propaganda had led the world to believe.

A speaker at the Israeli Symposium stated that Egypt possessed 653 fighters, 39 bombers, and 160 helicopters. According to IISS figures, the Egyptians had about 220 MiG-21s, 200 MiG-19s and MiG-17s, 120 Sukhoi-7 fighter-bombers, 18 Tupolov-16 medium bombers, and 10 Ilyushin-28s, which formed the main core of their offensive air power. The MiG-21s and MiG-17s were fitted with the Atol, stand-off air-to-air missile. The MiG-23s, which had been flown by Soviet pilots, were withdrawn when the Russians left. The remainder included trainer aircraft of the MiG, YAK, and L-29 types; Ilyushin-14 and Anatov-12 transport aircraft; and well over 100 helicopters, such as the Mi-1, Mi-4, Mi-6, and Mi-8. The Soviet helicopters developed many technical faults, and at one time nearly 50 percent were grounded for this reason.

In view of the weakness of their air force, the Egyptians understandably relied heavily upon the Air Defence Command, led by Major General Ali Fahmy, to counter the Israeli air force. They had constructed a strong air defence barrier extending in length about 70 miles along the major portion of the Suez Canal zone. Port Said, for example, had its own air defence as did certain vital airfields and other potential targets such as the Aswan Dam. Started in a small way after the 1967 War, the missile box (described in *The Electronic War in the Middle East, 1968-70* by Edgar O'Ballance) had just begun to prove effective when on 7 July 1970 improved equipment and new techniques and tactics came into use. The Egyptians claim they brought down fourteen Israeli planes before the cease-fire on 7 August. The War of Attrition not only gave valuable experience, but also pinpointed weak spots, mainly the need for all missiles, radar, and equipment to be housed in concrete shelters.

Intending to strike first, the Egyptians expected massive retaliation; their answer was to be the Air Defence Barrier, multilateral and multialtitudinal, a combination of surface-to-air missiles, SAMs, and guns. The missiles were the SAM-2, SAM-3, and SAM-6, the last completely new to the West. The static SAM-2 with a slant range of up to thirty miles was designed to deal with high-flying aircraft and had been used extensively in Vietnam against U.S. aircraft. Accordingly, the Americans had been able to develop electronic countermeasures (ECMs) against them. The ECMs consisted of sensors and other jamming and deflecting apparatus in pods which were clipped onto the wings of aircraft. They gave the pilot warning of an approaching missile, enabling him to take evasive action.

When the ECM was switched on, its jammer disrupted the missile's frequency, causing it to veer off course. In July 1970 the Egyptians received SAMs with a newer type of terminal guidance radar to guide the missiles onto the target. These had a greater range of frequencies than the ECMs held by the Israelis. Basically there are three types of radar on SAMs: the acquisition radar that searches for aircraft at long distance; the tracking radar that tracks the aircraft flight path when it is located; and the guidance radar that guides and fires the missile. The counters were ECMs which either blurred the blip on the radar screen or falsified its distance or its exact position—rather like a distorted television screen. Some aircraft used small decoy missiles with inbuilt ECMs launched on several flight paths different from the one on which the target aircraft was flying. As a counter, in July 1970 the Americans sent a batch of 200 of their latest ECMs with a greater range of frequencies and extra sensors that radiated electromagnetic waves on the same frequency used by the SAM's acquisition, tracking, and guidance system.

The SAM-3 was a similar type of missile, with a slant range of about seventeen miles, designed to counter aircraft at altitudes lower than those within the capability of a SAM-2. Both were cumbersome to operate and time-consuming to calibrate. The Egyptians had about forty SAM-2 sites, each with six launchers, and between seventy-five and eighty-five SAM-3 sites, each with four launchers. It was stated at the Israeli Symposium that the Egyptians had 146 SAM batteries. The engineers had constructed 650 individual launcher platforms reaching along the canal, with as many dummies, together with the necessary concrete shelters for men and ammunition. Many of the dummy sites had wooden dummy launchers and missiles, while the real sites were manned alternately to confuse the Israelis. Major General Benyamin Peled, commander of the Israeli air force, said that the Egyptian air defence consisted of 180 radar sites, 50 control centres, and 400 different radars. He said, "They are employing in that system some 200,000 people of the best quality." Later, President Sadat, talking of the number of Israeli Phantoms brought down by missiles, said, "Everything they boasted of came down because of the ground-to-air missiles of ours, and they were not up-to-date. They were the SAM-1 and SAM-2. The SAM-3 is up-to-date. The SAM-6s are also very up-to-date and very efficient, but the SAM-1 and SAM-2 are very old." By SAM-1 it is thought he meant the early model of the SAM-2, which he had in some quantity, as well as the more advanced SAM-2 itself.

The mobile SAM-6, mounted on tracks, had a slant range of about twenty miles and was designed to counter low-level aircraft attacks. The radar unit of a SAM-6 had a good frequency agility, its infrared homing device on the missile was not easily deceived by heat flares, but its radar had a limited search capability. Although mobile, the SAM-6 required up to eight hours after each move to recalibrate. Concrete shelters were constructed for them. Pajak says the Egyptians deployed 46 SAM-6 batteries, each having four launchers and three missiles.

Their antiaircraft gun was the four-barreled Soviet ZSU quad-23mm, radar-controlled, capable of firing over 4,000 rounds a minute, and the Egyptians possessed about 800 of them. When a number were fired together, a solid wall of lead was thrown up through which it was almost impossible for an aircraft to pass unscathed. Mounted on a tracked vehicle, this gun had a small saucerlike radar antenna. Its main disadvantages were that it took two minutes to warm up after being switched on, and that it could neither search nor fire on the move. The Air Defence Barrier could be switched on or off as an entity, a process that required split-second timing so as not to endanger their own aircraft, although there were flight paths through the barrier itself.

In theory the air force was the third element in the air defence system, but in practice it was not intended that it should be used to fight Israeli aircraft in an interceptor role. That responsibility was taken by the missiles and guns. The radar warn-

Egyptian SAM-2 base on the West Bank captured by the Israelis.

Israeli Army engineers recovering SAM-3 missiles on the West Bank.

ing network was backed by three lines of visual observers and so was thought by the Egyptians to be virtually unjammable. The Egyptians were relying upon their SCUDs, with a range of 160 miles, for retaliation in the event of Israeli deep-penetration bombing. The Egyptians additionally had 37mm antiaircraft guns with each ground formation; they also had 14.5mm heavy machine guns.

The Israelis relied heavily on the alleged technological gap between themselves and the Arabs. They openly boasted and firmly believed that it would be at least two generations before the Arabs could catch up. It was a mistaken presumption; the Egyptians were learning fast. For example, at their Technical Training Institute certain SAM-2 training equipment had been received and was still in crates when the Russians left in July 1972. The Russians estimated that it would take twenty-nine Soviet experts about nine months to install it. Egyptian instructors and students completed the job in fifty days. Also, when the Russians left, the Egyptians made certain modifications to the SAMs, radar equipment, and their electronic countermeasures (ECMs) which the Israelis did not learn about in time— another well-kept secret. The radar and electronic capability of the Egyptians was grossly underestimated by the Israelis—and others.

The Egyptians also had another antiaircraft missile, the SAM-7, operated by the infantry and designed to combat ground attack aircraft. A shoulder-held, short-range weapon, operated by one man, its main drawback was that it had only a small charge or warhead which, while it was capable of damaging aircraft, could seldom bring it down. It was heat-seeking, homing onto the aircraft exhaust, but it had to be fired as the plane was moving away from the infantrymen on the ground. The SAM-7 had been used in Vietnam against helicopters with some success, but it had been countered by dropped heat flares. The Egyptians possessed the newer SAM-7 fitted with infrared filters that did not react to flares, but the Israelis did not know this. A number of SAM-7s could be fitted on a tracked chassis and fired in salvoes.

Both the Egyptian and the Syrian air force had been re-equipped and trained by the Soviet Union, but, unlike that of Egypt, the Syrian air force, commanded by Major General Naji Jamil, still lay heavily under the technical presence of the Russians. The brusque independence of the Syrian character and the cold tactlessness of the Russians caused friction that interfered with smooth working and liaison. Syrian pilots were probably not as skillful as the Egyptians, and generally their technological gap with the Israelis was much wider. According to a statement made at the Israeli Symposium, Syria had 338 combat aircraft, all of Soviet origin, which included 200 MiG-21s, 80 MiG-17s, about 80 Sukhoi-7s, and some light Ilyushin-28s, (but no MiG-19s). Despite crash course training, Syria was short of pilots, and a percentage of those they did have were not fully trained or experienced.

Realising the shortcomings of their air force, the Syrians, like the Egyptians, relied upon an air defence barrier composed of missiles and guns to counter the Israeli air force. Syria's Air Defence Barrier was under the command of Colonel Ali Saleh. It was estimated the Syrians possessed twelve batteries of SAM-2s and SAM-3s and thirty-two of the mobile SAM-6s. In addition, Syria had about 160 ZSU quad-23mm radar-controlled antiaircraft guns. The Air Defence Barrier protected Damascus and covered the eastern portion of the Golan Plateau, but it did not reach as far as the River Jordan. Glassman says that "the Syrian SAMs had been emplaced on the Damascus Plain, thereby leaving strategic objectives in Syria open to air strikes." There were at least 2,000 Soviet personnel with the Syrian armed forces, at least half of whom were with the Air Defence Command, many in an operative role.

The Iraqi air force had about 190 combat aircraft and about 10,000 personnel, mainly regulars. Its aircraft were mainly, but not completely, of Soviet origin. They included eight TU-16 medium bombers, sixty Sukhoi-7 fighter-bombers, ninety MiG-21s, and thirty MiG-17s. There were also about thirty-two British Hunter FGAs. Three squadrons of Iraqi MiG-21s had been serving with the Egyptian air force on the Suez Canal front for almost a year. The Iraqis also possessed about forty-six Soviet helicopters (the Mi-1, Mi-4, and Mi-8) and about thirty transport aircraft (including Soviet Anatov-2s, Anatov-12s, Anatov-14s, Ilyushin-14s, TU-124s, and the British Heron). The Iraqi air force suffered similar drawbacks to those of Egypt and Syria, particularly in the shortage of pilots, although Iraqi pilots had been training in the Soviet Union for some time. During the first week of October 1973 a squadron of approximately fifteen TU-22s, supersonic strategic bombers, was sent from the Soviet Union to Baghdad. Considered superior to the Israeli Phantom, these were the first TU-22s to be stationed outside Europe. Only the Egyptian and the Iraqi air forces had a strategic bombing capability.

The Jordanian air force, which had been almost completely destroyed in 1967, consisted of about fifty aircraft of Western origin that included thirty-five British Hunters and fifteen American F-104As. In the face of Israeli size and superiority, it was puny and ineffectual and did not participate in the war at all.

The other air force marginally involved in the war was that of Libya; it was being modernised and expanded by Colonel Gaddafi. It consisted basically of ten U.S. F-5A Skyhawks, nine C-47s, eight C-130E medium transport planes, and eighteen French helicopters. Also, Gaddafi had placed an order with France for 115 Mirage aircraft; according to Pajak, over 100 had been delivered. France supplied them on the condition that they would be used only for the defence of Libya and would not be re-exported. The Mirage was a sophisticated single-seater, mach-2, delta-winged fighter, originally designed as a high-altitude interceptor. It was armed with a French Matra air-to-air missile, two 30mm machine guns, and two Sidewinder missiles. In June 1973 there were only ten Libyan pilots qualified to fly Mirages. Other Libyan pilots and a few Egyptians, together with technicians and ground staff, had been sent to France for training in a pilot exchange programme. The first batch of twenty-five trained Libyan pilots had just returned, and another group was being sent in its place. About forty-eight Libyan Mirages were sent to Egypt during the war, but they were flown by other Arab pilots.

The Israeli air force (Heil Avir Le Israel), given pride of place and priority, and a major allocation of the military budget, consisted of a variety of aircraft amounting to about 480 combat planes. They had been obtained as and when possible and formed the long arm that could stretch out to smack down any Arab nation that stepped out of line. Luttwak says the aircraft included 127 Phantoms, 160 Skyhawks, 60 Mirages, and 50 Super Mysteres (as well as some older Mysteres and Ouragans), 6 RF-5Es, 10 Stratocruisers (including two tankers), 20 Noratlas, and some 12 C-47 and C-130 transport aircraft. Israel also had about 75 helicopters, including 12 French Super Frelons and 20 Alouettes, the remainder being American CH-53s and AB-205s. The emphasis was on short-range bombing and ground support as the Israelis did not have any long-range bombers. Israel had a number of Teledyne Ryan-124 reconnaissance drones. The air force had received about twenty-five Barak planes (out of an order of 200); the Barak was a home-assembled plane.

Unlike the Arabs, the Israelis had an ample number of pilots, probably three per aircraft, since their process of selection and training had been perfected without interruption over the years. The air force consisted of about 10,000 regular personnel with another 1,000 in training at any one time. On mobilisation these numbers were doubled by recalled reservists, who mainly provided technical and ground support. A few piloted second-line aircraft. Pilot training was intensive, the pilots flying many more hours than was normal in other national air forces, and so the standard was high. For example, Arab MiG pilots seemed to average about forty hours of flying a month, less than half the time flown by Israeli pilots. However, the Arabs claim that only 50 percent of the Israeli pilots could fly at night, a state of training upon which the Israelis would not comment. The Israelis grouped their most skillful and experienced pilots into special squadrons known as hunter squadrons. They always went into action first, as the Israeli policy was based on a quick, short but decisive strike.

The Israelis had about ten airfields in the Sinai and over a dozen more in Israel proper. The two large ones in the Sinai were at El Arish on the coast and at Melize near Central Road, some fifty miles east of the canal. Others with good facilities included those at Thamada and Bir Hasana, and there were also a number of small landing strips such as the one at Tasa. The

Sinai air HQ was at Um Morgan near Melize. Generally there were about six Phantoms together with some Skyhawks and Mirages always on duty covering the Suez Canal front.

Difficulties in obtaining aircraft made the Israelis good at maintaining what they possessed. Ground crews had also reached a high standard of efficiency, and the Israelis in 1967 had claimed their turn-around time could be cut down to thirty minutes, as against a norm of about two hours. In theory this made four times as many aircraft available for operations. However, in practice, that was a pace the Israelis could not keep up for long. It had been shown in 1967 that even though a few pilots averaged nine sorties a day for one or two days, the mean average was slightly below three sorties daily. The Israeli claim for the record turn-around time for combat aircraft took a knock when it was seen that a Soviet team in Syria could unload and fully reload an Anatov-12 transport plane in a half hour. Also, the Arab turn-around time had been competitively reduced too, and the Israelis took a further knock when they learned the Egyptians were able to refuel and reload a single combat plane in six minutes, as against the new Israeli time of eight minutes. On 1 November 1975 General Moneim, who had succeeded General Mubarak as commander of the Egyptian air force, in a speech to mark the forty-third anniversary of its founding, claimed that "the time required for refuelling an aircraft was also reduced to a couple of minutes so that it was possible to make as many as eight planes take off simultaneously in a minute and a half."

The mad scientists' electronic war of missiles against ECMs, begun in Vietnam, was given an escalatory boost in the War of Attrition. As one improvement was discovered, a counter for it was sought and found, only to be nullified by another successive improvement. The Israelis had been sent about 200 ECM pods just too late for use in the War of Attrition. The ECMs, which always had to be carried at the expense of other weapon loads, were capable of countering the SAM-2s and SAM-3s in Egyptian service at that time. A warning light came on in the pilot's cabin, enabling him to take evasive action, or jam or divert the oncoming missile. His radar automatically transmitted counter signals tuned to Egyptian frequencies to distort their radar beams. It was a case of "beam riding" and "beam sliding." The Israelis used their Stratocruisers as airborne listening posts, packing them full of electronic detection equipment against which the Egyptians used what was termed electronic camouflage.

Progressive improvements had been made to the ECMs by the Americans after August 1970; yet they refused to let Israel have any more ECMs in case an aircraft carrying them was brought down in Arab territory. Neither would the United States let Israel have any of the newer weapons, such as the Lance, which would have been effective against missile batteries. As reported in *Aviation Week* of 29 October 1973, the Israelis had been banned from attending a classified ECM Symposium held in Washington, with U.S. Defense Department participation, by the Association of Old Cross. Representatives of NATO countries and others such as Australia had been present. The meeting was held only two weeks before the October War.

However, the Israelis were confident their pilots would be able to improvise defensive tactics against Arab air defensive weapons and believed that a combination of simple ECM equipment and skillful flying by experienced pilots would provide an answer. Having supreme confidence in their air force, the Israelis had not established an air defence barrier, but they did possess about eight batteries of the American HAWK missiles, amounting to about forty-eight launchers in all. The HAWK had a slant range of about twenty-eight miles.

President Sadat's later comments upon certain aspects of the relative merits of Arab and Israeli aircraft are of interest. In an interview in *The Times* of 4 June 1976, he said, "Before the war it was not superiority, it was supremacy, because they have Phantom and Mirage jets. I have got the MiG-21. If you compare these two types you will be astonished. In the MiG-21 the pilot has nothing except the compass. No facilities at all. In the Mirage, in the Phantom, in your planes, the Jaguar also, everything is computerized for the pilot. If he enters a missile zone there will be a lamp to tell him. If anyone is going to attack him from behind another lamp will tell him. He just puts a card in the computer. It will take him to the place where he is going. It will tell him to drop the bomb. It will bring him back to his airport. But all this is done, believe me, up till this moment in the MiG-21 and all Soviet military gear, by the pilot. Very primitive. So when I tell you that Israel has air supremacy, not superiority, it is true."

On 6 October 1973, almost before the 100 Syrian and 240 Egyptian (and Iraqi) aircraft had returned to their bases from their initial sorties into Israel and the occupied territories, the Israeli air force reacted like an angry hornet and flew swiftly to extract retribution. They found the Arabs had switched on their Air Defence Barrier into which the Israelis ran head-on with disastrous results. Within thirty minutes ten Israeli planes had been brought down, and more fell as other sorties were made. After one hour and fifty minutes the Israelis had lost about twenty-five Skyhawks and five Phantoms on the Golan front. On the Egyptian front, the first Israeli aerial sorties, which began at 1420 hours, also ran into disaster, although not quite of the same magnitude, when the Air Defence Barrier was switched on. The Egyptians claim that they brought down eleven Israeli planes by the end of the day. In their initial air strike, the Egyptians admit losing one aircraft. It was piloted by Captain Ahmed Sadat, the Egyptian president's half-brother, who was killed.

The Israeli ECMs were virtually ineffective against the Arab SAM-2s and SAM-3s and were completely powerless against the SAM-6s. Appalled by the unexpected and staggering losses, General Elazar, the Israeli chief of staff, suspended all Israeli aerial operations just after 1600 hours. He wanted breathing time while his air GHQ thought out what to do. About an hour later Elazar ordered the air force to resume operations, saying that new tactics were being employed—those of striking from a flank —but in reality this simply meant keeping away from the air defence barriers. The Egyptians claim to have intercepted an Israeli message ordering all Israeli aircraft to "keep fifteen kilometres from the canal." Israeli sorties were flown again, but cautiously; yet more losses were incurred. For example, the Syrians claim to have brought down four more Israeli aircraft about 1730 hours. The Israelis made limited night sorties, and the Syrians claim to have brought down another three Israeli planes about 2030 hours. On the ground, Arab infantry on both fronts, using the Soviet SAM-7, hit several Israeli aircraft but did not manage to bring any down.

By the end of the first day of the war the Israelis had lost from both missiles and ZSUs at least thirty Skyhawks, ten Phantoms, and a proportion of their best pilots, the cream of the hunter squadrons. The Syrian claim for the day was forty-three Israeli aircraft, which may have been about right. The government appealed to the Syrian people over the radio to "help our armed forces to capture Israeli pilots alive," as already some downed Israelis had been killed by villagers. The Egyptian claim for the day was twenty-seven Israeli aircraft (perhaps rather optimistic considering their new-style, low-profile reporting), and they admitted losing fifteen of their own. The shock to the Israeli government and GHQ was immense, and an example of the reaction was the almost panic move of the Sinai air HQ to El Arish.

The Israelis reported that at 1430 hours a Syrian aircraft dropped a bomb on Ayelet Hashaham in Galilee, and that at 1440 hours a Syrian plane came down inside the Lebanon, on the Bakaa Plain, the pilot being slightly injured. The Israelis reported that their aircraft, using Lebanese air space to avoid the switched-on Syrian Air Defence Barrier, were engaged in an aerial battle about 1530 hours over the Nabatiyeh Refugee Camp. Thirty Syrian aircraft were involved, but the Israelis said that a low cloud base made conditions unsuitable for aerial combat. They gave no more details. The Lebanese government later stated that an Israeli Phantom had crashed on a Lebanese village, injuring four people. Also, in the afternoon, the village of Majdal Shams was strafed by an Israeli aircraft and several Druse were wounded.

Later, on the fourteenth, it was alleged by Abba Eban at the United Nations that the Egyptians had fired a Kelt missile at Tel Aviv on the first afternoon. The Kelt, rather like a World War II V-1 missile, could be carried by a TU-16, and it was actually brought down by an Israeli pilot emulating RAF tactics. When I later questioned Field Marshal Ismail, he admitted this but insisted that "I did not fire at Tel Aviv," adding that he would have done so only if Egyptian cities were hit first.

During the seventh, the second day of the war, whenever Israeli sorties ran into air defence barriers, they suffered loss. A missile expert and U.N. observer officer, Major William Milinckrodt of the Dutch air force, in a U.N. observer post on the Syrian 1967 Cease-Fire Line, calculated that during the first three days of the war "three out of every five Israeli aircraft" that appeared in the sky overhead were hit, either by missiles or guns. An air raid warning was sounded in Cairo; the Israelis made three raids against Egyptian airfields, and at the end of the day the Egyptians, who admitted losing six aircraft, claimed another thirty Israeli planes. There was also at least one aerial clash over the Golan front.

Generally speaking, the air forces of both Egypt and Syria were held back, and the Air Defence Barrier remained switched on, a policy that paid off well. However, there were exceptions, and at 1200 hours Egyptian aircraft raided targets in the Sinai; they admit losing one plane. Egyptian naval forces claim to have shot down an Israeli helicopter near the northern Sinai coastline, and an evening attack was made on the area of Bir Gifgafa. That evening a film of aerial fighting and Israeli aircraft wreckage was shown on Egyptian television; the Egyptians claimed they held seven Israeli pilots. A Jordanian spokesman stated that at 1145 hours on the seventh its antiaircraft guns near Kuweila, twelve miles west of Amman, fired on an Israeli Phantom flying over Jordanian territory. He also said that the Amman International Airport was closed.

Emboldened, on the eighth, the third day of the war, Israeli aircraft made several raids but steered clear of the air defence barriers. For the first time they raided Port Said and area, which was not covered by the main Egyptian Air Defence Barrier. The twin bridges linking the city with the causeway to the south were hit and put out of action. Their destruction stopped all land movement from that direction. Persistent Israeli air raids on the Port Said area continued on most days, causing many casualties. Sometimes there was less than a three-hour respite between the attacks. Port Said had its own air defence based on the ZSU quad-23mm, other antiaircraft guns, missiles, and ECM equipment. Most were housed in brick-lined, igloo-like shelters banked with sand as protection against blast.

On several occasions on the eighth the Israelis again raided the Egyptian bridges across the canal as they had done since the war began. Although damaged, no bridge was put out of action for very long. Later, in an interview with *Al Akhbar* on 21 November 1973, General Shazli was to say, "The crossing operation could not have succeeded without the air and missile network covering the area. The air defence umbrella protected the infantry and engineers. The enemy's air attacks were severe and sustained. They did hit some points, but military bridges are built from linked sections, which are replaceable. Repairing a bridge usually took from half an hour to an hour. We also moved our bridges from one location to another to confuse enemy pilots who were working from reconnaissance information. We put up heavy smoke screens to make aiming more difficult for them while dense antiaircraft fire added to their difficulties. The enemy tried extremely low-flying tactics to get at the bridges, but the SAM-7 missiles proved a magnificent success in bringing down the attackers." Having lost another five aircraft by the end of the eighth, the Israeli effort in this direction slackened as losses were too heavy.

The El Al Fleet, according to Heikal, had quickly brought about 200 more advanced ECMs from America to Israel, together with quantities of *chaff* as the Israelis at the beginning had none at all. The chaff consisted of thin metal strips and was carried in the air brake recess of the Phantoms. When dropped, the individual strips showed up on radar screens as if they were aircraft. The Israelis also obtained chaff dispensers and chaff bombs direct from the U.S. manufacturers. The Israelis tried to neutralise the SAM-6 missiles by releasing decoy balloons of plastic, twelve to eighteen inches in diameter, carried in the ECM pods or strapped beneath the Phantoms. Coated with radioactive reflecting material, they also showed up on radar screens and attracted heat-seeking missiles—a method known in the jargon as "radar echo enhancement."

As the SAM-6 had a limited search capability, Israeli tactics were to dive onto it directly from a great height. The missile is initially slow to accelerate, although it eventually reaches a speed of Mach 2. This manoeuvre had some success, but the SAM-6 remained dangerous as it had frequency agility, which meant that it could operate on a wide range of frequencies making effective jamming extremely difficult. When they saw the firing flash of the missile and the white streak racing toward them, the Israeli pilots dropped their chaff, and then made a tight descending turn, but the missile batteries were so placed that the pilot's manoeuvre only brought him into range of another battery, so that by the fourth manoeuvre, he had lost all altitude and was caught by the ZSU guns.

The Egyptians made several bombing sorties on the eighth on targets that included the air bases at Melize and Thamada, HAWK batteries, and radar stations at Baluza, Thamada, Um Morgan, and Khaseiba. They also claimed to have brought down one Phantom and several helicopters. While the Israelis admitted these raids, they insisted that none of the targets mentioned had been hit by the Egyptians. The Egyptians admitted losing ten planes by the end of the day but claimed twenty-four Phantoms, while the Israelis claimed five Egyptian aircraft. On the eighth a batch of about 100 Egyptian pilots returned from their training in the Soviet Union.

On the Syrian front Israeli aircraft flew over Damascus for the first time in a dawn raid; some bombs were dropped. No air raid warning was sounded, but the people went into the shelters. The Israelis said that heavy cloud over the Golan limited air activity, but, in short, they still kept clear of the Air Defence Barrier as much as possible. In the evening, film of Israeli plane wreckage, pilot prisoners, and a shot of a Phantom crashing in flames was shown on Syrian television. Israeli losses were heavy, and on the eighth they probably lost thirty aircraft of different types on the Egyptian front and another twenty on the Syrian. More serious still to the Israelis was the fact that perhaps fifty or more of its hunter squadron pilots had already been eliminated by the Arabs.

On the eighth the Iraqis entered the war. That day two squadrons of its MiG-21s arrived in Syria and went into action almost immediately. However, four of the aircraft were shot down by the Syrian Air Defence Barrier because their IDFF (Identification - Friend or Foe) was not properly meshed in and the Iraqi pilots had not been properly briefed. The IDFF, the fixed response to a radar control challenge, was designed to prevent missiles and guns from shooting down their own aircraft. Also on the eighth Jordan claimed to have brought down two Israeli aircraft, but this cannot be substantiated.

Israel alleged that, since the war began, about twenty FROGs had been fired from Syria and the Lebanon into Israeli territory, causing damage. According to Glassman, the Syrians fired three FROGs on the sixth, seven on the eighth, and six on the ninth. The Israelis retaliated on the ninth at 1200 hours when six Phantoms appeared over Damascus and dropped bombs. A half dozen buildings were hit, including the ministry of defence, and one woman and a U.N. officer were killed. Other Israeli raids were made into Syria; one hit and set on fire the oil storage tanks at Homs. The fuel tanks and landing facilities at Adra, Tartous, and Latakia were bombed, and the Mediterranean terminal for Iraqi crude oil at Baniyas was hit and destroyed. The Israelis also claimed that their aircraft destroyed electric power generators at Damascus and Homs. In another raid two Israeli Phantoms bombed the radar station on the 7,000-foot-high Barouch Ridge in the Lebanon; the station was capable of scanning aircraft movement as far south as the Suez Canal.

Glassman writes that on the ninth the Syrian SAM-6s ceased firing through "a near exhaustion of missiles" when the Syrians withdrew some of their forward launchers to the Damascus Plain. Pajak writes that "in the first three days of hostilities the number of SAM missiles fired on the combined Syrian and Egyptian fronts reportedly totalled over 1,000, reflecting a deployment density surpassing that of any known SAM system in the world, the Soviet Union included."

At 0900 hours, in the south, Egyptian aircraft bombed airstrips at Melize and Thamada, claiming to put communication between them and air HQ at El Arish out of action. In the afternoon Israeli planes dropped bombs on the Mansoura and Khatmiya airfields in the delta. Port Said was again heavily raided.

The Egyptians claimed to have brought down sixteen Phantoms and Skyhawks that day, the ninth.

The Egyptians had constructed about five SAM sites on the east bank and by the tenth had moved a few SAM-6 batteries across the canal. That day General Shazli visited the east bank and said, "The Egyptian assault shattered the myth of Israeli air superiority and formed the east bank into a vast graveyard for the enemy." The Egyptian foreign minister alleged that American volunteers were serving in the Israeli air force; this was denied by both the United States and Israel.

Press correspondents visiting the Golan front still stated that Syrian missiles were hitting three out of five Israeli planes that appeared, and one comment was that it "was a familiar sight to see the white spiral of a SAM-6 in the blue sky every day, perhaps twice a day, then a puff of gray smoke, and, before it had begun to disperse, there was the fast-falling flame of the shot-down Phantom. It was rare to see parachutes." The Israelis, however, claim their air force remained active, and later General Peled said, "On the tenth we attacked Kressna, Abu Chamed, Damascus, Hales, Halhula, and Blei." On the eleventh an Israeli Phantom fell on the Lebanese village of Khiam, about two miles from the Israeli border, and General Peled later said, "On the eleventh, we attacked Blei, Saikal, Halhula, Dmer, Al Maza, Massariya, Damascus, and T-4 in Syria, and three airfields in Egypt, Salachia, Khatmiya, and Mansoura." On the twelfth Lebanese antiaircraft gunners opened up on Israeli aircraft flying over their territory. The same day another U.N. observer confirmed that Syrian missiles were still bringing down Israeli aircraft on the Golan front. Egyptian aircraft again raided over the Sinai; the Egyptians claim they destroyed radar stations at Tasa and Um Morgan. In the north, the Iraqis admitted the loss of twelve aircraft but said that six of the pilots were safe.

The Israelis gradually increased the number of sorties from a total, on both fronts, of 790 on the eighth, to 1,100 on the ninth, 1,164 on the tenth, and 1,318 on the eleventh. Meanwhile, they continued to raid the Egyptian bridges but did more damage to them with their long-range 155mm guns. The Arabs began using their SAM-7s mounted on vehicles (technically known as SAM-9s), firing them in salvoes of eight at a time. This firing procedure tended to nullify evasive movement by Israeli pilots and damaged many aircraft. Heikal says that from the sixth to the thirteenth the Israelis made over 2,500 sorties against Egypt: 70 percent against ground forces, 6 percent against airfields, 15 percent against independent missile concentrations, and 9 percent against Port Said and other towns.

The fourteenth was the day of the big tank battles near the Suez Canal when the Egyptians left the shelter of their Air Defence Barrier and the Israeli air force came into its own. Flying in pairs over the battlefield, its planes gave ground support, making good use of the recently acquired U.S. Smart bombs; during the Egyptian withdrawal they accounted for over fifty tanks. They also shot down two Mirages over the Sinai, and, as it was known the Egyptians did not possess any, it was alleged they were Libyan. Senior officers working in "Number 10" assured me that President Sadat only gave permission on the eighteenth for the use of Libyan planes—the "green light" in their jargon. Perhaps the pilots were over keen. The action was formally denied by both Egypt and Libya. In answer to criticism of Libyan inactivity during the October War, the Libyan newspaper *Al Fatah* of 19 May 1974 reported that "the Libyan air force made some 400 sorties against the Israelis," a fact that had been officially denied until then. After this, for identification purposes, the Israelis put large yellow markings on their own Mirages to differentiate them. At 1530 hours the Israelis, in three groups of twenty aircraft each, attacked delta airfields and were confronted by some thirty-five Egyptian fighter planes. In an air combat lasting for thirty-five minutes sixteen Israeli planes were brought down, according to the Egyptians, with the loss of nine of their own.

On the Golan Plateau the Israeli artillery was destroying SAMs by hitting their dish-shaped radar antennas with shell and mortar fire, thus making gaps in the Air Defence Barrier. Also, the operation of the barrier was becoming ragged and uncertain because of casualties and inexperience. On the fourteenth the Israelis claim to have destroyed half the Syrian air force, and that day they bombed Damascus Airport some fifteen miles from the capital. The Syrians alleged that American pilots with Vietnam War experience were flying with the Israeli air force; this was again denied.

On the fourteenth Israeli commandos made a heliborne raid on the Egyptian electronic monitoring station at Jebel Ataka. Later, at the Israeli Symposium, when commenting upon the Arab shortage of missiles, General Peled explained that "by the time we decided to land ground forces on the Ataka peak, the situation of the SAM defences in that area was very different from what it had been. It was almost nonexistent, but normal antiaircraft artillery was present." On being asked, at the same symposium, how the Israeli helicopters avoided the Egyptian Air Defence Barrier, General Elazar replied, "We have used ways and means to work our way through and land four times in succession, despite opposition and ground-to-air weapons, including SAM-6 missiles advancing from the Khatmiya airfield to try and stop us."

On the fifteenth Cairo had an hour-long air raid alert, and at 1210 hours the longest air battle over the northern part of the delta began and lasted for forty-five minutes. A formation of some twenty-four Israeli Phantoms and twenty-four Mirages launched an attack and were confronted by some forty-eight Egyptian fighters which beat off the invaders. The Egyptians claim the result was the loss of seven Phantoms and two Egyptian planes.

By the sixteenth the air lift from the United States to Israel was in full swing, bringing yet another batch of even more improved ECMs, known as Tiss, and some U.S. instructors to give the Israelis a crash course in their use. The air lift also brought the Sparrow air-to-air missile and Smart bombs that included Red-eye and Wall-eye. The use of these caused the Egyptians to speak of four bombs coming from one, each of which honed onto a separate tank. There were also reports of U.S. marines preparing eighty Skyhawks for dispatch to Israel; an official spokesman admitted that "forty-nine had been taken from the inventory for Israel." The Skyhawk was in particular demand by the Israelis as it had a good capability for strafing ground targets with its machine guns.

The sixteenth was the day that General Sharon damaged seven missile launchers, causing a gap in the Egyptian Air Defence Barrier through which Israeli aircraft were able to penetrate. Within a couple of days this gap had been widened. Kosygin, in Cairo, ordered 300 Russians to fly immediately to Egypt to stiffen the Air Defence Barrier as he feared Israeli raids on that country, especially on Huckstep, the armoured corps base. Other Russians took over ground control duties and the unloading of Soviet supply aircraft. Also, Soviet ground controllers, loadmasters, and other staff began to pour into Syria as the Russians thought the Syrians ground crews were far too slow. On the sixteenth the Syrians claimed to have shot down a U.S. Ryan Firebee (a pilotless reconnaissance plane) flying at 54,000 feet to the west of Damascus and that they had salvaged its camera intact. The following day a Ryan Firebee was shot down over the canal area.

On the eighteenth the Israelis again denied using American pilots, while the United States countered that thirty North Korean pilots were flying with the Egyptian air force. The Pentagon alleged that they were on an exchange visit, which was in turn denied by the Egyptians. Later, on 5 November, Deputy Defense Secretary William Clements stated at a press conference that the North Korean pilots "have been flying defensive patrols. They have not engaged in hostilities," and he added, "There were a few Pakistanis in the area who were engaged in instruction to the Egyptian air force." Glassman writes that "some twenty North Korean pilots flew passive air defense missions in the interior of Egypt. The North Koreans claim that they were on training exercises, not flying passive defense." Another group of North Korean pilots arrived in Syria after the war. The United States admitted there were a limited number of American servicemen in Israel helping with the air lift but insisted they were not combat troops. The Egyptians, who were using helicopters in the gap on the west bank to drop napalm on the Israelis, causing many casualties, claimed to have brought down 281 Israeli aircraft and 15 helicopters, but by this time their communiqués were completely unreliable.

By the nineteenth, the day the Egyptians alleged the Israelis had received an extra thirty-five Phantoms from the United States, the gap in the Egyptian Air Defence Barrier was further enlarged. General Sharon claimed to have destroyed ten missile launching sites, while the Israeli air force claimed to have knocked out another twenty-six sites, thus destroying the Egyptian forward air defence line. The Israelis had also captured the airfields at Deversoir and Fayid. From the nineteenth onward the Israelis launched 1,000 sorties a day for three days over their penetration on the west bank. On that day Dayan had a narrow escape on a visit to the west bank when an Egyptian Mi-8 helicopter came over suddenly at treetop height to drop napalm, missing him by only a few yards. The helicopter was brought down by ground fire.

On the twenty-first the Egyptians made a twenty-plane raid on the two Israeli bridges across the canal, catching a convoy of six tanks on one of them, all of which sank to the bottom of the waterway. When General Ismail withdrew his Air Defence Barrier batteries to prevent their weapons being captured or damaged, the Israelis were given more scope on the west bank. In the north, Israeli aircraft again raided Damascus, and there were dogfights between Israeli and Syrian planes.

On the twenty-second, the day of the first cease-fire, the Israelis claimed the Egyptians had lost 240 aircraft. At an Egyptian press conference it was said that the Israelis had lost 303 planes and 25 helicopters. Despite the Syrian acceptance of the first cease-fire, there were aerial dogfights over the Golan Plateau on the twenty-third, and on the twenty-fourth Israeli aircraft dropped leaflets over the Egyptian Third Army, urging it to surrender.

On the twenty-fourth foreign journalists were allowed into Port Said for the first time since the war began. The governor general, Abdul Tawab Hodiep, said that Israeli aircraft using Gueva bombs had raided the city for fifteen successive days. Although over half the population (then about 25,000) had been evacuated in the first days of the war, at least 200 civilians were killed and 500 wounded. The city was without electric power, and the fresh water system had been damaged. The Port Said garrison claimed to have brought down ninety-two Israeli aircraft but were officially credited with only forty-two. It was said that the total weight in bombs dropped was equal to one and a half twenty-kiloton nuclear bombs. The Israelis had generally bombed from high altitudes. A number of air defence posts were silenced in some of the raids but later came to life again to the surprise of the Israeli attackers.

On the twenty-fifth Israeli aircraft again raided Port Said. On the twenty-sixth they took part in the battle for Port Suez and again dropped leaflets urging surrender on the Egyptian Third Army. Although land movement stopped on the twenty-eighth, what the Arabs called the Wars of Attrition continued on both fronts almost until the disengagement agreements were signed. During this time there was air activity. For example, on 9 November an Israeli Phantom was shot down on the Egyptian front, and then on the twenty-ninth, the day Cairo International Airport reopened, three Egyptian helicopters were brought down as they attempted to land commandos on the eastern shore of the Gulf of Suez.

There are several sets of conflicting claims as to the aerial losses in this war. The Israelis say they flew in all over 11,000 sorties (Glassman says 18,000) and claim to have brought down 550 Arab aircraft with the loss of 350 Arab pilots. They say that 80 percent of their own losses was due to ground fire. The Israelis also claim to have destroyed thirty SAM batteries but say that only 10 percent of their own losses was due to SAM-6 missiles. They admit losing 115 of their aircraft (sixty in the first week of the war), eighty over the Golan Plateau and thirty-five on the canal front. Herzog writes that the Israelis lost only 102 aircraft.

The Soviets estimate that Israel lost 289 aircraft, the American estimate was 200, but whatever the true figures were, they amounted to a lot of aircraft in a short space of time. At the time the McDonnell plant in the United States was producing only three Phantoms a month. General Tlas told me that, according to a notice published on all notice boards in Israeli air force camps after the war, 160 Israeli pilots had been lost, but the Israelis will admit to only about fifty.

The U.S. Defense Department estimates that the Arabs lost

368 aircraft: 182 Egyptian, 165 Syrian, and 21 Iraqi. Herzog claims they lost 514. The Israelis claim to have destroyed 242 Egyptian and 179 Syrian aircraft, but President Sadat admits to losing only 120 planes. At the Israeli Symposium it was stated that Egypt lost 222 fighters, one bomber, forty-two helicopters, and forty-four SAM batteries, while Syria lost 117 aircraft and three SAM batteries, but Pajak states that Syria lost 222 aircraft and seventeen to twenty SAM batteries.

General Tlas told me that the object was to kill off the best Israeli pilots, those in the hunter squadrons, and that when this had been achieved "our own pilots were equal to the Israelis in training and skill." He went on to say that "if the Syrians had Phantoms and the Israelis had MiGs, be sure there would be no Israeli pilots flying over Syrian territory." President Sadat agreed with Tlas on the relative capabilities of American and Soviet aircraft. Tlas also told me that four or five Israeli pilots landed on Syrian airfields and gave themselves up and that he gave one of their Phantoms to the Soviet Union. Later, sixty-three Israeli pilots captured by the Syrians were exchanged for Arab prisoners.

Reports of the means by which aircraft were destroyed are also conflicting. Speaking at an International Symposium in Cairo in 1975, General Mohammed Fahmy, former Egyptian chief of staff, quoted a Western source that published an analysis of Israeli losses of aircraft which stated that 30 percent was due to antiaircraft missiles, 30 percent to ZSU quad-23mm and other guns, and 15 percent during air combats, but was unable to present a clear reason for the remaining 25 percent loss—a quote the general must have been in accord with. General Fahmy told me later that, of every five Israeli aircraft brought down, two fell to missiles and one to guns, and he claimed that the ECMs were not as effective as the Israelis made out. Glassman writes that, of the 120 Israeli planes brought down, some 80 fell to SAM-6s and most of the others fell to Soviet guns. As a matter of interest, about 17 percent of the U.S. aircraft brought down in Vietnam fell to missiles. President Sadat commented, in the *Times* interview, that "one-third of their [Israeli] Phantoms and everything they boasted of came down because of the ground-to-air missiles. We are in a missile era. Ground-to-air missiles deprived Israel of its supremacy."

A number of Arab aircraft were brought down by their own Air Defence Barrier, and one U.S. report stated that, owing to failures in the barrier, thirty-five Egyptian aircraft were brought down. Glassman says the Egyptians "apparently shot down a number of their own planes," and that "Egyptian planes apparently had greater difficulty [than the Syrians] in finding their re-entry paths." He also wrote that "some inaccurate missile launches did occur."

The SAM-6 clearly worried the Israelis, who did not have even the simplest ECM, the black box that alerts the pilot that his aircraft is caught in the tracking web of a radar. Also, they knew very little about Egypt's search and tracking radar, which could make rapid changes in frequency and so could not be deceived or blinded by jamming. The Israeli Skyhawks were especially vulnerable to the SAM-6. Although the Israelis captured six damaged SAM-6s, a Pentagon source later admitted they had failed to secure its guidance apparatus, and without an examination of the guidance mechanism, American technical experts could not devise an ECM to counter it. The Pentagon spokesman said the "retreating Egyptian troops had stripped the secret radar equipment from the Soviet SAM-6 missiles they abandoned during the Israeli attack on Egypt." The much-used Israeli handout photograph of a captured SAM-6, according to the Egyptians, was merely a wooden dummy.

The deduction must be made that, while the advanced U.S. ECMs were able to counter the improved SAM-2s and SAM-3s, they were ineffective against the SAM-6s, which were knocked out mostly by ground artillery hitting their antennas. Even so, the Israelis rightly claimed that the presence and effectiveness of their air force restricted the Arabs to limited objectives as they could not successfully advance beyond the cover of their air defence barriers. Luttwak makes the interesting observation that "there is reason to believe that, in the October War, the Arab armies fired more surface-to-air missiles than there are in the entire inventory of the European NATO forces."

The Arab tactics were to fire their SAM-6s and SAM-7s in salvoes to neutralise Israeli ability at rapid manoeuvre; the Israelis fired their HAWKs in pairs and claim that, in twenty-five such firings, they brought down twenty-two aircraft. Israeli aircraft carrying ECMs, at the expense of weapons, tended to fly at lower altitudes which brought them within range of both the SAM-6 and the SAM-7.

The Egyptian and Syrian air forces were never really committed to full-scale battle, and so they avoided crushing casualties, but many clashes occurred when the Israelis intercepted Arab aircraft making short-distance raids. Conflicting estimates are given of dogfight results. The Israelis officially admit to losing only four aircraft in this way (although Herzog says five). General Mubarak told me that two out of every five Israeli aircraft brought down fell to Egyptian fighters, and that more than eighty Israeli Phantoms and Mirages were shot down by Egyptian interceptors. When describing to me the battles of the seventh, eighth, and eleventh, General Tlas said that, when the Air Defence Barrier was switched off and his MiG-21s and MiG-17s moved in to attack the Israeli Phantoms, the result was "a three-to-two ratio in Syrian favour—better than we expected." It was officially stated that the Egyptians had flown 6,376 sorties from the sixth to the twentieth inclusive. General Mahmoud Shaker Abdul Moneim said that a number of Egyptian pilots made six or seven sorties per day, that "some participated in aerial combat on the same day after bailing out, and some pilots shot down four or five Israeli planes in one dogfight." Only the Egyptian and Iraqi air forces had a strategic bombing capability, but with minor exceptions they did not strike inside Israel proper.

The Israelis used their helicopters to rush ammunition and vital supplies to the fronts and to return with wounded. The Egyptians tended to regard their helicopters as gun ships, as the Americans had done in Vietnam, and accordingly suffered losses. They admit losing at least fifteen; the Israelis say forty-two. Later, the Egyptians used their helicopters, which were always giving mechanical trouble, to fly at treetop height to drop napalm on the Israeli bridges over the canal and also to pinpoint targets for their aircraft. The Egyptians claim that no single plane was hit or damaged while in its concrete shelter, but General Peled, at the Israeli Symposium, stated firmly that "to

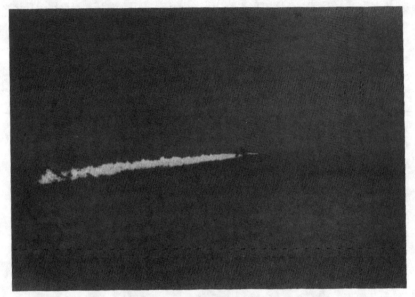

Egyptian MiG in flames over the West Bank battlefront, October 19, 1973.

our certain knowledge twenty-two Arab aircraft were destroyed in their shelters."

The customary flukes occurred. For example, an Egyptian helicopter shot down an Israeli Phantom with a rocket as it tried to fly beneath the helicopter. An Israeli antitank gun shot down an Egyptian helicopter attacking an Israeli bridge. As to rumours that arise and persist in war, one was that the Egyptians claimed that from the eighteenth onward a new type of pilot, who was far more experienced, was flying Israeli aircraft. They further alleged that the pilots were foreign mercenaries, meaning Americans. Perhaps the change of tactics forced on the Israelis, together with several days' hard experience, was partly the answer; another part may have been Israeli dual-nationality pilots.

The Syrians allege that toward the end of the war Israeli morale was so low that Israeli pilots had to be chained in their cockpits, but this can hardly be believed. A photograph was in circulation, of which I saw a copy, showing a dead Israeli pilot with one wrist handcuffed to the frame rail of his crashed aircraft, but no acceptable explanation has so far been put forward. The Israeli government later complained to the International Red Cross that at least six Israeli pilots who bailed out in Syria had been machine-gunned to death.

Summarising, one can say that the Egyptian and Syrian numerical superiority in aircraft over Israel was in the order of two-to-one, but the deduction must be made that Arab pilots were not an equal match for their Israeli counterparts in this war, although, especially on the Egyptian side, the difference had narrowed considerably. The technological gap had also narrowed as the Egyptians, for example, manned and operated the sophisticated Air Defence Barrier, and the fact that it worked at all, let alone so well, was indicative of their advance in this field. The Egyptians told me that the Soviet aircraft mechanism was very complicated, and that all other types were far easier to handle and maintain.

The one deduction that stood out, surprising to those who advocated the phasing out of conventional guns in favour of missiles, was that the best counter to attacking aircraft proved to be antiaircraft guns such as the ZSU quad-23mm, but they were very heavy on ammunition expenditure. A comment of Herzog's is of interest: "As far as the air force is concerned, it must be realised that the ground forces will be less pampered in the future. They will have to get used to not having quite the support they were used to." General Hod, a former commander of the Israeli air force, said that "an ounce of ECM is worth a pound of additional aircraft, in the presence of dense, sophisticated air defence." On the other side of the fence, General Gamasy said that "the war was begun and terminated by the Egyptian air force."

14

WAR AT SEA

> *The Egyptian superiority in the Red Sea was complete.*
>
> Rear Admiral Benyamin Telem,
> commander of the Israeli navy,
> at the Israeli Symposium

The naval forces of the combatant states did not materially affect the outcome of the October War, and only three of the countries involved—Egypt, Israel, and Syria—possessed naval forces of any significance. Those of Jordan were negligible, and Iraq had only a handful of patrol craft, all deployed in the Persian Gulf. The Egyptian navy, the largest, had both strategic and tactical capability. It might have affected the outcome had the war lasted longer, as it was enforcing an embargo of supplies, especially of oil, to Israel—a blockade that was beginning to tighten its grip on that country. The smaller Israeli navy can be thought of as a tactical offensive force. That of Syria, smaller still, could be regarded only in a concept of local coastal and harbour defence.

Somewhat naturally, navies in the Middle East took a much lower priority in military budgets and prestige than armies and air forces because ships, as compared with modern aircraft, for example, are slow in moving from place to place. The fact that, in the 1967 War, there had been no spectacular naval clashes with positively confirmed losses also tended to downgrade any naval demand.

The Egyptian navy, which embraced the Coast Guard service and a small marine commando group, had both a Mediterranean and a Red Sea coastline to protect. Having a strength of over 15,000 personnel, it consisted basically of twelve submarines (the Israelis insisted sixteen), eight destroyers and frigates, nineteen missile boats (the Israelis insisted twenty-five), thirty-four motor torpedo boats, fourteen minesweepers, and other small vessels, including landing craft. Naval headquarters and its main base were at Alexandria; other large bases were at Gharghada, Safaga, and Koseir on the Red Sea coast, and there were several other small naval stations and refuelling facilities along both the Mediterranean and Red Sea coasts. Because of its proximity to Israeli military units and the Bar Lev Line forts, especially Budapest on the Mediterranean coastline, the Egyptians were not able to utilise their naval facilities at Port Said.

The Egyptian naval college at Aboukir provided a four-year training course for cadets, catering for over 470 at a time. The term was less for reserve officers, most of whom, as was the case in the army and air force, had been retained on the active list since the 1967 War. This meant that the Egyptian navy had its full complement of experienced officers. Ordinary ratings were conscripts who served for three years and then became reservists for another nine. Volunteers, accepted for longer engagements, provided the petty officer class and the skilled technicians such as radar operators. There were always ample volunteers for long-service naval engagements.

Rear Admiral Fuad Zukri, commander of the navy, explained to me that in the beginning it had absorbed British methods and traditions, but even in the 1950s it had tended to be regarded as the "poor relation of the armed forces." He said that, in the 1948 War against the Israelis, there had been only a few naval skirmishes, merely brushes, but no serious clashes. When the 1956 War started, he said, the navy had just begun to receive Soviet equipment but "had no time to master it."

In 1967, when the prehostility tension began to mount, the Egyptian navy had larger ships than the Israelis. The Egyptian naval role was to protect harbours and coastlines and also to control the Straits of Tiran (the extremely narrow and vulnerable passage from the Red Sea that led to Israel's southern port of Eilat and also to the adjacent Jordanian port of Akaba). Zukri told me that "at the outbreak of war we had no ships in Israeli waters, and there was no time to deploy them. In this war our navy was not offensive enough; it was not given any offensive mission." He went on to say that the Egyptian navy did not make use of its superior naval strength at a time when it was the only navy (except that of the Soviet Union and certain of the Warsaw Pact powers) to have surface-to-surface missiles on its ships.

The highlight for the Egyptian navy came on 12 July 1967 when it sank the Israeli destroyer *Eilat* (formerly H.M.S. *Zealous*), thus making naval history by being the first navy in the world to sink an enemy ship with a guided missile. Two Egyptian Komar class missile boats had engaged the destroyer off the northern Sinai coast and, firing three Soviet Styx missiles at a range exceeding twelve miles, sank it with the loss of forty-seven lives. Extremely proud of this exploit, Admiral Zukri told me, "There were no Soviet advisers on our missile boats at the time. It was entirely an Egyptian affair, and the Soviets did not find out about it until sometime afterward."

One line of thought advocated phasing out guns and installing guided missiles because, unlike ordinary shells, the projectiles, after being fired, could be diverted or altered from their set course. Impressed by the number of sinkings of capital and medium Allied ships in World War II, the Russians, who were in the process of creating a huge global navy, also tended to favour guided missiles instead of conventional guns. They had developed the concept of small, fast ships, armed with surface-to-surface missiles, that would operate in the area of their own or friendly coastlines. These were designed to engage enemy naval craft at ranges between twenty-two and twenty-eight miles, distances that were considered to be advanced in the technical field in that era of the 1950s. The generally accepted naval dictum, inherent in naval thought since the days of Lord Nelson and before, was that in any engagement the first ship to fire would be the victor, and it naturally followed that the one with the longest-range gun had a vital advantage.

Describing this new type of small ship and its main weapon in a talk at the Israeli International Symposium, Rear Admiral Benyamin Telem, commander of the Israeli navy, said, "The Russian concept is based upon simplicity for the operator, on large numbers of boats and missiles, and on high range and hit probability." The missile boats produced for the Soviet navy were armed with the Styx surface-to-surface missile, which had a range of about 40,000 metres (about twenty-five miles). They had the speed to rush in and strike quickly, relying upon early identification, and once having fired their missiles, they would rapidly disengage.

Two main types of missile boats appeared in Soviet naval service: the 100-ton Komar class, armed with a single pair of Styx missile launchers, which the Egyptians began to receive in 1962, and the 160-ton OSA class missile boat with two pairs of Styx missile launchers, which began to arrive at Alexandria in 1966. Both types also had light naval weapons. They had a speed exceeding forty knots, which was considered to be quite fast at that time. These Soviet Komar and OSA class missile boats were the first to be sent to any non-Warsaw Pact country, and by mid-1967 Egypt possessed twelve OSAs and six Komars, all armed with the Styx missile.

After the 1967 War there was a reorganisation and a weeding out in the Egyptian navy, but its victory over the Israeli ship *Eilat* saved it from wholesale dismissals, as happened in the army and the air force. The navy's primary task was redefined as protection of naval bases against Israeli attack. During the War of Attrition, from 1968 to 1970, the navy came into action on several occasions, bombarding land targets in northern Sinai and occasionally firing back at attacking Israeli aircraft. Its marine commando element made raids against Israeli coastal positions and oil installations along the east side of the Gulf of Suez using non-guided rockets on their small craft.

Admiral Zukri had, of course, been included in the senior planning group for Operation Spark and Operation Badr and indeed, since his appointment as commander of the Egyptian

navy, had been preparing it for action. In particular he had reinforced and trained the Red Sea Squadron, which had been in
existence as such since 1969 and had been holding a number of
communication and deployment exercises in the Red Sea area.
Zukri's plans had to be completed and presented to President
Sadat by January 1973, and, once they were approved, he began
his preparations. For example, certain submarines were sent to
Safaga on the Red Sea and had to steam there by way of the
Cape of Good Hope because the Suez Canal was closed. Arrangements also were made for Egyptian destroyers to use Aden
harbour in South Yemen, and facilities were negotiated with
Pakistan for naval repairs and dry dock facilities. It was decided
that, because the navy did not have its own aircraft element, its
medium ships would operate only outside the radius of action
of the Israeli air force, and that its smaller ships would operate
mainly at night.

Secrecy and careful positioning were important, and by the
end of September 1973 a number of Egyptian ships had been
deployed over a wide area. In the week beginning on 1 October
over fifty naval units were sent to sea. One group was dispatched
to Libya to threaten the Mediterranean route and to attract
Israeli missile boats, while three Egyptian destroyers were sent
to Aden harbour. The prime task was to disrupt maritime shipping to and from Israel and to deprive that country of supplies
and oil. In short, the navy was to blockade Israel from the sea,
but this strategy was more moderately described to me by Admiral Zukri as merely "taking action against sea communications." He would not admit to such crude language as an all-out
blockade such as Britain had mounted in the two World Wars.
At 1300 hours on 6 October Admiral Zukri sent a signal to his
submarines in Safaga harbour and his destroyers in Aden harbour to commence hostilities at 1800 hours and to close to all
shipping the Straits of Tiran, the Gulf of Suez, and the Bab el
Mandeb Straits. As mentioned previously, the Egyptian government defined combat zones at sea and warned shipping to keep
clear of them.

There is little to say about the Syrian navy except that it was
minute and inexperienced, having been formed only compara-

tively recently. It had fewer than 3,000 personnel in all and consisted (according to the Israelis) of some forty light craft that included at least nine missile boats and seventeen motor torpedo boats. Certainly, it possessed six Komar class missile boats, armed with the Styx missile, three Soviet T-43 minesweepers, and at least three of the latest Soviet Nanuchka missile corvettes. They had just arrived in Syria, and were the most modern Soviet type of missile craft to appear in the Mediterranean, under other than a Soviet flag. A small group of Russian advisers was at Syrian naval headquarters at Latakia, but there is no firm evidence that Soviet personnel were actually on board any of the ships that went into action during the October War. The task of the Syrian navy, which again was a poor relation and a belatedly unwanted one, was to protect its main ports—Latakia, Tartous, and Banias—and its Mediterranean coastline.

More can be said about the Israeli navy, although it too was small when compared with its sister services and also considered itself to be a poor relation when it came to priority, equipment, and prestige. Cheered by its capture of an Egyptian destroyer in battle in the 1956 War, it was depressed by its comparative inaction in 1967. Commanded by Rear Admiral Telem, it consisted of about 3,000 regulars, with another 1,000 or so conscripts in various stages of training, and it could be expanded to the 5,000 mark on full mobilisation. It also had a 500-strong naval commando group that included frogmen. It possessed at least three submarines, two destroyers, and about forty smaller ships; among these were twelve Saar class missile boats armed with the Gabriel missile, four motor torpedo boats, ten landing craft and two Reshev class ships.

The sinking of the *Eilat* by a Soviet missile made a deep impression on Israeli naval thought and prompted the search for new concepts of naval warfare. This resulted in Israel, too, producing a missile boat prototype, the *Mivtach,* in December 1967. Then followed a period of trial and development which produced specifications that led to the Israeli government's ordering twelve small, fast patrol ships, known as the Saar class, from the French government at a time when Israeli relations with President de Gaulle were cordial. Seven of them had been delivered to Israel when de Gaulle placed an embargo on the delivery of the others. This resulted in the dramatic escape of the five 220-ton boats from Cherbourg harbour on 24 December 1969; they arrived a few days later at Haifa. The Saar missile boats, with a claimed speed of forty-two knots and a crew of forty, had a patrol capability of over 600 miles and each was armed with eight Gabriel missiles and a rapid-firing cannon.

Further research and experiment, especially in relation to a combination of radar detection, weapons, and electronic countermeasures (ECMs) eventually materialised in the Reshev class missile boat concept. A primary consideration was that it be produced in Israel, which had a fairly advanced home armaments industry by Middle East standards. The first Reshev keel was laid in 1970, and, according to the Israelis, two such boats were in commission when the October War began. The Egyptians, however, insist that only one was active, the other not being delivered until after hostilities ceased. The 260-ton Reshev missile boats carried eight Gabriel missiles, had two quick-firing cannon, and claimed a speed in excess of forty knots.

The Israeli armament industry had produced the Gabriel surface-to-surface missile, which had a range of 20,000 metres (about twelve miles) and which began to come into service in late 1969. It was primarily designed to combat and out-range the 4.5-inch guns on the Soviet Skory class destroyer, the main naval unit in use by the Egyptians in the 1960s. In fact, the first prototype of the Gabriel had been mounted on an Israeli Z class destroyer, but it was immediately seen that a small, faster vessel was required. The Israelis claimed the Gabriel missile was a skimmer in that it had a very low trajectory when in flight and remained close above the surface of the sea, which enabled it to remain below the lower detection capability of the normal radar detection apparatus. According to the *Jerusalem Post* of 16 November 1973, the "Gabriel missile had a 90 percent on-target rating."

Naval activities did not commence on 6 October until after 1800 hours, when darkness fell, because of possible aerial intervention. That night the first of a half dozen clashes of missile boats occurred. The Israelis anticipated a Syrian missile boat

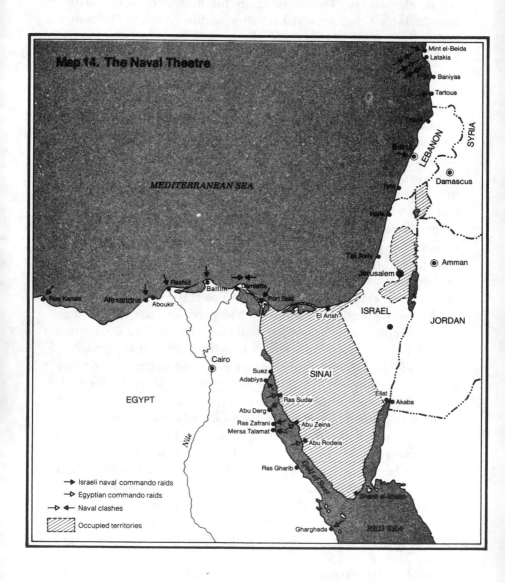

Map 14. The Naval Theatre

MEDITERRANEAN SEA

Mint el-Beida
Latakia
Baniyas
Tartous
Tripoli
Beirut
LEBANON
SYRIA
Damascus
Tyre
Haifa
Tel Aviv
Jerusalem
Amman
ISRAEL
JORDAN
El Arish
Ras Kanais
Alexandria
Aboukir
Rashid
Baltim
Damietta
Port Said
Cairo
EGYPT
Suez
Adabiya
SINAI
Ras Sudar
Eilat
Akaba
Abu Derg
Ras Zafrani
Abu Zeina
Mersa Talamat
Abu Rodeis
Ras Gharib
Gulf of Suez
Sharm al-Sheikh
Gharghada
RED SEA
Nile

→ Israeli naval commando raids
→ Egyptian commando raids
→ ← Naval clashes
Occupied territories

task force might attack Haifa or other targets on the northern part of the Israeli coastline, so an Israeli five-boat force—four Saars and one Reshev—was sent northward on an offensive patrol. First contact was made about 2230 hours with a Syrian K-123 torpedo boat, and one T-43 minesweeper were sunk, all some manoeuvring, was attacked by gunfire. Then the Israelis detected a T-43 minesweeper and three missile boats to the east of the Israeli task force, so, leaving one Saar to deal with the Syrian torpedo boat, the Israeli craft changed direction and made for the Syrian ships, detecting and identifying them positively at 40,000 metres range. An engagement south of Latakia developed when the Syrians opened fire with missiles at 37,000 metres, but none hit their targets. The Israeli boats continued to advance until they were within 20,000 metres, when they opened fire with their Gabriel missiles at their extreme range.

The Israelis claim that one Syrian OSA, two Komars, one K-123 torpedo boat, and one T-43 minesweeper were sunk, all by Gabriel missiles, and that a Komar missile boat that ran aground was fired on by the 40mm gun of another Syrian missile boat, with no Israeli losses. The Syrians, on the other hand, say that in this engagement, which began about 0100 hours on the seventh and lasted for two hours, their coastal batteries took part and sank four Israeli boats. Syrian communiqués were unreliable. So ended cloudily the first missile boat engagement in naval history.

The Egyptians say that in the Mediterranean from 1800 hours onward they carried out "fire missions on control targets and radar posts in the Sinai," which meant, in fact, that they provided artillery ground support. At 0100 hours, because of this bombardment, Israeli aircraft had to be deployed against Egyptian ships. After darkness on the seventh a group of Egyptian naval commandos in five ordinary fishing boats landed to the east of the Israeli Budapest fort on the coastal road. In the south on the Gulf of Suez, the Egyptians landed a number of fishing boats near El Tur, an action they claimed was a feint.

That night, the seventh, the Egyptians again shelled ground targets in northern Sinai, and, as a counter, the Israelis bombarded Port Said from the sea. In the Gulf of Suez, Egyptian commandos made a number of raids on the east coast. On the following night, the eighth, Egyptian commandos mounted a raid on the Balmein oil rig, which was set in the sea near Abu Rodeis. They crossed the sixteen-mile wide gulf after 1800 hours, arriving on the east side only to discover that, instead of having only four sea legs, the rig had eight, which meant the sabotage task would take twice as long. It was accomplished by dawn, and the boats returned across the open gulf in daylight, a dangerous, vulnerable voyage, but they were not detected by the Israeli air force, which at that stage was both busy elsewhere and perplexed. One of the commando boats sank on the return journey, and the men had to swim back through waters in which there were sharks, but all made it to safety by the afternoon of the ninth.

Having first struck at the Syrian navy in the north, the Israelis next turned toward the Egyptians. Anticipating they would move a missile boat task force from Alexandria to reinforce Port Said, the Israelis sent six Saar boats to intercept it. The Israeli task force arrived off Damietta at 1846 hours on the eighth and then cruised around until it identified an Egyptian group of four OSA missile boats at 2110 hours, after which there was some manoeuvring. The first Egyptian salvo, of twelve missiles, was fired at 0015 hours on the ninth from a range of 40,000 metres, but none hit their targets. The Israelis quickly closed to 20,000 metres, the maximum range for their Gabriels, to fire their missiles; they claim they instantly destroyed three of the Egyptian boats and caused the fourth to run aground near Baltim. The Israelis say they suffered no loss at all in this engagement, but the Egyptians, who fired more missiles and their guns, insist the Israelis suffered losses on this occasion from gunfire. Admiral Zukri told me that this missile boat clash had been carefully planned by the Israelis, who had used helicopters to help locate the Egyptian boats and had aircraft flying overhead to give cover against possible intervention by the Egyptian air force.

Next, two missile boat clashes occurred on the night of the tenth. This was the day the first ship of the Soviet sea lift, which had left Odessa laden with ammunition and spares on the seventh, arrived at Latakia. In one incident, as a group of Israeli Saars bombarded installations at Tartous, Syrian missile boats suddenly emerged from the harbour to attack the Israelis. After firing some missiles, the Syrians quickly broke off the engagement and returned to the shelter of their harbour and the cover of their coastal guns. The Israelis, who had fired back, claim to have sunk two Syrian missile boats. The same night six Saar missile boats ran into a group of Egyptian missile boats off Damietta. The Israelis claim to have sunk three Egyptian boats in the exchange of fire, but the Egyptians deny this.

The next night, the eleventh, there were two more missile boat clashes at sea. As an Israeli missile boat task force was moving toward Latakia harbour, Syrian missile boats suddenly emerged, fired their missiles, and then escaped back to the shelter of their coastal batteries, taking refuge among the freighters of several nationalities at anchor. The Israelis continued firing and hit three of the merchant ships. One, the Greek ship *Tsimentarchos,* sank; two of its crew were killed and another seven injured. The second was the Soviet ship *Samir Cote,* and the third was a Japanese freighter, *Yamama Shipomaru,* which was set on fire and later sank. Glassman writes that "some inaccurate [Israeli] missile launches did occur." The Israelis claim to have destroyed four Syrian missile boats in this engagement, but the Syrians countered with a claim of sinking eight Israeli craft.

The second missile boat engagement on the same night was off Tartous, wherein the Syrian navy employed similar tactics. As soon as the Israeli Saars were sighted, the Syrian missile boats would rush out of harbour at full speed, fire their missiles, and then withdraw into the shelter of the international merchant ships at anchor. That night the Israeli navy again bombarded Syrian coastal installations, leaving oil storage tanks on fire at Banias.

From the twelfth onward the Israeli navy had a free run of the Syrian coastline. They were able to go in close and, with their 76mm guns, shoot up oil and other installations, shore batteries, and radar posts, at Latakia, Tartous, and Banias. For example, they shelled the key Al Abrash road bridge just north of Tartous, doing damage and causing alarm. Anticipating that this might be a prelude to an amphibious landing on the Syrian coast, two Syrian brigades were moved from the Golan front down to the coastal plain to counter it. After the twelfth there were no more missile boat clashes at sea, but on that date the Soviet freighter *Ilya Mechnikov* was sunk by a Gabriel missile near Tartous. The Israelis hastily claimed it was accidental, but after this incident they were extremely careful and fired few other missiles. In any case, they had fired off a fair number and were becoming short of them. Israeli missile boats roamed the Egyptian Mediterranean coastline too, but to a lesser extent, even though Egyptian missile boats did not venture out to engage them again.

The war at sea now devolved into what can be regarded as small shadowy actions, some of which have been emphasised, or ignored, by one side or the other. Conflicting versions have been given to me in this still wide grey area in which it is not yet possible to delve too deeply or to double-check. Perhaps positive details may never emerge, and broad hints will either cease and be forgotten or be magnified and distorted into legend by one or the other of the adversaries. Both Israelis and Egyptians, and indeed also the Syrians, claim they initiated naval operations daily. These involved shelling land targets, commando raids, and frogman activities in enemy harbours. For example, the Israelis say that on the fourteenth they shelled Damietta and on the fifteenth mounted a commando raid on Ras Gharib in the Gulf of Suez in which they destroyed eighteen rubber assault boats. They also say they bombarded Port Ibrahim and Port Tewfik on several occasions.

On the sixteenth the Israelis launched a large frogman raid on Port Said harbour which ended disastrously. They lost at least nineteen men. Later, the sister of one of the missing Israeli frogmen made an enquiry seeking information about his disappearance, and on 14 February 1974 Mrs. Sadat, wife of the Egyptian president, wrote a letter of sympathy in response.

On the seventeenth the Israelis put a landing craft into the Gulf of Suez to see if it would be possible to send ships safely through to take on oil from the wells on the east side of the Gulf, but it was sunk by the Egyptians. There were two other

Blazing oil tanks at Latakia Harbour after an Israeli missile boat attack on the Syrian oil port, October 9, 1973.

The traditional broom hoisted on the mast after a successful mission of an Israeli missile boat in the October 1973 war.

similar test attempts by Israeli small craft to run through the Gulf; they also failed, but the Israelis do not mention them at all. I later saw a copy (in translation) of extracts from the interrogation of an Israeli sailor who had been picked up by the Egyptians after his craft had been sunk in the Gulf. If true, the reports tend to confirm these Israeli losses and the reason for such risky attempts.

On the sixteenth three Soviet freighters arrived at Latakia, only hours after Israeli ships had shelled it. By this date the Syrians were desperately short of ammunition and antitank missiles. They had a large convoy of trucks on the dockside waiting to take them instantly to the front, but the ships would not commence unloading until orders to do so were received from the Soviet ambassador in Damascus. As a Soviet ship had been damaged in an air raid, and at least one other had been sunk by the Israelis, the Soviet ships were told to put to sea again immediately without discharging their cargo. The Syrians did not get their much-needed ammunition and missiles, and Soviet-Syrian relations suffered further deterioration.

The Israelis claim that during the night of the eighteenth their ships in the Port Said area and in the Gulf of Suez hit Egyptian targets. The same night Israeli frogmen caused an underwater explosion just off Beirut, which severed two submarine cables, one of which went to Alexandria and the other to Marseilles. This put out of action both the telex and telecommunications from Damascus to the West. This was a blow to the Arabs because both the Syrian and Egyptian governments had used this method of communicating with each other in preference to using the radio, which was monitored by Soviet, American, and Israeli intelligence surveillance organisations. Egypt and Syria then communicated with each other by way of the radio station at Ajlun, Jordan, bouncing its signals off a U.S. satellite. The Beirut underwater cables were not repaired until the twenty-seventh, when communication was restored with the West.

On the twentieth the Israeli navy claimed to have again shelled the military installations near Damietta and for the second successive night to have set fire with rockets the supply dumps near Rosetta. In the last week of the war there were three or four raids on Eilat by Egyptian frogmen. They caused little damage, but some alarm. No precise details have been released by the Egyptians, and the Israelis were evasive about the matter, denying in vague terms that any such raids had ever taken place. The Egyptians say that on the twenty-first they fired missiles and rockets from shore bases at Israeli craft; they did not claim any hits.

At dawn on the twenty-second, the day of the first cease-fire, the Israelis launched an amphibious attack on Gharghada harbour, on the Red Sea. Their purpose was to destroy what they believed to be the last Egyptian Komar missile boat still operating in that area. Two Israeli commando boats (the Israelis would not confirm they were Saars, although the Egyptians insisted they were) managed to manoeuvre undetected into a roadstead between reefs and sighted the Komar at anchor near the quay. The Israelis fired at the Komar with antitank rockets from a distance of fifty metres. They did not hit it, but this alerted the Egyptians, who opened fire on the Israeli boats from the shore, causing one to go aground on a reef near the Komar missile boat. Meanwhile, an Israeli antitank rocket struck the Komar, which caught fire and exploded. The Israeli boat was levered from the reef, and both craft returned to their base near Sharm El Sheikh.

After the first cease-fire, aggressive activity at sea slackened, but both the Egyptian and Israeli navies remained tensely on the alert. On the twenty-fifth a Greek 3,000-ton freighter, flying a Cypriot flag and sailing from Alexandria to Benghazi, was sunk off Alexandria with the loss of fourteen out of its crew of eighteen. Allegedly it was torpedoed by an unidentified vessel. The Israelis deny responsibility. On the twenty-sixth the 45,000-ton Liberian oil tanker *Sirus,* under charter to Israel, was sent from Eilat to take on oil at Abu Rodeis, but, when nearing its destination, it hit a mine and sank.

Those seem to be the main naval operations, actions, and incidents of the October War for which there is some degree of confirmation. In interviews and discussions, hints of other actions by small ships and commandos have been given to me by both sides, invariably with the hasty addition that they could not be enlarged upon for reasons of "security" or because they were "classified." Finding little or nothing to substantiate such hints, they cannot be seriously considered. On the strategic side, Admiral Zukri told me Egyptian submarines came into action three times—on the seventh, the eleventh, and the twenty-second —but he did not know whether they hit, damaged, or sank any Israeli craft, "nor was it possible to know." He also added that there were "a few missile actions and some helicopter operations with the navy according to a conventional plan in which the strategic and political aim was coordinated for the first time."

In the naval sphere, as in those of the air force and the land forces, there are conflicting claims which are impossible to reconcile. Many claims made by both sides have either been quietly amended or presented in a different form. The Israelis claim to have destroyed fourteen Arab missile boats in battle and others at their moorings. The Egyptians admit the loss of only one missile boat sunk on the night of the sixth and two others hit and damaged but not sunk. The Israelis insist that only one of their Saar missile boats was hit, being slightly damaged by shrapnel, and that none were sunk or lost in any other way. The U.S. Pentagon, however, estimated that the Israeli navy lost at least two, perhaps three, Saar boats which were sunk, and that one or two others were damaged. Soviet estimates indicate the Israelis lost five craft of all types.

Additionally, the Israelis claim that, in the Red Sea, the Gulf of Suez, and along the Mediterranean coastline, the Syrians and Egyptians lost a number of other vessels, including minesweepers, MTBs, and a variety of auxiliary naval craft, ranging from armed tugs to ammunition carriers. Precise details are not forthcoming about dates, places, or craft. The one exception was the Israeli claim that the Egyptians, on the night of the thirteenth, lost three OSAs "from the safety of their harbours."

An analysis of the half dozen missile boat clashes indicates that the Israelis were the absolute out-and-out victors. They boasted that neither the Egyptians nor the Syrians managed to land a single Styx missile on an Israeli target, despite the fact that the range of the Styx was twice that of the Gabriel. The Israelis say their successes in these missile clashes at sea—the first in naval history and, therefore, ones which obviously would be closely studied by naval commanders and staffs in naval colleges the world over—were due entirely to superior seamanship, better missiles, better and more manoeuvrable boats, and better trained, more skillful crews. They further claim that the Arabs were hopelessly outclassed in this new form of naval warfare. In doing this they are creating a mythology of naval superiority which they do not necessarily have, and the situation seems reminiscent of the overwhelming overconfidence assumed on land and in the air after the 1967 War.

The Israelis say that their activities in the October War with their small missile boats had demolished the premature conception that the days of surface vessels, especially large ones such as destroyers, were numbered, and that they had shown that even small countries could afford to have effective, if small, fleets of missile boats that could counter ships many times their size. Having a keen eye on their export market, the Israelis claimed the speed and versatility of their Reshev and Saar class missile boats made them excellent submarine hunters, convoy escort vessels, and floating weapon platforms to support combined operations. However, the Egyptians mutter accusingly that the Israelis were crediting their missile boats, especially the Reshev, with more capability than they possessed, not only to give an impression of superiority over Arab navies and ships, but also so they could be sold overseas.

The truth, unpalatable to Israel, is that, just as the Israelis had been caught out on 6 October by inferior ECMs on their aircraft, so had the Egyptians and Syrians also been badly caught out by the fact that the Israelis had superior ECMs on their missile boats. This electronic advantage was the sole reason none of the Israeli craft was hit by Styx missiles. It accounts for the fact that the Israelis could steam unscathed for 20,000 metres toward the Arab missile boats until their Gabriel missiles were within reach of the enemy craft, and why the Israelis achieved so many kills, and the Arabs none, by missile fire. In the face of advanced and superior ECMs on the Israeli missile boats, the Soviet OSA and Komar missile boats with their Styx missiles were impotent. There was not a great deal to choose between skill and seamanship, and the Soviet missile boats were as manoeuvrable as those of the Israelis and, indeed, faster in the water.

The Gabriel missile carried ECM equipment able to jam the Styx missile on its ballistic curve, and it also had an automatic homing device that operated in rough seas and weather without loss of accuracy or technical efficiency. The Soviet ECMs were inferior in effectiveness because rough weather and seas caused a clutter that affected their performance. In short, the Soviet ECMs could not counter the Israelis' Gabriels, but the Gabriels could deflect the Styx missiles, a fact that caused satisfaction to NATO and American designers and planners and dismay to the Russians. Both missiles were deadly and efficient in their own way, but there was a distinct ECM gap on the Arab, which is to say the Soviet, side, and the Israelis had allowed the watching world to draw wrong deductions. The Lord Nelson adage may still be valid, but it appears to be a maxim that has been modified by the efficiency of opposing ECM capability.

An important point made by Admiral Telem was that "boats under no circumstances [should] become big or expensive in equipment to the extent that their own defence becomes a first priority requirement in itself. This would inevitably negate their offensive capability"—a point upon which designers of aircraft and tanks would do well to ponder.

The Egyptians claim the blockade by their Red Sea Squadron was complete, and that from the evening of the sixth until the twenty-eighth no ships destined for Eilat entered the Red Sea nor did any from that Israeli port leave the area. The Egyptians stopped over 200 ships at the Bab El Mandeb Straits; only four were allowed to pass to ports in either the Sudan or Yemen. The *Jerusalem Post* of 2 November 1973 reported that "no ships have entered the port [Eilat] since the outbreak of war and the subsequent closing of the Bab El Mandeb Straits at the entrance to the Red Sea. Only one ship sailed, the Japanese freighter *Kuo Maro*, which was reportedly let through the blockade; the other thirteen are still there." Perhaps one ship did get through. The blockade was mainly enforced by the three Egyptian destroyers based on Aden harbour, supported by smaller ships. They were assisted by landing craft of the tiny South Yemen navy, which itself consisted of two submarine chasers, two minesweepers and three landing craft. The thirteen merchant ships caught on the sixth at Akaba, the Jordanian port, had to remain there throughout the war.

The Arab Mediterranean blockade was not quite so watertight, and the Egyptians admit that seventeen ships reached Haifa during the war. They point out that this must be compared with 198 ships arriving at that port during the corresponding period in 1972. The Israelis disagree with this figure and insist that over eighty freighters and passenger ships arrived at their ports during the war but decline to give details. Admiral Zukri told me again that "we were actually using the international right to visit and examine the merchant shipping, which would show us whether they were carrying strategic material needed for the Israeli war effort." He also said that "our flow of merchant shipping was very normal in and out of Alexandria, and, as our Egyptian merchant fleet was small, it was mostly foreign shipping. This showed international confidence in us, as no nation would risk their ships unless confident of their safety. It was not so with Israel."

One incident of interest in the blockade should be mentioned because it nearly caused international repercussions. It became known as the La Salle Affaire and began during the first days of the war when the U.S. freighter *La Salle,* moving southward in the Red Sea, signalled that it had been fired on in the Bab El Mandeb Straits by an Egyptian destroyer. A shot had been put across its bows, and the ship was turned back to the Ethiopian port of Massawa. At this time the U.S.S. *Charles Adam,* a destroyer, was in the French port of Djibouti, in the Red Sea, but the French authorities prevented its leaving port to go to the assistance of the *La Salle.* The rather tactless American handling of its NATO allies in this crisis had caused friction, which provoked the comment from Michel Jobert, the French foreign minister, that "the superpowers are humiliating European countries." After this incident a U.S. naval task force, consisting of the U.S.S. *Hancock,* an aircraft carrier, and five escorting destroyers was sent into the Indian Ocean to keep a watch on the Middle East from that direction.

The Israelis resolutely refuse to discuss their oil problem during the October War, but there can be no doubt that it worried them far more than they can ever bring themselves to admit. Owing to the Egyptian sea blockade, no oil went into Israel, and it is known that the forty-two-inch oil pipeline from Eilat to Ashdod, on the Mediterranean, was empty at the end of the war. It is not known how much oil remained in Israeli storage tanks and dumps—it could not have been much. In view of this, one can only speculate how many more days, or even hours, the Israelis could have fought on, especially if the combined Syrian-Iraqi-Jordanian five-division assault had been launched on the twenty-third as planned, or Egyptian resistance on the battlefield had stiffened.

The urgent Israeli need for oil was indicated by the frantic efforts of Premier Meir during the negotiations before, and after, the cease-fires, and her insistence on the primary condition before the Israelis would agree to anything—a condition that must not be communicated to the press—of lifting the oil blockade at the Bab El Mandeb Straits. The Israelis also made desperate efforts to get oil tankers into Eilat and to obtain oil from the Sinai oil wells. When the Egyptian Third Army was encirlced and wanted medicines and other vital supplies, the Israeli paramount condition was that the Egyptian oil blockade in the Red Sea first be lifted. The Israelis also tried to persuade the United States to bring in oil tankers under an American flag, but the U.S. government was not prepared to go that far, partly because of possible Soviet escalation and partly because the Arab reply would have been an instant and total oil embargo on the whole of the West. It was obviously not a practical proposition to airlift in enough oil to make any significant contribution. The Arabs did not have an oil supply problem; even Syria was supplied by Kuwait by way of Iraq, a temporary friend. Libya sent oil to Egypt, but charged for it at the full commercial rate.

Realising the power they held in their hands, the Arab oil-producing states began to use it to help the war effort against Israel. As a result, an international oil crisis arose and developed dangerously after the October War ended. The Americans and the Dutch, for example, were extremely unpopular with the

Arabs, while certain other countries, such as Britain, Spain, and France, came into the "most favoured" category of Saudi Arabia and Abu Dabai at least, which ensured that their oil deliveries remained about the normal level. Saudi Arabia made it clear that any country that passed on crude oil or its refined products to a country under embargo would be penalised, and Holland's pleas for oil were ignored.

When they met on 4 November in Kuwait, the Arab oil ministers intended to tighten the squeeze and to consolidate the measures already taken. They contemplated a 25 percent cut in production (not delivery) with a further 5 percent to be introduced in December. They vaguely promised that normal supplies would be maintained to favoured countries. The Dutch banned Sunday motoring, the Germans were considering a similar measure, and the British prepared a scheme for petrol rationing. As the Arab oil-producing states remained united, and as they had already increased their prices by some 70 percent, predictions indicated it would be February 1974 before they actually received less income from the sale of oil than before the cuts were imposed in October 1973. King Feisal of Saudi Arabia told Secretary of State Kissinger that he would prefer to stop oil production completely, rather than give up his ambition to pray at the Aksa Mosque in Jerusalem before he died, and he made it known that his country had sufficient cash reserves to live on for more than three years without receiving any oil royalties. The October War had unsheathed the Arab oil weapon. The Arabs looked at it, tested it, and found that it was a sharp one.

15

IN RETROSPECT

The war was a near disaster, a nightmare.

Premier Golda Meir

Both sides claim to have won the October War. Neither will admit defeat, and, as there was no clear-cut military decision on the battlefield, myths are being manufactured to be written into national history books. The Israelis now give the impression that they were merely caught by surprise, and that, once they had recovered their balance, all was well. They insist that their "quality" was still superior to Arab "quantity" and that their young, energetic, capable generals were superior to those of the Arabs as was the Israeli soldier to his Arab counterpart. The Israelis like to say they drove back the Arabs on both fronts, crossed the Suez Canal, penetrated into Africa, and surrounded the Egyptian Third Army with ease. They further claim that only intervention by the superpowers saved the Third Army from surrendering and the Israelis from advancing further into Arab territory, as the road to Cairo lay open before them. This was by no means the correct picture, and, by perpetuating it, the Israelis are in danger of falling into the same errors of self-deception and overconfidence that they did after the 1967 War.

On the other hand, the Egyptians are also trying to persuade themselves, and others, that they won the war. They point to

329

the fact that the Israelis are no longer on the east bank of the Suez Canal, that the Bar Lev Line no longer exists, and that the Suez Canal is now open to normal traffic. In doing so, however, they blind themselves harmfully to Israeli military achievements and the fact that they penetrated no more than some sixteen or seventeen miles into the Sinai. Even Syria has convinced itself that its defence of the Sasa Line was a victory, while both Iraq and Jordan feel the cease-fire was premature, preventing them from driving the Israelis back to the River Jordan.

The truth is that the October War, militarily speaking, was a standoff. Even though the Egyptians gained some 300 square miles of Israeli-held Sinai on the east bank of the canal, the Syrians lost almost the same amount of terrain in the north. Politically speaking, the war drastically changed the situation in the Middle East from the almost crystallised one of No Peace, No War, to one of No Victor, No Vanquished. In short, both sides gained advantages and suffered disadvantages, the Arabs perhaps gaining far more than the Israelis. The Palestinians, in whose cause the Arabs fought, also gained politically, and by mid-November 1973 the Soviet Union was calling for implementation of Palestinian "national rights," as opposed to the customary but less definite "legitimate rights." The U.S.S.R. was followed by Japan which recognised the "legitimate rights" of the Palestinian people, while in March 1974 Italy recognised their "national rights."

The Israelis lost the military superiority they had enjoyed over the Arabs for so long, and their military power alone was no longer great enough to deter Arab attacks. While the Arabs have since appeared to have gained more from subsequent negotiations, the Israelis have had their armoury filled to overflowing by the Americans as never before. The greatest Arab gain from the war was the fact that the haunting spectre of the Israeli "invincible soldier" was shattered. Premier Golda Meir writes, in *My Life,* "The war was a near disaster, a nightmare that I myself experienced and which will always be with me. . . . I found myself as prime minister, in a position of ultimate responsibility at a time when the state faced the greatest threat it had known."

A number of sharp lessons, some unpalatable, have come out

of this war. One that affects the NATO Alliance as much as any other is that the almost traditionally accepted and expected period of "rising political tension," part of current Western military doctrine upon which NATO relies to mobilise, muster reserves, and deploy troops, may not necessarily precede an enemy attack. There was persistent tension in the Middle East, and it fluctuated only in degree before the bombshell burst.

The prominent lesson that stands out is that surprise can still be achieved in modern times, despite sophisticated means of obtaining intelligence, and remains perhaps the most valuable principle of war in the book. General Gamasy said at the International Symposium in Cairo in October 1975 that "this [war] proves that surprise can be achieved in modern war." Lulled into a sense of superiority, the Israelis had not thought it conceivable the Arabs would be capable of mounting an offensive against them, let alone on two fronts simultaneously, and neither did they dream the Arabs could make such deceptive plans or keep such secrets. It must follow that a nation's armed forces must be on their guard at all times and be ready to react instantly.

Some tend to blame the intelligence services for the failure to give due warning, but the Israeli Mossad was an extremely efficient one, which had noted and reported the Arab moves. The failure lay not in assessing capabilities, but in differentiating them from intentions. The American intelligence services thought highly of the Mossad, and one suspects they worked closely together; perhaps the Americans relied on it too much. Heikal writes, "The Americans were able to confess to Egypt afterward that they had got hold of the plans for Badr in May [1973] but did not believe them."

The next shock to NATO planners, the Soviet Union, and others was the incredible amount of material destruction that occurred in such a short period of time. Precise figures are still elusive, but it may be safe to say that not less than 500 aircraft and 2,500 tanks were destroyed, together with an untold number of guns, vehicles, and other equipment. All this happened at a time when American war production plants had been scaled down after the ending of the Vietnam War. One official report (House of Representatives Armed Services Committee, Subcommittee Report on the Middle East in 1974) says that "there is only one producer of tanks in the United States for the U.S. Army, and the present production rate is thirty a month, or 360 a year." It is believed that France, for example, was producing only about 300 tanks a year, and it is thought that the Soviet Union was producing only about the same number.

When one considers that the ZSU quad-23mm antiaircraft gun is capable of firing 4,000 rounds a minute, and that many did so for fairly lengthy periods, one can begin to appreciate the magnitude of the supply problem in ammunition alone. Herzog writes, "The Israeli expenditure of ammunition was inordinately high." Generally, ammunition was used up at a rate far greater than anticipated, and it would be of interest to know exactly how many missiles of all types, Soviet and American, were actually fired in this war, and their results analysed. It has caused NATO planners, whom one suspects were working on World War II experiences, to hastily revise their estimates for European and other stockpiles while the Soviet Union must also have had to recalculate furiously on similar lines.

When the United States decided to openly mount an air lift across the Atlantic of material vital to Israel, it ran into an unexpected difficulty. It found that individual members of NATO had minds of their own regarding the Arab-Israeli problem and were not prepared to accept American policy unthinkingly. Generally, Western Europe, Great Britain, and Japan favoured the Arabs, perhaps influenced by their dependence upon Arab oil; only Holland openly supported Israel. Arrogantly, or thoughtlessly, the Americans began using their leased airfield facilities in the Azores without initially informing the Portuguese, who, when they found out, were persuaded to allow this to continue only because they wanted support on an unpopular colonial point in the United Nations. Without this grudgingly given Portuguese facility, the United States would not have been able to air-supply Israel. One NATO country, Turkey, actually gave the Soviet Union permission to fly over its territory to take military supplies to Arab countries. Again, on the tenth, the British refused to allow the Americans to use Cyprus as a base for the American SR-71 spy planes, and it was not until the thirteenth that the United States could persuade Iran to give it this facility. The Americans felt that the NATO Allies had let them down badly. The assistant secretary of state for Europe, Arthur Hartman, openly criticised their reluctance to support the United States in the October War and spoke of "our keen disappointment with some of the allies during the Middle East crisis."

Also, during the course of the war the Americans took weapons, especially TOWs, ammunition, and materiel, from NATO stockpiles in Europe without asking or telling the host countries. When this was discovered it caused resentment and raised the question of whether American bilateral interests took precedence over NATO's, and what was the primary purpose of NATO stockpiles anyway? The Americans discovered their NATO allies were not servile satellites on the Soviet pattern, and their action had made another deep crack in the alliance.

No NATO country can carry on normally in peacetime without Arab oil for its domestic and industrial consumption, and even the United States needs a little to keep up its high standard of living. For NATO a most important factor in the war was the Arab oil embargo. Western economy had been based upon the assumption that there would be ample, cheap Arab oil for some years ahead. The war showed that this was no longer the case as Arab oil suddenly became expensive, financially and politically, and, more important still, the Arabs could afford to withhold it completely for periods of time as they had enough monetary reserves to survive. This condition indicates that the NATO alliance could not wage war against the Warsaw Pact powers without an unstinting supply of Arab oil. As Arab oil-producing countries are no longer "occupied," or have their economy controlled by Western colonial powers as in World War II, NATO would have to win Arab approval and support, probably at the expense of Israel, when difficulties might arise should the United States continue to underwrite and support Israel.

Other general lessons include the danger of preparing for a short war; if it is not won within the stipulated time, it is invariably lost because plans and stocks of material do not cater for extra time. There must be tight, central control of aircraft closely linked with the air defence to coordinate the split-second

switching on and off of an air defence barrier. Air tactical headquarters should be as far back as possible so that it can control a
whole front or more. On the other hand, the general headquarters of land forces and formation commanders should be well
forward on the ground to be able to react instantly to any emergency. General Ismail's GHQ at "Number Ten," for example,
was too far back once the battle was joined and operations became fluid. When I asked him why he did not have a field GHQ
forward, he replied that "the distances were too small and a
corps headquarters would have required an extra 100 staff officers which we did not have. I did have a forward HQ, which
both myself and Shazli visited from time to time, and also a
field GHQ, designed to move forward if we advanced." The
maxim seems to be that air control should be further back and
ground control further forward.

This was the first war in which the battlefields were regularly
monitored by reconnaissance satellite which could take and
send back photographs that could be so enlarged that individual
vehicles, guns, and positions could be identified. The Russians
had a huge advantage in gaining a clearer and more accurate picture of the progress of the war than did the actual combatants,
who were befogged by the smoke and dust of battle, and the
Americans, who, owing to economies in their space programme,
had neglected the Middle East area for Europe. There was the
instance of Kosygin showing satellite photographs to President
Sadat on the seventeenth to prove to him the extent and strength
of Israeli penetration of the west bank. In future wars, superpowers, by means of reconnaissance satellites, will gain more
accurate battlefield information about the enemy than has ever
been gained before in history, bringing new and urgent problems
of flexibility and camouflage.

Air reconnaissance and surveillance are commonplace in war
today, and, although good at them in this war, both Israelis and
Americans were hamstrung by the efficiency of the Arab air defences. One pilotless U.S. Ryan Firebee was sent over the Suez
Canal area on the seventeenth, only to be shot down, which
brought this method to a stop as being too vulnerable and costly.
It seems that the power with the best reconnaissance satellite

system will have an outstanding advantage in any future war, while a country without one, or without access to one, will be at an acute disadvantage.

Yet another innovation of this war was the alleged use of the "truth drug" on Israeli prisoners by the Syrians, who delayed the exchange of prisoners until they had drained them of all useful information. According to some sources, the Israeli prisoners talked freely. The drug used was succinyl choline, and one source alleged Soviet military interrogation teams questioning Israeli prisoners of war had employed medical and other techniques to break down resistance. Should the truth drug techniques prove to be successful and be developed in a big way, which a cynic would say must be the inevitable progression, it would be yet another valuable aid to intelligence gathering we might see as a commonplace feature of future warfare.

Few wars are devoid of secret agreements, forced by expediency, and this was no exception. It was, for example, strongly suspected that King Hussein, through French intermediaries, made a secret agreement with the Israelis not to attack Israel in the early part of the war. This enabled Israel to move formations away from the west bank of the River Jordan for use elsewhere at a vital time. The Jordanian open bridges policy tended to substantiate this agreement, although its existence was denied by both governments. Again, some of the French Mirage aircraft received by Libya were used in battle by the Egyptians, a fact that was denied by both governments until some time after the war when Colonel Gaddafi asked for them to be returned. President Sadat was reluctant to do so because there was friction between the two heads of state at the time, and Sadat was not sure how the unpredictable Gaddafi would use them. Gaddafi had promised France the aircraft would not be exported or used other than in the defence of Libya, so the secrecy was understandable; if the fact were known, France might not have sent the remainder of the promised aircraft consignment or the vital back-up supply of spares.

The Arabs accused the Americans of helping the Israelis, and the Israelis accused the Soviet Union of helping the Arabs. Each alleged that without such unstinting aid the other would prob-

ably not have been able to fight the war, and certainly not for
so long. Both were correct as the Soviet Union and the United
States poured in material replacements in quantity; it was a
moot point who received the most. Support for any military
action tends to escalate, be it in reinforcements, arms, or supplies, and the Vietnam War is a typical case in point. Neither the
Soviet Union nor the United States originally wanted the war,
being interested in *detente,* but, once it began, neither wanted
its clients to be defeated. Consequently, they began to supply
them, an act that escalated wildly owing to the massive material
destruction that occurred, becoming an escalation that neither
could stop until a cease-fire was imposed. Heikal writes that on
the seventeenth Kissinger told President Nixon that Israel could
not fight alone for more than nine days, and after that period it
would be entirely dependent on the United States. When inter-
viewed by *Al Anwar* on 22 June 1975, President Sadat said,
"When I wanted to liquidate the Israeli pocket [on the west
bank] in December 1973, and I was ready to do this, Kissinger
came on the eleventh and twelfth of December, and I told him
the situation, and asked what would be America's position. Kissinger replied, 'We will enter the war with Israel against you,
because we will not allow Soviet weapons to win over American
weapons *again*' " (author's italics).

Neither the Soviet Union nor the United States sent in combat personnel as such, either pilots or soldiers, but there was in
both cases a wide grey area. When the war began there were
about seventy Soviet personnel with the Egyptians, who insisted
that none were advisers but all were specialist technicians, either
training Egyptians or repairing sophisticated equipment. Up to
1,000 more Soviet personnel came into Egypt during the war.
There were probably some 2,000, or even more, Soviet personnel
in Syria when the war began, of whom a number were obvious
advisers and of whom 1,000 were distributed out to air defence
units. Glassman writes that "Soviet advisers were present in
Syrian command posts at every echelon, from battalion up, including supreme headquarters." Some actually went into battle
with the Syrians, and it is thought that at least twenty Russians
were killed in action, with presumably a conventionally accepted

higher proportion being wounded. Shimon Peres, speaking in the Knesset on 2 July 1974, said that "high-ranking Russian officers were killed on the battlefield in Syria," without specifying how many. There were also strong rumours in circulation at the time that a handful of Russians had been captured by the Israelis, but this was denied and played down. It was noticeable that just after the war certain Jews were allowed to leave the Soviet Union, the suspicion being that a covert exchange had been effected. The *Observer* tended to confirm this rumour, saying that "seven Russian soldiers in uniform were captured by the Israelis in the first week, the Russians surrendering when Israelis overran their bunker in the first line of Syrian defences." It added that this incident was treated by the Israelis with the greatest secrecy, and that the Russians were whisked off to Ramat David airbase for interrogation. There was another influx of Soviet personnel into Syria during the war to deal with the Soviet air lift and help repair the SAMs and radar equipment.

On the other side of the fence Israel received similar but not such extensive American help. The Arabs loudly alleged that American pilots, some veterans of Vietnam, were flying with the Israeli air force. This accusation was denied, but it was later admitted by the Americans that a small number of U.S. servicemen were in Israel to handle the air lift. A large number of Israeli reservists returned from abroad during the war, of whom a number had dual nationality—that is, possessing both Israeli and American passports. This was a wide grey area about which the Israelis are silent and in which Arab allegations may have had substance.

If the strongest card played on the Arab side was the initial surprise attack, that on the Israelis' was their counter of speedy mobilisation. Within twenty-four hours the elements of four reserve divisions were on the battlefields. It was a reversal of 1967, as this time it was the Arabs who had been mobilised for several days and who had the advantage of refresher and collective training, while it was the Israelis who were unprepared and unready. The initial hours of mobilisation were chaotic, but matters quickly sorted themselves out.

While the Israeli strategic aim was to win decisive battles

quickly, that of the Arabs was the more limited one of simply recovering the occupied territories. General Gamasy explained that "on the strategic level it [the war] has shaken the theories and doctrines embraced by the Israelis and has shattered the Israeli 'security theory' as well as their theory of 'preventive war.' " He went on to add that "it [the war] was planned. I want to stress from the start that it was a purely Egyptian strategy that was neither imported from the East nor the West." The Egyptians crossed the Suez Canal on a broad front and stormed the Bar Lev Line; this was the first time in military history that such a defensive barrier had been overcome by military means. Others, such as the Maginot Line, were bypassed. Once on the east bank the cautious General Ismail would probably have remained under his Air Defence Barrier, content to wait for a cease-fire, appreciating the strength and advantage of his position while the Israelis destroyed themselves on "his rocks." He probably would not have moved forward at all if he had not been compelled to do so by a political decision. The Egyptian soldiers were trained to do just that one operation, and they did it magnificently, but Ismail knew they were not conditioned for mobile warfare. Things got out of hand as neither his GHQ nor his field formations were flexible.

General Ismail's decision to bring over a proportion of his strategic armoured reserve to the east bank on the eleventh and twelfth must be questioned, for he admitted to me that he anticipated an Israeli airborne landing on the west bank and that he knew of the Israeli plan to cross the canal and "roll up" the Air Defence Barrier. His armour would have been ideal to counter such operations.

General Shazli, the chief of staff, who argued with General Ismail, urging him during the first week to run for the passes, was, in my view, quite wrong. Away from the shelter of the Air Defence Barrier, the Egyptian army would be at the mercy of the Israeli air force, which was still superior to that of the Egyptians. However, General Shazli's recommendation, made after his visit to the front on the eighteenth when he realised the strength and depth of the Israeli gap, was to quickly bring back the strategic armour from the east bank to deal with it. This was, in my view, correct as armour could have been effective in this case. Another wrong decision, perhaps also Shazli's, was to withdraw the paratroop brigade and artillery units threatening and shelling the Israeli bridge and bridgeheads on the eighteenth and nineteenth. Their absence enabled the Israelis to become more firmly established on the west bank with fewer casualties.

The Egyptians gave their infantry first priority and kept their armour to the rear. This was a good disposition and the opposite of what the Israelis expected and hoped for, but, once they advanced, their formations were too rigid, their sights too narrow, and all eyes looked forward only. In short, the Egyptians developed the concept of elevating the infantry, armed with antitank weapons, to a leading, instead of a supporting, role. However, formation commanders had little liaison with flank formations, the passing back of information was poor, and the reaction to anything unexpected was slow. There was clearly the need for a corps commander in the field. In brief, the Egyptians had planned and practiced their first great bound in detail, but had only thought, and not planned and practiced, their second one, which was to advance to the passes.

The Syrian strategy was to bulldoze their way across the Golan Plateau to the River Jordan, but the mass assault, at first successful, halted through lack of confidence and realisation of the vulnerability of their armour once beyond the Air Defence Barrier. They then failed to advance and were driven back by the reinforced Israelis, who had recovered from their initial shocks. To the proud Syrian character, all advice, especially from foreigners, was odious, and it was four days before Soviet advisers were allowed into the GHQ operations room, by which time disaster had befallen the Syrian divisions. The Soviet advisers recommended a swift withdrawal to the Sasa Line. This was fairly well done, except that all guns and vehicles were abandoned. Once there, the Sasa Line held well, and the Israelis could not break through it.

For political reasons the Iraqis were invited onto the battlefield only in the "hour of panic" to help stabilise the situation. Once they arrived, the Jordanians followed, also for political reasons. The two combined Arab attacks were failures owing to no coordination or trust between the three armies and lack of a firm command. The fighting on the Syrian front was rather in the nature of a slugging match, demonstrating little finesse or skill.

General Tlas told me, "We were politically ready, but not militarily ready," and said, "When considering our struggle with Israel, I think of the Syrians as Russians and the Israelis as Germans in World War II." He was clearly haunted by the debacle of 1967. Tlas seemed to me to be a pleasant, but hesitant, character, who does not like immediate trouble and has many second thoughts. The blame must rest on the senior Syrian leadership, and a thought must be that political leadership of an army in battle is no substitute for sound generalship. A flair for politics is not a substitute for a flair for battle.

Before the October War the tendency of larger nations was to gradually replace their guns with missiles. The theory behind this was that, once a shell is fired, it is irreversible and must continue on its course even though the target, perhaps a tank, has moved from the spot originally aimed at. With an antitank missile, for example, no matter how the tank moves about, provided it remains within range and sight, the missile can follow it. Similar reasoning was applied to surface-to-air missiles, which were designed to home onto aircraft by a variety of means, as it was thought that conventional antiaircraft guns were obsolete. To the protagonists of either missiles, aircraft, or tanks, the war prompted some surprising and disturbing deductions. Complete analysis of the effects of the various weapons is not yet available, and perhaps may never be, but partial and selective figures are, and they have become the ammunition of protagonists. For example, traditionally the Israelis are interested in playing down the deadly effect of missiles, both surface-to-air and antitank, and boosting the superiority of their air force and tank gunnery, while the Arabs are on the side of missiles.

Steeped in the belief that it takes a tank to kill a tank, and their own superiority in mobile armoured warfare, the Israelis had a contempt for antitank missiles, which had a very low priority with them. Even now they are perhaps not keen on admitting their potency for psychological reasons mainly, to which can be added that of vested interest. General Herzog states that less than 25 percent of Israeli tanks were hit by missiles. Brigadier Eytan, speaking of the Israeli advance into Syria across the 1967 cease-fire line, insisted that not one of his tanks was hit by missiles. Proud of their armoured corps tank gunnery and their first shot kills, the Israelis played down their liberal use of TOWs in the second part of the war. The Egyptians admit the TOWs destroyed many of their tanks. Certainly tanks unsupported by mobile infantry were easy prey to the missiles fired by opposing infantrymen.

With the rise of the fashionable trend for infantry to be carried in armoured personnel carriers that gave protection against shell splinters and small arms fire, it was thought that the need for conventional HE shells, originally designed to break up infantry formations, was unnecessary. Initially the Israelis had none which would have been effective against Arab infantry manning antitank missiles, nor did they have any mortars with their forward tanks. Once the Israelis realised what was happening, they reverted to all-arms combat teams in which there were tanks, guns, mortars, missiles, and infantry and were more successful. The Syrians were forced into this pattern as all their arms became jumbled together on the Golan Plateau; the Egyptians had never really departed from it. And so the deduction drawn by NATO experts and armoured warfare protagonists is that the tank is not an obsolete weapon but must be used in conjunction with other arms. I feel that tradition and vested interest are conspiring to maintain its importance.

In the air the Arabs tend to emphasize the lethal quality of their SAMs and to play down the importance of the ECMs attached to aircraft, while the Israelis try to persuade one to see it the other way round. Selective sets of figures are bandied about by both sides to gild their views. In the sophisticated sphere of aircraft, missiles, radar, and ECMs, in the mad and extremely expensive race for technical superiority and one-upmanship, the slightest advantageous progression could mean disaster to the other side. Also, a great number are required and even so can cover only a comparatively small area of territory, so that elsewhere other methods, less sophisticated, of combating air attacks would have to be employed. It was shown how deadly was the solid lead wall, also expensive, but less so than SAMs and ECMs, thrown up by the conventional antiaircraft guns. Those with thoughts that antiaircraft guns, and, in fact, all guns, are obsolete, are perhaps having second thoughts.

The aircraft and the tank are big business nowadays. They have dominated the theory and practice of warfare for some years, so much so that it is difficult to imagine a war without them playing the dominant part. We may have to do just that. Herzog writes that "one of the mistakes we made was that we assumed after the 1967 War that all you need is a tank and an aeroplane, and you can do anything with them—you can't." General Ismail said to me, more moderately, "Aircraft and tanks have lost their mastery of the air and the battlefield, but not their value." Perhaps their value is falling faster than many care to admit.

In regard to vehicles, the Arabs say they like the Soviet tanks better than the American or British. Although they are noisier and offer less comfort for the crew, they are more "soldier-proof" and have a greater radius of action than Western tanks. The Arabs say they are quite happy to retain them. On the other hand, the Israelis like the American and British tanks, saying they are superior to those of the Soviet Union. It seems to be a case of the representative cobblers talking about the quality of their own leather, making it difficult to draw analytical comparisons. Most NATO nations say it takes eighteen months to train a tank crew, but the Egyptians claim it takes only nine months to train theirs, as Soviet tanks are comparatively simple to operate and maintain. There was an exception, and Jordanian officers who had taken part in the fighting on the Golan Plateau said that Soviet equipment in use with the Syrians was superior to their own.

Much has been said about Israeli officers—their dedication, high degree of training, and competence—which was certainly true in 1967; yet there is the suspicion that their standards had slipped slightly since. Mutterings and rumours in Israel after the October War that it had been a "private soldiers' war" caused the Israeli government on 12 March 1974 to issue a statement to the effect that 23 percent (some 600) of the 2,522 killed in battle were officers and that only 123 of them were private soldiers. However, once the officers got over their initial shock, they soon recovered their determination.

It was on the Egyptian side that the greatest improvement in the officer cadre was seen, and, since their defeat and demoralisation of 1967, they had steadily improved in dedication, efficiency, and fitness. The Road to the Pyramids (the street of the night clubs in Cairo, the slur and stigma of 1967) was no longer the place for an officer to be seen. The demand for specialisation had been met as witnessed by the fact that Egyptian officers, unaided as far as is known, worked a highly sophisticated air defence barrier with some considerable success.

The Syrian officer cadre was not quite in the same class because it was a political army of a small country; many senior officers had more of an eye to a political future than to a purely military one. The young officers I saw seemed to be tough, dedicated, and keen, but in the middle grades, from major to colonel, I sensed a lack of interest in their profession. The flair and enthusiasm for battle seemed to be absent. Pride prevented them from accepting Soviet advice readily, from admitting mistakes and shortcomings, or taking criticism. Although the Syrian Air Defence Barrier was more effective than that of the Egyptians, it was because of the presence of so many Soviet technicians.

On the part of the soldiers, from a Spartan military point of view, the Israelis had tended to go soft since 1967. There were many instances of avoidance of the call-up and annual training, of slackness, indiscipline, and indifference, glossed over by a superiority complex and a belief that "Arabs always run away in battle." To the Israeli conscript, the Arabs were a nuisance, not a danger. Herzog writes, "It is clear today that part of our shortcomings at the start of the war stemmed from the lack of discipline . . . from an atmosphere of negligence and who-gives-a-damn that spread throughout the nation and infected the army." However, when they got their second wind, things went better.

The Egyptian soldiers were well trained, disciplined, and tough. There were more urban soldiers in the ranks, together with numbers of those with secondary or even higher education, which had not been possible in Nasser's day, and they gave a leavening which enabled Egyptian soldiers to manipulate anti-tank missiles and to become competent tank crews and gunners. The Syrian soldier was also well trained, disciplined, and tough, but the educational leavening was not there.

While generally it must still be conceded that the Israeli soldier is better trained, better educated, and more flexible than his Arab counterpart, the vaunted technological gap, upon which the Israelis relied for another two generations to maintain quality over quantity in battle, is fast narrowing, and may have disappeared in some spheres by the time this book appears in print. In making comparisons, perhaps the Egyptian rangers were better than their Israeli counterparts and the Syrian commandos were also equal to them. While the Egyptian and Syrian infantry may be tougher than the Israelis, the latter is more flexible. The Israelis still retain their superiority in armoured warfare and in the air, but this may disappear. An Egyptian armoured corps brigadier, when I asked his opinion of Israeli and Arab tank crews, said the Egyptians were taught more self-reliance, while the Israeli tank crews relied too much on their recovery service to help them and did not automatically carry out minor repairs to keep their tanks running. He said he had seen many Israeli tanks abandoned because of some small technical fault which the driver should have been able to put right.

The Israelis lost heavily in tank crews and it takes them eighteen months to train replacements. The Arabs could absorb their armoured personnel losses much better for they had a training target of only nine months. In the air the Israelis lost heavily in pilots, practically all those in the Hunter Squadrons becoming casualties, while the Egyptians, and also the Syrians to an extent, held back their air force and so minimised their losses of pilots. This would mean that Egypt, with pilots having completed a period of some seven years' training, is now producing and should be able to produce and maintain pilots of a calibre equal to those of the former Israeli Hunter Squadron.

No paratroops were dropped by parachute during this war, but both sides expected the other to make an airborne landing of some sort in their rear areas. The Israelis generally used their helicopters as soft-skinned vehicles to ferry ammunition and urgent supplies to the fronts and to return with wounded. There were exceptions, such as when they were used to put troops down into positions for the final attacks on Mount Hermon, their raid into Syria against the moving Iraqi column (if indeed one actually was made), and their attack on Jebel Ataka. The Arabs also used helicopters for the same primary purposes, but they tended to regard them more as fighting vehicles. The Egyptians used them to transport rangers on their missions, and to bombard and drop napalm on the Israeli bridges across the Suez Canal and on their vehicles and troops on the west bank. The Syrians also used helicopters on occasion to bring troops to the battlefield.

The discipline of the Egyptians and Syrians seems to have been good, both among officers and men in the field, although there were exceptions. The Arabs gave rewards, promotions, honours, and medals for meritorious service with some publicity, but they carried out their demotions, dismissals, and punishments, and inflicted their penalties quietly and without comment. The Israelis followed much the same pattern, the exception being that they seemed, due to some inborn inverse snobbery, to be extremely coy over issuing medals for valour. An unknown number were awarded, but without publicity—a system not liked by all Israelis.

One instance of an Israeli court-martial punishment that slipped through the net to hit the headlines was that of two technical sergeants who were sent forward to repair some vehicles and were caught in a Bar Lev Line fort when the war suddenly began. They refused to help or take part in the defence of the fort for two days, and, although they did so on the third day, the fort fell and they were taken prisoner. They were charged with disobeying orders, demoted, and sentenced to seven years' imprisonment, perhaps a fitting and salutary punishment in the circumstances, but one that caused unease to the Israelis, who looked even harder and more critically at the conduct and failings of their leaders in the war.

Because of his conduct, it is amazing that General Sharon was not at once removed from his command, but it is not clear whether the GOC had the power to do that alone. Even more surprising is the way his indiscipline and insubordination were dealt with by Moshe Dayan, the minister of defence. Dayan had allowed Sharon to contact him on military matters over the head of the GOC and to persuade him to countermand certain of the GOC's orders. Claiming he was an exponent of mobile warfare, Sharon said he left the army "partly because he was opposed to fixed defences." During the war, although a member of a political party, of which he took full advantage, he was not a member of the Knesset until elected in December 1973. Just before he was finally released from the army to take his seat in the Knesset, Sharon was emboldened to give a critical interview, which was published in the *New Yorker* of 11 February 1974. Talking of General Bar Lev's recall to active service, Sharon called him "a political opportunist put in place by the government to justify poor actions and to deny credit to any other officer," presumably meaning himself. Sharon was still not disciplined, and so it is difficult not to suspect political favouritism, even though he and Dayan were in opposing political parties. On the Egyptian side President Sadat, when he thought it necessary, had no hesitation in removing General Shazli on the nineteenth. Certain senior Syrian officers who had failed in battle also were instantly dismissed, but reports of wholesale executions must be discounted.

All three of the principal combatant states had great disappointments: the Syrians because they had so narrowly failed in their initial advance across the Golan Plateau and were driven back again; the Egyptians because they had not reached the passes and because the Israelis penetrated the west bank; and the Israelis because of their initial failure to hold the Bar Lev Line, and their subsequent failures to break all the Egyptian bridges, to drive the Egyptians from the east bank, to force the Egyptian Third Army to surrender, and to break through the Sasa Line. Another Israeli disappointment (and an American one as well) was their failure to capture intact the radar directional guidance system of the SAM-6.

Neither side is willing to discuss openly its shortcomings or mistakes. In this respect Egypt seems to be the most forthcoming, admitting at their 1975 International Symposium in Cairo that "tactical failures did take place, there was a mishandling of mass armour by the Syrians, discoordination between the two offensives, and an uncoordinated gap between the Second and Third Armies." Another speaker at the same symposium talked of "tactical mishandling, coordinational failures, or any other *contretemps* which reduced the peak period of Arab superiority from the ratio of 8:13 down to 8:10 only." The Syrians will say only that they were "not militarily ready." On the other side, the Israelis will admit only that they were caught by surprise, insisting that, once they got over their initial shock, all was well, and they jostled the Arabs backward in fine style.

On the Arab side, the Egyptians blame the Syrians for letting them down. Shazli is blamed for the Israeli penetration on the west bank. In Syria the senior officers on the battlefield were blamed for the reverses, but the Syrian regime was unshaken. On the Israeli side, considering that its government and society generally are more open and akin to Western ones, it seems remarkable that none of the political leaders was prepared to accept any blame or feel any guilt for the shortcomings, nor were there resignations on a ministerial level as might have been expected in a Western democracy. The premier, Golda Meir, steadfastly hung onto office to fight the December election. It is true that on the evening of the seventh Dayan weakly offered his resignation to the Premier. She wrote of this incident that "I told him—and I have never regretted this—that he had to stay on as defence minister."

Aware that they had become Jewish historic figures, none of the Israeli leaders, political or military, would openly admit he was wrong, had been mistaken, or had miscalculated, or that he was not absolutely the right person in the right post at the right time, and these included Premier Meir and Moshe Dayan, and the generals Elazar and Gonen. The politicians tended to blame each other while the generals openly squabbled and bickered among themselves. In the circumstances, the quiet dignity and acceptance of dismissal by General Shazli is particularly commendable. The only minister to resign from the Israeli government after criticising the conduct of the war, on 30 October, was Yacov Shapiro, minister of justice.

As has become customary nowadays, propaganda is openly used by all combatants, but, as sometimes happens, "black" propaganda creeps into the picture as well. For example, during the first week of the war the West was regaled with tales of General Shazli going forward to personally shoot Egyptian officers and soldiers who had run away in battle. There was not the slightest element of truth in this account, but it is still believed by some, and others are suspicious (or hopeful) that it might have happened. Another black propaganda exercise was to deliberately misquote a vital word from a quotation from the Koran in the pamphlet entitled "Our Religious Belief - Our Road to Victory," which was an exhortation by General Shazli on the eve of battle to all his officers and men. The black translation read, "Kill them [the Israeli soldiers] wherever you find them, and be careful they do not trick you." The vital Arabic word was *khartel,* which means "to fight" and was used by Shazli; the Arabic word for "kill" is *uktal.*

More attuned to Western reaction, the Israelis were more cautious and shrewd, taking care that translations from the Hebrew were suitably bowdlerised, as it is known that sections of the Old Testament are written in strong language. The Israeli magazine *Haolam Hazeh* after the war published a photostat of a document that purported to show that the chief rabbi of the IDF had during the war issued a religious dispensation to Israeli soldiers to kill Arab civilians. One authority wrote that a book in tribute to the Israeli war dead included a contribution from the chief rabbi of central command in which he stated that in his judgement the Jewish religious law did permit the killing of civilians in the course of military action, and that "before the document was published, somebody in central command who knew what propaganda was all about had the document cancelled and pulped all the versions in print—except for one which got away."

At the beginning of the war morale was almost in an inverse ratio to what it had been in June 1967. This time it was the Arabs who were delirious with elation, and it was the Israelis who were more despondent than ever before. In Egypt, for example, as the war progressed popular enthusiasm took on a religious fervour to such an extent that President Sadat released the fact that General Ali Ghali, GOC of the 18th Infantry Division, one that had made a spectacular crossing of the Suez Canal, was a Christian, and not a Muslim.

In Israel there was alarm, despondency, and unease throughout the war. All Israeli soldiers carried their own transistor sets and were able to listen to foreign news broadcasts, as well as their own, which, together with internal rumours of reverses and heavy casualties, tended to establish and broaden a credibility gap. As has so often been said, truth is the first casualty of war.

The Arabs were conditioned by their own television and radio news bulletins, which in the first days were restrained and made comparatively moderate claims. Such Arabs as listened to foreign broadcasts did not believe anything that was contrary or adverse. As the war progressed the accuracy of the Arab news bulletins faded. Many facts were kept from the people, such as the extent of the reverses on the Syrian front, the Israeli penetration of the west bank of the canal, that the Third Army was surrounded, or the extent of Soviet help.

The Israelis, too, were not told many of the facts, such as the fall of their observation post on Mount Hermon on the first afternoon (until several days later), the squabblings of the generals, the Kelt missile fired by the Egyptians, the crisis of confidence in the military leadership, or the Arab oil blockade at the Bab El Mandeb Straits and how empty the Israeli oil pipeline and oil storage tanks had become. The Israelis were not told their true casualty figures, but then neither were the Egyptians or the Syrians. The Israeli government issued only one interim figure, on the fourteenth, of 656 dead. This presumably excluded the large number killed that day in the tank battles on the Egyptian front so as to try to allay the wild and alarming rumours that were circulating, stimulated by hospitals overflowing with wounded. Individual Israeli soldiers later spoke of muddle and administrative confusion, of shortage of arms, equipment, and ammunition, of conflicting orders, and of lack of liaison and accord between their political leaders and the IDF. On 23 October 1973 the Israeli Central Bureau of Statistics announced that during the war some 16,000 Israelis had returned home from abroad but that some 4,000 had left Israel in the same period. The latter figure caused some raised eyebrows in Israel and elsewhere.

Military censorship was imposed in the combatant countries, and a firm hold was clamped on foreign correspondents. Their dispatches were censored, and they were generally kept away from the fighting areas, being taken only on carefully routed visits to selected parts of the front. The foreign press generally had to rely upon such visits, supplemented with official bulletins and briefings which were often vague, contradictory, and confusing. In previous wars Arab communiqués had been bombastically misleading, often far removed from fact, and those of the Israelis had reflected more skillful public relations techniques. While being more factual, their omissions and vagueness were overshadowed by their selective candour on other matters.

The internal security situation also gave the Israelis some cause for concern because several thousands of the Arabs living on the west bank of the River Jordan and in the Gaza Strip, who normally worked on Israeli projects, refused to do so. There was also a series of terrorist attacks on Israelis in Jerusalem, Hebron, Nablus, and other Arab towns.

Of the more prominent personalities who had some influence or control over events during this October War, on the Israeli side probably the staunchest figure was that of the premier, Golda Meir, who remained calm throughout and overshadowed her defence minister, Dayan. The hero of two previous wars against the Arabs, Dayan, by reason of his past military and political experience and the authority of his appointment, might have been expected to emerge as the strong man of Israel in its hour of need and to be proclaimed as its saviour. However, he seems throughout to have been hesitant, indecisive, and pessimistic. The top Israeli generals—Elazar, Eytan, Peled, Mandler, Gonen, and Adan—formed a team of only average ability and a team that did not always pull together, seeming to lack a dominant personality to unite them above their petty promotion prospects, prestige precedent complexes, and personal intrigues.

Recalling senior generals who had entered the political field, which had probably been a thoughtless panic measure intended to inspire the nation with confidence, seems of doubtful wisdom. By their seniority and rank alone they tended to overshadow the team of serving generals, whose job it was to fight the war. They had no command powers, and their presence aroused the suspicion that politics was intervening in the military machine to the detriment of its efficiency. Recalled generals included not only ministers, such as Bar Lev, but also others like General Weizman, a former commander of the Israeli air force.

On the Egyptian side, pipe-smoking President Sadat, like Golda Meir, remained solid, calm, and collected throughout as did General Ismail. General Shazli proved to be more mercurial, alternating extreme optimism when things were going well with extreme pessimism when they were not. He was counterbalanced to a large degree by General Gamasy, the director of operations, who remained cool and levelheaded. On the Syrian side, President Assad and General Tlas did not seem to have the same iron nerve, confidence, and decisiveness. Their team of generals was less effectual than the Egyptians, and without Soviet advice, influence, and aid their fortunes might have been disastrous.

What of the prospect? Will Fortress Israel still prevail in Spartan strength, or will its political independence eventually disappear from the Middle East scene? For some years to come, with its overstocked armoury and the measures taken to sharpen and harden its armed forces, Israel in any future clash with the Arabs should be able at least to hold its own, if not be the outright winner. The proviso is that it would be increasingly difficult each time to assert its military dominance, which could only be achieved at a great cost in human lives—the Achilles' heel of Israel.

As to the more distant future, many long-term factors are working in favour of the Arabs and against the Israelis—population trends, improvement in Arab technology, the rising standard of Arab education, development of industrialisation, a diversification of arms supplies with perhaps the establishment of their own armament industries, and better relations with Western

Europe and America. One day these factors, and perhaps others too, may tip the scales against tiny Israel. At the moment it has only one real friend, the United States, prepared to stand up and be counted and has many disadvantages, not the least being the dramatic fall in immigration and the rise in emigration. As Herzog writes, "In 1973 the Israeli doctrine of deterrent had proved to be a failure"—indeed, a dismal conclusion.

An opportunity exists for negotiation of a long-term settlement which would ensure that Israel would always remain in being as an independent country, accepted by its Arab neighbours, and so ensuring its infinite survival. But the Israeli government and political leaders would have to relax some of their implacable conditions, become more tolerant, and perhaps lower their sights a little. If this opportunity is not taken, it may soon be too late, as attitudes may ossify, especially if American foreign policy changes back to an isolationist stance. This raises the spectre of the fate of the Christian crusader kingdom that once ruled an area of Palestine greater than is encompassed by Israel within its pre-1967 boundaries, only to be eliminated after ninety-nine years by the timeless erosion of the Middle East. Should that happen, once again a world Jewish problem would arise to supersede the present Israeli one, and which nation would take up cudgels in the Jewish cause? Fears and prejudices of today must be overcome to obtain a secure tomorrow.

Index

354   INDEX

Formations and Units

Equipment

AIRCRAFT

HELICOPTERS

ARMOURED VEHICLES